The Roughshooter's Handbook

The Roughshooter's Handbook

DAVID HUDSON

SWAN HILL
PRESS

First published in the UK in 1995
by Swan Hill Press an imprint of Airlife Publishing Ltd.

British Library Cataloguing in Publication Data
  A catalogue record for this book
  is available from the British Library

ISBN 1 85310 456 6

Typeset by Litho Link Ltd, Welshpool, Powys
Printed in England by Butler and Tanner Ltd, Frome and London

Swan Hill Press

An imprint of Airlife Publishing Ltd.
101 Longden Road, Shrewsbury SY3 9EB

Contents

Acknowledgements

It would be an impossible task to list all those who have, in some way, had an influence on the preparation of this book. My appreciation and understanding of the pleasures and problems of rough shooting have grown over the years with the help of, and in some cases in spite of, the advice and example of a great many people.

That the advice was sometimes good, occasionally bad and often downright contradictory is undeniable, but good or bad it was usually well-meant. As for practical examples, I am perhaps most indebted to those who, sometimes unwittingly, gave a demonstration of dangerous or un-sporting behaviour. When it comes to, for example, safe gun handling, there are few things more certain to concentrate the mind than the head-on view, from a range of a couple of feet, of the twin muzzles of a loaded shotgun.

I must though say thank you to many friends who have allowed themselves to be photographed during shooting days, and to their various gundogs who have posed for me — often with greater alacrity than their owners. In particular I must thank John Ormiston for giving me access to his magnificent collection of firearms and for enthusiastically demonstrating a flintlock blunderbuss for the camera, and Colin McKelvie for advising on both the initial layout and the final manuscript.

To them all; to Brian Hopewell who read the first draft and made a number of helpful suggestions and to Georgina who never complains at the time I spend in the darkroom and at the keyboard; I am truly grateful.

David Hudson

Introduction

'Begin at the beginning, and go on till you come to the end: then stop.'

Those of you who made the acquaintance of *Alice in Wonderland* during their childhood may remember the King's answer to the White Rabbit's plaintive 'Where shall I begin, please your Majesty?' I would prefer not to become too entangled with Lewis Carroll's story; particularly remembering that the cry of 'Off with his head' tended to greet the conclusion of each tale.

Nevertheless, what better place to start than at the beginning, and since this is a book about rough shooting, let us begin by deciding what, exactly, is meant by rough shooting?

There is, as far as I know, no universally accepted definition of the boundaries of rough shooting. Fieldsports differ from games such as football and cricket in that they have no rule books; no international associations and by and large, no umpires or referees. No ruling body establishes the number of players, the size of the pitch, the length of each match, the method of scoring and rules of the game for fieldsports. There are certain codes of conduct which are followed, there is an increasing volume of legislation setting out what may be shot, hooked or hunted, where, when, and by whom, and of course, there are centuries of tradition to guide the modern fieldsportsman.

But there are no books of rules. Nowhere is it laid down that a rough shoot shall consist of a team of 'w' number of guns, accompanied by 'x' number of dogs; that the shoot shall take place on a pitch measuring 'y' number of acres, or that the duration of the shoot shall be 'z' number of hours, plus extra time in the event of the result being a draw. A rough shoot is pretty much what you want to make it. By the same token a book about rough shooting can be fairly flexible in setting its parameters. Given such licence therefore, I intend to throw quite a wide net and perhaps touch on some areas that others would not consider to be strictly within their definition of rough shooting. I make no apology for this, beyond saying that, as a lifelong rough shooter, they are within mine.

The word shooting is easily defined. It means, in this instance, the pursuit of live quarry using a shotgun. It is the adjective that poses the problem: that word 'rough' which we use to distinguish this particular form of the sport from the other disciplines. Driven game shooting; walked-up shooting; roost shooting; wildfowling; decoying; shooting over dogs: they are all different forms of shooting, but not necessarily of rough shooting.

Tell me you are invited to a day's driven pheasants and I will know that you will be spending your time standing at a series of covert sides while a team of beaters flush pheasants over you. Ask me to come pigeon decoying, and I know that we will be sitting in a hide with a pattern of decoys set, waiting for pigeons to drop into them. If we are to

Formal — standing on a woodland ride at a driven pheasant shoot.

And informal — rabbit shooting on a rocky hill-side.

walk-up grouse then I can immediately visualise the line of guns advancing in open order across heather moorland. Talk of bolting rabbits with ferrets, flighting woodcock at dusk or geese at dawn, ambushing pigeons as they come to roost among the stark woods of February or waiting in gathering darkness for the sound of mallard wings whistling over a flight pond and I know exactly what you are describing.

But rough shooting? A day's rough shooting might embrace any of the above situations: a lifetime's rough shooting will probably include all of them, and then some more.

Which leads us back to the original question — what, exactly, is rough shooting?

The word 'rough' has some rather unfortunate connotations. To describe something as rough is often to imply that it is in some way inferior; second-class; undesirable even. Golfers try not to end up in the rough; we describe something which is crudely made as being rough and ready; a brawling boxing match as a rough and tumble. Living under harsh or uncomfortable conditions is roughing it. A horse may be rough shod, a man may suffer rough luck or be a rough diamond. Think about feeling rough, rough passage, rough hewn, rough cast, rough in, rough out and rough up. None of them are exactly desirable conditions.

And so does rough shooting mean inferior or second-class sport? Is it the poor man's alternative to better, more desirable methods; something to serve as an introduction to the sport before passing on to better things? Something that we do, but which we don't talk about in polite society; the next best thing; a near enough, more or less, bit of a sort of a branch of fieldsports? It may be for some; but as far as I am concerned rough shooting is the pinnacle of the sport, not the pits; the first choice rather than Hobson's choice. Given the rough shoot of my choice I would aspire to nothing finer: the highest of driven pheasants, the fastest of driven grouse could all take second place.

Shooting live quarry means (now that live pigeon trap shooting is no longer practised) shooting wild quarry. Since the maximum range of a shotgun is somewhere around fifty yards it is necessary for the shooting man to make some arrangement that will bring him and his wild quarry within that distance of each other. There are three ways of doing this. The sportsman can go to where the quarry is; he can wait in an ambush (possibly aided by some form of decoy) for the quarry to come to him, or he can attempt to have the quarry sent in his direction. Of the three, rough shooting is primarily, though by no means exclusively, concerned with method one: the rough shooter goes out and hunts for his quarry.

It is, perhaps, the sense of rough shooting as first and foremost a hunting activity that leads us closest to a means of identifying the boundaries between rough shooting and other forms of shooting. The driven game shooter waits at a pre-arranged point for his quarry to be persuaded to fly or run past him: the decoy shooter relies on the illusion that his decoy birds impart to convince others that food and safety lie within range of his gun. The rough shooter though will usually rely on his legs to carry him and his dog to guide him to his quarry. A rough shooter is primarily a hunter of game. In contrast, a gun at a driven shoot may need no fieldcraft beyond that required to find his butt or peg. Shooting driven game is primarily a test of marksmanship.

There are, of course, no hard and fast rules to distinguish one form of shooting from another. Certain situations are easily recognised: when ten guns, twenty beaters, five pickers-up and a head keeper meet after breakfast in anticipation of shooting three hundred pheasants before dusk, there is little difficulty in categorising this as a driven pheasant shoot. When a solitary gun sets out for a field of laid barley carrying fifty shell decoys, half a dozen lofting poles, a patent flapping device, twenty yards of camouflage netting, a gun plus two hundred cartridges, face mask, thermos flask, folding seat and enough sandwiches for three square meals then it is almost certain that a day's pigeon decoying is planned.

And if a single gun, or three or four friends with their dogs are planning a wander round the shoot, hunting out the hedgerows, looking for rabbits in that field of rough grass, pushing a snipe up from the boggy bits near the river or surprising a half dozen mallard on the flight pond, then the sport is unquestionably rough shooting.

But suppose two of the guns wait at one end of a spinney while the other guns take the dogs and beat through the trees to drive the pheasants over them. Suppose two wait behind at one end of that strip of kale while the others walk it through, knowing that the birds will probably lift on the wind and head back towards the home wood. Is this rough shooting or is it impinging on the preserves of driven game shooting? Perhaps because only three or four guns are involved it still qualifies as a rough shoot — but if so, how many walking and how many standing guns can take part before our rough shoot ceases to be a rough shoot and becomes a driven day?

Let us imagine that, having worked the hedgerows, the rough grass and the snipe bog, and having completed a couple of impromptu drives, our sporting quartet notice that there is a steady stream of woodpigeons flighting in to feed on a field of winter wheat. There are already a few pigeons in the game bags from earlier in the day. Suppose that they decide to build a couple of rough hides under the hedge which borders the wheat field; set up the dead pigeons as decoys and spend the rest of the afternoon shooting pigeons. Has our rough shoot now been transformed into a afternoon's decoying? Perhaps the boundaries which separate one form of shooting from another are not as clearcut as might seem at first sight.

It is, for me at any rate, part of the attraction of fieldsports that there *are* no formal books of rules; no rigidly defined boundaries between one sport and another. Customs and traditions vary from country to country, from one part of a country to another, and indeed may even differ widely between neighbouring shoots. Such variety may not find favour with some, particularly those politicians and civil servants who are so frantically trying to legislate the whole of Europe into a single, characterless, homogenous mess; but for the shooting man, and for the rough shooter in particular, variety is undoubtedly the spice of life.

The rough shooter is, has to be, flexible. Certainly plans can be made for the day's sport, but the plan may have to be be altered at short notice. Rough shooting involves a lot of tactical manoeuvring, a willingness to adapt the overall plan to meet sudden changes of circumstance. This flexibility is often denied to those who participate in other forms of live shooting.

An individual gun at a driven shoot has little or no control over the events of the day. Having drawn for position before the first drive, his day is set out before him in detail. His task is simply to remember his correct position at each drive, ensure that he is in that position as and when required, and then to shoot as safely, sportingly and capably as he is able; mark any birds which are killed or wounded for the pickers-up, and then present himself on time for the next drive.

This is not to underestimate the amount of forethought and planning that will have gone into the organising of the driven day, nor the amount of tactical manoeuvring that will be required from the head keeper or shoot captain during its course. There are beaters, stops, flankers and pickers-up to organise, quite apart from those with a peripheral involvement such as transport drivers, game collectors and luncheon providers. It is just this sheer volume of planning that can often restrict the driven shoot organiser's room to manoeuvre if things are not running entirely according to the plan.

The decoy shot is also restricted to some extent by the amount of equipment he carries. Setting out a decoy pattern and building a hide takes time and creates disturbance. The idea is to get it right first time, and even if things fall short of perfection the temptation to stay put may well be stronger than the desire to effect a marginal improvement in sport at the expense of lifting hide and decoys and decamping to another site.

So the rough shooter is usually a man in charge of his own destiny, with the chance to chop and change the game plan when things do not turn out quite as anticipated. Naturally, the amount of variety that can be introduced into a rough shooting day will depend largely on the type and extent of ground which you have to shoot over. A thousand acres of forestry plantation might actually offer less real variety than a hundred acres of fields and woodland.

I was lucky enough to spend my schooldays living in rural Suffolk where my father was the landlord of a village inn. The inn was rented from a brewery, who in their turn rented it from the Lord of the Manor. And along with the inn came a small agricultural holding.

It might once have formed the basis of a productive smallholding to supplement the landlord's income from the sale of beer, wines and spirits, but at the time which my father took the tenancy it had long fallen into neglect. The hedges were tall, thick and overgrown; the meadow had been left to grow wild, ungrazed and unmown for a decade, and the old sandpit which had once produced building materials for the village had degenerated into a wilderness of thorns, hardwood saplings and weeds. The arable land had been planted to barley each year, since the subsidy yielded a small return even if the crop was negligible. In a word, the land was neglected.

But it was precisely that neglect that had transformed it into the ideal place for a boy to learn to shoot; and, incidentally, to fish as there was a river running along one boundary. There were pheasant and partridge of course, though these were strictly off limits to me since the estate retained the game rights. But there were rabbits in the meadow and the sandpit was one huge warren. There was usually a hare somewhere in the field, there were always woodpigeon, feeding on the stubble or roosting in the hedgerow trees, there were mallard and moorhen on the river, snipe in the meadow after floods and woodcock in the scrubby thorn bushes.

I started shooting there with an air-rifle at about the same time that I started at the local grammar school. Over the years I graduated to bigger and more powerful air-rifles, then to my first shotgun — a Lee-Enfield rifle bored out to accommodate a .410 cartridge — and on through a series of potentially lethal museum pieces until I finally owned a double-barrelled, hammerless twelve bore shotgun. It was a very old Webley and Scott; I sold it for twelve pounds when I joined the RAF, and I have regretted parting with it ever since.

I walked-up rabbits in the meadow, flushed them with a dog along the overgrown hedges and stalked them as they sat outside their burrows on summer evenings. I shot pigeons as they flighted through a gap in the hedge, fighting against a winter gale, or sat under that same hedge in a carefully contrived hide and waited for them to fly into the tall elms at the bottom of the field.

Accompanied by a friend who kept ferrets I spent hours hunting rabbits in the sandpit warren; sometimes tangling them in purse nets, sometimes shooting them as they bolted and all too often digging to recover the liner when it laid up on a kill.

I killed my first hare there as it bolted from the harvester; shot mallard when they flushed from the flooded water meadows which bordered the land and was almost shot myself by a shooting party on the neighbouring estate. I killed a fox which ran right past me one day as I was crouched among the thorn scrub waiting for pigeon, shot rats in the hedgerows after harvest and even killed the odd coypu down along the river.

Of course, things were much simpler in those days: a gun licence came over the counter at the local post office and required the applicant to furnish no more than his name, address and a ten shilling note. At twelve years old I could quite legally wander down the lane to 'my' shoot with a pocketful of cartridges and that old .410 converted rifle over my arm. It kept me out of mischief and also kept me engrossed for endless hours and days.

I learned to shoot there, and to handle a gun safely. I learned an awful lot about fieldcraft, and hunting, and how keeping quiet and still meant that you saw a whole lot more than you did if you spent all day charging about. A childhood spent out in those fields and meadows gave me a love of fieldsports and the countryside which has never diminished in the years since. And the whole of that little shoot: field, meadow, sandpit and river bank amounted to a total of just eight acres.

Naturally I hankered for bigger and better things. Every February saw me out in the big woods for the pigeon roost shoots, and no chance to shoot on other ground was ever turned down. I don't know what has become of those eight acres now, though I suspect they will have long since been incorporated into one large field, the hedges grubbed out, the sandpit bulldozed level and the river dredged to prevent the water meadows from flooding every winter. I prefer to remember it as it was; a tiny eight-acre holding, but a whole world of adventure to a small boy with gun.

I am not suggesting that eight acres of neglected farmland is all that is required to form the basis of a rough shoot. I spent whole days on my tiny shoot precisely because it was all that I had. If my eight acres had just been one corner of a five hundred-acre holding then I would probably have spent no more than a few minutes there in the course of each day. I longed to have five hundred acres in those days: now I think perhaps it was much better for me to have been restricted to the tiny patch that I did have.

It is hard to say what might be the minimum acreage that could fairly be labelled a 'shoot'. Everything depends on the type of ground; what game there is on the ground, and probably more pertinently, what potential the ground has to hold game. No rough shoot is ever likely to be too large, but even the smallest piece of ground can form the basis of a shoot, provided the potential is there.

Colin Willock, who, as 'Town Gun' must have written thousands of articles for the *Shooting Times*, once had a shoot centred on a sewage farm and a market garden only a few miles from central London. The late Major Archie Coats used to organise a day's driven shooting on a total area of about twelve acres. Given the right ground and a determination to succeed it is surprising what can be organised by the resourceful rough shooter.

In rough shooting as in all other forms of live quarry shooting it is the nature of the ground that determines the amount and the quality of sport that can be achieved. How much ground is available; is it moorland, commercial forestry, mixed woodland, farmland, heathland or foreshore? Is it mountainous or low-lying; hilly or flat? These basics control what it *may* be possible to achieve from the ground.

Almost any area of open ground has at least the potential to be turned into a rough shoot. Some, obviously, are more promising than others, and some very promising areas are unlikely ever to become available. There are public parks in most cities which would form the basis of excellent shoots. Think of the thousands of pigeons that could be decoyed with a handful of cake crumbs; the ducks and geese which abound on the ornamental ponds, the rabbits grazing down the flower beds. Of course, there might be a few practical difficulties, even supposing that the city fathers felt like assigning the shooting rights to you, but the potential is certainly there.

One of the difficulties in reaching a precise definition of rough shooting is that there is such a wide variety of sport that can wear the rough shooting label. It is not easy to draw the line at which driving, flighting, decoying, dogging or walking-up stop being a part of the rough shooting day and qualify as a sport in their own right.

The amount of game involved must have a bearing; a series of 'impromptu' drives which produced a fifty-bird bag would begin to look suspiciously like a 'pukka' driven shoot. On the other hand, the rough shooter who spots a good flight line might well shoot fifty pigeons in a couple of hours simply by standing quietly in the corner of a wood, while even the most countrywise pigeon decoyer will experience days when little or nothing is drawn to his decoy pattern. Numbers alone are not sufficient guide.

The keys which indicate a rough shoot are words like 'informality', 'variety', 'uncertainty' and perhaps most importantly of all, 'fun'. If you are going to spend your time, your energy and your money on shooting then for goodness sake enjoy it. There is such a variety of sport to be enjoyed.

Rough shooting can be found anywhere in the British Isles from the south-western tip of Cornwall to the northernmost counties of Caithness and Sutherland and even beyond to Orkney and Shetland. There are shoots in East Anglia and on the west coast of Ireland

Sport can be found in the highest mountains — gun, dog-handler and a pointer above Loch Choire in Sutherland.

and pretty well all points between.

There is sport to be found on the tops of the highest mountains and on the foreshore below the high water mark. Flat fenland or rocky hill, intensively farmed arable land or open moorland, forestry plantation or ancient woodland, marshes, bogs, washes, heathlands and water meadows; all of them, to some degree, offer sport to the rough shooter.

The type of sport on offer will depend very much on the type of ground which forms the shoot. On the high tops, which are the home of the ptarmigan, a shooting day is almost certain to be spent walking-up; probably after the first couple of hours have been spent walking up a mountain. Ptarmigan shooting is very much a sport for the fit and hardy, and not one which is likely to yield large bags.

A covey of grouse springing in front of a gun in Sutherland.

A little lower down the hill from the ptarmigan (although there is considerable overlap in their territories) we should start finding grouse. Heather moorland in the north of England, Wales, Ireland and of course Scotland is the home of the red grouse; arguably our finest sporting quarry. The best moors, with the highest density of birds, are normally devoted to driven grouse shooting; possibly the best and certainly the most expensive shooting available in these islands.

But not all moors are driven moors. Where the grouse are in short supply driving becomes uneconomic, even at the sort of prices charged per brace for driven grouse shooting. Now the rough shooter comes into his own; walking-up the birds; perhaps with a spaniel to hunt the heather ahead of him, or with a pointer or setter quartering way out

15

to either side. If there are enough birds a walking line of guns will find sport even without the aid of dogs, though many coveys will be missed, particularly early in the season, and it may not be easy to pick any wounded birds.

Snipe and golden plover are found out on the heather as well as grouse; there may be hill partridge, hares both blue and brown and of course rabbits. If there is woodland around the margins of the moor then blackgame, woodcock, pheasant, pigeon, perhaps even capercaillie may feature in the game bag by the end of the day.

Ponds, rivers and lochs; whether high up in the hills or right down at sea level will attract wildfowl; particularly if a little food is distributed on a regular basis. A moorland shoot might not seem very promising at first sight, but given the right conditions it can actually provide the sportsman with a greater variety of both quarry species and types of shooting than any other environment.

Where there is open moorland there are often forestry plantations. A lot of hard things are said about these, often huge, blocks of conifers. At their worst they are almost useless for sporting purposes, consisting of little more than a giant monoculture of exotic trees planted so tightly together that few birds or animals inhabit them. Fortunately the modern forester is beginning to adopt a more sympathetic approach to forest design, incorporating deer lawns and open spaces, a variety of species and a generally encouraging attitude to other birds, animals and plants. The sight of a geometric block of gloomy sitka spruce looming threateningly across the hillside is gradually becoming a thing of the past.

A forestry shoot, particularly when the trees are first planted, can be both varied and productive. Later, when the dark green canopy closes over and slowly chokes the life from the underlying flora there is less scope, though the rides and margins can still give a certain amount of shooting. It can be hard earned sport, but it may well be cheap sport; and if nothing else is available . . .

As moorland gives way to farmland so upland shooting changes to low ground shooting. Grouse are seldom found far from heather, but many moorland species can still occur among the rough grazing, the grass parks and the birch woods that border the moors. The ubiquitous pheasant is found here, as are snipe and woodcock, perhaps blackgame, certainly pigeon and of course rabbits. There is still scope for dogging and for walking-up game.

Moving down from the moors and the hill farming country into the richer ground below brings another change in the type of rough shooting on offer. The grouse family will no longer feature in the bag, except possibly under freak weather conditions, but other species will replace them. Arable crops provide food and shelter for pheasant, partridge, woodpigeon and rabbit, with deciduous woodland offering a far more welcoming environment than the upland evergreen plantations.

Shoots tend to be much smaller down here. A thousand acres of low quality moorland might provide no more than a couple of day's sport dogging or walking-up grouse before the danger of overshooting threatens future sport. By contrast, there are plenty of low ground pheasant shoots which can offer eight or ten good driven days from a much smaller area.

The climate is generally milder and the availability of food, shelter and nesting cover much increased on this lower ground. Equally importantly, pheasants and partridges can be reared for release to boost the wild stock; something that is not possible with grouse.

A far greater variety of ground exists within this arable farming belt of course, and the quality and quantity of sport will vary enormously according to the crops that are grown, and the way in which they are grown.

It is almost impossible to describe a typical rough shoot of the type which can be found among low ground farms. To begin with, farming practice varies widely in different parts of the country; crops which are common in East Anglia may be a rare sight further north. Modern farming practice has changed some holdings beyond recognition with hedges grubbed out, ditches and ponds filled in and woods and spinneys felled. Parts of the Suffolk which I explored as a boy have changed from small fields bordered with trees and hedgerows to the wide open spaces of prairie farms. Where these featureless fields are farmed with a regime that makes extensive use of insecticidal and herbicidal sprays they can be as barren as the endless dark green ranks of the softwood plantations.

But recent years have seen a change in farming practices that should have huge incidental benefits for wildlife in Britain. No longer are farmers encouraged by grants and subsidies to produce vast quantities of grain, meat and dairy products for which there is no European demand. Instead of paying for hedges to be ripped out, ponds to be filled in and marshes to be drained the government is now diverting funds into the creation of new woodlands and wetlands. The set-aside scheme actually pays farmers *not* to grow crops.

It may be difficult, when half the world's population is malnourished, to follow the logic of schemes which aim to reduce the production of food by developed countries. Nevertheless, set-aside and small woodlands grants are with us, whether or not we approve of the principle behind them. Their application has enormous potential for improving our environment, and as an associated benefit for greatly improving the prospects for the rough shooter.

Depending on the type of ground that you have to start with, the degree of control that you can exert over the way the land is used, and also the depth of your pocket, an enormous amount can be done to improve the sport that a shoot provides. There are three primary ways to enhance the sporting potential of a shoot: habitat improvement, vermin control and releasing reared game. They are not, of course, three alternative methods of shoot improvement. Though the emphasis would switch between one shoot and another, it would be normal for all three to be tackled together as part of an overall strategy.

Many of our native birds and animals have suffered disastrous declines in their population during the twentieth century. There is little doubt that changes in farming practices must bear a great burden of responsibility for this. Herbicides and pesticides have contributed both directly and indirectly; sometimes by actually killing birds or animals, sometimes, as in the case of dieldrin and birds of prey, by stopping them from reproducing.

The destruction of insect 'pests' and weeds from crops has eliminated whole levels of vital food chains, often with disastrous consequences for species which were considered desirable. A hundred years ago partridges thrived under the normal farming routines; in the last fifty years they were decimated as their nesting sites were destroyed and their insect food poisoned in the interests of growing unwanted grain.

Over the past few decades the bureaucrats in Brussels have wasted billions of Euro-dollars on a Common Agricultural Policy that encouraged farmers to grow crops for which there was no market; spent a small fortune on storing the surpluses and then another fortune destroying them to make room for yet more in overcrowded warehouses. Now the emphasis has switched to paying farmers *not* to grow crops; to replant the hedges and woodlands that were destroyed in order to increase the surpluses a few years before. You may be able to see some sense in all this; I cannot. I can, however, see it resulting in a richer and more varied landscape and a reduction in the amount of poisonous chemicals which are sprayed around: and that must surely be of benefit to the countryside. And by and large, what is good for the countryside is good for the rough shooter.

A couple of hundred years ago there were thousands of acres of marshes and wetlands in the country, from the salty wastes around the coasts and estuaries to the silent, secret world of the fenlands. Most of it has now gone forever; drained and dyked to provide some of the richest farmland in the country; but pockets still exist, and are largely protected from further development by conservation bodies.

Wildfowl abound here of course; snipe spring from under your feet and jink away with their harsh scraping call. There may be pheasant, partridge, hare and rabbit to be walked-up on the flat, windswept fields or hunted out from reed fringed ditches with a questing Spaniel or Labrador. Heavy rains can cause flooding that may bring armies of duck flighting in to feed on the newly created lakes while a frost can turn the whole area into one vast skating rink. It is a wonderful environment for the rough shooter, and at times a dangerous one: flooded dykes and thin ice have claimed many lives over the years.

Beyond even the bounds of the saltmarsh lies the foreshore and the inter-tidal sand and mud flats. This is the land of the wildfowler; a place of muddy gutters and deep channels, violent storms and lashing rain, and always the danger of being cut off by the tide or lost in a sudden fog. Far out on the mud is the haunt of the wildfowler, but the rough shooter may find plenty to entertain him along the periphery of the foreshore, where the sea wall keeps the tide from flooding across the land.

There are other places where sport can be found with a gun provided that permission to shoot can be obtained. There are huge areas given over to military training for firing ranges; tank testing and battle simulation; and these have great potential for rough shooting. Market gardens, golf courses, disused railway tracks, old gravel workings and

Sport at the edge of the sea — a reedy fringe on the Solway Firth.

quarries: almost anywhere that has a few acres of open ground has the potential to provide some rough shooting.

The quality of the sport will vary enormously of course. Five acres of disused gravel pit on the edge of a city may not bear comparison with a hundred acres of mixed farmland; a couple of miles of mixed woodland or a thousand acres of heather moorland, but given the ground, determination, a little ingenuity and a lot of hard work something worthwhile can be achieved almost anywhere.

You will, of course, need more than just some ground on which to shoot. A gun, the right sort of clothing, a gundog to do some of the work for you, and something at which to shoot. Just as there is no simple definition of rough shooting, so there is no such thing as a rough shooting gun, rough shooting clothes nor a rough shooting dog. We will be looking at all these in more detail in later chapters.

But before going on to look more closely at rough shoots, at dogs and keepers, guns and clothing, at learning to shoot, at the laws that govern the rough shooter and the clubs and organisations which exist to encourage shooting and to protect sportsmen from their political opponents, we should perhaps return to our initial question. What, exactly, is rough shooting?

A definition remains elusive because of the very nature of the sport. It is shooting without the formality of the driven game shoot; without the single-minded dedication of the pigeon decoyer and without the dangers and deprivations of the specialist wildfowler. It is the informal, unpredictable, widely variable and always interesting side of the sport.

Man was a hunter-gatherer for aeons before he first began planting seeds to grow crops and took the first steps along the road to becoming the tame, domesticated creature that we are today. Somewhere deep down in the psyche of all of us though remains that primitive hunting instinct that was vital to survival until quite recent times. Rough shooting is essentially a sport for the hunter; a game for the man (or woman) whose hunting instincts are not too deeply buried to surface from time to time.

Give us a piece of ground, a gun and a dog and for a while at least we can address those ancient instincts and revert to the role of hunters.

And have a hell of a lot of fun in the process.

A gundog to do some of the work . . . Viszla retrieving a pheasant.

2 Mountain and Moorland

Upland areas; moorlands, mountains, hills and bogs; cover a surprisingly large percentage of the total land mass of Britain and Ireland. A relief map of such areas would highlight vast tracts of land in mainland Scotland, the Western Isles, Orkney and Shetland, Wales, Ireland, the north of England and the West country. Incidentally, a map indicating the areas of highest rainfall in Britain and Ireland would cover almost exactly the same ground — a fact that will be well known to anyone who has lived, worked or spent their holidays among the hills.

These sparsely populated regions, particularly the Highlands of Scotland, the Welsh hills and the moors of the West country, are often referred to as wilderness areas, though the term is not strictly correct since the landscape has largely been created by the action of man. The mountains may seem timeless and immutable but they have changed greatly in the past three thousand years or so, and are changing still today.

When the glaciers retreated at the end of the last Ice Age the uplands reverted to scrub woodland with birch, Scots pine, hazel and alder the dominant species. During the Bronze Age man began the process of felling and burning the forests for fuel and to clear land for agriculture, and this continued until relatively recent times, when much of the ancient Caledonian forest was used to feed to iron smelters.

As communications improved during the nineteenth century the more remote areas became accessible to sportsmen who came seeking grouse, salmon and deer. They also became accessible to vast flocks of sheep which brought radical alterations in their wake, both to the native population and, more slowly, to the landscape. In parts of the Highlands, crofters were simply turned out of their homes and forced to leave to make way for the thousands of sheep. The evils which occurred during the infamous Highland Clearances are well documented, and there remains a strong sense of injustice among many Highlanders even today.

Increasing rainfall played a part in preventing the regeneration of the felled woodlands and in many places they were replaced with heather moorland or blanket bog. Intensive grazing by sheep meant that seedlings could not mature and the open, heather or grass moorland that is typical of so much of today's uplands was created.

From the mid-nineteenth century sport began to have an increasing influence on land usage in upland areas. Land was managed primarily for the good of grouse or deer, and the practice of heather burning to replace old, woody plants with succulent young heather helped to ensure that the land stayed open and that the trees were held at bay. Thus the so-called 'wilderness' areas are not truly wild landscapes, but have been created and maintained by the influence of man.

The landscape is still changing. Vast areas of upland have been afforested during the last seventy years or so, largely as a result of grants and tax breaks provided by the government. Subsidies to hill farmers which are based on the numbers of sheep they run, have resulted in many areas being grossly over stocked and the grazing pressure itself, coupled with frequent burning, changes the nature of the land, heather being replaced with grass, and grass with rush and bracken.

Drainage schemes, re-seeding, liming and fertilising all alter the nature of the hills, as does the influx of visitors drawn by leisure-based developments such as ski lifts and visitor centres. There is an increasing pressure being brought by conservation bodies to force landowners to follow particular management policies in order to satisfy their own ideas of what the uplands should be like.

These ideas are often somewhat contradictory. We are told that planting trees is a bad thing, but that deer and sheep should be removed from millions of acres of the Highlands in order that trees can regenerate. In contrast, the sheep in the English Lake District are a good thing because they graze down the fells to the short grass which delights the hiker and opens the views of the hills and fells. Vast amounts of public money are paid to landowners to encourage them to plant trees and to compensate them when the government decrees that they should not plant trees. There are grants for keeping sheep and grants for getting rid of them, just as lowland farmers are paid both to plant hedgerows and to grub them out; to grow cereals and to leave good land lying fallow.

But whatever may happen to the land in the future; whatever influence town-based conservationists may have with their sometimes crackpot ideas; the uplands of Britain and Ireland cover millions of acres which offer some of the finest, most spectacular and most demanding sport for the rough shooter which can be found anywhere in the world. It can, to be fair, also provide the sportsman with long, hard, cold, wet days tramping over sodden acres of mist-shrouded moorland during which he may see nothing more than a couple of meadow pipits and a rake of hoodie crows, but even then the exercise will probably do him good.

Although I have lumped all the uplands together under a single chapter heading there are considerable variations in the type of landscape which falls into this category. The grouse moors on the eastern side of the country are covered primarily with heather,

Pointer galloping for the sheer joy of running.

whereas the lakeland fells consist largely of grass and bracken. Flatter sweeps of blanket bog may have bog myrtle and cotton grass as the dominant species along with sphagnum and other mosses and rush, deer grass and bent.

The flow grounds of the north are a maze of shallow, peaty pools; there are bare, rocky tops and scree slopes, strips of scrub woodland along valley sides and loch edges, scattered remnants of the ancient forests that escaped the fire and the axe, and in many places vast areas of cultivated conifer forests.

The high ground and moorlands are not only beautiful on the grand scale. Vegetation which may seem at first glance to be almost a mono-culture of heather or deer grass, bracken or rush can yield a host of delights on closer inspection. Orchids by the million carpet parts of the Highlands from June to August; tiny lichens and mosses form miniature forests of their own at ground level; there are bilberries and cranberries to tempt the palate in late summer and several species of insect-eating plants.

The hills and moors may look bare and empty at first sight, but they offer the rough shooter a wide variety of quarry. Some species such as grouse and ptarmigan are exclusive to these areas and can only be found on the moors, or on the high tops, but most of the low ground species are also available to the rough shot along the margins of the moors and in the valleys and scrub woodlands.

Quarry

There is a story, possibly apocryphal, of a grouse drive in the course of which one of the guns, becoming carried away by the excitement of the moment, shot a sheep which happened to pass by his butt. The gun was an Arab gentleman of considerable wealth, and when his error was explained to him he sent the head keeper to apologise to the owner of the dead sheep and to deliver some cash in an envelope by way of compensation. Initially somewhat disgruntled, the farmer opened the envelope and perused the contents carefully. 'How many more would he like to shoot?' he asked. 'You put him back in the butt, and I'll get the dog and drive the whole damn lot past him.'

Sheep are not, of course, a recognised quarry species. If you feel, possibly with good reason, that there are a damn sight too many of them on the hill, then you may regret that fact. The number of sheep on the ground is controlled at the will of the shepherd. He can add more or reduce those that are already there at will. Unfortunately the birds and animals which are of interest to the rough shooter on the mountains and moors cannot be regulated in quite such a simple manner.

GROUSE

The principal upland quarry for both the rough shot and the driven shot is the red grouse (*Lagopus lagopus scoticus*). Once considered a separate species, and the only bird species found exclusively in the British Isles, the red grouse is now said to be simply a sub-species of the willow grouse. Highly territorial birds, they are found wherever there is heather moorland in Scotland, Wales and Ireland, the north of England, Dartmoor and Exmoor.

Grouse numbers leapt dramatically during the nineteenth century when the benefits of strip burning were discovered. By burning the oldest heather in long, narrow strips on a regular rotation the grouse were provided with an ideal habitat: short, young heather for food with areas of longer heather close by for nest sites and cover from predators. With

*Swinging to take a grouse
as it curls over the hill.*

First of the season: gun with Setter, Labrador and grouse.

the introduction of grouse driving, as opposed to shooting over dogs, the latter part of the century saw enormous bags of grouse produced. Inevitably the over-concentration of a single species led to disease problems — the 'grouse disease' *strongylosis* being caused by a parasitic worm — and a series of population crashes. The grouse initially seemed to recover subsequent to a disease year, but around the nineteen-thirties a decline set in which was exacerbated by the effects of the war, and from which grouse numbers have never really recovered.

A great deal of research has been, and is being done into the causes of the decline. The blame has variously been attributed to the reduction in the numbers of gamekeepers, predation by foxes and crows, over-grazing by sheep and over-burning by shepherds, loss of habitat, disturbance by ramblers, tick borne disease such as louping ill and a number of other reasons. As yet there is no single factor identifiable as the root cause of the decline, though it is often possible to isolate the particular cause for population depletion on individual moors.

Even though it is unlikely that we will ever see a return to the numbers that existed up to the late thirties there are still ample grouse around to provide the rough shot with some superb sport. Unlike pheasant, partridge, (and sheep!) grouse cannot be reared and released successfully. They can be encouraged by heather burning, by predator control, and by the provision of grit and the siting of dewponds on dry moors, but the stock on the ground, come the Twelfth of August will consist only of those wild birds which have bred and reared their broods naturally. There will be no incubator-hatched, hand-reared and artificially-released grouse to supplement the wild stock.

This forced reliance on wild birds is, to me, one of the delights of shooting on the uplands. Like wildfowling, it is hunting in the truest sense, taking a crop from the natural surplus of a wild species and leaving a stock to reproduce and provide sport in subsequent seasons. It must also be said that over-shooting, over-grazing by sheep, lack of predator control or poor heather management can seemingly push grouse into a terminal decline from which recovery is a long and slow process — if indeed it is possible at all.

But where there are grouse what wonderful sport they provide. Their natural defence against predators is to flatten themselves in the heather where their superb camouflage will make them invisible even from a few feet away. When a covey of grouse bursts from the heather right beneath your feet on a bright August day and wings away with that curving, ground-hugging flight that is so typical of the bird I defy any sportsman to deny the surge of excitement that courses through his veins. The red grouse is, quite simply, the best of a pretty good bunch.

PTARMIGAN

The ptarmigan (*Lagopus mutus*) is a cousin of the grouse. A slightly smaller bird than the grouse, the ptarmigan is found on the high tops of the hills living year round among the rocks and scree in the harshest environment to be found anywhere in the British Isles.

In Britain it is found only in the Highlands of Scotland and the Inner Hebrides, though further afield it can be found right around the polar regions of the northern hemisphere. Its range and that of the red grouse overlap to some extent and ptarmigan will sometimes be found quite low down, particularly when they have been pushed off the tops by a hunting eagle.

A covey of ptarmigan away on the high tops.

Their plumage changes to suit the season. In summer they are a mottled grey which matches the rocks and scree among which they hide. Almost impossible to spot while they remain stationary, they give themselves away by their croaking call as they run ahead of you. Even then they can be difficult to see: until they take to the air and the wings flash brilliant white against the sky. In winter the plumage is almost pure white, apart from the black tail and a red wattle above the eye.

They look deceptively easy targets as they float away into a vast, empty sky but I have never found any difficulty in missing them. Their flight is faster than you may think and ptarmigan will often be curving downwards to disappear over the edge of the hill making it all too easy to shoot over the top of them.

Cautiously approaching a Pointer working ptarmigan above Badanloch in Sutherland.

Ptarmigan shooting will almost certainly be walked-up; the walking-up process often beginning only after a long, hard slog uphill has been completed. Their habit of running ahead of the shooting party makes them an irresistible temptation for all but the best trained dogs. They may fly around the hill for a short distance after being disturbed and then settle, but they may equally well set their wings for some distant top and disappear for the rest of the day.

Probably more dependent on the weather than any other form of shooting — no-one in his right mind tries ptarmigan shooting in the mist, low cloud or heavy rain that are all too frequent in the Highlands — a ptarmigan shoot is less an exercise in bag filling than a chance to savour the magnificent scenery of the high tops while retaining the possibility of a shot or two to keep your interest alive.

BLACK GAME

The black grouse (*Lyrurus tetrix*) has suffered a considerable decline in both numbers and range since the end of the last century. It was once found in the south and east of England but its current distribution more nearly follows that of the smaller red grouse being restricted to Scotland, northern England, Wales and the West Country.

The male, or blackcock is unmistakable with his black plumage and lyre-shaped tail, though the smaller greyhen can easily be confused with the red grouse. Dedicated bird watchers may snort at this, but it is one thing to identify the species at leisure through the lens of a telescope and quite another to realise that the bird which has just risen in front of your dog is a greyhen rather than a grouse. This is particularly difficult when you are shooting on a moor where a voluntary ban on shooting blackgame is enforced, or in the short period from the twelfth to the nineteenth of August when grouse are in season and blackgame are not.

The size is one clue, and a slower, more deliberate wingbeat is another, but it is all too easy to realise that the grouse ahead is of the black rather than the red variety only at the instant in which you squeeze the trigger. I need hardly add that such shots are invariably fatal to the blackcock or greyhen.

They like woodland rather than open moorland and can be found in birch woods, young conifer plantations and open pine forests as well as on moorland, rough grazing and agricultural land. They were once a considerable nuisance to farmers as they flew in to feed off corn stooks in the autumn, but the decline in their numbers and changing agricultural practice has long since altered that.

They will often be found on open, grassy areas of moorland, particularly where there is nearby birch or conifer woodland. In the early spring they gather at traditional lekking sites where the cocks compete for mates, and their spectacular display is well worth the effort for anyone who takes the trouble to go and observe them. The Game Conservancy are currently carrying out research into the reasons for the decline in blackgame populations, and many shoots have imposed a voluntary ban on shooting them until this decline is arrested.

CAPERCAILLIE

The capercaillie or capercailzie (*Tetrao urogallus*) is both a native and an introduced species to Britain. This huge grouse had become extinct at about the end of the eighteenth century, but was re-introduced some fifty years later using stock captured in Sweden. Credit for this is generally given to Lord Breadalbane though there were other re-introductions at about the same time. The story of the expedition to capture a stock of these great birds is vividly told in *The Banville Diaries* (Collins 1986); a fascinating account of the life of Larry Banville, the keeper who was responsible for catching and transporting them.

Attempts were made to release caper in Norfolk as well as in Scotland but the efforts failed. They are found now mostly in the eastern and central Highlands among mature pine forests. As with blackgame there is a considerable difference in both size and plumage between males and females, the huge, almost black male bird being like no other species except the domestic turkey. The female is smaller and a mottled red-brown in colour, and could be confused with a greyhen.

Like blackgame the male caper display at lekking sites to attract females during the breeding season, and make an extraordinary range of clicking, popping and rattling noises during the process. In flight they are deceptively fast, their great size disguising the fact that they are travelling quicker than even grouse or blackgame.

There has been a considerable decline in caper numbers over the past ten to twenty years, and many shoots have imposed a voluntary ban, or a very strict limit on them until a reason for the decline has been identified and, hopefully, a cure found and implemented. Where they are still shot they are often driven to standing guns. Continental sportsmen will pay large sums for the chance to shoot a cock caper in order to have it set up as a trophy, and it is possible that this in itself may have contributed to the fall in numbers.

On the continent they are stalked like deer and shot with rifles. This is generally frowned upon by the more conservative of British sportsmen, though it is hard to see why it is considered good sporting practice to stalk and shoot roe deer, but bad form to do the same thing to caper. Curiously, continental roe deer are driven to standing guns, but the British roe is, or should be, primarily a target for the rifle only. The old practice of loosing off at passing roe in the course of pheasant drives is, thank goodness, illegal since much suffering was caused by 'sportsmen' peppering deer with birdshot which was woefully inadequate against an animal of this size.

WOODCOCK

The woodcock (*Scolopax rusticola*), unlike the members of the grouse family, is not exclusively a bird of the uplands; indeed they are found practically everywhere in the British Isles. They breed here, and right across Europe and northern Asia, and the resident population is greatly boosted by the arrival of migrants during the autumn and winter months.

They are mainly nocturnal birds, resting during the day and flighting out to probe for worms with their long bills during the hours of darkness. The resident birds can be seen making their roding flights during spring and early summer, flying slow circuits round and round a particular part of their territory and uttering little grunts and squeaks as they go.

Their camouflage is perhaps the most effective of all the game birds, and often only the huge, liquid eye will betray the presence of a sitting bird however closely you look. Their pin feathers — tiny, stiff feathers which occur on the wings — were once used by artists as brushes for finely detailed work, and are popular now as hatband decorations. The wings are very large in proportion to the body and endow the woodcock with both speed and a remarkable ability to jink and weave through trees which makes it a very difficult mark.

They can be flighted for a few minutes around dusk if you can discover where they leave the woods on their way out to feed. The flight will only last a few minutes before gathering darkness makes it impossible to see them, but in those few minutes you will experience some extremely challenging shooting. They have a tendency to fly out through the tops of the trees rather than over them and this, coupled with their silent flight, means that there is precious little warning of their coming. You will see a flicker of wings against the sky and then they will be gone.

During the day they can be hunted with dogs as they rest on the ground. They are found in birch woods and among young conifer plantations as well as in bracken banks and rushes. Holly bushes and rhododendrons will often shelter birds during the day, and there are certain favourite spots which will produce birds time after time. Woodcock shooting is a very opportunistic sport, particularly when they are migrating, as the woods may be full of birds one day and completely empty the next.

THE MOUNTAIN HARE

The hills have their own species of hare, the mountain hare (*Lepus timidus*). Smaller than the brown hare (*Lepus capensis*) which is found on lower ground the mountain hare is a beautiful smokey blue colour in summer. At the end of summer they moult and, depending on their locality, the winter coat may be almost pure white, blue, or a mottled, skewbald mixture of the two.

Like the various grouse species, mountain hares are generally far less common now than they were in times past, though they are still found in considerable numbers on some moors. As with caper and blackgame, hares are afforded voluntary protection in many places where they have become scarce though there are still moors where they exist in sufficient numbers to be considered a nuisance.

They will sometimes sit very tightly, tucked into a form among the heather and quite invisible until they spring up under your feet or right in front of your dog's nose. A sitting hare seems to give off very little scent and I have often seen dogs run right over them, seemingly oblivious of their presence, though at other times they may be winded at considerable distances.

If you are walking-up on a moor where hares are found it is obviously vital to check before you start whether or not hares are to be shot. I would suggest that you might also consider the distance you are expecting to walk and whether you will be personally responsible for carrying any hares that you shoot. They are quite a bit smaller than their lowland cousins, but two or three hares in the gamebag at the start of a long day is not a prospect that I would relish.

Where hares are very abundant they are sometimes driven to standing guns, and bags of several hundred have been recorded. It is not a type of shooting that holds much appeal for me, but there is plenty of demand, particularly from continental guns, and where the hare population is high enough to require an annual cull it adds variety to the shoot.

GOLDEN PLOVER

At one time there were a whole host of waders on the quarry list including curlew, lapwing, knot, redshank, greenshank, whimbrel and more. Now, apart from woodcock and snipe, only the golden plover (*Pluvialis apricaria*) remains on the list of those waders which may be shot legally. This is something of an anomaly, since some other waders which are now protected are at least as abundant as the golden plover. Nevertheless, the law is the law, and while former quarry species such as the curlew and the lapwing are now protected the golden plover is still a legal quarry.

They are handsome little birds with their gold flecked plumage, their plaintive calls and their characteristic, plunging and wheeling flight. They can also be an infernal nuisance to the trainer of pointing dogs with their habit of peeping and running along provocatively just ahead of your half-trained pup. They breed inland on upland moors and pastures, but are much more widely spread in winter when their numbers are swelled by migrants from Iceland and the continent.

SNIPE

The common snipe (*Gallinago gallinago*) is not just a bird of the uplands. It can be found almost anywhere where there are damp, boggy patches from high moorland through wet meadows right down to the foreshore. Only the common snipe may be shot: the smaller jack snipe and larger great snipe are both protected in Britain, though the jack snipe is still a legal quarry in Ireland. Both are much rarer than the common snipe.

The snipe is a resident, and large numbers are present throughout the year, these being augmented in winter with migrants from Iceland, northern and eastern Europe and Scandinavia. It has the longest season of any gamebird, being legal quarry from the twelfth of August through to the thirty-first of January. That said, breeding pairs may still have dependant young from a second brood in late August and for this reason some guns will prefer not to shoot any which are flushed while walking-up grouse at the start of the season.

They can be walked-up, driven or shot over dogs and are guaranteed to provide testing shooting with their small size and jinking, twisting flight. They rise with a characteristic scraping cry; zig and zag rapidly for the first few yards of their flight and then may either drop back down into cover or climb high into the sky and perhaps swing back over the guns to provide a testing, driven shot.

Like woodcock they may be here today and gone tomorrow, particularly if a sharp frost locks up their feeding grounds and drives them off to low ground or estuaries in search of nourishment. They favour the wetter, rushy patches of moors but will still be found in among heather, grass and bracken. Drainage and the ploughing of grassland has removed much of their habitat and while still relatively abundant the snipe is much less common than it was in years past when professional hunters, particularly in Ireland, shot thousands every year.

OTHER SPECIES

If you are fortunate enough to have a rough shoot which blends heather moorland with mixed woodland, some boggy pasture and a bit of farmland with a flight pond and perhaps an estuary not too far away, then it is possible that you might be able to shoot practically every species in the book in that one area. The rabbit can be found practically everywhere and the brown hare's range will overlap with that of the mountain hare in places. Pheasants are not averse to life on the hill, particularly if there is woodland around the margins of the moor, and grey partridge will live quite happily on upland shoots.

Woodpigeon can be found everywhere except on the highest tops and the collared dove has spread its range to all areas of the country in the past forty years. A flight pond will attract the local wildfowl if it is fed regularly; teal, wigeon and mallard could all feature in the bag as well as other less common species. Greylag and pinkfooted geese will flight in to feed on upland grazing and even that American import the Canada goose is continually extending its range.

These will all be looked at in more detail in later chapters.

Shooting the Uplands

Driven grouse shooting on the moors of Scotland and northern England is among the best, the most well known and the most expensive shooting in the world. Those fortunate to have a gun on such a shoot will see only a fraction of the effort and organisation that is needed in order to persuade grouse to fly over their butts. Beaters will walk miles and bring in thousands of acres of ground in order to persuade the grouse to skim over the guns. Flankers work with the beaters to stop birds leaking out of the sides of the drive, pickers-up wait back behind the butts to gather the dead and the wounded; transport and lunches have to be arranged, the final bag must be sorted into old and young and readied for the game dealer. The more smoothly the day runs the greater the efforts that the head keeper and his staff will be making behind the scenes.

But shooting days organised and run on such a grand scale have little to do with the rough shooter. At its most basic a day's rough shooting on moor or mountain may require you to bring no more than your gun, some cartridges and a game bag. The game bag may well turn out to be superfluous to requirements.

On the high ground, no matter what your plans are for the day, they are likely to involve a certain amount of walking. Indeed, the simplest form of shooting is walking up: a gun, or a line of guns walking across the moor and shooting their quarry as it flushes on their approach. Nothing could be simpler, and an lot of sportsmen shoot in just exactly that manner. On a good day it can provide them with excellent sport; on a bad day you are guaranteed a good long walk. Walking-up is one alternative, but it is a poor alternative when compared with some of the others.

On typical open moorland or fell there is little cover to offer concealment to game. Rough grass and heather, ground hugging shrubs such as bilberry and bog myrtle, mosses and lichens offer shelter only to those birds and animals which are well camouflaged and adept at skulking low to the ground. Perhaps not surprisingly that is a fair description of most of the quarry species which are normally found on open moorland and mountains.

In contrast, a man with a gun stands out for miles, and there is no cover to hide his approach. If they choose to do so then bird or beast could simply up and leave at the first sight of man, and the walking gun would find precious little sport. That they do not do so is because of their inherited instincts which put concealment above flight as the best means to defeat their predators.

Bolting rabbits in the heather on the margins of the moor.

Grouse shooting high up on a Ross-shire hillside.

Intense concentration as the pointer scents grouse.

Lady handler and a brace of Labradors ready for action.

Guns and Labrador going to the next beat on a rough shoot in Scotland.

German Shorthaired Pointer and gun; grouse shooting.

The eagles and peregrine falcons, harriers and buzzards which prey on the moorland and mountain birds and animals all hunt by sight, either stooping on their prey in flight or swooping down to pin it on the ground. When a bird of prey appears in the sky the potential victims crouch down among the grass and heather and trust in stillness and camouflage to protect them. Only when it becomes obvious that they have been spotted do they take to their legs or wings and try to outpace their enemy.

These are deeply ingrained patterns of behaviour, and it is precisely these behaviour patterns that make it possible for a man with a gun to walk to within the thirty yards or so of his quarry which is necessary to give him a sporting chance of a clean kill. The problem for the walking gun is this. The camouflage of most of the quarry species is designed to fool the eyes of eagles and falcons looking down from above. The eyes of man, only a couple of yards above the heather are a poor substitute for those of a soaring eagle. Provided that their nerve holds the majority of grouse, hares, snipe and rabbits can crouch quite safely in their forms and allow man to walk past a few feet away. Unless he practically stands on them he will never see them at all.

Walking-up without a dog can be a most unrewarding task. If the birds are sitting tightly you may walk past nine out of ten and never suspect that they were there. On the other hand, if wet, windy conditions have made them flighty they are quite likely to rise well out of gunshot and never give you a chance at all. The walking-up gun can sometimes see excellent sport on the hill, but only when conditions are just right.

But let him take a dog along with him, and the balance is altered. The dog's eyes are not better: indeed they are worse, and operating at an even lower altitude: but the dog has one sense which totally transcends the equivalent one in man. I refer of course to the sense of smell.

All birds and animals give off a characteristic scent. We can identify many ourselves, providing that they are strong enough and close enough to our nostrils. A dog though can locate a sitting snipe at fifty or more yards; can track a running grouse through heather and peat hags; can follow the trail of a wounded pheasant long after it has gone. It is impossible for us to appreciate just what a wealth of information a dog receives through its nostrils; we have no comparable sense to measure it against. What we can appreciate though is the difference that a good dog, or team of dogs, can make to the rough shooter, particularly the rough shooter on moors and mountains. The dog can do what you cannot; and that is to find quarry without being able to actually see it.

Dogs may be divided into two types according to what they do when they scent game. The flushing breeds, of which spaniels are the best example, do what their name suggests and hunt up the scent of the game until it is flushed. This means that they must work close enough to the gun for the quarry to be in range when it runs or rises. In contrast, the pointing breeds react to the presence of game by standing motionless until the handler urges them to go forward and flush it. Because of this pointing instinct they can be allowed to range well out of gunshot, since the birds will not be flushed until the guns have got into position. At least, that is the theory of which more in the Gundogs chapter.

If you are shooting alone, or with one or two friends, and the ground you are shooting is sparsely stocked, then there is nothing to match a pointing dog at finding game for you. If however, you are part of a larger party — say six or eight guns — or you are shooting on ground with a heavy stock of quarry, then a flushing dog, or a team of them, may be the better choice. Mixing pointing and flushing breeds is not a good idea. A spaniel will quickly learn what it means when the pointing dog freezes on game, and you may find that you need to be pretty quick across the ground to get there before the point is 'stolen' and the birds flushed. And there is always the danger that your pointing dog will take exception to seeing his good work undone by an interloper and decide to start a little flushing on his own account.

Shooting over pointing dogs can be a relaxed and sociable way to spend the day. You can walk along with your friends, with your gun unloaded and enjoy the dog work in the knowledge that you will have plenty of time to get into position and load your gun once the dog has come onto point. You can proceed pretty much at your own pace, though it helps both you and the dog if you don't lag too far behind. You can chat to your fellow gun as you go, though excessive noise is invariably counter-productive. And when game is found you will know pretty much where it is and when it is going to rise.

Contrast this with the walking guns who do not have the services of a pointing dog to assist them. They must walk in line abreast, and take care to maintain that line throughout the day for safety reasons. If you are a kindly lot then the fitter guns will be dawdling in order to match their pace to that of the slowest member of the party. Of course, it is also possible that your leader may be the type of macho man who will press on regardless of all others until the weaker members are courting coronaries. Either way it is inevitable that progress will be too fast or too slow for at least some of the party.

The need to maintain a disciplined line makes for hard walking. If you are shooting alone, or with just one or two companions, then you can pick the easiest route. There is no need to wade through the longest stands of heather, cross the deepest parts of the gullies or scramble along the vertical faces of cliffs. This is another advantage of using a pointing dog: the dog can be sent to work the steep faces and the long heather while you take the easy route. Once you are part of a line of guns though you must follow the path dictated by the rest of the line. Over the course of the day you should all get your share of both good and bad walking. You won't really end up by having the deepest, steepest, roughest and wettest ground throughout the day — it will just seem like it!

Because you have no way of knowing when your quarry is likely to be flushed you must carry loaded guns throughout the day and be constantly alert for the sight or sound of a bird or animal breaking cover. It helps a lot if you have dogs to flush the game since their behaviour should warn you when there is game about, but if you are simply walking in line then the first indication you are likely to get is a clatter of wings or a sudden glimpse of rabbit or hare dodging through the undergrowth.

Conversation is difficult: the next gun is likely to be anything from thirty to a hundred yards away, and loud talking will do nothing for your prospects. There are circumstances when walking in line is the only option: for ptarmigan shooting high up on the tops of the hills it may even be the best option: but generally, and particularly if you have no canine assistance, walking-up is a hard, hard way to shoot over open moorland. That said, it is much to be preferred to no shooting at all.

But of course, the uplands are not just open fells and moorland. There are woods and spinneys, bracken banks, coombes and corries which can hold a variety of game from snipe to capercaillie, from rabbit to goose. The rough shot may lack the resources of the driven shot: the beaters, flankers, stops and pickers-up: but he does have the advantage of flexibility. Even with only a couple of guns it is possible to arrange impromptu drives: one gun slipping forward while the other works through a clump of trees; one waiting for birds to break back while the other hunts out a bracken bank. Try and put yourself into the mind of your quarry and think where it is likely to run or to fly, then think how you can take advantage. You won't be right all the time: you may not be right most of the time, but it will be immeasurably satisfying when you do get it just right.

And when you don't the experience will be invaluable — next time.

Obtaining Shooting

Much will depend on where you live. If you are based in the south and east of the country then any shooting you do among the hills is likely to be part of your holidays and require considerable planning and forethought. If you are fortunate enough to live out in the hills then you obviously have more scope for fitting in odd days as chance permits, or even taking a shoot of your own.

The one factor above all others that will govern the availability of shooting is the amount of money you can afford to spend. At the very top of the scale there are whole estates of twenty, thirty, fifty thousand acres available to buy or to lease by the day, the week or the season. At the other end you may be able to get a bit of rabbit and pigeon shooting simply by getting to know the keeper, or by banging on the farmer's door and asking permission.

There are any amount of estates which will rent shooting, stalking and fishing out by the week. The package may include the use of a lodge, the services of household and keepering staff and even the provision of guns, rifles and fishing rods. It can be surprisingly cheap, particularly if a party of friends get together and share the costs between them. Obviously the price will vary according to the quality of the sport and the accommodation, and to some extent on the greed of the owners or their agents. There are real bargains to be had if you are lucky enough to find them, but it is also possible to be grossly overcharged for inferior sport. Dealing through an established and reputable agent is one safeguard, looking carefully at what is on offer is another.

Hotels also offer sporting breaks, often in conjunction with their local estates, and may be able to provide a variety of shooting, from driven game to wildfowling in the course of a single week. There are regular advertisements in the sporting press.

Shooting rights can be rented, and will vary from fully keepered shoots which will cost you a small fortune to blocks of marginal ground which may be had for a few pounds per season. Land agents and sporting agents, the local press, sporting magazines and forestry companies are all sources to investigate if you hanker after a shoot of your own. If you can find ground close to your home it can provide you with sport and interest throughout the year, not just in the shooting season. Consider forming a small syndicate to share the costs and the work if time and money are at a premium

Keepering

Professional keepering services are expensive. It is not that keeper's wages are high for they are often ridiculously low for the work that a keeper is expected to do, but when housing, a vehicle and the various perks such as fuel, clothing, cartridges and dog food are added in a full-time keeper's cost will be at least double that of his wage packet. The rough shooter then, unless he is blessed with a very deep pocket, is likely to have to be his own keeper.

The rearing of pheasant, partridge and duck which accounts for so much of a keeper's duties will be looked at in another chapter, though depending on the ground there may well be a case for releasing a few birds onto your shoot. For the hill keeper though, full-time or part-time, two other aspects of keepering are likely to occupy much of his time. I refer of course to habitat improvement and vermin control.

Heather burning, *done properly*, will do nothing but good to the upland habitat. The heather is burnt in small patches or long, narrow strips which will regenerate to provide fresh, young growth to feed the grouse while leaving longer heather within easy reach for shelter from weather and predators. The dates during which heather may be burnt are limited by law in order to protect nesting birds.

Heather fires are controlled by beating the edges with brooms made of birch twigs, wire mesh or rubber, or by metal plates attached to long poles which are used to smother the fire. Great care must be taken when burning: it is never hard to start a fire but it can be almost impossible to stop it again if the wind changes. The hill should be burnt in rotation so that there is a patchwork of old and young heather, and long term planning will create fire breaks with one year's burning which can be used to control the next year's fires.

Sheep and deer are attracted to burnt ground like filings to a magnet, and where the ground is heavily stocked may severely retard regrowth by pulling out the young heather shoots. An over-enthusiastic shepherd with a box of matches can also do lasting damage to the hill by burning vast areas, and burning too frequently. This can quickly reduce heather moors to wastes of white grass and bracken which ironically are of reduced value to the sheep as well as to grouse and other game birds.

*Heather burning — hard,
hot work, but vital for the
good of the moor.*

Heather burning — hard, hot work, but vital for the good of the moor.

Excluding grazing animals from existing woodland and from the margins of the moor will encourage the regeneration of scrub woodland which will benefit blackgame and woodcock, and incidentally provide winter shelter for deer and sheep once it has grown tall enough to survive being grazed and browsed.

Wet, boggy patches will attract snipe and even the smallest pond can be fed to encourage wildfowl, so drainage schemes should avoided unless they are absolutely vital. On a larger scale there are grants available for planting trees, and while there is little benefit to the sportsman in the commercial forestry plantations there are also schemes which encourage the development of native species such as birch, rowan, Scots pine and oak. How far you may wish to go along this road will obviously depend on the terms and the length of your lease and, once again, the depth of your pockets.

Vermin control is the other factor that can have an enormous influence on the quality of your sport. Your aim is to harvest a surplus from the quarry species on your ground, and the foxes, crows and other predators will be trying to do exactly the same thing. The more eggs and chicks that disappear down a crow's gullet; the more sitting grouse that go to feed a litter of fox cubs, the less there will be for you to shoot when the season opens.

Years ago it was the practice for many keepers to see predator and prey in simple, black and white terms. If it was a quarry species you encouraged it: if it was practically anything else you shot it, trapped it or poisoned it. Those days have gone thank goodness and a combination of research, education and legislation has ensured that the majority of keepers now take a more enlightened view of the birds and animals on their ground.

The main predators which must be controlled are foxes and crows, though mink can be a serious problem in some localities. The keeper has three options in his fight against predators: he can shoot them, trap them, or in the case of foxes, use terriers to kill them underground or bolt them so they can be shot.

Trapping is undoubtedly effective — a trap works for twenty-four hours a day — but there are legal and moral restrictions to be considered before you set any form of trap for a wild animal. It is a legal requirement that all traps and snares must be inspected at least once every day. If you cannot be sure of making time to inspect your traps daily then do not even contemplate starting a trap line. It is illegal, and more importantly it is needless cruelty to expose any animal to the risk of prolonged suffering.

If daily inspections can be arranged, possibly on a rota basis with other guns, then there are several options open to the DIY keeper. Small predators such as rats, stoats and weasels can be taken by Fenn traps set in tunnels, and mink are susceptible to cage traps baited with fish or rabbit. Fox snares account for thousands of foxes every year provided you know what you are doing, or can get someone who does know to advise you, then they are an effective means of fox control. Be warned though, that they will also catch badgers, deer, dogs and cats and farm livestock if they are set in the wrong places. It is all too easy to tie a wire to a gap in the fence, but the victim may not be one that you wanted. Learn to use wires properly or don't use them at all.

Cage traps will account for crows and magpies. There are several kinds ranging from quite large, permanent structures to the portable Larsen trap which has proved most effective in Game Conservancy trials. The great advantage with traps which take their victims without injuring them is that the trapper can release any protected species that he takes by mistake. There is no second chance for a dog or a deer which gets hung in a wire.

Shooting crows and magpies can provide a little off season sport, and where it is safe to do so foxes can be taken with the aid of a lamp and a rifle and a little judicious squeaking. Remember though, that it is extremely dangerous to use a rifle at night unless you know your ground very well and can be sure where the bullet is going to end up if you miss the fox. Good communications with your local police are also advisable if you are not to be arrested as poachers or worse. The police are understandably sensitive about people wandering the countryside at night with lamps and rifles.

The use of poisons, except against rats and mice is illegal. (Moles are another exception, but they are of little interest to the DIY gamekeeper.) Don't even consider it: besides being illegal, poison is indiscriminate and will kill eagles and red kites just as easily as it kills foxes and hooded crows. It will also kill dogs, cats and conceivably humans. If you are stupid enough to set poison baits and are caught then you might well find yourself facing a prison sentence. Don't do it!

Conclusions

The hills and moors can offer us some of the best and wildest sport in Britain. There is tremendous scope for the rough shot and a great variety of sport from rabbits to grouse, geese to woodcock, pheasants to pigeons and much more besides. It can be a very different type of sport to that which the rough shooter will find among the woods and fields of the low ground, but it is none the worse for that. It helps to be fit, particularly on the wilder moors and steeper hills, and you may have to accept the cold and wet as part of the price of your sport, but if you live among the hills, or can arrange to spend a few days or weeks shooting there, then sport of the highest quality is available.

3 Fields and Woodlands

How do you begin to describe a 'typical' low ground rough shoot? There is no such thing. Certainly there are shoots which will be typical for a particular part of the country, but how can you compare the flat, windswept fens of Lincolnshire with the rolling grasslands of the Borders: the hedges and ditches of Suffolk to the marshy expanses of the Norfolk broads: open, rolling downland to the laid hedges, gorses and coverts of the shires?

Wherever there are woods or fields, marshes or meadows there is the potential for sport with the gun. A great deal of the countryside has been laid out with just that aim in mind. Shooting and hunting were not the prime movers behind the forming of the British landscape, since the ancient forests were cleared primarily to free land for food production, but the modern patchwork of woodland and fields owes a great deal to the hunting and shooting activities of landowners in the last couple of centuries.

There are other, older influences too. The Normans were great hunters, and huge areas were given over to the chase. The New Forest was created as a hunting preserve the better part of a thousand years ago, and many of the ancient rights and customs survive to this day, though it is perhaps ironic that pressure groups are now seeking to ban hunting in the forest — the very reason for which it was created. Even more ironic is the fact that changes in agricultural practice created a landscape which was the ideal habitat for game and thus permitted the development of shooting as a sport in the British Isles. Now, modern agricultural methods are as effective in destroying the potential for sport as our ancestors were in creating it.

Aside from a few stretches of ancient woodland and the tops of the highest mountains there is virtually nowhere in these islands that can be called a truly natural landscape. In pre-historic times much of the land was forested but the need to grow food for a steadily rising population meant that the trees were gradually but inexorably, felled to clear land for agriculture.

Medieval strip farming gave way to a system of fields and hedgerows in the wake of the Enclosure Acts, and by the time that firearms were reliable enough and accurate enough for shooting as a sport to become established, the countryside had itself developed into an ideal habitat for game to flourish.

For the grey partridge the patchwork-quilt landscape of small fields divided by hedgerows was the perfect environment. There was nesting cover and shelter from predators under the hedges and abundant food in the form of insects and weed seeds. Coupled with farming practices which were, at least in part, designed to encourage game production, plus an abundance of gamekeepers, the farms of the eighteenth, nineteenth and early twentieth centuries produced bags of partridge which were enormous by today's standards.

Eager concentration from this Springer spaniel.

But times change. Farming has become more and more 'efficient': so efficient in fact that our farmers can now produce enormous quantities of food for which there is no demand, beyond the artificial demand created by the Common Market which buys grain, meat and milk at intervention prices; stores it for a while and then either destroys it or sells it off at a thumping loss to countries outside the European Economic Community. Indeed, so ludicrous has this situation become that even the bureaucrats that rule Europe finally and belatedly have begun taking steps to prevent it continuing.

Three things contributed to the changes in farming that have produced these huge surpluses while despoiling millions of acres of the countryside. Mechanisation; the agri-chemical industry and soaring labour costs between them revolutionised agriculture in Britain. Since it was a revolution largely inspired and funded by successive governments it was, in the final analysis, a revolution whose costs were met by the tax-payer. As to what proportion of the tax-paying public might approve of the ways in which their money has been spent I can only speculate.

Mechanisation was inevitable. Once reliable tractors were available the days of the horse were numbered. With progress machines grew ever larger and more powerful, and in the process became less manoeuvrable. Small fields which had been suited to the horse were hard to work with tractors and combine harvesters so the fields were made bigger. And the same process of mechanisation which had produced the tractor and the combine had also produced the digger and the bulldozer. Grubbing out hedges and woods, filling in ponds and ditches, draining wetlands and bogs was suddenly easy. The government would even pay you grants to help cover the cost of doing it.

While the engineers were developing their machines, the chemists were also busy producing herbicides, pesticides and artificial fertilisers. Fertilisers maximised the yield from each acre; herbicides and pesticides controlled weeds and insects that might have competed with or preyed on the crops. Farms became increasingly specialised as the chemical industry replaced the need for traditional husbandry involving crop rotation and the use of stock to produce muck in order to maintain the fertility of the soil.

It is debatable whether rising wage levels were a cause or an effect of the changes in farming. Mechanisation and agricultural chemicals meant that much less labour was needed in order to farm, while at the same time soaring wages meant that less labour could be afforded. A farm is, first and foremost, a business and like all businessmen farmers must make a profit or go under. Farms which employed a dozen men when I was a boy are now farmed with a workforce of one or two. And the dozen men that I knew were in themselves a reduction from the twenty or so that would have worked the same farm in their grandfather's day.

The changing face of agriculture affected wildlife in a number of ways. Loss of habitat was the most obvious. The hedgerows and woods which provided cover for nests and shelter from predators were disappearing; the ditches and ponds that were home to aquatic and amphibious animals were filled in; wetlands were drained, hay meadows ploughed up and rivers dredged to prevent the flooding which was once an essential part of wetland management.

Less obvious, but potentially more damaging was the effect of the chemicals which were poured onto the land. The herbicides and pesticides killed off plants and insects which were vital steps in the food chain for a myriad of birds and animals. With their food supply thus restricted the decline of many species, including the grey partridge, was inevitable. There was also other, more direct damage caused by the spreading and spraying of agri-chemicals. Poisons which were ingested by prey species would accumulate in the system of predators higher up the food chain. The damage that was done to birds of prey by dieldrin and the like is well documented, and almost led to the extinction of several of our most attractive raptors.

Silage replaced hay as the method of storing grass for winter feed for livestock. This meant that grass was mown earlier and more frequently than for hay production, and as a result many ground nesting birds were destroyed. Stubble burning killed insects and destroyed another food source while autumn ploughing removed the stubbles that once provided cover for game birds, hares and many other species.

Changes in habitat mean that changes in the species which live there will be inevitable. Some cannot adapt to the new farming methods and the changing landscape and enter an irreversible decline — corncrakes and barn owls are as much victims of the changes in farming as are partridges or snipe — but others will adapt and increase, or move in to exploit the new environment.

I am no Luddite: change is inevitable, and the process of change is continuous. It may be a pleasant exercise in nostalgia to hark back to the countryside as it was a hundred years ago, but the exercise is fruitless. Until we have exhausted all our supplies of fossil fuels, farming will not revert to the horse and the scythe, so the tractor, the combine harvester and the chemical sprays will remain with us. There is some hope though that the worst of the government-inspired excesses of the past thirty years may be curtailed, and even reversed in some degree.

Farmers can now be paid not to grow crops, to leave arable land to lie fallow and to plant woods and spinneys. Conservation bodies such as the Nature Conservancy will attempt to prevent the destruction of those hedges, woods and wetlands that remain. And, if and when it happens, a reform of the ridiculous Common Agricultural Policy may finally see an end to the nonsense of millions of tons of surplus foodstuff being grown every year at the tax-payers' expense and then destroyed to make room for more unwanted surpluses.

Whatever the layout of your shoot it is almost certain that it will have been created by man as much as by nature. If it is primarily farmland, then the more old-fashioned the farming methods employed the better it is likely to be for the game on the shoot.

The ideal lowground rough shoot will be situated on farm land where there are still small fields surrounded by hedges and ditches and mature trees growing along the hedgerows or even out in the fields themselves. There should be areas of woodland, preferably a mixture of broad-leaved varieties rather than a mono-culture of soft-woods, and the woods should have thick undergrowth for warmth and shelter. A mixture of crops with roots as well as cereals and meadows which are cut for hay rather than silage will help, as will ponds in the corners of fields, occasional rough patches of uncultivated land with docks, thistles and other weeds flourishing and stubbles which are left unploughed during the autumn.

Trees like beech and oak provide food which will both attract game to your shoot and help to prevent the resident game from straying. Rough banks with rabbit warrens and bigger woods where pigeons roost will help to boost your sport as will low-lying ground beside a river which should flood onto water meadows in winter. If there are hills and valleys, the chances of showing high pheasants from the occasional drive receive a boost, though the contours of the land are one factor that is fixed — strip miners and motorway builders aside.

But of course; you may not have the ideal ground for your shoot. At worst you may be faced with a prairie-type farming operation growing mile upon mile of barley on flat fenland without a hedge, ditch or coppice in sight. You have my sympathy, which will not help much, though later I will suggest a few things that might. Even here, though certainly limited, there is still the potential to enjoy a rough shoot. Just about everywhere else has a head start.

Cock pheasant retrieved to Colin Organ, picking-up along a ride in thick woodland.

Quarry

PHEASANT

The pheasant (*Phasianus colchicus*) is undoubtedly the best known and most common of the game birds in Britain. The bird was originally Asian in origin and the native range of various pheasant species spreads from the Caspian eastwards to China, Burma and central Siberia. It is said by some to have been introduced by the Romans; it was definitely brought here by the Normans, and has since spread, or been introduced to, practically every part of the British Isles except for the highest mountains and some of the more remote islands.

In their native habitat there are a number of different species of pheasant but years of inter-breeding have produced a wide range of hybrid plumage variations from near black to practically white, with the majority of males being the familiar mixture of rich chestnut, gold and black barred body with bottle green or blue heads and necks. The eyes are distinguished by a bright red wattle and some have a distinctive white ring around the neck. In contrast the females are much more plainly coloured though there is still considerable variation of shade and pattern.

Millions are reared and released every year to augment the natural stock and inevitably some of these released birds will survive to breed in the wild the next spring, though the vast majority will fall victim to the gun, the motorcar or the jaws of a predator. They are the mainstay of the majority of shoots outside the grouse moors, from the smallest of rough shoots to the largest and most exclusive of driven shoots. Without the pheasant there would be precious little sport on some shoots.

It might be argued that it was precisely because pheasants can be artificially reared and released with such relative ease that the decline of the partridge was allowed to proceed unchecked for so long. Partridges can be reared and released too, but it is a much more difficult procedure, and the great partridge shoots of the last century relied on wild birds for their stock, though it is fair to say that nature was given considerable aid and encouragement by the keepers of the day.

Fashion at the end of the last century saw the great driven shoots become the focus of attention, with enormous bags the aim of many landowners. Pheasants were (relatively) easy to rear, with good management they could be held in the coverts and produced over the guns in whatever numbers the shoot owner wanted and was prepared to pay for. As partridge numbers declined so the emphasis shifted to pheasants and continuity of sport was maintained, though it is interesting to speculate what the effect might have been on the spread of intensive farming practices had the pheasant not been available to fill the gap left by the partridge.

Though it is undoubtedly an introduction, the pheasant is now so well established that it would remain a part of our native fauna even if shooting and keepering were to cease. It would not of course be present in anything like the numbers that it is now. Unless your rough shoot is remarkably well stocked with other game it is likely that you will want to hold the pheasant stock at an unnaturally high level — i.e. at a higher level than would be the norm if no stocking, no feeding programme specific to the pheasants and no

Pheasant family — note both cock and hen are looking after the chicks.

*Safely brought to hand —
Vizsla with a hen
pheasant.*

keepering was carried out. Which means of course that by introducing new stock, by providing food and by judicious gamekeeping you should be able to achieve your aim.

Stocking the shoot with pheasants is not difficult. Depending on the time and money which you wish to spend there are a number of different ways in which you can do this. There are any number of game farms which will sell you poults by the hundred, the thousand or the tens of thousands if you so desire. The poults will need to be released into a pen which will both keep them from straying out and keep vermin, particularly foxes from getting in. They will require regular feeding and watering, either by hand or by some sort of hopper system, and must be watched carefully for any signs of disease.

As they grow up they will spread out around the shoot, and if you do not provide them with what they consider to be the proper food and shelter they will continue to spread onto neighbouring shoots. Provided that you can avoid this, and nip in the bud any outbreaks of disease such as gapes, and limit the losses to vermin to a reasonable amount then you should have some pheasants to shoot during the season. If bad weather or poachers haven't killed them all beforehand.

If you wish you can start higher up the production chain by buying day-old chicks or by getting hold of an incubator and hatching your own. The eggs can come from the game farm or you can catch-up pheasants at the end of the season and let them produce them for you. As a variation on this some game farms will undertake to incubate your own eggs for you, or will take the caught-up pheasants in return for a percentage of the chicks they produce.

At the other end of the chain you can buy ex-layers from the game farm at the end of the laying period and release these adult birds onto the shoot. Putting down ex-layers avoids some of the problems that poults present: they are hardier and more canny, so less at risk from predators and foul weather, but exposes you to others. Ex-layers are notorious for wandering and considerably more difficult to manage than poults. This is probably less of a problem on a rough shoot than on a driven shoot where the keeper may want to exercise fairly direct control on where his birds go and when.

Feeding does not stop when the poults leave the release pen, unless you are exceptionally lucky with the natural food supplies on your shoot. If time permits it is hard to beat daily hand feeding, scattering wheat onto well-strawed feed rides. The fact that someone will be about the shoot every day is a useful deterrent to poachers and to predators, and the feeder, seeing his birds daily, will have an early warning of any problems which are starting up.

Feed hoppers fashioned from old oil drums or the like can be hung up so the birds can help themselves, and there are battery operated feeders which broadcast grain at set intervals if you prefer a more high-tech solution. The important point is that there is continuity: if you run out of feed then you may also run out of birds and your neighbours will benefit. It helps if the birds have to work for their suppers; by scratching through straw to find grain or by having to peck at the slot in the feeder rather than finding heaps of loose grain all ready to be gobbled up. A hungry pheasant keeps busy feeding, but a pheasant which can fill its crop too easily is a pheasant with time to spare, and may end up going walkabout.

If there are natural food sources such as oaks and beeches, berry bearing shrubs, stubbles and nursery crops it will be a tremendous help in holding and attracting game to the shoot. If you are lucky enough to have a co-operative farmer there are commercial game cover crops which will both hold and feed birds, and which can be planted in strips around field margins or where there is no natural holding cover.

Provided that your release pen is fox proof then predators should not be an enormous problem when putting down poults, though rearing from day-old leaves you open to attacks from many smaller predators such as rats, weasels and corvids. It is in the spring and early summer when the survivors from the previous season are nesting and raising chicks that the crows, jays, magpies, rats, foxes and stoats will do the most damage to your prospects.

The most important time for predator control is just before and during the nesting season when eggs, chicks and sitting hens are all easy targets for a variety of hungry mouths. One hen taken from the nest is a potential loss of a dozen or more birds for the season. Incidentally pheasants have the reputation of being careless mothers and absentee fathers, with the hen often said to be indifferent to the well-being of the rest of her brood as long as one chick stays with her, while the cock is supposed to play no part in rearing the chicks. This was certainly not true of the pheasants which raised their young near to our home in Sutherland; both parents appearing every day for food with the chicks in tow, and both cock and hen shepherding the chicks into cover if there was a threat from dog, human or winged predator.

GREY PARTRIDGE

At one time the grey partridge (*Perdix perdix*) was the most common low ground gamebird and was the main quarry for sportsmen from one end of the country to the other. They were shot over pointers and setters, walked-up through the roots and stubbles of the autumn countryside or driven to guns waiting behind hedges or hurdles. Found everywhere except the Highlands and some of the Islands of Scotland, parts of Wales and Ireland, the partridge is still present over much the same range as it was a century ago, but the numbers have declined drastically.

The reasons for the decline are the subject of much research by the Game Conservancy and others, and are generally attributed to loss of habitat as hedges were destroyed, reduction in food supply caused by insecticidal and herbicidal chemicals and changes in farming practices. In some places sympathetic farming coupled with good keeping has succeeded in holding the decline at bay, and it may be that changes in the agricultural grant system coupled to the increasing value of shooting rights may help to arrest and even reverse the decline in the fortunes of this most attractive gamebird.

Both cocks and hens are a delicate mixture of brown and grey with chestnut bars on their flanks, orange faces and a dark chestnut horseshoe on their breasts. Unlike the pheasant, partridges are monogamous and generally noted for their dedication to their brood.

Partridges can be reared and released to supplement wild stocks but it is a more complicated process than the releasing of pheasants. They need to be put out in small groups which will form coveys and attach themselves to a territory. If large numbers are concentrated in one release pen they are likely to remain in a single large pack after release and provide little shooting. Individual pens of fifteen to twenty birds should be scattered around the shoot in places where there is both food and cover, then a few birds at a time are let out leaving the rest as call birds to hold them in the area until they have accepted it as 'home'.

The problem with this is that it is obviously far more time consuming to feed twenty separate and widely scattered pens of twenty birds each than it is to feed a single pen containing four hundred pheasant poults. It may not be a problem for the shoot with a full-time keeper, but for the part-time keeper, trying to plan his keepering around a full-time job, the chances of getting around twenty or thirty pens every day are probably nil.

One of my neighbours manages to release young partridges directly onto his shoot from the rearing pen without the use of intermediate pens by turning them down in small groups in different parts of the shoot where there is good cover and natural food available. However, the shoot covers a huge area and has three full-time keepers on the books who keep the vermin well within bounds. It is in any case prime partridge environment, so the birds have little incentive to stray. If this is tried in places where the released birds find their new environment lacking in some respect then they are quite likely to disappear completely.

The old ways of keepering on a partridge shoot were extremely labour intensive. Under the Euston system the keepers attempted to find every possible partridge nest in order to remove the eggs and replace them with dummies. The eggs were then brought to the point of hatching in an incubator or under broody hens and then substituted for the dummies as the chicks began to chip out from the shell.

The eggs were therefore only at risk from predation for a relatively short time, and if a sitting hen was taken by fox or cat then 'her' eggs could be added to another clutch. Eggs were exchanged between estates in different parts of the country in order to prevent in-breeding and also imported from the continent (usually said to come from Hungary but actually from a number of different countries). The keepers trapped, shot and poisoned predators; marked nests to save them from being destroyed by mowing machines; provided water in dry seasons; discouraged poachers and discouraged trespassers who would disturb the nesting birds.

There is no doubting the value of good keepering even today, though few shoots will employ even a fraction of the keepering staff that were kept fifty or a hundred years ago. A Game Conservancy trial which effectively divided a shoot into a keepered and an unkeepered portion; then reversed this after a set time; showed vividly how important is predator control, particularly in springtime, to the success of ground nesting birds like the partridge. The part-time keeper is unlikely to be able to match the work of a dedicated professional when it comes to controlling foxes, crows and the like, but any reduction in the enemies of game will help to produce a shootable surplus when the season opens.

Partridges are heavily reliant on insect food to feed their chicks in the first couple of weeks after hatching, and as adults will take a wide range of seeds from grasses and weeds. Any reduction in the use of poison sprays is likely to benefit the partridge, and the practice of leaving the headlands of fields unsprayed, or even uncultivated, has been shown to have considerable benefits for game, and indeed for many other species.

RED-LEGGED PARTRIDGE

The red-legged partridge (*Alectoris rufa*) was brought to Britain from the continent at the end of the eighteenth century, earning its alternative name of French partridge in the course of the introduction. Inevitably the more conservative elements were opposed to the introduction and the red-leg was blamed by some for the decline of the native grey partridge.

The red-leg is similar in size and flight to the grey partridge and not easily distinguished at a quick glance, though at close range the black eye stripe and white face, the barred sides and the absence of the chestnut horseshoe on the breast will all help to identify it. Not surprisingly the legs and feet are red, as is the bill. There is little to distinguish cocks from hens apart from the spurs on the legs of the cock bird.

They are found mainly in the south and east of England and seem to prefer a drier climate than grey partridges. A charge that was frequently levelled against them, particularly when shooting over dogs was the norm, was that they preferred running to flying and were therefore unsuitable as quarry for pointers and setters. Certainly birds which run ahead of a pointing dog can cause problems but grey partridge, grouse, pheasant and even woodcock will all do the same, so it is hardly fair to condemn the red-leg on this basis alone.

There are a number of differences between red-legs and greys which will be more apparent to those who do their own keeping than to the gun who only sees the birds on shoot days. The hen will sometimes lay two clutches of eggs, one of which will be incubated by the cock. This potential for prolific production is somewhat offset by the fact that they are far more careless of the eggs than are greys and liable to greater losses from rats, hedgehogs, crows and other predators.

Like the greys they can be reared and released in small groups which will form coveys and hopefully stay in the release area. And like greys they will up stakes and walk off into the sunset if they decide that the new situation is not to their liking. Their tendency to run rather than fly can make them a difficult quarry when you are walking up, their initial burst of speed on foot taking them out of range before they rise. If there is more than one gun present then an impromptu drive may be arranged.

If you are shooting over pointing dogs then working them downwind may produce a better chance at red-legs since at the point the birds should be between you and the dog with their options to run somewhat limited. Much will depend on the type of ground you are shooting: it is obviously easier to sneak within range of birds where there are small fields bordered with hedgerows than when the coveys are feeding out in the middle of fifty acres of flat fenland.

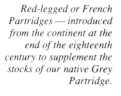

Red-legged or French Partridges — introduced from the continent at the end of the eighteenth century to supplement the stocks of our native Grey Partridge.

Until quite recently many of the red-legged partridges which were bred for release were actually a cross between the true red-leg (*Alectoris rufa*) and the Chukar partridge (*Alectoris chukar*). This cross-breeding and release has now been banned by EEC regulations which forbid the release of 'alien' species into the wild. One effect may be to make red-leg poults more expensive, since the Chukar-cross was supposed to lay better in captivity than pure-bred birds. Incidentally, had the regulations been in place in 1790 the red-leg would never have arrived here at all: a few centuries earlier and we would have no rabbits, no pheasants, no Sika, Muntjac or Chinese Water deer, and incidentally no grey squirrels and no wallabies of which there is a small wild population in Derbyshire.

BROWN HARE

The brown hare (*Lepus capensis*) is another species that has declined in numbers during recent years. It is tempting to place the blame for this decline on 'modern farming practices' in the same manner as for the decline in partridges and skylarks and other birds of the fields and hedgerows, but it is less clear why this should be so in the case of the hare. Hares still flourish, albeit in lesser numbers, in parts of East Anglia where modern farming is at its height, yet have declined badly in parts where the changes in agricultural practices have been less marked.

I remember seeing hares by the dozen from the windows of the school bus, and huge numbers being shot during the end of season hare drives. By the time I was old enough to be invited the numbers of hares were already declining, and today, far from being considered a pest the hare enjoys voluntary protection on many shoots.

They are often considered as animals of open farmland, possibly because it is in spring corn or on autumn stubbles they are seen most easily. The sight of hares boxing and cavorting about during the breeding season is a familiar one to all countrymen, though the old belief that the boxing matches took place between rival males has been corrected and it is now known that it is part of the courting ritual.

They are most common in the south and east of England and Scotland, generally on lower ground than the blue or mountain hare, though the species will overlap. The brown hare has been introduced to Ireland and to some of the Scottish Islands which is said by some observers to be detrimental to the native blue hares.

RABBITS

There can be few mammals more familiar than the rabbit (*Oryctolagus cuniculus*), even though these days, since myxomatosis has become endemic in Britain, they never reach the numbers that were common before the mid nineteen-fifties. Strangely, though now one of our most common animals, the rabbit was almost certainly introduced by the Normans who kept them in warrens as a source of food and fur rather than as a sporting quarry.

They were apparently difficult to rear when the species was first brought here and needed careful husbandry. Obviously successive generations were able to adapt to their new environment and by the time they began to escape from their warrens and spread into the wild they had become so used to the conditions, and so prolific, that despite all the efforts of man to control them they pestered farmers and gardeners for several hundred years.

Myxomatosis was responsible for a short term decline in many predators as well as the decimation of rabbit stocks. Foxes, buzzards, stoats and weasels all relied heavily on the rabbit and buzzards and stoats particularly were hard hit by the loss of their main food source — an interesting example of the principle that it is the abundance of prey that governs the number of predators and not the reverse.

Attitudes to rabbits differ widely. To some it is an unmitigated pest and should be destroyed in any way possible, including poisoning, gassing underground and even the deliberate dissemination of that vile disease myxomatosis. A recent attempt by anti-fieldsports campaigners to ban hunting with hounds specifically excluded the rabbit, though why it should be so cruel as to make criminals out of those who would pursue a hare with a greyhound but quite acceptable for them to hunt rabbits with a terrier I was unable to discover.

For the rough shooter though rabbits offer the chance of sport almost the year round. They will be found on grassland and among arable crops, in woods and on open moorland, along railway tracks and road verges, in hedges, ditches, quarries and sandpits, on downs and breckland, heaths and parklands: in fact everywhere there is space to dig a burrow and greenstuff to eat there are liable to be rabbits.

You can walk them up and shoot them over dogs — and not just gundogs. Some of the best rabbiting dogs are terriers, though they will probably do their best to save your cartridges for you. You can bolt them with ferrets during the winter and stalk them with gun or rifle during summer evenings. Provided you don't shoot too many — and if there is a big rabbit population it is very, very hard to shoot too many — they will also help to feed the buzzards, foxes, stoats, badgers and mink which might otherwise be turning their attentions to your pheasant poults or partridge chicks.

DUCKS AND GEESE

There are three ways in which to add duck or goose to the bag on your rough shoot. They may occur naturally, coming in to rivers, ponds and flooded meadows; to feed on stubbles or to graze. If there is a lake, reservoir or estuary within the shoot boundaries there may be both resident wildfowl and migrants during the winter which can provide you with some shooting from the first of September onwards.

If you are not fortunate enough to have duck coming in naturally, but have a pond, however small, that you can feed regularly with barley, wheat, chat potatoes, stale bread or whatever else you can get hold of, then there is a strong possibility that you can draw duck in to feed and thus add an evening flight to the end of the day's shooting.

Finally you can buy young ducks from game farms and release them if you have a suitable area of water. This is probably the least satisfactory method and has led to some sharp and well deserved criticism of certain shoots in recent years.

It is not particularly difficult to rear the ducklings, subject to the usual caveats about disease and predation, but it may be difficult to get them to fly well enough to provide sporting shooting. If they have become too tame they will only rise from their pond with a great deal of provocation, and then are quite likely to circle round a few feet above the ground and settle in again. To shoot what are almost literally sitting ducks in this manner is not sporting; it is no test of either woodsmanship or shooting skill, and ultimately it can be used by those who oppose fieldsports as ammunition against us.

Regular feeding of a flight pond can attract duck throughout the season provided that you do not shoot it too hard or too often. Once a fortnight is about as much as most ponds will stand, and it is best to leave before the flight has ended so that the last birds in will be able to settle and feed. By providing food for these wild birds you are also paying your dues for those that you shoot during the season. It should never be the aim of any sportsman to take without putting something back, be it food for wild birds as in this case, or adding birds to the wild stocks as when releasing pheasants, partridges or ducks, or by improving the habitat which will benefit both quarry species and others.

WOODPIGEON

There must be many thousands of fieldsportsmen (and women) who started their shooting by sitting in a hide or standing in the middle of a wood waiting for a pigeon to fly within range. The largest, and by far the most common, of the British pigeons the woodpigeon (*Columba palumbus*) is both a serious pest to farmers and nurserymen and the most common, most available, and at times the most difficult of our sporting quarry species.

The woodpigeon is found practically everywhere, though it is most abundant where there is a combination of woods for roosting and a variety of food available to sustain it throughout the year — in other words it is most abundant in just those areas where the best lowground rough shooting is to be found. They will eat a huge variety of foodstuff including acorns and beechmast, ivy berries and oak-apples, kale, rape, mustard, young corn, clover, beans, brassicas, peas, maize, barley . . . But the list is practically endless.

For years the woodpigeon was considered such a serious agricultural pest that the Ministry of Agriculture provided subsidised cartridges for pigeon shooting — some of them were actually used for pigeon shooting — and many farmers would even supply free cartridges to anyone willing to shoot pigeons on their crops. A number of men, of whom the best known was undoubtedly the late Major Archie Coats, made their living pigeon shooting, and during February each Saturday was devoted to roost shooting when practically anyone who could raise a gun was welcome to enter the woods and coverts and blaze away at the flocks of pigeons as they came in to roost.

There is some doubt now as to whether all that effort did anything to reduce pigeon numbers overall. It may well be that only a certain number of pigeons would survive through the winter to breed the following year and that shooting pressure simply did what predation and starvation would have done in any case. It may even have helped the survivors by reducing competition for food at an early stage and leaving more for those that escaped the guns. Certainly any analysis of pigeons killed compared with cartridges expended would probably conclude that the greatest beneficiary from the whole exercise was messrs Eley Kynoch.

There is no need to encourage woodpigeon to your shoot: indeed if your landlord is the farmer he may well want you to do precisely the opposite. The woodpigeon has phenomenal eyesight and is, understandably, one of the wariest of our sporting birds. Where most of the quarry on the rough shoot can be hunted out with dogs or walked-up where it is sitting or feeding, with the woodpigeon it is usually necessary to arrange for your quarry to come to you rather than for you to go in pursuit of it. You may get the odd snapshot at pigeon as you walk the hedgerows or the edges of woods, but in general they will spot you or hear you long before you get in range. And once a pigeon knows that you are there it will leave. Immediately. And usually there will be a tree between you and it for the first hundred yards of its departure.

If you are arranging to drive a wood there is often a chance at pigeons right at the beginning when the beaters first enter the cover. It helps if the guns and beaters get into position quietly with conversation kept low and dogs restrained without the use of shouts and Thunderer whistles. This is the moment when standing guns are often caught out, talking to their neighbours, lighting cigarettes or standing with guns unloaded when the pigeons wheel over them and away. And unless it is a very big wood every pigeon is likely to be gone with that first flight.

In general though, if you want to shoot pigeons you will need to conceal yourself somewhere where they will come to you. You can decoy them to feeding or drinking areas; wait in the woods in the evening as they come in to roost; or identify a flight line and ambush them along it. I had a favourite corner of a wood under a stand of beech trees which seemed to attract pigeon like a magnet. They followed the line of the wood along, then swung high over the beeches, and by standing still among the bracken it was possible to get some really testing shooting through the openings between the trees. It wasn't easy because as soon as I lifted the gun they would see me and swerve in all directions, but from time to time I would hit one.

I particularly liked that spot because there was no need to build a hide or set out lofters and decoys. I just wandered across with the gun and a dog and stood there. If nothing was moving I could try somewhere else or go and hunt a rabbit along the hedgerows or just enjoy standing there under the beeches and seeing what happened. There was always something to see and to learn from and to enjoy. I never got bored when I was pigeon shooting in that wood, even when I didn't shoot any pigeons.

Talk to the farmers on the shoot; watch the flight lines which pigeons use even when you are not pigeon shooting and see where there are crops under attack be it spring sowings, laid corn, peas, beans or greens. If you can drop everything and get down to the shoot at short notice then you may be able to help out the farmer and get a bit of sport at the same time.

OTHER QUARRY

Snipe can be found practically anywhere there is damp, boggy ground and the residents may be augmented by migrants during the winter months. Woodcock too, are both residents and visitors, and as you get to know your shoot you will know those places where woodcock are likely to be found.

The collared dove (*Streptopelia decaocto*) has spread all over the country during the past forty years and is now on the list of quarry species for England, Scotland and Wales, but protected in the Irish Republic and only allowed to be taken under licence in Northern Ireland. Fond of parks and gardens, farm buildings and grain stores, they may not have the same sporting potential as the woodpigeon, but may add variety to the shoot where they exist in sufficient numbers. Feral pigeons may be shot, but you must be sure that they really are feral (i.e. domestic stock gone wild). There are penalties for shooting racing pigeons.

Coots (*Fulica atra*) and moorhens (*Gallinula chloropus*) are both still on the list of legal quarry though there is less interest in shooting them now than there was in years past. They are broadly similar in appearance, the distinguishing feature being the white face of the coot compared to the red forehead and yellow bill of the moorhen. Both can be eaten, and provided that you intend to eat them, or give them to someone who will, then they can add further variety to the shoot. If you don't want them for the pot then leave them alone. There is no point in killing something you won't eat, unless it is to protect crops or other species that you will eat.

IMPROVING THE SHOOT

The extent to which a low ground shoot can be improved obviously will depend on the state in which the shoot begins. As with mountain and moorland environments there are a number of routes to enhancing the sport which you get from a shoot and these may be broadly summarised as the provision of shelter and food and the reduction of predation. How much can be done will depend on the time you have to spare, the money you are able to spend and your relationship with the landowner.

We have already seen that wild stocks of game have suffered in recent years from farming methods that have destroyed hedgerows, woodlands and wetlands; that have eliminated plants and insects that were vital to chick survival and that have disturbed nesting birds during silage cutting and the like. Any steps which can reverse these trends should therefore have a beneficial effect on game stocks.

While it is not likely that any farmer will welcome the suggestion that he abandons all his modern machinery and hi-tech farming practices in order to improve your rough shooting, there may be room for compromise. It is the field margins which are most important to gamebirds. Restricting the use of sprays to the centres of fields and leaving the headlands to flourish with weeds and insects, can boost the breeding success of many species of birds of which partridges and pheasants are just two. The Game Conservancy has done a great deal of research into these Conservation Headlands and can advise their members accordingly.

There are several types of game cover crop available which can be planted in narrow strips and which will provide both cover and food for gamebirds during the season and can be used to feed stock when the season ends. Again, the Game Conservancy have conducted a number of trials and can advise the best mixture to use depending on your particular location and farming pattern.

Working out a point from a German Pointer in a turnip field.

On a larger scale, planting of woods and spinneys, digging ponds and creating wet places, underplanting woodland and leaving wild areas in odd corners of the shoot will all help to a greater or lesser extent, and will benefit many species other than just game birds. There are grants and loans available to assist with many of these types of habitat improvement and it will certainly strengthen your hand with the farmer or landowner if you can show him a financial as well as an aesthetic benefit in implementing a new scheme.

It may be easier in the short term to simply hang feeders around the coverts and supply wheat for your pheasants, and this will probably still have to be done if you decide to rear any number of birds. The benefits from game cover crops, headland conservation, creating new woods and ponds and other habitat improvements are slower to come through but over a period they may well prove to be more effective, both in holding your reared poults and in maintaining and increasing the stock of wild birds.

PREDATOR CONTROL

The predators of the low ground shoot are much the same as those that beggar the moorland gamekeeper: foxes and crows, mink, stoats and weasels, plus magpies, jays and poaching cats. The same laws apply to the use of poisons, the inspection of traps and the protection of certain species, and to a large extent the weapons that may be used against low ground predators are the same.

Rats are likely to be a problem on low ground shoots, both as predators on eggs and chicks and for the feed that they steal and spoil. Baiting with Warfarin is one way to account for them provided that it is carried out properly and responsibly. Baits must be placed where the are out of reach of dogs and farm stock and must be replenished regularly until they cease to be taken. Tunnel traps and cage traps sited near feeders, around release pens and along hedgerows will also account for rats as well as stoats and weasels.

Crows and magpies can be shot or trapped in cage traps baited with eggs or carrion. Best of all is a cage trap containing a live crow or magpie, suitably supplied with food and water, which will entice others of the species to join it. The traditional cage trap was normally a fixed structure but the recent innovation of the Larsen trap can be moved around the shoot. Plans are available from the Game Conservancy if you decide to make your own, or complete traps can be bought ready to use from shoot suppliers.

Snares can be effective against foxes, but as we have already seen, they are also effective against dogs, cats, deer, badgers and farm stock. One stupid mistake with a wire snare may well be enough to lose you your shooting should the farmer's prize ram or champion sheepdog be the unfortunate customer.

Running an electric fence around the release pen won't kill any foxes but it may well persuade them to leave that particular area alone, despite the enticement of the poults. Winged predators are more difficult to discourage and the law does not permit you to deter them permanently with an ounce of shot, however infuriating their attentions may be. Any bird-scaring devices that might keep owls or sparrowhawks away from your poults might also tend to panic the poults, though if you should become subject to a regular visit from a protected predator it might be worth trying a few children's windmills on the top of the release pen posts. Hopefully the poults would soon get used to them — of course the owl or hawk might get used to them as well.

FINDING SHOOTING

It may be a depressing fact, but it is a fact that must be faced: the ease with which rough shooting can be obtained will depend to a considerable extent on the amount of money you have to spare. If cost is no object then there should be no real problem in finding a place to shoot either by using the services of a sporting agency or by studying the advertisements in trade magazines. For those of us with less spare cash it may be more problematical, but it should not be impossible for anyone to find some shooting. It may not be exactly the shoot of your dreams, but once you have located the first step on the ladder you can begin to think about climbing a little higher.

Shooting magazines are the obvious place to look for shooting to let, but your local paper may well be a better source for shooting in your area. There are plenty of hotels which offer sporting breaks and an increasing number of farms which let out rough shooting by the day — though I would advise caution in these cases or you may find yourself paying fifty pounds for the pleasure of walking round all day in search of the last rabbit left after a hundred similar day's 'sport'. Get to know your local syndicate; perhaps offer to do some beating or picking-up if you have a steady dog. If there is a wildfowling club or gun club in your area they may have some shooting rights for their members.

If you are a stranger in the area, new to shooting and not able to spend a lot of money then it is not going to be easy to find shooting. Offers of work; beating, helping with feeding or building pens, perhaps feeding a flight pond; may help to get you accepted, and will give you a useful insight into the background work of running a shoot. If the occasional invitation should follow, and you handle yourself and your gun safely and politely, then acceptance may not be too far away.

4 Forestry Plantations

There were lots of woods in and around the village where I grew up. They all had names — I remember Ben Hunt's Plantation, Birdsedge Wood, Dorman's Wood and less interestingly, Big Wood, Hall Wood and 'A' Wood. There was no 'B' Wood, but I suppose there may have been one planned by the same, unimaginative Lord who had 'A' Wood planted. None of them were big enough to qualify for the title of forest, even to a boy with a bow, arrows, and a head full of the adventures of Robin Hood. The nearest forest was thirty miles away at Thetford — the evocatively named Thetford Chase.

The Chase consisted of several thousand acres of Forestry Commission softwood plantation, spread out across the rolling Brecklands of Norfolk. There were deer and squirrels among the trees, mile after mile of forest rides to walk down, open beech glades for picnicking and stalker's high seats to climb. There were also quite a few pheasants along the edges of the trees and partridges where the forest ran alongside farmland. It was certainly not a natural landscape — trees all of one species planted in long straight rows, piles of logs to mark the site of forestry operations — but it was attractive enough to draw bird-watchers, picnickers and Sunday afternoon drivers from miles around. But Thetford Chase is one of the older Forestry Commission woodlands.

Until the beginning of this century the management of woodland had been pretty much in the hands of landowners. Trees were felled for their timber and to clear land for agriculture; coppice woodland provided fuel and charcoal and new woods were planted, often specifically to provide coverts for hunting and shooting. The richer landowners would import rare and exotic species from all over the world to enrich their parks and gardens and to add to the variety and beauty of their woodlands.

But although individual landowners may have been planting trees and creating new woodlands the overall area of woodland in Britain was declining, and had probably been declining for the past thousand years. The industrial revolution hastened the decline and the first world war made massive inroads into what was left. In 1917 the government set up a committee under Sir Richard Acland to examine the problem and as a result the Forestry Commission was formed in 1919, charged with the task of restoring Britain's woodlands.

Obviously any project involving timber production is essentially a long term undertaking and by the time that the first of the new forests began producing timber another half a million acres or so of native woodlands had been felled — a process accelerated by the second world war. Targets for the Forestry Commission were raised and grants and tax breaks were introduced to encourage the private landowner to plant trees.

That the policy has been successful in increasing the area of Britain under tree cover is undeniable — there are currently around four million acres of Forestry Commission and private woodlands that have been planted since its introduction. What is doubtful though, is whether the type of trees being planted are of any real aesthetic or amenity value, or whether they can be considered in any way a substitute for the older woodlands which they have replaced.

Natural woodland is an extremely rich and diverse habitat. Trees of different species and different ages are mixed together and support a variety of plants, birds, animals and insects. Wind, fire and natural wastage open up clearings and let the light in to encourage shrubs and wild flowers which are in time supplanted by mature trees. There is a slow but sure progression in the life of a forest as it matures from scrub to broad-leaved woodland. The problem with modern forestry plantations is that there is no time for that slow progression to take place.

The forester is quite naturally concerned with producing a crop of timber and seeing a return on his investment. The fastest return comes from softwoods, therefore the vast majority of those four million acres planted since 1919 consist of conifers such as sitka spruce, lodgepole pine, Norway spruce and larch. Hardwoods such as oak, beech and ash are much too slow growing to produce cash crops within a reasonable time for the forestry companies.

Thetford Chase was planted with pines, but they were planted far enough apart to let some light through to the forest floor. The modern plantation is generally a much less pleasant place. To begin with the ground is first cultivated with a drainage plough which rips deep furrows down through the topsoil. The trees are planted in tightly packed ranks along the tops of each furrow; fertilised and sprayed with insecticides and left to grow.

Initially the newly planted forest can support a variety of plant and animal life, but the situation soon changes. As the trees mature they jostle closely together shutting off the light from the ground beneath. Once the canopy closes over, the ground under the trees becomes a sterile carpet of dead conifer needles: no flowers, no shrubs and precious few birds or animals will live there.

The timber is cropped by taking out intermittent rows of trees in order to let the others grow larger. This no doubt maximises the tons of timber produced per acre and the cash value of the forestry project, but it does nothing to provide the richness of the natural woodlands which the new forests are supposed to replace. This method of growing trees has little to do with woodland management as it was practised in past centuries.

Intensification in forestry has produced monocultures of exotic trees which are most closely identified with intensive cereal growing and the open, prairie-like fields of the heavily subsidised barley barons

The tax breaks offered by the government became so attractive during the nineteen seventies and eighties that sportsmen, television personalities, rock musicians and businessmen could invest heavily in forestry and be assured of a paper profit irrespective of the eventual cash value of the timber. This led to widespread protests as wild areas such as the flow grounds of the far north were ploughed and planted, and eventually to changes in the grant system.

There are signs now that a more sympathetic approach to forestry design and management is being adopted by both the public and private forestry agencies. Deer are managed for their sporting value instead of being shot as vermin; trees are planted to blend with the landscape instead of in giant rectangular blocks, and a mixture of species, particularly around the woodland edge, adds beauty and variety to the newer forests.

*Young beater with
pheasant in a mature
forestry block.*

When considering forestry plantation shooting in this chapter I am thinking of the type of shoot where all, or a very substantial part of, the ground is given over to intensive forestry production. Many shoots will have some forestry blocks within their bounds and will probably incorporate them into their shoot management, perhaps as holding cover or as sites for release pens if the trees are suitably spaced. In those situations the forestry is just one part of the shoot; a resource to be exploited or perhaps a relatively useless area to be left alone. Here though it is the type of shoot which is leased by the Forestry Commission or private forestry companies that we are concerned with: all trees and not very much of anything else. As we shall see there are particular problems associated with this type of shoot.

To the rough shooter in search of a place to shoot, a forestry plantation may offer the best chance of finding some ground of his own. The shooting rights over blocks of forest

Three guns about to enter a block of young trees.

are advertised in the press, usually inviting tenders from interested parties. The rents are sometimes quite staggeringly low, a few pounds per annum securing the rights over hundreds, and perhaps thousands, of acres of ground. Beware though of buying the proverbial pig in a poke — even a few pounds per annum may be more than the shooting rights are worth. A lot will depend on the age of the trees and the ways in which the plantation is being managed.

When it is first ploughed and planted, forestry land may even be at an advantage over the surrounding countryside in providing a habitat for game and other species. In areas where fencing is needed to keep deer and sheep away from the young trees there may be a dramatic resurgence of growth within the fence as heather and grasses, brambles, scrub birches and other trees take advantage of their protected environment. This new cover and relative lack of disturbance may attract and hold game in the area for a few years until the growth of the conifers begins to shut out the other species. It may not be easy ground to work: walking across forestry ploughing is notoriously hard on man and dog alike: but in the first ten to fifteen years after planting you may enjoy some decent shooting.

What follows will depend very much on the way the plantation is being managed. If the whole area of the shoot is covered with trees of roughly the same age, and they have been planted in the modern 'pack-'em-in-tight' style then you may be reduced to scratching around the forest rides for the odd pheasant or rabbit or waiting for wood pigeons to drop in to roost in the evenings. Between the rides the trees are sometimes planted so closely together that it is practically impossible to force your way through them, let alone see, much less shoot among them.

Nevertheless, with around four million acres of them across the country, forestry plantations are an important part of our landscape. They may be far from ideal ground for the rough shooter but at the same time they may be all that is available.

That the dense rows of trees act as reservoirs for vermin is a fact of which keepers who have blocks of forestry on or around their patch will be only too aware. Crows can nest among the trees, secure from the eyes and the gun of the keeper and foxes lie up during the day, coming out to hunt in darkness. Trapping, snaring and shooting using a lamp may account for any number each season but somehow there is always another fox or another pair of crows to take their place. Clearing a large forestry block of predators is a bit like trying to empty the sea with a bucket — however hard you work at it you are never going to succeed.

Stalker's high seats can be useful to the keeper as well as to the stalker. Being set up above the ground seems to allay the suspicions of foxes as well as deer and sitting quietly in a high seat at dawn or dusk is a good way to cull foxes. You will probably need a rifle rather than a shotgun — the range at which a fox can be killed by a shotgun is very limited and there is no excuse for firing at any animal in the knowledge that you can only wound it and not kill it cleanly. Be sure that you clear your actions with the stalker: they are his high seats, he may be rightly suspicious of a stranger armed with a rifle occupying one of them and more than a little upset if you blaze away at a fox and ruin his stalking for the day.

Newly-planted trees have good potential for holding game and, provided that they have been sufficiently thinned out, blocks of mature timber may allow enough undergrowth to become established to attract pheasants, partridges and rabbits. When the trees are felled there will be piles of brashings and stripped bark to shelter game, and pioneer plant species will quickly establish themselves in the newly-cleared areas.

The most important part of a forestry shoot is not the interior of the blocks of larch, spruce or pine trees. Dense and dark, there is little to attract game and quite probably little hope of finding the birds even if they were there. The blocks are too thick to shoot walking-up and often too large to drive. It is the margins that will produce your birds: the boundaries of the forest where it meets farmland or moorland, the edges of rides and fire breaks, the open areas where wind blow or felling have cleared the trees and let through some light and air.

Many forestry blocks have strips of broad-leaved trees planted around their borders to disguise the uniform ranks of the conifers and these are attractive to game. On low ground pheasants will utilise these strips while in upland plantations blackgame are attracted to them. If oak or beech trees are established, pigeons as well as pheasants will come to feed on the acorns and beechmast.

Woodcock will use conifer plantations to rest in during the day, flighting out to feed at dusk. They can often be seen along the edges of roads and forestry rides in the headlamps of cars, or in the spotlight when lamping foxes, and will sometimes be present in quite surprising numbers. Flighting at dusk may give you some exciting shooting, but it will only last a few minutes before it is too dark to shoot. If the trees will permit you to hunt through them with a good dog then you may be able find woodcock during the day. Where the trees are young and the 'cock fly above them when flushed the shooting is relatively easy, but where they are twisting and turning between the trunks of mature trees it is another matter entirely.

Pigeons like roosting in the fir trees, protected from wind and rain and safe from the eyes of most of their predators, including man. Even so, they have to fly out to feed and to drink, and siting a hide under a flight line can provide good sport during the day as well as at roost time in the evening. The ponds which foresters establish as part of their fire precautions will attract pigeons seeking drinking water and may be suitable for feeding as flight ponds for ducks.

Walking the rides with a dog hunting ahead of you may not give you a very full bag but it will give you plenty of exercise and the chance of a shot at rabbit, pigeon, pheasant, woodcock, perhaps partridge, snipe, hare or blackgame, and even capercaillie in some areas. Crows and foxes are not what you want to see on a shooting day but they may also provide a few shots for you. Unless the rides are very wide one gun can usually cover everything that gets up within range and two is probably the maximum before you begin to get in each other's way.

Releasing pheasants into a big forestry plantation is an operation fraught with danger, but it can be done and many established shoots do it every year. A fox-proof release pen is an obvious priority as is the provision of a constant supply of food. If your poults once start wandering there is no telling where they may end up, so every effort must be made to keep them safe from predators, free from disturbance and occupied with scratching for food. In calculating the number of birds that your shoot can hold, take care not to pay too much attention to the total area alone. A thousand acres of intensively-managed forestry might only have a couple of hundred acres along rides and around the borders which were actually suitable pheasant habitat.

This means that your couple of hundred acres may consist of a strip of scrubby woodland five miles long and a hundred yards across, with open farmland or moorland on one side and a thick blanket of trees on the other. Instead of aiming to hold your birds in the middle of the shoot to stop them straying over the boundaries you will have to contend with them being spread out right around the boundary itself.

This obviously has a potential for fairly stressful relations with your neighbours, depending on whether birds are drifting from your shoot onto their ground or being attracted from their shoot by your feeders. Or more importantly, depending on whether you each *think* that birds are drifting one way or the other. You are not going to relish the idea of rearing poults simply for them to be shot by your neighbours any more than they are likely to approve of your feeders being sited all along their boundary — even if the boundary is the only practical place for them.

This is the type of case when discussion at an early stage, and certainly *before* the start of the shooting season, may lead to some sort of amicable arrangement between you which will save a lot of ill-feeling later on.

Shooting lets over forestry plantations usually do not include the stalking rights, though this is not an invariable rule. Roe deer can be a considerable nuisance to the pheasant rearer as they will quickly learn that your feeders are a source of supply for deer as well as pheasants. Roe quickly become adroit at butting and rattling feeders to shake out the wheat or pellets, and a family of roe can get through an awful lot of expensive food in a very short time. Some kind of fencing around the feeders which will let pheasants through but exclude deer is the one answer, or you may be able to find or

Guns among Rosebay Willowherb in recently felled woodland.

design a feeder that is impervious to the attentions of deer. If not your feed bill is going to be a lot higher than it need be.

The long-term nature of forestry means that it is more difficult to make changes that will benefit the shoot than it is on farmland where crops are rotated every year. Often the sporting rights are let in order to make a few extra pounds of revenue each year and are seen as only marginally affecting the management of the forest. A good relationship with forestry staff, both at management and forester level, can help enormously in preventing poaching, disturbance from walkers exercising dogs and in avoiding expensive mistakes such as siting a new release pen next to an area about to be felled.

The amount of sport that you can get from a forestry shoot will depend mainly on the way in which the trees have been planted and managed. If they are set out in small blocks, with frequent rides criss-crossing them; if there is a mixture of old and young trees with blocks being felled and replanted; if there are deer lawns, open glades, hardwoods along the edges and patches of dense undergrowth here and there then you should enjoy some good shooting, and have the potential to improve it by stocking and predator control. On the other hand, if your shoot is a dense monoculture of tightly packed spruce, unrelieved even by access rides (many forests are planted with the minimum of rides, access roads for forestry operations only being made when the trees are ready to be felled) then your sport will be limited to hunting around the borders with little chance of making any real improvements to the number or variety of quarry species. The only consolation is that the rent should reflect the value of the sport on offer.

Even so, you will have a place where you can wander around with dog and gun hunting-up the odd rabbit or pheasant, flight pigeons as they come in to roost and perhaps woodcock as they go out to feed at dusk. The forests are usually quiet when timber operations are not being carried out; the trees tend to blank out the sounds of traffic and farm stock; and a peaceful stroll among the pines can help to relieve the stress of a busy life-style.

At their worst forestry plantations are dark, gloomy, foreboding places with no bird song, no animal life and precious few plants beyond the rows and rows of trees all straining for light and air. To many people they are moody, depressing places, devoid of the richness and variety that exists in natural woodland. There is certainly no comparison with the ancient forests that once covered much of the country, but for better or worse the forestry plantations are here to stay. The rough shooter can only make the best of what is on offer.

A pheasant shot on the edge of the moor. Even in such open country an open boring should be adequate.

Shooting grouse over a pointer – range at this moment perhaps ten yards.

Guns with Springer Spaniels walking-up pheasants through rough grazing land.

In the thick of it. One bird in the hand and the Labrador is already back with the next.

5 Foreshore and Marsh

The salt marshes and mudflats, creeks and estuaries which are found around the coastline of Britain would normally be considered more the province of the wildfowler than the rough shooter. Anyone familiar with the writings of Colonel Hawker, Abel Chapman, Sir Ralph Payne-Gallwey and more recently 'BB' will have a mental picture of the loneliness of the windswept mudflats, the sound of the wind through the reedbeds, the gentle lap of the tides and the whisper of wings in the moonlight even if they have never lain out themselves waiting for fowl to flight.

There is a desolate beauty about the foreshore; a loneliness and an element of danger that attracts a certain kind of sportsman to the cold and wet, the gales and rain, the early mornings, late nights, and the plowtering mud which plasters boots, clothes and equipment alike. The true wildfowler is supposed to be at his happiest only when there are flakes of snow being driven before a gale of wind, the glass is falling like a stone and the temperature is only marginally above absolute zero. For myself, I suspect that all that cold, wet and discomfort is at its most attractive when seen in retrospect, preferably through the bottom of a glass, but to each his own. Wildfowling in the depths of winter is definitely for the fittest and hardiest of sportsmen.

But leaving the open mudflats aside there are still many places around the coast and along rivers and estuaries which offer a chance of sport to the rough shot as well as the fowler. The rocky coasts of the north and west where steep cliffs and sandy beaches mark the transition from land to sea are of relatively little interest as far as rough shooting goes, but there are other places where the meeting of sea and land is more gradual, less clearly defined, and here the rough shot can look for a surprising variety of quarry.

A sand dune is perhaps not the most promising of places to start. Dunes piled up by wind and tide and shaped and reshaped by gales offer little purchase for plants. It is a long, slow process but sooner or later pioneering species such as marram grass will take root and begin to stabilise the dune. This colonisation is sometimes speeded up by planting grasses and pegging down netting to the surface of the dune in order to create sea defences or to protect established dunes from erosion.

Once the pioneering plants have taken hold and their roots have begun to spread through the top layers of sand other plants begin to colonise. At first salt-tolerant species like sea holly move in but in time grasses and heathers, thorn bushes and birch scrub will become established on the landward side while new dunes begin to grow to seaward.

Rabbits are among the first animals to inhabit the dunes and the easy digging offered by the sand allows them to excavate extensive warrens. Constant nibbling helps to encourage finer grasses to supplant the coarse marram and the dunes take on their familiar appearance of humps covered in long, rough grass surrounding finely cropped hollows. Such areas are ideal for golf links; the game is supposed to have originated among sand dunes; and it may be possible to obtain rabbit shooting on your local course. Greenkeepers and golfers are not fond of rabbits and their tendency to scratch holes in carefully tended putting surfaces.

Sand dunes are also popular with holiday makers, and it should hardly be necessary to remind you to take great care never to shoot unless you can see clearly what is in line with your muzzles. A picnic party or a courting couple peppered with shot will probably mean the end of your shooting rights and quite possibly the revocation of your shotgun certificate. A degree of tact with regard to when you shoot is also advisable — you may have a perfect right to be shooting rabbits but to members of the public reared on Beatrix Potter stories you will be seen as a cruel monster. Save your shooting for the winter months, or for days when the trippers are not around.

Further inland the grasses and mosses may be supplemented with shrubs and trees and the extra cover can be attractive to pheasants and pigeons as well as the ubiquitous rabbit. The ground behind the dunes is often wet and boggy and should attract snipe and woodcock as well as wildfowl. Much of the shooting may be opportunist: woodcock are notorious for being here today and gone tomorrow: and in many areas will become increasingly regulated by conservation bodies as the dunes and their associated marshes are made Sites of Special Scientific Interest or Environmentally Sensitive Areas.

Shingle beaches provide nest sites for a variety of gulls and shore birds but offer little else in the way of food or shelter, the constant shifting of the stones and the swift

Gulls and oystercatchers flighting over the Solway.

drainage making sure that few plants can become established. The shingle is constantly shifting under the influence of the tides, this longshore drift moving from north to south along the North Sea coast and from west to east along the English Channel. Groynes built at right angles to the coast are often used to try and arrest this drift and protect the land from erosion. In places huge shingle spits have built up, such as the the the one at Orfordness and salt marshes or lagoons may be formed in the relatively sheltered area to landward of the shingle.

Rabbits will be found almost anywhere there is grass for them to eat, but the birds which congregate behind the shingle banks will depend to a large extent on the salinity of any water lying there. Pheasants do not mind damp conditions underfoot, their native habitat being marshland and swamps, and can be found right down to the edge of the shingle, and in the reedy dykes and drains behind the sea walls. Snipe will be found wherever there is damp ground for them to feed on and several species of duck will take advantage of the food and cover offered by the dykes.

If the danger of flooding is not a limiting factor then pheasants can be released, though holding them may be a problem if there is a more attractive alternative just inland. The possibilities of duck flighting are obvious, the number and types of duck that you may find depending very much on the part of the country. As with any flight pond, regular feeding and freedom from disturbance are the main factors in attracting and holding a good stock of duck, and of course the flight pond should not be over shot. Once a fortnight is generally held to be about the maximum and once a month would be better.

The slower flowing rivers which deposit tons of silt and mud along their estuaries are the mecca of the wildfowler. Small animals and plants living in and on the mud provide food for millions of wading birds, geese and ducks which follow the tides in and out as they feed. Huge areas like the Wash in Lincolnshire and Norfolk, the Solway, the Severn Estuary and Morecambe Bay are the wintering grounds for mallard and wigeon, pink-footed and grey geese, shelduck and teal as well as knot, dunlin, oyster-catchers, brent and barnacle geese, and a host of others. In the old days the market gunners — professional wildfowlers — made their living from what they could shoot with their punt guns, supplemented at times by fees for guiding gentlemen gunners who came to shoot

Mallard on the margins of an estuary.

for the sport. The mudflats and gutters are still the preserve of the fowler and even the occasional punt gunner, but it is to the area above the mudflats that we must look for sport for the rough shooter.

Plants which can gain a footing in the mud are few, but some such as cord grass, sea manna grass and marsh samphire do succeed in colonising the more sheltered areas of the estuaries. The vegetation traps silt and slowly the mudflats are transformed into salt marsh and new land is formed from the sea. The process is speeded up by man; building sea walls, digging dykes and planting colonising species in order to hasten the growth of the marshes. At first the marshes will flood on spring tides and only salt-tolerant plants will survive but gradually the sea is excluded entirely and the land given over to agriculture.

Snipe will be found on the salt marsh as well as on the reclaimed land in-shore. The salt ponds on the marsh and the drainage dykes will attract duck of many species while geese will flight-in from the open water to graze the sweet grass on the meadows. They can be intercepted as they fly in if they are crossing the sea wall at a low enough height, or ambushed from the cover of a rough hide as they drop in to their feeding grounds. Decoys may help to bring them within range and the skilful use of a goose call, though it is also possible to drive them away.

Stalking geese as they are feeding is rarely easy; they like to feed well out into the middle of fields away from any cover, and there are always some heads raised as lookouts while the rest are grazing. If you are shooting alone a stalk or an ambush are the only options, but if you have one or more companions then it may be possible to arrange a 'drive' with one gun putting the geese up while the others conceal themselves along the anticipated line of flight. Naturally geese do not co-operate in these matters with quite the same alacrity as hand-reared pheasants, but luck and careful attention to the wind direction may provide you with the occasional success.

The draining and reclaiming of land is not by any means a modern phenomenon. The Romans are known to have carried out land reclamation in the Wash, and Dutch engineers drained thousands of acres of marsh and fen to create the fertile farmlands of Norfolk and Lincolnshire. These flat, open fens with their long, straight drainage dykes and huge fields of corn, vegetables, flowers and fruits have a haunting beauty that is all their own.

Winter floods can bring thousands of duck inland to feed on the flooded washes and some exciting flight shooting is possible if you can be in the right place at the right time. Snipe love the wet, boggy washes and can provide testing shooting as they spring out of cover and twist and jink away. Small shot such as eights are often recommended for snipe, and if you are going out with the sole intention of snipe shooting then eights are certainly adequate and will improve your pattern density and possibly your kills-to-cartridge ratio if such things interest you. Usually though, snipe will be encountered as just one among several quarry species, and while small shot may be good for snipe it is far from ideal for the duck, pheasant and hares which may also feature in the bag. Number sixes, properly placed, will kill most of the snipe you shoot at, and if you should miss an occasional one because the pattern has failed then good luck to the snipe.

I once used to train my dogs along the shores of a Suffolk estuary where salt marsh was separated from the adjacent farmland by a steep earth bank reinforced by pre-cast concrete blocks. Behind the sea wall the bank was covered with a mixture of rough grass and bramble, and it was a sure place to find pheasants. Sheltered from the wind by the wall and fenced off from the cattle that grazed the meadows, they had cover, food provided by seeds and insects, and apart from my dog-training forays, peace and quiet for most of the time. The meadows behind the sea wall were generally grazed pretty short, and were more likely to hold brent geese than pheasants, but that strip of sea wall was a sure place for a find.

A lot of the washes and wetlands have disappeared in the past few years; drained, ploughed and then turned over to cereal production. More recently though, the conservation authorities have acted to prevent further loss of these wetland habitats, setting up management agreements with landowners to conserve the traditional ways of managing the flood meadows. While this is undoubtedly better than seeing them drained and ploughed there is always the danger that shooting will be banned by the conservationists when the management agreement is in place.

There have been a number of cases in recent years where wildfowlers have lost their shooting rights after a change in the ownership, or the management, of an area of the foreshore. Too often this has happened in an entirely arbitrary way with the fowlers simply being notified that as from a certain date shooting will be prohibited. Such unilateral declarations are extremely difficult to reverse.

Whether it is the Local Authority, one of the Government funded conservation organisations, or a charity such as the Royal Society for the Protection of Birds, it will almost certainly be harder to persuade them to lift a ban once it has been imposed than to prevent the ban being imposed in the first place. If there are any signs of a change in management, or ownership, of your shooting ground then the sooner you get involved in negotiations with the new management the better it is likely to be.

The responsible rough shooter or wildfowler, far from being a threat to wildlife, should be seen as an ally of the conservationist. Allowing shooting by authorised sportsmen will restrict the activities of those who have no authorisation to shoot but who will take advantage of the lack of a gamekeeper to poach the marshes and foreshore. Perhaps worse than the traditional poacher who will generally confine his activities to the recognised quarry species is the sort of lout who, armed with air rifle or shotgun, will

raft of mallard resting ear a river mouth.

blaze away at anything he sees; rare and protected species not excepted. The element of policing that will result from an sporting tenant keeping an eye on his preserves should be enough reason to continue shooting, apart from any other benefits that may accrue.

Control of predators, particularly where there are ground-nesting birds, is another valuable service that the shooting man can perform for the conservationist. Foxes, crows, magpies and the like are not just the enemies of gamebirds. By reducing their numbers through trapping and shooting the rough shot will be improving the prospects for all the other species which nest and feed on the shoot. Co-operation, rather than confrontation, is far more likely to benefit both sides in any dispute over the continuance of traditional shooting rights.

The laws which deal with shooting rights on the foreshore in England and Wales are substantially different from those which apply to Scotland. North of the border the foreshore — that is to say the area between the high and low water marks — is considered to be public ground, and the public have the right, among others, to shoot wildfowl. In England and Wales the foreshore is owned by the Crown and no such public rights exist. For many years wildfowlers shot on the foreshore and were allowed to do so in that the Crown did not attempt to prevent them. Following negotiations between the Wildfowlers Association of Great Britain and Ireland (then known as WAGBI but since re-named the British Association for Shooting and Conservation — the BASC) and the Crown Commissioners, permission was given for members of WAGBI to shoot on the foreshore, unless of course the shooting rights had previously been assigned by the Crown to some other body.

As we have already seen, this right to shoot on the foreshore has been under attack by conservation bodies and local authorities in recent years. In addition the shooting rights over many areas are now restricted to the members of wildfowling clubs and associations affiliated to the BASC. If you are planning to shoot on the foreshore, other than in Scotland, it is essential that you make sure that you have the right to do so before setting out with gun and dog.

It may be, of course, that you have the rough shooting rights on ground which marches with an estuary or with the coast. Obviously there may be problems if wildfowlers have the right to shoot on the foreshore immediately below your release pen, particularly if the shooting is not controlled by a responsible body such as a local wildfowlers association. At the best, constant disturbance will be a nuisance; at worst you may find your stock of game being depleted by every poacher in the neighbourhood. Of some help may be the fact that neither in Scotland, nor in England and Wales, is there a public right of access to the foreshore through private ground. Any attempt to do so without permission will probably amount to armed trespass.

Wherever your shoot is, be it inland or on the coast, low-lying marshland or high moorland, the best antidote to the poacher is undoubtedly the presence on the ground, as often as possible, of a keeper, the shooting tenant or some other interested party who will both see and be seen by anyone planning mischief. If your shoot is miles from your home and you are only going to be there on alternate Saturdays from November to February then poaching problems are always likely to arise. If the shoot happens to be bordered by foreshore where the public can shoot as and when they choose then the problems are likely to be worse. It is unfortunate but it is a fact of life.

There are special problems likely to be found on a marshland shoot, but like all problems they can be overcome with a combination of determination, ingenuity, hard work and hard currency. Only you can decide what combination of these you can provide. It certainly helps if you live close enough to have regular access to the shoot. Problems or not, a shoot along the foreshore can be as interesting and as varied as one further inland, and just as rewarding.

6 Guns and Cartridges

Take a few grains of gunpowder and apply a match. The result may be disappointing, particularly if you were expecting an explosion. There will be no loud bang, just a fizz, a brief, bright flame and a cloud of smoke.

But take a similar pinch of gunpowder and confine it tightly in an enclosed space before setting light to it. This time you will get your explosion. Small quantites of gunpowder, tightly confined in small cardboard tubes, can be obtained ready-made from any fireworks manufacturer. In my day these were called Penny Bangers, though no doubt inflation and Health and Safety legislation has since transformed them into something more expensive and less effective.

Gunpowder, when used as the propellant in a firearm, does not strictly speaking, explode. It simply burns very quickly, producing heat and a quantity of gas of considerably greater volume than the original powder. Ignite it in the open and the gas simply disperses into the surrounding air. However, if you seal one end of a piece of tubing, pour gunpowder down the tube and then ignite it, the gas will follow the line of least resistance as it expands: and that is along the tube and out through the open end.

If there is anything in the tube between the burning powder and the exit then the expanding gas will propel it along the tube and fire it out of the end. And you will have just invented the gun, albeit several hundred years too late to obtain a patent.

Having preceded us with the invention of the gun, our ancestors developed two distinct types of weapon. A shotgun is a smooth bore weapon firing multiple projectiles at each discharge. This distinguishes it from a rifle, which has spiral grooves in the bore (rifling) which impart spin to a single projectile in order to increase its range and accuracy. There is a rather muddled middle ground between the two since it is possible to obtain for example .22" cartridges containing shot, or shotgun cartridges loaded with a single, rifled slug, and there used to be a rifled shotgun, known as a Paradox, which was popular with big game hunters, but for the purposes of rough shooting we are concerned only with true shotguns; that is, those which fire a large number of small projectiles (shot) rather than a single bullet.

A shotgun or rifle is basically little more than a length of tubing, a handle and a device for igniting gunpowder: a barrel, a stock and a lock. Drop some gunpowder into the closed end of the tube, follow it with some lead shot, or a single lead ball, or a handful of tin-tacks if nothing else is available, and when you set light to the powder the shot, lead ball or tin-tacks will come flying out of the open end of the tube, causing death and destruction to anything unfortunate enough to be in the line of fire. The main problem which occupied the early gun-makers was to find a simple and reliable way of igniting the gunpowder.

The earliest guns had a tiny hole drilled through the barrel at the point where the powder charge lay, and ignition was made by use of a match — in this case the smouldering end of a short piece of rope. These guns were called match-locks.

The accepted way of lighting a fire in those days was to strike sparks into tinder using a flint and a piece of steel. The next refinement was to add a tiny pan below the hole in the barrel and prime this with a few grains of gunpowder. A piece of steel was fixed above the pan and a spring used to strike the steel with a piece of flint. The subsequent sparks lit the powder in the pan, which ignited the powder in the barrel. The guns were known as flint-locks, and besides revolutionising sport, and war, they gave us a whole series of new expressions to enrich the English Language.

Lock, stock and barrel, as mentioned earlier, were the three main components of a gun and meant something complete. A flash-in-the-pan occurred when the flint struck the steel and sparked off the powder in the pan but failed to ignite the main charge.

When the powder and shot were poured into the barrel they were tamped down with a long, straight stick called a ramrod. If you want to describe something as perfectly straight you can call it 'as straight as a ramrod'. The hammers of a gun were drawn back to compress the spring which impelled them onto the steel. There were two positions for hammers; fully back — at full cock — and an intermediate position which gave access to the pan but from which they should not fall and ignite the charge — half cock. Sometimes they did fall, thus something that starts prematurely 'goes off at half cock.'

Flintlock ignition was slow; there was a discernible delay between the sparks igniting the powder in the pan and the subsequent flash setting off the main charge. Around 1805 the minister of the village of Belhelvie, near Aberdeen, invented a 'scent bottle' lock which used fulminate of mercury to ignite the main charge instead of gunpowder. The Reverend Forsyth's invention was soon replaced by a small cap containing the fulminate of mercury which fitted over a nipple on the end of the barrel. The cap was struck by a hammer; the fulminate exploded and sent a spark down the middle of the nipple to ignite the powder.

But the gun still had to be loaded by pouring powder down the barrel, followed by a wad which had to be tamped down with the ramrod before the shot was added, then a

A flintlock with the cock in the fired position.

second wad, then more tamping before capping the nipple and cocking the hammer ready to fire. Rapid fire it was not. There were ways to increase fire-power: guns were made with multiple barrels and Sam Colt patented his single-barrelled pistol which had six charges contained in a revolving cylinder: but there was always the problem, after one shot, or after half a dozen, of stopping to pour powder, wads and shot or bullets down through the muzzle.

The answer was simple. Incorporate powder, wads, shot and percussion cap into a single container and introduce this into the barrels by arranging for them to open at the blunt end. The modern cartridge and breech-loading weapon had been invented, and apart from a few minor changes nothing much has altered in the past one hundred and twenty or so years.

Having taken a very brief look at the history of firearms in general let us now take a closer look at shotguns. What are the choices facing the sportsman when he steps through the door of the local gun shop? Let us make our way past the fishing rods and the dog whistles, the waxed jackets and the hunting knives, and turn our attention to the new and secondhand gun display.

Buying a gun means making a number of decisions. The most important one is probably deciding how much money you are prepared to spend; and here the choice is very, very wide. At one end of the market you can pick up a single-barrelled shotgun for around fifty pounds and quite possibly less. If you prefer, and if your pockets are deep enough, you could part with fifty thousand pounds for a single weapon. Both, if pointed in the right direction, will kill with almost equal efficiency.

So let us assume that you have somewhere between fifty and fifty thousand pounds; you have your gun licence, and you have the time and the inclination to purchase. What are the alternatives, and what is the best choice of gun for you?

Shotguns

The general design of the modern shotgun has changed little in the past century. This is not because gun-making has stagnated, nor because the gun buyers are hidebound traditionalists, but because the double-barrelled, breech-loading shotgun is such an efficient and elegant piece of design that very little improvement is possible. Many guns around a hundred years old are still in regular use, are virtually indistinguishable from, and perform as well as, or even better than, a brand new weapon.

It is almost certain that every gun on the display shelves will have either one or two barrels. Occasionally you may come across a sort of hybrid shotgun/rifle with three barrels; usually a double-barrelled shotgun with a rifle barrel between and below the shotgun barrels. These are called 'Drillings' and are less common in Britain than on the continent where boar and deer are shot at the same stands as smaller game.

SINGLE-BARRELLED GUNS

The simplest of shotguns is a single-barrelled breech loader. Load it, fire one shot and the gun must then be opened, the spent cartridge removed and a new one inserted and the gun closed before a second shot can be fired. They are generally plain, no-nonsense, work-horses of guns; the sort of thing that was kept standing in one corner of the barn, ready loaded to loose off at any rat foolish enough to show itself among the corn sacks.

They are almost invariably cheap guns. If you can afford a double-barrelled gun then why settle for a single shot weapon? Their limitation is obviously that only one chance is offered at the bird flying or rabbit running past. In their favour it must be said that you will waste less ammunition with a single shot; particularly when your judgement of range is uncertain. A high pigeon that is just too high will cost you just one wasted cartridge; with a double barrelled gun it would have been two.

Single shot weapons are less common now than they were a few years ago when I and practically all my contemporaries started their shooting career with one of the many ancient singles that circulated around the village. Part of the theory was that, having only one chance, a boy would learn to shoot better with a single-barrelled gun. There may have been something in it. It certainly made a box of cartridges last a little longer.

Not all single-barrelled guns need be single shot weapons. Bolt action, pump action and semi-automatic shotguns are all designed to offer the chance of a second shot to the gunner. Of the three the bolt action is the least common, and probably the least efficient.

The blunt end of the barrel is closed by the 'bolt' — a metal cylinder containing a firing pin which bears against the rear face of the cartridge and is operated by the gunner's right hand. When the gun is fired the bolt is drawn back to eject the spent cartridge case, then brought forward to cock the firing mechanism, collect a fresh round from a magazine fitted below the breech and slide it into the breech ready for use.

It is the system which was used on military rifles for many years, and it is robust, reliable and capable of rapid fire and quite swift reloading. When built into a shotgun the bolt action has a tendency to jam; particularly when you try to reload rapidly. The magazine lies below the barrel, and a spring lifts the cartridges up so that the forward movement of the bolt should slide them up a ramp which leads into the breech. Rifle ammunition, being pointed, locates itself naturally in the breech, but the flat front end of a shotgun cartridge has an infuriating habit of jamming — especially when you hurry.

Pump action repeaters have a tubular magazine located beneath the barrel and are reloaded by 'pumping' the fore-end. This ejects the spent case, cocks the firing pin and locates the new cartridge in the breech. Semi-automatic weapons use the expanding gases from the previous shot to perform the eject, cock and reload cycle.

The armaments industry in North America has produced pump and semi-automatic shotguns by the million in the past century, and they are used extensively by American hunters. In Britain there has always been a certain prejudice against such weapons. At the better class of driven shoot it was, and probably still is, akin to social suicide to turn up armed with a pump or semi-auto. Indeed, in many cases the use of an over-and-under would raise eyebrows if not actually attracting adverse comment from one's fellow guns: a pump, or worse a semi-auto would be would be completely beyond the pale.

Social snobbery aside there are a number of good reasons for the relative lack of popularity of single-barrelled repeating shotguns. Their balance and handleability can never compare with that of a well-made double gun, and although five rapid shots could be taken with a loaded gun it then took a considerable time to reload. At a driven shoot, where a gun might be expecting to fire twenty, fifty, perhaps a hundred cartridges in rapid succession at a single drive there was no way they could match the rate of fire of a conventional breech loader.

More recently legislation in Britain came close to banning the use of semi-automatic shotguns and limited the magazine of all repeating shotguns to two cartridges. There is still a place for single-barrelled guns on the rough shoot, the foreshore and for the pigeon shooting enthusiast, but the natural choice for anyone contemplating purchasing a shotgun for sporting shooting is almost certainly a double-barrelled, breech-loading gun.

The two barrels can be oriented in two planes: one above the other, in which case the gun is called an over-and-under, or side-by-side, in which case, not surprisingly, the gun is called a side-by-side. The majority of clay pigeon shooters use over-and-under guns: the majority, but it is a decreasing majority, of sporting shots use a side-by-side. There are a few quantifiable differences between the two.

An over-and-under is slightly slower to reload since it has to open to a wider gape in order to give free access to the lower barrel. Over-and-under guns tend to be a little heavier than side-by-sides. This has the positive effect of reducing recoil, but also means that there is much more weight to be carried. A few ounces won't seem much at nine a.m., but they may have taken on a wholly different significance eight hours and sixteen miles of walking later. On the other hand, many shots believe that the narrower sighting plane of an over-and-under is a significant aid to accurate shooting. In the end you pays your money and you makes your choice.

There are in fact a lot more choices than simply the number and orientation of the barrels to be considered when purchasing a gun. The matter of price will probably resolve itself quite simply. Most men know how much they can afford when they are making their purchase and will naturally stay within the bounds of their budget — give or take a factor or two. Or perhaps three. Tell yourself that it is an investment. As a matter of fact a top quality English shotgun is one of the best hedges against inflation it has been possible to buy over the past few years. That may not be strictly true of the fourth-hand, five-year-old, Eastern European blunderbuss that you are about to purchase, but it is a useful excuse to offer your wife/husband/bank manager. Monetary considerations aside though, what other choices must be made before becoming the proud owner of a new gun?

BORE

The size of a gun is known in Britain as its bore, and in America as its gauge. When someone refers to a twelve bore, sixteen bore, twenty bore and so on they are

An over and under shotgun. Note the wide gape needed to clear the lower chamber for loading.

classifying the weapon by the size of cartridge that it takes. The higher the number the smaller the gun, thus a ten bore or ten gauge is a considerably bigger weapon than a twenty bore. The measure represents the number of perfectly spherical balls of lead of a size to fit the breech of the gun which would weigh one pound. In other words, a ball of lead weighing one tenth of a pound would fit into the barrel of a ten bore gun; a twenty bore would require a ball weighing only a twentieth of a pound.

The system dates back to the old days of muzzle loaders, when a barrel could be made in practically any diameter that suited the gun-maker. Now that cartridges are mass produced the range of bore sizes available has standardised to about nine, of which perhaps four are in relatively common use.

The nine I have in mind are, starting at the largest, four, eight and ten bore, which are primarily wildfowling guns: twelve bore — the size in most common use — sixteen, twenty and twenty-eight bore, and then two odd ones, the .410 and the Number Three. The .410, usually referred to as a 'four-ten' gets its name from the measurement of the diameter of the bore — 0.41 inches — and the Number Three is what used to be called a garden gun, firing 9mm cartridges. It is a wonder that our masters in Europe haven't decided to standardise and metricate all cartridge sizes but so far they haven't, and long may it continue thus.

The twelve bore is by far the most common gun used for game and for clay pigeon shooting. The larger bores; ten, eight and four bores are rarely seen other than on the foreshore. Their weight, size and the cost of cartridges all tell against their use in the rough shooting field. I am not saying you can't walk-up grouse with an eight bore, but I'm glad I don't have to carry it for you.

The Number Three is not suitable for use as a sporting weapon; it is too small to kill efficiently except at close range. It was commonly called a garden gun, and was intended for killing rats in the hen run and small birds among the fruit bushes. The four-ten is the smallest practical size of shotgun for sporting use. It is often bought as a first gun for a youngster learning to shoot — my own first shotgun was a Lee-Enfield rifle bored out to take a four-ten cartridge — but is probably not the best choice for this purpose, of which more later.

This leaves us with four other bore sizes to consider: the twenty-eight, twenty, sixteen and twelve bores. It also brings us to the stage at which we should consider some very basic ballistics. The first thing to understand is that for every gain there will be a corresponding loss.

A shotgun doesn't fire a single bullet like a rifle,; it fires a number of small pellets of lead which are called shot. The shot charge leaves the muzzle in a compact ball and then spreads out wider and wider the further it travels from the gun. This removes the need for exact aim by providing a margin of error for the gunner, and it is this margin of error that makes it practical to shoot birds flying or animals running. It also imposes severe limits on the practical range of shotguns.

As the shot charge spreads out so there are bigger and bigger gaps between each individual piece of shot. These gaps will widen until and beyond the point at which we can no longer rely on hitting a target even though the shot charge is centred accurately on that target: in other words the gaps will eventually become so wide that the target can literally slip between the shot.

If we loaded a twelve bore cartridge with a single lead ball; which we know would weigh one twelfth of a pound, or 1.33 ounces; then that lead ball would be lethal at a range of several hundred yards. Since our barrel lacks rifling it would not be particularly accurate, and with only a single ball to hit our quarry we would have to be spot-on with our aim or we would miss. The answer; divide up the single ball into a lot of little balls; in effect change our musket into a shotgun.

The problem now is this. To kill a quarry, or to break a clay pigeon, we must strike it with a certain force. We measure this as the energy with which the shot strikes it; and the energy is the product of the weight times the velocity of the projectile. Shot leaves the barrel with a certain energy and this energy is dissipated due to the effects of gravity and wind resistance, growing less and less the further the shot travels. The smaller the shot size, the lower will be its initial energy as it leaves the barrel: therefore the shorter will be the distance over which it retains suffcient energy to kill the quarry.

If we load our cartridge with an ounce of the smallest possible shot then we will get an extremely dense pattern in which the individual pieces of shot will lack sufficient energy to break our clay or kill our quarry. Let our one ounce load consist of just half a dozen bigger lead balls and each ball will retain the necessary killing energy for much longer — but there is no guarantee of hitting the target even when the gun is pointed in the right direction.

So why not load the gun with a couple of pounds of big lead balls and get the best of both worlds: penetration plus pattern? The answer is that you can: it has been done and the resultant weapon was called a punt gun or perhaps a cannon. To drive that two pounds of lead needs a lot more powder: that means a bigger and heavier gun to cope with the pressure generated when all that powder burns. You might be able to lift it but you certainly couldn't carry it around all day, and if you did manage to get it up to your shoulder and fire, it you would probably break your shoulder. The answer has to be a compromise.

The bigger the bore, the more shot you can load into your cartridge; the denser your pattern can be for any given shot size. A bigger bore and more shot requires more powder; more powder means more pressure and more pressure means a stronger — and thus heavier — gun. Make the gun too heavy and not only does it become an excessive burden to lug around all day but it also becomes harder to swing, thus reducing the chance of you hitting your moving target.

Modern technology means that it would be possible to construct a very light gun which would have sufficient strength to fire a very heavy load. A good idea perhaps? I'm afraid not. Let me introduce the question of recoil to the equation.

For every action there is an equal and opposite reaction. Fire the gun and an ounce or so of lead is propelled forwards at about 1,250 feet per second. At the same time seven pounds of gun tries to go backwards with much the same energy. Your shoulder prevents this backward movement. The heavier the gun, the greater the inertia that must be overcome before it begins to recoil. The lighter the gun the harder the recoil will be for any given load.

For practical purposes the muzzle velocity — the speed with which the shot leaves the barrel — does not alter significantly as the bore alters. Bigger bores mean guns which can handle heavier shot loads, but the energy of each individual piece of shot will be much the same whether it is fired from a four-ten or a four bore. What changes is the amount of shot which it is practical to fire at each discharge. And if you have more shot in your cartridge then you can have a denser pattern, or a wider pattern of the same density that you get from a lesser shot load. The first gives you a longer effective range; the second a greater chance of hitting your target. The amount of choke in your barrels decides which you get.

CHOKE
A shotgun barrel is not normally a simple, parallel tube. The muzzle is narrower than the breech. This narrowing of the bore is known as choke, and has the effect of altering the rate as which the shot spreads once it has left the barrel. The tighter the constriction of the muzzles the denser will be the concentration of the shot charge, and the longer the effective range of the gun.

But. There is always a but; always a price to pay for every apparent gain. A tightly choked gun will have a longer range than one firing the same charge from a more open bore, but it will be correspondingly more difficult for the user to hit the target.

Practically all barrels will have some choke, the true cylinder barrel being a rarity, Choke is normally referred to as Full Choke (the tightest pattern), then in descending order, Three-quarter Choke, Half Choke, Quarter Choke and Improved Cylinder. Gunmakers measure the nominal choke by gauging the diameter of the barrels, but the proper measure of choke is the percentage of the shot charge which will strike within a thirty inch circle at forty yards range. Improved cyclinder should put about fifty per cent of the charge into the circle; full choke around seventy per cent.

Ideally the shot should be evenly spread so that when the gun is test fired at a pattern plate there are no wide gaps in the pattern and no thick clusters of pellets. Anyone can assess the pattern thrown by their gun; all that is required is an open space and something to serve as a pattern plate. Ideally use a square of sheet metal coated with whitewash, but a few sheets of newspaper, tacked to a sheet of plywood will serve at a pinch. Remember though that firing a single shot and studying the resultant pattern may well prove deceptive. Take half a dozen shots and look at the results overall. Remember too, that different loads, different velocities and different makes of cartridge will also effect the tightness and quality of the pattern thrown by a gun.

A competent gun-maker can alter the choke without much difficulty, though it is obviously easier to reduce the constriction than to increase it. If you wish to have a fully-choked gun reduced to quarter choke there should be no great difficulty: having a quarter choke altered to full choke would be more problematic though not necessarily impossible.

Many manufacturers now offer guns fitted with detachable choke cones which screw into the ends of the barrels. These offer a degree of versatility denied to the owner of more conventional weapons, though I doubt that the patterns they throw will consistently compare with that thrown by a properly regulated conventional barrel.

ACTIONS
The action is the mechanical means by which the gunner delivers the sharp blow to the cap which will fire the cartridge. The blow is delivered by a firing pin, which is in turn energised by a compressed spring. In a bolt action gun or rifle the pin is driven against the cap directly by a coil spring, but in all other actions the power of the spring drives a hammer against the head of the firing pin.

The first breech loaders had external hammers which were cocked by drawing them back with the thumb, thus compressing the springs. Modern side-by-side and over-and-under guns are referred to as hammerless, but in fact they too are hammer guns. The 'hammers', now known as tumblers, have simply been concealed within the body of the gun. Instead of being cocked by the gunner's thumb their springs are compressed by levers operated by opening and closing the gun.

Actions fall into two main categories: the sidelock and the boxlock. There are others: the elegant round action for one: and there are different details of design from individual makers. And of course, there are still many excellent hammer guns available for those who wish to use them. Indeed, there is no reason why the rough shot should not arm himself with a muzzle loader, percussion or even flintlock if he so desires. There are a number of firms producing excellent replicas of these old weapons, and a growing band of enthusiasts who shoot with them.

However, assuming that the majority of readers are likely to be interested in a more conventional choice of gun, let us simply look briefly at the main differences between boxlock and sidelock actions.

The boxlock or Anson and Deeley action has its working parts housed below and behind the breech while the sidelocks' components parts are attached to the side plates and extend well behind the ends of the barrels. The more expensive guns are usually sidelocks since this action lends itself to producing more elegant, aesthetically pleasing weapon. In comparison with a well made sidelock, boxlock guns look a little lumpen; a little 'country cousinish'. That said, the Anson and Deeley is a strong, reliable, well proven and robust action. Certain refinements such as self-opening actions and detachable locks are generally the prerequisite of the sidelock.

In general sidelocks are more expensive than boxlocks — but that is a dangerous generality. A top grade boxlock from a good English maker may cost many times the price of an excellent sidelock from an overseas manufacturer. 'Best' guns, by which I refer to the top models from any given manufacturer's range, will almost invariably be sidelocks, but this does not mean that a boxlock is an inferior, or second choice, of weapon. A good boxlock is infinitely to be preferred to a poor sidelock.

CARTRIDGES

The modern shotgun cartridge is simply a plastic or paper case containing the powder, shot and wads which were once poured down the barrels of a muzzle loader by the sportsmen of the past. The front end is closed by some form of crimp or turnover and the rear is usually of brass-plated metal containing the ignition cap.

Plastic cases have the advantage in that they do not swell up when damp and then either refuse to enter the breech, or more annoyingly, prove impossible to dislodge after firing. In their favour paper cases are bio-degradable and will not litter the countryside in the way that the largely rot-proof plastic cases do. That said, there is no reason why the rough shot should not pick up all fired cases and take them home for proper disposal. Some shoots insist that all cases are picked up, often to prevent them causing digestive problems to livestock which have a tendency to chew them.

The powder and shot are separated within the cartridge by a wad. This acts as a seal (to prevent the burning gases from bursting through the shot charge) and drives the shot down the barrel ahead of the expanding gas.

Plastic shot cups which are designed to improve patterns by protecting the shot from abrasion against the barrel walls, and by concentrating the shot charge until it leaves the muzzle have largely replaced the old cardboard wads. I suspect that shot cups may have the effect of concentrating patterns; that is to say they may exaggerate the degree of choke in the barrel. This may or may not be a good thing and must be considered when choosing a gun and cartridge combination.

Cartridges come in many different sizes. Twelve bore cartridges can be obtained in two inch, two and a quarter inch, two and a half inch, two and three quarter inch and three inch lengths. Obviously the larger sizes are designed to hold more shot, or more powder, and probably both, with the aim of increasing range, velocity or pattern density, and probably all three.

A word of warning. Guns are chambered for a particular length of cartridge. While it is safe, if not necessarily desirable, to fire a two inch cartridge from a gun chambered for three inch cartridges it is most definitely NOT safe to attempt to fire three inch magnum loads from a gun chambered for shorter cartridges. The chamber length will be stamped on the barrels with the proof marks. Oversized cartridges will cause excess pressure which could result in a burst barrel.

When I was learning to shoot, along with the other lads from the village, it was our invariable fashion to purchase the heaviest loads and highest velocity cartridges which were obtainable. Noise and recoil were our benchmarks for judging the efficacy of ammunition. If it had a good loud bang and a kick like a mule then it must be a good cartridge. That was the basis of the theory. I shudder to think now what strain we must have put on some of those old guns which were required to cope with our magnum and maximum loads. Perhaps the occasional — the very, very occasional — pigeon was killed at some enormous distance thanks to our over-loaded weapons, but in hindsight we would all probably have shot a lot better with lighter loads which kicked less, cost less, and killed just as efficiently as all normal ranges.

There is no doubt that some of the guns with which I learned to shoot fell somewhat short of perfection. That old Lee-Enfield rifle conversion was an interesting-looking gun. but its balance was atrocious, the alignment of stock and barrels meant that, unless consciously aimed, it delivered its shot charge high and some way to one side of the quarry, and the cartridges invariably jammed below the chamber if I tried to utilise the magazine instead of treating the gun as a single shot weapon. Later guns were invariably fully choked, usually too heavy and often in a state of repair which bordered on downright dangerous. Nevertheless I had a wonderful time wheeling and dealing my way through a catholic assortment of weapons; never caused any serious harm to myself or any of my companions; and, come to think of it, did only negligible damage to the local pigeon, rabbit and duck population.

Proud though we were of our motley arsenal we were only too well aware of its limitations. Since the pool of weapons available to us was limited by price, most of our acquisitions took the form of swaps and part exchange deals, with the same dozen or twenty guns circulating among the youth of the village for year after year. Our insistence on straining both guns and shoulders with the highest velocity, heaviest loaded cartridges available was primarily an attempt to compensate with power for our weapons' lack of refinement. In so doing we probably made things worse rather then better. A novice shot allied to a clumsy and inaccurate weapon is never likely to impress with his kills-to-cartridge ratio.

Overloading both gun and handler may induce a flinch in the one and possibly a burst barrel in the other, but it will not put more game into the bag. A clean miss with one and a half ounces of high velicity shot will look no more impressive than a clean miss with an ounce and an eighth travelling at normal speed. It may sound louder and kick harder, but the end results are identical. All that the extra kick of the magnum cartridge does is to make missing a little more probable.

The choice of guns available to the rough shooter is dauntingly wide. What type of gun; single barrel, repeater, side-by-side or over-and-under? Should it be a twelve bore or a twenty; a four bore or a four-ten? How heavily choked? New or second hand; a cheap import or an expensive English make? Sidelock or boxlock; light or heavy; short or long barrels; single trigger, pistol grip, easy opening, selective ejecting, beaver tailed fore end . . . or what?

Now that we have had a look at the rudiments — and I stress that we have only looked in the briefest of detail at bore, choke, cartridges and the rest — we should consider what the ideal choice of gun for the rough shooter might be.

7 Choosing a Gun

The purpose of a shotgun is to fire shot at a target. When choosing a gun therefore it is reasonable to assume that the best gun for any individual shooter is the gun that will give him or her the best chance of hitting that target.

The wider the dispersal of the shot, the greater the likelihood of hitting the target — provided that the shot is not so widely dispersed that the target can slip through the gaps in the pattern. The more shot contained in the load, the more widely it can be dispersed before gaps in the pattern render it ineffective. Will the ideal choice of gun automatically be the one that can fire the heaviest possible shot load through barrels with the least possible degree of choke?

When I suggest that the answer to my question is a qualified 'yes', I can imagine the howls of protest that will emanate from experienced shots; particularly those who favour light loads and small bore weapons. But bear with me for a few pages and remember that I said a qualified 'yes'. The important point here is that we are considering a matter of choice — and choice of gun and cartridge is necessarily subjective.

The first proper shotgun which I owned did not come into my possession as the result of any particular choice on my part. It was at the start of a particularly hard spell of winter weather and the regular non-appearance of the school bus meant that I and a couple of friends were free most days to station ourselves around the borders of a forty-acre field of sprouts and attempt to keep the hordes of pigeons away. So much damage was being done to the sprouts that the owner of the field would issue free boxes of cartridges to anyone who was prepared to face the cold — and it was bitterly cold that year — and spend the day shooting, and more importantly from his viewpoint, scaring the pigeons.

There were two flaws in this otherwise excellent arrangement as far as I was concerned. At the time I was still using the Lee-Enfield conversion which was a four-ten. The free cartridges came in twelve bore size only. More importantly, with the initial pride of ownership long since worn off, I was beginning to appreciate the limitations of the gun as a sporting weapon.

It was, after all, still a rifle in every respect except the boring of its barrel. Handled like a rifle it placed the shot charge right where I aimed it, but it had to be aimed. It was heavily choked so the shot spread was minimal and since it was designed as a rifle there was no cast-off and very little drop on the stock. Try to swing on to a rabbit running or a pigeon flying and the most likely result was a wasted cartridge. And unlike the other lads, I was paying for those cartridges myself.

Some diligent intelligence gathering in the bar at the village pub (where I was living at the time) soon located a possible successor to the four-ten. One of my father's customers had an old single twelve bore lying in a garden shed. I borrowed it on the understanding that I would clean the rust off it and out of it. Having cleaned it and checked that it was in proof (by firing it! It didn't blow up so it was obviously okay.) I was able to take part in the free cartridge bonanza. And incidentally to begin hitting a few more of the things I aimed at.

It could hardly be said though that I made any particular choice in getting my first real shotgun. It was available when I needed it and it never occurred to me to wonder if it fitted me properly, or whether there was too much choke. There was of course: it was a Harrington and Richardson single-barrel hammer gun and was fully choked. I bought it after a couple of weeks use, paying thirty shillings if I remember correctly, and I had a lot of fun with that old gun. Whether I would have chosen to buy it if an alternative had been offered is another matter.

But let us assume that our aim is to purchase a gun for rough shooting, and that the choice is no longer limited to unwanted weapons that can be scrounged from the depths of garden sheds. Where should we begin to make our choice?

Swinging on to a grouse — range about fifteen yards at this point.

The purpose of our gun; of any gun; is to provide the means by which a target may be struck by a projectile. In rough shooting, as in any other shooting sport, it is what the shot or the bullet does that signifies success or failure; the gun is merely the delivery mechanism. Our objective is to bring at least three or four individual pellets of shot into contact with our quarry, while the shot still has sufficient striking energy to ensure a quick, clean kill.

Heavier shot will retain its energy over a longer range; but the heavier the shot the less individual pellets there will be in any given load. As the shot spread increases with range so the pattern becomes less and less effective, until it is quite possible to miss the target even though the gun has been aimed correctly. There are two ways to combat this: load the cartridge with more shot or employ an increased amount of choke to tighten the pattern.

If you elect to increase the number of individual shot then you must use either smaller shot or a heavier shot load. But smaller shot will have a lower striking energy at any given range. It is quite possible that reducing shot size enough to provide an effective pattern will also reduce the striking energy of the shot below the level at which a clean kill be made. This will inevitably result in birds being pricked but lost, possibly to die later of their wounds. Not at all the result which we want.

Increasing the overall weight of the shot charge will provide us with a greater number of shot of the original size, and will increase the density of the pattern, but the greater weight of shot will need a heavier powder charge to impel it. This means either using a heavier gun or being subjected to increased recoil. Alternatively, introducing a degree of choke to the barrels will concentrate the shot charge and thus decrease the number of gaps in the pattern but at the same time it will reduce the overall spread of the pattern and reduce the margins of error. Clearly we have to accept some degree of compromise when selecting the ideal charge to fire from our rough shooting weapon.

It is an over simplification of the facts, but in general the larger the bore of the gun the heavier shot charge it can handle and the longer will be the effective range. Unfortunately the larger the bore of the gun, the heavier it will be — again there are exceptions to the 'rule' but it is generally true — and the harder will be the recoil. Recoil can be reduced by making the gun heavier still: conversely, any saving in weight will be paid for by an increase in recoil.

What then if we accept a relatively light shot load and enhance the pattern density by increasing the degree of choke in our barrels? Those readers with good memories will note that this is the exact opposite of the heavy shot load, minimum choke hypothesis which I offered at the beginning of this chapter. Heavy choke will indeed have the desired effect of removing the gaps in the pattern which would cause us to 'miss' even though our aim was correct, but in tightening the pattern overall we are also certain to miss many birds which would otherwise have been hit by the fringes of the original, wider pattern.

Our final choice of gun will inevitably represent a degree of compromise. It has to be light enough to be carried all day without undue strain, but heavy enough to keep recoil within acceptable limits. It should throw a pattern which will ensure a clean kill of the type of quarry we expect to shoot, at the range at which are going to be shooting it, with the shot size we intend to use. And, unless we know for certain that all our future shooting is likely to be at one particular quarry then it would be well to select a weapon which is adaptable.

Let us consider the choices facing us in a little more detail.

Of the nine possible bore sizes open to us I would suggest that only three represent a sensible purchase for the novice rough shooter. The three big bores: four bore, eight bore and ten bore: are all too heavy for general rough shooting; their ammunition is prohibitively expensive, and they are generally too unwieldy for use when any form of snap shooting is required.

On the foreshore, particularly where constant shooting pressure has educated wildfowl to fly above normal shotgun range, there is a place for the big guns. On the rough shoot they are more likely to be a handicap than an asset. Of course, if you envisage doing a lot of your shooting on the foreshore then there may be a case for a big gun, though a magnum twelve, proved for three inch ammunition, will fire a shot load approaching that of the bigger guns while still allowing the shooter to use standard loads for normal shooting.

At the other end of the scale the four-ten has a strictly limited range unless it is very tightly choked, and tight choking combined with the limited shot load of even the three inch four-ten cartridge means that very accurate shooting is a prerequisite for consistent success using one of these little guns. In the hands of a first-class shot a four-ten can be a very effective weapon, even against quite high pheasants, but as a gun for a novice shot it imposes unnecessary handicaps. And the novice shot has problems enough without adding to them where there is no need to do so.

We are left then with only four bore sizes to choose from — the twenty-eight bore, the twenty bore, the sixteen and the twelve. Of these, the twelve bore is by far and away the most common; sales of twelve bore ammunition outnumbering the combined sales of all other cartridges in the ratio of around six to one. The twenty-eight bore is a considerable rarity, and even the sixteen bore seems to be much less commonly used now than it was a few years ago.

In contrast, the twenty bore has enjoyed something of a revival in popularity in recent years. It is lighter than a twelve bore, weighing five and a half to six pounds compared to the six and a half to seven pounds of the larger gun — a significant saving when the gun has to be carried throughout a long day in the field. The lighter loads used in a twenty bore should mean that there is also a considerable reduction in recoil, provided of course that standard loads are used and not heavily loaded magnum cartridges.

The sixteen bore falls neatly between the twelve and the twenty bore, occupying the middle ground with both weight and shot load. If light weight is an important factor in the choice of calibre then I would suggest that the extra advantage which can be gained with a twenty bore will probably influence the purchaser away from the sixteen. That said, a good sixteen bore will do everything a twenty bore can, and is capable of matching the performance of a twelve bore — up to a point.

Choosing a shotgun means deciding between a number of conflicting ideals. It may be that particular circumstances will dictate that one factor will assume a level of importance that overrides all the others. If increasing age or some form of physical disability means that you *must* use a very light gun then all the other choices are secondary. Perhaps you intend to use the gun only on a foreshore where the wildfowl invariably fly high. Then a gun which can handle heavy shot loads through tightly choked barrels may be an absolute must for you. If, as I did when I bought the old Harrington and Richardson single-barrel, you find there is only one gun available, then your choice is the simplest one possible. There are no set rules; no guns which are right for everybody. All we can do is to try find the right gun for ourselves.

Let us start narrowing down our choices by considering the question of range. As a boy, I set great store by guns and cartridges that would kill at the longest possible ranges. The four factors which will increase range are well known. Heavy shot loads; large shot; high velocity and tight choke. Big shot, fired at high velocity, will retain sufficient striking energy to kill over greater distances than smaller or slower pellets. Heavy loads fired through tightly choked barrels will throw dense enough patterns to ensure kills over greater distances than light loads fired through open bored barrels.

I believe my early obsession with guns that would kill at the maximum range was triggered by a boyhood spent hunting with a succession of air rifles. With certain reservations, such as accuracy and weight, the best air rifle as far as I was concerned was the one which would kill at the greatest range. We were forever comparing air rifles, checking the power by comparing the penetration of the pellets on the wooden garden shed, or seeing how effectively the pellets would flatten when the muzzle was pressed against a piece of steel. In our minds good meant powerful and powerful meant high muzzle velocity. What was more natural than that we should extend our thinking to cover our first shotguns? We did, and I can still recall the sore shoulders and missed birds that resulted from it.

Let us consider this question of shotgun range. In general, discussion of the range of a particular gun and cartridge will be concerned with the *maximum* distance at which the combination is effective. Bear in mind though that there is also a *minimum* range to consider. By minimum I refer to the distance below which game shot by that gun and cartridge combination will be so badly damaged as to be unfit for the table. Heavy loads and tight choking will both have the effect of increasing the minimum as well as the maximum range of a gun.

Minimum range is rarely a limiting factor since quarry which is too close can normally be allowed to run or fly a little further before being shot, or in the case of incoming quarry taken a little earlier before it closes the range too much. Even so, there may be circumstances such as shooting woodcock among dense woodland or bolting rabbits in thick cover where quarry must be shot at close range or not at all. For most practical purposes though, range limitations are concerned with the maximum rather than the minimum distance at which quarry can be killed.

If our sole objective in choosing a gun and cartridge is to maximise the range at which the combination will kill then there are few problems. Large shot will retain sufficient striking energy to kill at greater distances than smaller shot. The more shot there are in

Grouse, dead in the air: range perhaps twenty-five yards.

the load the greater distance at which the pattern can retain sufficient density to ensure a kill. And the tighter the choke in the barrels the more concentrated the pattern will be.

To maximise range therefore, buy the heaviest gun which you can carry, prime it with the maximum load of large shot and ensure that the barrels are fully choked. Taken to its logical conclusion a four bore firing a single slug would have a theoretical range of several hundred yards. You would have a gun and cartridge combination that absolutely maximised killing distance. As a sporting weapon for the rough shooter it would be totally useless, other than as a poor substitute for a stalking rifle. And if it is a stalking rifle you want there are any number on the market, all of them far more suitable for the task than an over-loaded four bore would be.

There is no question that using heavy shot and tightly choked barrels will increase the maximum range at which a gun can kill. However, by concentrating the shot charge in order to minimise gaps in the pattern we must, inevitably, reduce the overall spread of the charge. And the less the charge spreads, the less chance we have of hitting our target.

This means that in order to increase the maximum distance at which, with any given shot load, we *can* kill our quarry we must also reduce the probability that we *will* hit that quarry — at *all* distances. The question which we must consider then, is whether the extra range gained by increasing the degree of choke will offset the extra misses which will occur at all shorter ranges.

So what sort of distances are we considering? The accepted maximum range of a twelve bore among the village lads of my youth was fifty yards. Bearing in mind our bias towards heavy loads and full choke this may even have been a slightly conservative estimate, but let us assume that fifty yards was indeed a fair estimate of the range at which a fully choked twelve bore firing a heavy load will kill quarry with an acceptable degree of certainty. If you fire at enough birds which are just beyond the normal range you will inevitably manage a few 'fluke' kills where a single pellet hits a vital spot. You will also wound a lot of quarry which will escape to suffer and perhaps die later. An acceptable degree of certainty occurs at ranges where, if you centre the charge on your quarry it should, excluding 'fluke' pattern gaps, be hit by sufficient pellets of high enough energy to ensure a clean kill.

Grouse rising and gun — a 20 bore — being brought to the ready position.

Obviously there is not an exact distance at which pattern and energy fail for any given load. A pheasant will not be in range at forty-five yards and out of range at forty-seven. Even if a precise distance for maximum range could be calculated, who could estimate the distance to a running hare or flying pigeon with sufficient accuracy to benefit from it?

The extra range which may be gained by increasing the shot load has been estimated at around three yards per one eighth of an ounce of shot. The standard load for a twelve bore game cartridge is one and one sixteenth ounces. A light load for the twelve bore is fifteen sixteenths of an ounce; a heavy load anything over one and a quarter ounces. The difference in range between a light and a heavy load is therefore only around six or seven yards.

It is not a simple matter to quantify the extra range which choke boring will give to a gun. Maximum range is reached when either the density of the pattern or the energy of the shot falls below that required to ensure a clean kill. If you are shooting geese with number six shot then the penetration of the pellets will fail long before the pattern becomes too widespread to ensure a reasonable number of hits. Conversely, if your target is snipe, then the same load of number six shot may be failing because of inadequate pattern density while individual pellets still retain ample striking energy to ensure a kill. Increasing choke would be effective against snipe but would do nothing to help kill the geese.

Certainly, having loaded with number three shot instead of sixes, we might then find that the energy was high enough to kill geese but that the pattern was failing. Now an increase in choke would help to ensure a clean kill — but it would also make geese or snipe a little bit harder to hit.

Juggling with shot size, shot load and choke combinations can certainly alter the maximum range of a gun. The difference between improved cylinder and full choke is probably about ten yards of range for a given shot load. Add this to the distance which can be gained by increasing shot size and shot load and there is perhaps a matter of fifteen yards 'extra' range to be gained by using a fully choked twelve bore firing a heavy load over an improved cylinder gun firing a light load.

In order to gain that extra ten to fifteen yards of maximum range you will have to tolerate a higher recoil and accept that your gun will be a pound or so heavier than would be necessary to fire the lighter loaded cartridges. And remember; that fifteen or so yards represents the difference between a *light* load fired through an improved cylinder barrel and a *heavy* load fired through a full choke. Use a normal game load and a barrel with light choking and the extra range of the heavily loaded gun drops to no more than eight or ten yards. So what about all that extra weight and recoil? Is it worth it?

As far as the rough shooter is concerned the answer is almost certainly not. By its very nature rough shooting suggests variety. The quarry is going to be shot at a variety of distances from about twenty yards upwards. Most of our shooting is likely to be a quarry between twenty-five and forty yards away, with only a small proportion taken at greater ranges. Unless you have reason to expect most of your shots to be taken at maximum range then there is little point in handicapping yourself with a heavier than necessary gun, and putting up with an unacceptable degree of discomfort from the recoil. Remember, the tight choking needed to maximise range will make effective shooting that much more difficult at all ranges. Maximum range is available — at a price.

The weight of the gun is an important factor for the rough shot. Driven shooting, shooting over decoys and clay pigeon shooting — even wildfowling — differ from rough shooting in one important respect. The rough shooter may have to carry his gun over considerable distances; and he has to carry it so that it is ready for instant use. Wildfowlers often have to walk long distances and a driven grouse shoot may well involve some brisk exercise between drives, but in both cases the gun can be carried in a slip hung comfortably from the shoulder. Only when you have spent six or eight hours walking up grouse on a steep hill will you begin to realise just how heavy even a light gun can feel by the end of the day.

A standard side-by-side twelve bore game gun will weigh about six and a half to six and three-quarter pounds. A gun built with two and three-quarter inch chambers and proofed to handle heavy loads will scale seven to seven and a half pounds, and a full magnum twelve bore intended to fire three inch magnum loads might well touch eight pounds. Over and under guns are usually a little heavier than their side by side equivalents.

Now; a pound to a pound and a half of extra weight may not seem that much, but believe me, by the time you have lugged it over half the county every extra ounce will count and you will have a bruise on your forearm to prove it. If you must fire heavy loads then get a heavy gun by all means, but for normal shooting ranges it just isn't necessary.

At the other end of the scale — literally — it is sometimes possible to find exceptionally light guns. A twelve bore chambered for two inch cartridges could weigh less than six pounds and yet not recoil excessively. The saving in weight though would be offset by a certain loss of flexibility. While a two and a half inch chambered gun could happily fire two inch cartridges it would certainly not do to feed two and a half inch cartridges into the lightweight gun.

So what should the rough shooter look for in a gun? There is no such thing as a perfect gun for all occasions, whatever your choice it is certain to have limitations. And it is also worth remembering that even an 'unsuitable' gun can provide good sport for the owner. Over the years I have shot with any number of guns that differ, sometimes widely, from what I would consider the ideal rough shooting gun. Those differences never prevented me from enjoying my shooting though no doubt I would have shot a lot straighter with guns that fitted me properly, that had a lot less choke, weighed a bit less and handled a little more sweetly.

If you already own a pump action repeater or a three inch magnum twelve bore, a single barrel ten bore or a bolt action four-ten and you plan to use it for your rough shooting — fine. It may not be the gun that I am going to suggest as the ideal rough shooting gun, but that is no reason why you should not shoot with it and enjoy your shooting. If you are used to the gun and shoot well with it then it may well be the best possible gun for you. And even if it isn't, as long as you enjoy your shooting the 'right' gun is probably the one you are using.

But suppose that you are about to buy your first gun, or are thinking of changing your old one. Here is the gun shop with row upon row of shotguns, new and old, racked up on the shelves. Of all the possible permutations of bore and choke, barrel configuration and action, manufacturer and price; which is the one combination that would be the ideal gun for rough shooting?

The simple answer to the question is that there is no such thing as an 'ideal' gun; far less an ideal gun for such a varied sport as rough shooting. But then, if you have been paying attention over the past couple of chapters you will already know that. However, I can tell you what I think might approach somewhere close to that ideal, for me, and then leave you to exercise your own judgement. Let us try to build up a picture of the most suitable gun for the rough shot.

Bore

At a rough guess about ninety per cent of the guns currently used in this country are twelve bores. If there was any great advantage to the average shot in using one of the smaller or larger sizes of shotgun then the twelve bore would not enjoy such massive numerical superiority over all other bores. When muzzle loaders were replaced by breech loaders it was the twelve that emerged from the transition period as far and away the most popular boring. An awful lot of sportsmen over the years have chosen twelve bore shotguns, and unless there is a pressing reason to do otherwise it is the twelve bore that I would recommend to the aspiring purchaser.

That said, there are a lot of shotgun users who may be better served by a lighter gun than a conventional twelve bore game gun. Youngsters starting to shoot, ladies, the elderly or those with physical limitations may well shoot better with a light gun. If this is the case then I would suggest that a twenty bore offers a greater weight saving, combined with appreciably lower recoil than a twelve or a sixteen bore.

Be wary though of trying to extract twelve bore performance from a light game gun. Certainly there are twenty bore magnum cartridges available which have the same shot load as a conventional twelve bore cartridge. Combine these loads with a very light gun however, and the recoil is likely to far exceed that which would be experienced using a standard game load in a normal twelve bore. There is no point in providing a youngster with a light gun which is going to subject him or her to excessive recoil at every shot. A twenty bore, firing normal twenty bore loads of just under an ounce of shot has the dual advantages of lightness and low recoil. Cram the equivalent of a twelve bore load into the breech though and that same lightness becomes a handicap by promoting excessive recoil.

I may appear to have dismissed the sixteen bore in rather cavalier fashion, and if so I apologise to devotees of this particular gauge. There are some beautifully made sixteen bores about, and there is no reason at all why the rough shooter should not be equipped with a sixteen bore. In practical terms there is little to differentiate the field performance of a sixteen bore and a twelve bore with normal game loads. My choice of the twenty bore as my preferred 'light' gun was simply because, if weight saving is a major reason for selecting a smaller bore, then the twenty offers a greater saving than a sixteen.

Choke

A twelve bore shotgun firing a normal game load of an ounce to an ounce and one eighth of number six shot through a barrel bored somewhere around improved cylinder to quarter choke should be capable of killing practically all normal quarry up to a range of about forty-five yards. Geese and hares are the main exceptions to this and the use of larger shot — fours for the hares and perhaps threes for the geese — would mean that the combination was quite capable of making a clean kill on either.

I will repeat: the great majority of the quarry which will be found on a rough shooting day is likely to be shot at ranges between twenty-five and forty yards. If you are using a twelve bore shotgun the effect of choke, certainly up to the forty yard range, will be to handicap you rather than to assist you. So why opt for anything other than improved cylinder barrels, when the addition of choke will simply make it less likely that you will hit the majority of the birds or animals at which you shoot?

There is certainly a valid argument for minimising the degree of choke in any gun intended primarily for sporting shooting. But choke has been around for a long time now, and the majority of guns will have some degree of choke boring in both barrels. If choke is an unnecessary handicap, then it is a handicap that has been borne by nearly all shotgun users over the past one hundred and more years. There must be something to be said in its favour.

Choke extends range: both the maximum range of the gun and the range at which the larger shot sizes will pattern sufficiently densely to take advantage of their extra power

A pheasant away on Ford Moss, Northumberland. No need for tightly choked barrels here.

and penetration. Having different degrees of choke in either barrel of a side-by-side or over-and-under gives an instant choice to the shooter and adds a little bit to both ends of the effective range of the gun. And for the devotee of the smaller bores; the twenty, twenty-eight and four-ten; choke tightens the pattern of their lighter shot loads so that they are effective at almost the same distances as a twelve or sixteen bore.

Remember though, that the lighter and more concentrated the shot load, the greater the test of marksmanship. A four-ten may be easily handled by a slightly built youngster, but it will make the task of connecting with quarry that much more difficult than with a larger gun with open boring. A boy or girl learning to shoot needs the encouragement that a successful shot brings, and starting them with a fully choked four-ten is not the best way to ensure that success.

More choke means greater certainty of killing with a correctly aimed shot, slightly longer effective range but also the certainty of more misses. Less choke means more birds killed at all except extreme ranges. What proportion of your birds will be shot at extreme range? More choke also means birds spoiled if they are shot at too close a range.

The multi-choke system, where choke tubes can be screwed into the ends of the barrels allowing choke to be varied for different types of sport is popular with many shooters, and it certainly extends the possible uses of a single gun. It does though, add weight at the very ends of the barrels, which does nothing for the handling properties of the gun.

The 'best' choice of choke is a subject guaranteed to provoke discussion among any group of shooting enthusiasts. In the end it is a matter of individual preference. Well worth remembering though is the fact that it is a simple task for any competent gunsmith to reduce the amount of choke in a barrel: making an open bored gun produce choke patterns can be done, but it is likely to be both difficult and expensive. My own choice would be for quarter choke in one barrel and improved cylinder in the other, but for every expert who would agree with me I will guarantee there is another who would not.

Barrels

There is no reason why you *cannot* shoot with a single-barrel gun, or with a repeater, provided that the repeater is modified so that the magazine will only accept two cartridges. The usual choice of gun for the rough shooter though is a double-barrelled weapon. The advantages are obvious: ease of reloading; the possibility of maintaining a rapid rate of fire if such should be necessary; the instant choice of choke offered by having each barrel bored differently; the ease of demonstrating that the gun is safe by carrying in the open position and the fine balance and handleability which can be obtained from a well made double shotgun.

Add to the above the, possibly unreasonable, tradition that a double barrel is the correct weapon for quarry shooting, and there are compelling reasons for choosing conventionally when selecting a gun for rough shooting. Two barrels it is to be then; but should they be aligned in a horizontal or in a vertical plane?

The choice is yours. A few years ago I would have suggested that an over-and-under might be frowned upon at the more formal type of shooting day, but increasing use has made them acceptable everywhere — as far as I am aware. At one time the side-by-side was considered to be the gun for the live quarry shooter with over-and-under guns largely the preserve of clay pigeon enthusiasts, but that distinction has long since blurred.

There are differences: the side-by-side may be a little quicker to load because of the lesser gape at the breech; it may be a little lighter than its over-and-under equivalent. It is argued that the narrow sighting plane of the over-and-under gives it superior pointability. Only you can decide which you prefer. Try both; at clays if possible; and then decide. If you have a subjective preference for one above the other then follow your instincts. You can always change your mind next season.

The standard length for the barrels of a game gun is twenty-eight inches, though naturally guns can be found with longer or shorter barrels. The minimum length is twenty-five inches, and several manufacturers make guns to this specification. Short barrels mean a light gun which can be swung very quickly and easily. Some shots find this is an excellent arrangement and a positive aid to good shooting. Conversely; the shorter barrels reduce inertia and may cause some shooters to poke rather than swing at their target. Longer barrels, of thirty or even thirty-two inches are also available, often in heavier, magnum-chambered weapons where the extra length will reduce muzzle blast and the extra weight reduce recoil. If you have a tendency to poke at birds and stop your swing then longer barrels may be the cure for you.

Actions

Whole books have been devoted to the relative merits of boxlock and sidelock actions. I intend to deal with them in a couple of paragraphs; not because I have no interest in the mechanics of sporting guns, but because I believe that the action, provided that it is has been properly made by a reputable manufacturer, need make little real difference to the suitability of a gun for the rough shooter.

Briefly, sidelocks are generally considered to look more elegant than the utilitarian boxlock, though the boxlock is said by some to be a more robust design. Best guns are generally sidelocks, though I would far sooner have a good quality boxlock than a cheap sidelock. Only an expert will detect any real difference in performance. The Dickson round action is an elegant and well tried alternative to the two more common actions, though definitely not a cheap alternative.

Few hammer guns are seen in the field these days, but that is no reason to eliminate them from your consideration. Superb hammer guns by top English makers can sometimes be picked up relatively cheaply, and provided the rules are followed they are just as safe as a hammerless weapon. Indeed, the fact that the hammers are exposed may even serve to make the handler a little more conscious of the need to handle the gun correctly. If you aspire to a Purdey or a Holland and Holland but are a little under-deposited at the bank, then a hammer gun might be the answer. Remember; the term 'hammerless' is really a misnomer; the hammers are still there, albeit tucked out of sight inside the action. You can lower the hammers on a hammer gun; a loaded hammerless gun is *always* at full cock.

Details

There are quite a lot of other choices to be made apart from the main ones of bore, choke, barrels and action. Most game guns have double triggers which give the shooter instant choice of barrels. Single triggers, and single selective triggers which can be adjusted by a button to fire either barrel first, are found on some guns, particularly over-and-under weapons. They may be easier to use when wearing gloves, but are slightly more prone to malfunction than guns with a trigger for each barrel.

The classic game gun has a straight hand stock, which allows easy adjustment of the right hand grip to select either trigger. Pistol grip and half pistol grip stocks are normal on over-and-under guns, and are not uncommon on side-by-sides. Pick whichever feels right for you.

The cheapest guns, and some older guns, are non-ejectors; more expensive weapons have a spring mechanism which throws out fired cartridge cases when the gun is opened after firing. There is no question that an ejector will allow you to reload much faster than a non-ejector, and if the pheasants are coming thick and fast this may be a very desirable feature. That said, it doesn't take that long to remove a fired case and replace it with a fresh cartridge; and if the birds are that thick on the ground you should have plenty of other chances.

So what, in the end, is the right gun for the rough shoot? The simple answer is that there is no simple answer. What is right for one shooter may be completely wrong for another. There are plenty of books around which will advise you on your choice of gun, and if you read enough of them you will probably find every single piece of advice contradicted at least once by some other writer. Rather than trying to tell you what sort of gun you should buy I shall content myself with describing the weapon I would choose if I were thinking of adding to the contents of the gun cabinet.

I would look for a double barrelled twelve bore; a side-by-side ejector with double triggers and a straight hand stock. This is the weapon that has been the natural choice of game shooters for the past century or more and I see no reason to differ from all the thousands of shooters, good and bad, who have selected just such a gun in the past. The barrels would probably be a conventional twenty-eight inches, though it would be more important that the gun felt right for me when I handled it than that the barrels were a specific length.

The weight would be around six and a half pounds: light enough to carry all day but heavy enough to absorb the recoil of the ounce and a sixteenth of number six shot that I

Grouse missed cleanly — probably just as well at this range as it would have been unfit to eat if shot.

would use for the majority of my shooting. Two and a half inch chambers are all that I need, though I would not reject a gun simply because the chambers were longer. I am tempted by the thought of improved cylinder boring in both barrels, since I suspect that it might be the most effective choice for my often erratic shooting, but a combination of improved cylinder and quarter choke would be a little more versatile. It could always be altered later.

The gun would need to be a good fit, or be close enough so that it could be altered so that it became one, and I would like it to throw its pattern just a little high, which should help with the going away shots which are common for the walking gun.

My choice of maker would be determined by the depth of my pockets. At the top of the list would be a best quality English game gun by one of the top makers. It might not have been built with rough shooting in mind but we are firmly in the realms of fantasy here so I might as well enjoy the dream. Being practical, and thinking in terms of what might be possible, I might be tempted to choose a second-hand, English boxlock rather than a new, continental sidelock at the same price.

I am, at least as far as game guns are concerned, somewhat conservative. I can admire fancy engraving, deeply figured walnut stocks and gold plated triggers but not if they are present at the expense of quality and workmanship of the functional aspects of the gun. No amount of engraving will make a good gun out of a weapon with a poorly engineered action or badly regulated barrels. It is the working parts of the gun that enable us to kill game; not the grain of the stock nor the pattern engraved into the lock plates.

I would want to see the gun fired at a pattern plate so that I knew what the real, as opposed to nominal, degree of choke was, and then I should like to try it out on some clay pigeons to confirm that the fit was as it should be and that the gun really did shoot where I was looking. Then I could take it home and stand it in the gun cabinet and look forward to the first day of the new season.

You may not agree with everything, or anything, about my choice of gun. If you want a single trigger, over-and-under, twenty bore with full choke in both barrels, gold inlaid engraving, a full pistol grip stock, beaver tail fore-end, raised, ventilated rib and thirty two inch barrels then go ahead and buy one. Provided that it is what you want then it is the right gun for you — and if you have confidence in your choice of gun then you are likely to shoot well with it.

Guns with their Labradors and Springers going to the next drive.

Yellow Labrador retrieving a grouse among heather and deer grass.

The Pointer is indicating game at hand: the gun is ready with his weapon pointing safely away from the dog.

Working out a point with the gun muzzles well clear of the dog and the photographer.

8 Clothes and Equipment

Fashion writers have never, as far as I know, shown a great deal of interest in clothing for the rough shooter. There was a brief time in the nineteen eighties when waxed jackets became the 'in' thing for town-dwelling Yuppies, and smart shops would sell you one with a designer label for three times the price of the real thing. Mostly they had pretty patterns on the lining, 'game pockets' that were hardly big enough for a couple of snipe, and little gilded brass badges on the lapels. They looked pretty, and so did the models that posed with the shiny guns and show champion gundogs and tried to look as if they knew which end of the barrel was up. No doubt Mr and Ms Yuppie were suitably impressed.

But clothes for the rough shooter have little to do with the dictates of fashion. There are three main requirements that must be satisfied when choosing clothes to go shooting. They must keep you dry when it is wet, keep you warm when it is cold, and they should be inconspicuous. Once those three conditions are met there are others almost as important. The cut of the coat must leave you free to mount and swing your gun; the material must be tough enough to stand up to thorns, brambles and barbed wire and the boots must be suitable for long days out walking. The cost is likely to exert an influence as well, which is why the over-priced, designer-labelled creations favoured by the Yuppies are rarely seen in the shooting field.

I had a good look around at the clothes that the guns were wearing at our last shoot of the season and the only word that really seemed to sum them up was 'nondescript'. No-one looked much like the models in the adverts. Come to think of it, none of the dogs looked the part either. All of them; guns, dogs and our three honorary beaters, looked businesslike, but I fear none of us will ever feature in the pages of *She* or *Elle*. Nondescript may even be erring on the side of generosity.

At first glance there was little to distinguish any of the guns from each other, the ubiquitous waxed jacket being almost universal, mostly in shades of olive green, mud green or a sort of greeny khaki. Only when I looked closely were the little differences apparent: boots of rubber or boots of leather, gaiters or leggings, caps or broad brimmed hats, gloves made of wool, gloves made of leather or perhaps no gloves at all. Cartridge belts for some, cartridge bags for others, and a couple of pockets full of cartridges for the rest. Not smart certainly, but not scruffy either; just comfortable, well worn shooting clothes that would keep the rain, the cold and the mud, the thorns, the brambles and the barbed wire at a respectable distance from the wearer.

Despite the apparently nondescript uniformity of the various guns at the shoot there was actually quite a variety of styles and materials on display. Some were undoubtedly better than others; some cost a great deal more than others without necessarily being

Shirtsleeve order on a hot August day shooting over pointers.

better. I doubt whether any of the guns would claim to have arrived at the perfect shooting outfit. There is usually something that could be improved.

It is unusual for the fieldsports enthusiast to set out to equip himself from top to toe at one time. Items of clothing are added when we need them, or when we can afford them, and discarded as they wear out or as something better is bought to replace them. Mistakes can stay with you for a long time — I have a jacket that is a little tight in the sleeves, but I have been wearing that jacket for the past four seasons and will carry on until it has worn out sufficiently to justify a replacement. Having paid out good money for it I intend to get my money's worth, even if it isn't quite right.

The choice of materials, and styles open to the rough shooter is considerable, and there is no such thing as the 'right' outfit. You must make up your own mind, depending on the depth of your pocket, the type of ground you plan to shoot over and your personal preferences. I can offer no more than a guide to what is generally available, leaving the final decision in your hands. Bearing in mind that most rough shooters spend a considerable amount of time walking, I propose to start with boots and work upwards. If you prefer to begin with hats and work downwards I suggest you start at the end of the chapter and work back. We should meet again somewhere about the waistline.

Boots

When I first started shooting there wasn't a great deal of choice of shooting boots. Mostly we wore wellington boots; real wellies made out of thick black rubber and costing about thirty shillings at the hardware shop; except in the summer when we made do with what were called baseball boots. They had canvas tops and bouncy rubber soles and were usually pretty well worn out by the end of the summer holidays. If you had a hankering for 'real' boots, the Army and Navy Stores would sell you a pair of ex-Army ammunition boots complete with nailed soles and stiff toe-caps, or you could buy work boots at the shoe shop. Either way they cost very little, needed weeks of patient breaking-in and, properly treated with dubbin, neatsfoot oil and boot polish, would last for years.

Nowadays you can still make do with a pair of wellies, though baseball boots come with designer labels, pretty patterns on the soles and a price that would keep me in cartridges for a season. There is a far wider choice of materials, styles and prices now, though we have a long way to go before we get anywhere near the choice offered to sportsmen in the United States. I have an American mail-order sporting catalogue in front of me and there are literally hundreds of different boots and shoes on offer, designed to cope with every possible variation in terrain and weather. There are boots guaranteed to protect your feet in temperatures of minus forty; boots with special, snake-proof uppers for use in rattlesnake country and boots for just about every circumstance you might imagine. The only thing the catalogue doesn't have is a pair of bog-standard black wellies — but you can get them over here.

The best choice of boot will depend on where and when you plan to go shooting. A dry moor in August will call for something rather different to a muddy foreshore in January — though a pair of wellies would serve in either case at a pinch. There is no question of recommending any particular type or make of boot — only you know where you will be shooting — but we can look at the different boots which are available and consider their advantages and disadvantages.

Rubber boots, provided they haven't perished or been holed, will keep your feet dry — from the outside. Since the rubber is impervious to water they will also make your feet sweat, and that sweat will have no way of evaporating, so they will also make your feet wet — from the inside. Some people are quite happy to walk all day while wearing wellies; others find them hot, uncomfortable and tiring. A lot depends on their weight and on how well they fit.

There have been a lot of improvements to the design of rubber boots in recent years and you can buy them now in softer, lighter rubber, with hard-wearing and absorbent linings. The better ones are shaped at least approximately like a human foot and have good, grippy cleats on the bottom. If you are feeling really rich you can spend well over one hundred pounds on a fancy, leather lined pair with zips up the sides and impress your shooting partners no end — but they will still, basically, be a pair of welly boots.

If you choose a pair that fit you properly; remembering that you will be wearing thick socks in them on shooting days; then they should be reasonably comfortable for walking. The old type of welly which fitted only where it touched was prone to slop around on your feet and cause blisters, and the tops rubbed against your calves as you walked. Modern 'field boots', as the advertisers have dubbed them, should fit as well as an ordinary pair of shoes and have a strap or lace at the top of the leg to tighten them. Being made of softer rubber they flex when you walk, which is fine for comfort but also means that they are prone to crack and perish around the instep and ankle. They are also more vulnerable to thorns, brambles and barbed wire so you need to watch your step in thick cover or be prepared to buy replacements on a regular basis.

Lace-up rubber ankle boots offer a compromise between wellies and the traditional leather boot. Made of pure rubber, or of rubberised canvas, they are light, comfortable and waterproof, and need no breaking-in. Like all rubber boots they are maintenance free, needing nothing more than a quick splash to wash away the mud and then drying out ready for the next day. They will only keep your feet dry as far as the ankles of course: if you are going to be floundering about in estuary mud or standing in eighteen inches of water at the flight pond then you either wear wellies or get wet: but for most purposes they have all the advantages of ordinary rubber boots while being lighter, warmer and more comfortable. They also tend to wear out rather rapidly. If they are moulded from pure rubber the soles are very soft, and once the treads have worn away they are absolutely lethal on any slippery surface. The rubberised canvas type have harder soles, but the rubber and the canvas are liable to part company where the boot flexes.

You can avoid most of the problems associated with rubber boots by choosing boots made of leather. Leather will let your feet 'breathe' instead of cocooning them in impervious rubber. Leather is far more resistant to wire, thorns and sharp edges generally; will stretch and mould to fit the peculiar contours of your feet; can be laced more or less tightly according to how many pairs of socks you decide to wear and can be re-soled when the grip starts to wear away. Those are the good points. On the other side of the balance sheet, leather is not waterproof unless treated with dubbin, oil, wax or silicone, and whatever you rub into the outside of your boots in order to keep the wet out will eventually be worn off by friction against grass, heather or bramble. Then they will not be waterproof any more.

Of course, you can repeat the treatment and re-proof them, which brings us to the matter of maintenance. Leather boots have to be cleaned and polished, waxed and dubbined, dried carefully when wet and generally molly-coddled in a way that rubber boots never are. If you take care of them a good pair of leather boots can last for years and get more comfortable with each year that passes; but if you neglect them; dry them out in front of a hot fire, throw them into a cupboard when they are wet and muddy; then they will stiffen and crack, the stitches will rot and you will soon be reaching into your pocket for the price of a new pair.

The price you will pay can vary from a few pounds to a few hundreds of pounds. The cheapest boots, made in Eastern Europe or the far East, will not compare with a hand-stitched, custom built pair from a traditional bootmaker, but they can represent excellent value for money, and if you look after them properly should be good for several seasons of hard work. At the other end of the scale, a pair of hand-mades might well last you a life-time, again provided you look after them properly.

In between the two extremes there is a wide range of styles and prices to suit every pocket. Some of the more high-tech boots incorporate a waterproof lining of Goretex or something similar and are claimed to be completely waterproof but not to trap perspiration in the way that rubber boots do. If they work they would seem to offer an excellent compromise between the comfort of a leather boot and the dry feet given by rubbers, but all those I have seen have been too expensive for my pocket and no manufacturer has yet plied me with free samples for me to review.

The growth of the rambling and climbing industry has meant that a wide range of new walking boots has reached the market place. Walkers' magazines 'road-test' boots in the same way that auto mags test cars. There are boots now which are made more like sports shoes than traditional walking gear, with nylon and soft leather uppers bonded to light, well-sprung soles. They are ideal for long days on the moors in August and September where lightness combined with good ankle support and a grippy sole puts them way ahead of the alternatives, but I have some doubts regarding their resilience in the mud and muck of a winter shoot day. I spent a whole August wearing a pair of football boots, designed for use on astro-turf, and very good they were, except for letting the water in.

Leggings and Gaiters

If you elect to wear ankle boots and knee length breeks, plus twos or plus fours, then the area between the top of the boot and the knee is left pretty much exposed to the elements. This isn't too much of a problem as far as rain is concerned because a decent pair of woollen socks will keep your legs warm even if they get wet and will soon dry in the breeze. However, woollen socks will not stop brambles, thorns and midges from doing battle with your shins and calves, and it is the shins and calves that will come second. The answer is to invest in a pair of canvas gaiters.

Climbing shops sell them in a range of colours and materials. Opt for something suitably subdued in green or khaki and make sure that you choose a material that will let your legs breathe and also stand up to thorns and brambles. Nylon gaiters create a mini sauna for the lower legs and will soon get ripped in thick cover. Goretex and the like will do the job much better and cost a small fortune; canvas is cheap, strong and just as good.

On the moors in summer they keep the midges out of your socks (and you have to have experienced that particular torture to know just how bad it can be) as well as keeping bits of heather out of the tops of your boots.

In the wet they will also provide a bridge between your feet and the bottoms of your waterproof leggings, without which you must either switch to wellies or put up with all the rain which falls on you descending under the influence of gravity and being decanted neatly into the tops of your boots.

As for leggings, they also fulfil the twin functions of keeping you dry and saving your legs from thorns and brambles. Out on the hill there is a lot to be said for the very lightweight nylon waterproofs which can be carried in the pockets and pulled on when rain threatens. Once the shower is past they will dry in minutes and can be put back in the pocket until the next one begins. In thick cover though they will be shredded by the first bramble you encounter. Something much harder wearing is needed, in waxed cotton or perhaps one of the Goretex type fabrics.

Full over-trousers keep you warm and dry from the waist down; especially useful if you are sitting in a ditch waiting for duck or pigeon to flight, or just sitting to eat your lunch. They are bulky to wear and bulky to carry; hard work to walk in and sometimes extremely hot to wear.

Leggings are lighter, airier and easy to tuck away in the gamebag. Your coat should cover the bits that they miss, so provided that you don't wish to sit on the damp ground they will keep you just as dry as over-trousers. But of course, you may want to sit on the damp ground, in which case . . .

Whichever you choose make sure that you can get them on and off *without* removing your boots. Wide legs, zips or snap fasteners are essential, otherwise you are effectively locked into (or out of) your waterproofs for the whole day, no matter how often the weather changes. And as you know, one of the delights of our British weather is its changeability. But not when you have sit down in a thunderstorm to take your boots off before you can put your waterproof leggings on.

Breeks and Trousers

The most practical choice is probably a pair of loose fitting breeks in a good quality heavyweight tweed. Tweed is tough, warm and pretty well waterproof, comfortable to wear and easy to clean. Knee length breeks (or plus twos/fours) are to be preferred to trousers because they don't flap around your ankles when wet and collect mud from your boots. You can always tuck full length trousers into your socks of course, or wear gaiters over the top of them.

Next to tweed there is the choice of corduroy, moleskin, cotton and a range of man-made fibres. Comfort and warmth are the main considerations since you will normally be wearing waterproofs over the top of them when it rains. Leather breeks, which are popular on the continent, are warm, water resistant, very tough and very expensive. Moleskin is soft and comfortable but will soak up water like a sponge. Denim jeans look a little out of place on a shoot but if it is wet and you are wearing over-trousers all day they will be out of sight in any case.

Dressed for the hill. Cap, tweed jacket and breeks, canvas gaiters and a stout walking stick.

Coats and Jackets

Waxed jackets get everywhere. Even grouse shooting in the middle of summer, on scorching days when the pointers flopped down into the burns to cool off between points and I was wandering along in my shirt sleeves, there was a fair chance that one of the guns would sweat throughout the day in one. A more unsuitable garment for a hot, dry day would be difficult to devise, but every August they take to the moors in droves. If your shoot is in the sort of place where you expect to be walking-up grouse in August, then take a tip from the clothes that Highland stalkers and keepers wear to work. If you can afford it, and if you are going to do enough summer shooting to justify the expense, then a good quality tweed jacket is undoubtedly the best choice for the hill.

It will keep you warm in the cold but allow perspiration to evaporate on hot days. It will keep you dry for a considerable time even on wet days, and it will blend into the background far better than a waxed coat which looks black at any distance. If you make sure that is big enough to accommodate several layers underneath it will serve pretty well during the winter too, and if you happen to enjoy stalking as well as shooting it will double as a stalking jacket. But it will cost you quite a lot of money, particularly for a jacket in the heaviest quality tweed.

Most rough shooters though will be content with a waxed coat, or one made of the modern 'breathing' waterproof materials. The prices vary alarmingly, especially when you consider that the materials used vary little between one manufacturer and the next. Waxed cotton coats vary from twenty pounds to perhaps one hundred and fifty, and coats made of Goretex, Ventile and the like can cost considerably more. The actual construction of the cheapest coats is often suspect, with seams badly stitched and pocket linings skimped and zips which will rust and jam after a few weeks wear, but even so it is hard to see how such a variation in price can be justified on economic grounds.

Look for a coat which has ample room inside for you, plus two or three layers of warm clothing and whatever you put in the game pocket. You need plenty of freedom to swing a gun, even when you are cocooned against the weather. Pockets should be wide enough to let you get gloved hands in and out of them easily; the zip must be tough and rustproof and the hood, if fitted, should be loose enough to fit over your cap or hat. I prefer fixed hoods which can be pulled up as and when they are needed to those which are hidden in a pocket at the back of the collar or fastened and removed by zips, buttons or snap fasteners. The hidden hood always ends up as a uncomfortable, wet lump in the back of my neck, while detachable hoods are invariably lost early on, only re-surfacing long after the coat has worn out and been thrown away.

Waxed cotton will undoubtedly make you sweat on a hot day while the more modern waterproof fabrics claim to keep rain out while letting perspiration escape through a semi-permeable membrane. They are generally better than simple waxed cotton, but if it is hot enough then sweat you will, and no waterproof fabric yet invented will prevent you from getting damp and clammy inside your coat. Whatever your choice, remember that you may soon be thrusting your way through thorns and brambles, climbing fences and scrambling across ditches while wearing it. If the idea of subjecting several hundred pounds worth of tailoring to such abuse will worry you then buy a cheap waxed jacket. It will probably serve you just as well while preserving your peace of mind and saving your bank balance.

Hats and Gloves

Everyone should wear a hat to go shooting. The human face shines out like a beacon, particularly when it is pointed upwards to watch pigeon, duck or the like flying into range. For that reason alone some sort of hat with a brim which will shield the face is most essential. Serious decoyers go even further and wear face masks or balaclava helmets. This can sometimes have unfortunate consequences when some public spirited citizen spots a masked gunman lurking in the undergrowth and calls the police. At such times it may be as well to have your shotgun licence to hand and not to make any sudden moves when the helicopter appears and the loud-hailer starts up.

An ordinary flat cap is probably the most common head-gear and serves perfectly well. A deerstalker has the added advantage of a peak at either end to keep the rain off your neck as well as your face, and the flaps can be tied down to keep your ears warm and anchor the hat in place during a gale. There are several variations on the stetson or bush hat theme made in waxed cotton which are excellent in wet weather, keeping the rain right off the head, face and neck. They may also attract a certain amount of abuse from your fellow guns, but this is best ignored. You may look like an idiot but you will be a dry idiot.

A towelling cravat is a great comfort on really wet days, not only keeping the rain from trickling under your collar but also helping to trap the heat inside your jacket.

Gloves are very much a matter of individual choice. The special shooting gloves made of paper thin leather are excellent in that they don't interfere with the handling of your gun, but not so good at keeping your hands warm when it is really cold and wet — which is the time when you most need them. Woollen gloves are warmer but less sensitive and can get slippery when the gun is wet. Special shooting gloves often have trigger fingers which can be folded back leaving the fore-finger bare for shooting — a device which also exposes the trigger finger to the cold and wet and may negate any good that the gloves were doing.

Some people wear gloves from the moment that the weather becomes unsuitable for sun-bathing. I prefer to manage without until it becomes so cold that shooting without them becomes impractical, if not actually impossible, shoving my hands into my pockets rather than wearing gloves. That said, I have never found actually handling a gun particularly difficult with gloves on, but do find it harder to get cartridges out of my pockets and into the breech.

Cartridge Belts and Bags

The simplest way to carry cartridges is loose in the pockets of your coat from where they are easily reached for re-loading. This is fine as long as you are wearing a coat, and assuming that is has big enough pockets to hold a box or so of cartridges. On the debit side, cartridges are quite heavy — there is a pound and a half of shot in a box of twenty-five, never mind wads, powder and cases — so two big pockets full of cartridges are going to hamper your swing quite considerably. And if you are out on a summers day in shirt sleeves you are going to have to make some other arrangement anyway.

The usual alternatives are a cartridge belt or a cartridge bag. The belt has the advantage of being strapped around your waist and so is effectively weightless, while a bag hung from the shoulders will make its presence felt by the end of the day. Most cartridge belts hold one box of cartridges because twenty-five cartridges in line abreast are about as many as will stretch round the average human waist. A reasonably sized bag will hold more — probably a couple of boxes — though you can of course wear a belt full round your waist and fill your pockets as well.

Pockets and bags will keep the wet off your cartridges when it is raining. Obviously a cartridge belt doesn't, unless you wear it under your coat in which case access to the cartridges is somewhat restricted. Again, a belt-full underneath and a few in the pockets ready for use is an acceptable compromise. If you opt for a bag be sure you can get your hands in and out easily, even when wearing gloves.

Gamebags

The main reason for having a gamebag is, obviously, to carry game. You may have a poacher's pocket in the lining of your coat, but its capacity will probably be limited to a couple of cock pheasants or two brace of grouse. Once you get beyond that you are going to need something to carry what you shoot. At properly organised driven shoots the problem doesn't arise. There will be a team of pickers-up to collect the game and a game cart to carry it back to the larder. Rough shooting is a little different and generally requires you to carry what you shoot. And since you will want both hands free for the next shot a gamebag is the obvious answer.

The usual design is a stout canvas bag with a net attached to the front, and usually with a rubberised lining. It is not a good idea, especially in warm weather, to cram everything you shoot into the interior of the bag. Game can spoil very quickly, and sweating in a jumbled heap inside a gamebag is a good way to accelerate the process. Put your birds, rabbits or whatever into the net and let the air circulate around them and they will cool faster with less danger of going off.

A wide strap is essential, particularly the part which will transfer the weight of the bag to your shoulder. Half a dozen pheasants or five brace of grouse will weigh fifteen pounds or more, and a narrow strap that cuts into your shoulder will appear to double or treble that after a few miles walking. Ten brace of grouse — say thirty pounds — may not sound very heavy but it is more than enough to carry on a hot August day. Add gun, cartridges, walking stick, waterproofs and perhaps camera or binoculars and you will be heartily glad to see the lodge or the Land-Rover come evening — I write from bitter experience!

Besides bringing your game home in the evening the gamebag will double as a container for all the junk you decide to take out with you: lunch, tins of beer, spare cartridges, waterproofs, an extra pullover, spare dog lead, Mars bar for the dog, ditto for self, camera, binoculars, mooring spike for dog, cartridge extractor, map, shotgun licence and whatever else I may have forgotten. Always remember that, food apart, whatever you take out in the gamebag in the morning you will be bringing home in the gamebag at night — plus whatever you shoot during the day. It is not a good idea to take everything but the kitchen sink.

The gamebag also serves as dry seat at lunchtime, something to spread across the barbed wire if you or your dog are worried about getting spiked while climbing fences and a handy container for wheat or barley if you are scattering a bit of feed for the ducks or pheasants. The net does have a tendency to snag every twig, branch, bramble or bit of wire that you pass, and the strap will slip down and trip you when you are crouching low to get under branches in the woods, but these are minor inconveniences which are more than offset by the gamebag's general usefulness. Do make sure that you are not the only gun with a bag or you will end up acting as porter for the others. This is something that they will appreciate far more than you.

Odds and Ends

There are any amount of other bits and pieces which you can take with you when you go shooting. Your local gun and fishing tackle shop will stock loads of patent gadgets that you can carry, wear, or stuff in the gamebag and some of them might even prove useful from time to time. Your idea of getting ready to shoot may consist of nothing more than tucking your feet into your wellies, taking the gun down from its peg and dropping a handful of cartridges into your trouser pockets. Others may require a couple of hours with frequent references to a check list before they feel ready to leave the house.

One thing that all sportsmen should carry is a knife. You can spend anything from a couple of pounds for the most basic penknife to a couple of hundred pounds for a something really fancy with engraving on the blade, the horns of an endangered species for the handle and a velvet-lined presentation case which you can keep the knife in when you are not using it. Provided you keep them sharp both will gut rabbits, cut string, peel an apple or whittle a stick with equal efficiency. If you like gadgets one of the excellent Swiss Army knives will provide you with two blades, a pair of scissors, a corkscrew, a screw-driver, a marlin spike, a pair of tweezers, a thing for getting stones out of horses hooves, a tooth pick and a couple of other things the function of which is a mystery to me, but which are undoubtedly essential to a Swiss squaddie. Pay your money and take your pick, but do carry a knife: it is the one accessory which is genuinely useful.

A cartridge extractor is something that was once considered as almost essential for the rough shooter. In the days of paper cartridge cases, which would swell slightly if they got wet and stick firmly in the breech, it was undoubtedly a useful thing to have with you. I have never yet needed one in thirty something years shooting; probably because the modern, plastic case is pretty well impervious to moisture. If you do get a stuck case you may be able to cut a long stick, using the knife which you are carrying (see above), and poke it out from the muzzle end. Should you get frequent stuck cases then take a look at how you are storing your cartridges, and if there is no problem there then get a gunsmith to examine your gun.

The sound of a gun can damage your hearing. It is a cumulative process and the chances are that you won't be aware of any problems until it is too late. Once the damage is done it cannot be reversed. You can protect your ears by reducing the amount of noise which reaches the ear drum. The simplest way to do this is with a couple of bits of cotton wool; the most sophisticated ear defenders have electronic wizardry which is supposed to filter out loud noises but still let you hear normally. In between there are various types of plugs and mufflers, some of them invisible and others which make you look like Mickey Mouse. If you value your hearing then some sort of ear defender is a wise investment.

It is true that wearing ear plugs will make it harder to hear rabbits rustling in the undergrowth, pigeons wings whistling over the wood and the distant cry of geese in flight. Remember that gun deafness will have exactly the same effect, and once it has happened it cannot be reversed.

While on the subject we might consider safety glasses. Wearing a pair of these will protect your eyes from a ricochet or a careless shot; from a blow back from the breech of your gun and from a branch whipping into your face as you push through a wood. They are undoubtedly a sensible precaution and I should recommend you to purchase a pair and to wear them whenever you go shooting. That said, I have never worn a pair for shooting and doubt that I ever will, unless our political masters pass some law that insists that I do. I suspect that some day they may do just that.

If you suffer from cold hands there are a number of useful little devices which you can carry in your pockets and which will release heat slowly throughout the day. There are little metal cases in which you can burn a fuel stick rather like a fire lighter and gel packs which release heat via a chemical reaction when they are triggered off. These come as both disposable packs which work once only and multi-use packs which are re-charged by boiling them in water.

There are lots of other bits and pieces which you might want to take along. A length of string can come in useful for all sorts of things: spare bootlace, makeshift dog lead, game carrier, hide building accessory, belt, gun sling, whistle lanyard etc. Binder twine is strong and available, if not exactly elegant, while a couple of leather bootlaces will do just as well and look slightly less rustic.

Shooting rabbits over a Labrador in winter. Warmly dressed in tweed breeks and waxed jacket.

If you prefer not to kill wounded game by breaking its neck there are patent humane dispatchers available. I know several sportsmen who carry a small screwdriver or a set of turnscrews in their pockets ready to effect running repairs to their guns if the need should arise. A compass and a map may be useful if you are out on the moors without a keeper, and the compass is almost essential for wildfowlers where they are far out on the mudflats of a big estuary. Indeed, distress flares, life jackets and survival blankets may be in order as well, but these are more the province of the wildfowler than the rough shooter. Bear in mind though, that it is the occasional wildfowler — the man or woman who is not familiar with wind and tide — that is most likely to get into difficulties out on the foreshore.

A pair of binoculars is sometimes useful; spotting incoming pigeon or wildfowl or following the flight of a pricked bird. Though not necessary, they can add to the enjoyment of a day on the foreshore, out in the hills, or when waiting in a hide for pigeon, by helping you to watch the birds and animals around you. Standard sized binoculars can be heavy and awkward to carry, but there are miniature pairs that will slip easily into a pocket yet still have first class optics, even if they lack the light gathering power of their big brothers.

There are cameras of course, there are pipes, cigars and cigarettes; matches and cigarette lighters. You may want to take sunglasses, bottle openers, a clicker to count the shots fired, a patent cartridge dispenser for fast re-loading, a hip flask for sloe gin and one of those patent, collapsible cups to drink it from. You can, if you so desire, and if you are strong enough to carry it all, take everything up to and including the kitchen sink. The choice is yours.

If you are warm, dry and inconspicuous; have your gun and some cartridges and something to shoot at; then you have all the necessary ingredients for a day's rough shooting. Whatever you add after that for your convenience, comfort, safety and general enjoyment of the day is entirely up to you. I will settle for my dog, a knife and a gamebag. Sometimes I don't bother with the gamebag.

9 Gundogs

Every rough shooter should have a dog.

Now that is a pretty unequivocal statement; it is not by any means original; and it is not necessarily true. There are certain situations for the rough shooter in which a dog is not any great asset. They are few and far between I will admit, but there are times when you can manage quite well without a dog. Bolting rabbits with ferrets perhaps — provided there isn't any thick cover nearby where you might need your dog to hunt out and retrieve a wounded rabbit. Shooting crows which you don't intend to retrieve anyway. There are probably other situations, though none spring to mind at the moment. But there it is: you don't absolutely *have* to have a dog: it is just much, much better if you do.

A dog will find game that you never suspected was there. Walk through a strip of cover without a dog and I guarantee that at least half the game hidden there will simply crouch low and let you walk past. Make that a heather moorland in August and I would put the figure at closer to ninety per cent. A good dog will find nearly all of that game for you.

A dog will retrieve dead and wounded game that would be otherwise be lost. Shoot a grouse which falls wounded into long heather and see if you can find it without a dog to help. Drop a duck out into the ebb tide on a January morning and try swimming after it yourself. Or perhaps you would like to track down a winged cock pheasant as he legs it through the brambles in the middle of a hundred-acre wood. A dog will do all those things while you lean on your stick and admire the view.

One moment there is just you and the pointing dog . . .

. . . then suddenly the air is full of grouse.

There are somewhere in the region of sixty recognised breeds of gundog, worldwide, of which twenty or so may be seen working in Britain. In addition there are various other breeds and cross breeds which are worked to the gun or used as beating dogs — I have seen Jack Russell terriers used to bolt rabbits and a Lakeland cross terrier retrieving grouse. The first dog which I shot over was a spaniel crossed with a collie. Allegedly. It had every fault in the book plus a couple it had patented personally, but it was an expert at pushing rabbits out from hedge bottoms. It was also more than a bit useful at catching them for itself, so shooting over it sometimes meant just that. It wasn't ideal but it was what we had, and we made the best of it.

Gundogs serve two functions — finding and fetching. Some specialise in one or the other; most will do both. When I say finding I mean hunting out game so that the guns can shoot it. Fetching means retrieving dead and wounded game after it has been shot. Obviously retrieving will also mean hunting when searching for a runner or looking for a bird which has fallen into cover, so there is no clear distinction between the two functions. The game-finding dogs can be sub-divided further into pointing breeds and flushing breeds, giving us three categories of gundog — those which hunt game and point; those which hunt game and flush it; and those which are primarily retrievers.

In Britain and Ireland gundogs are classified slightly differently to the above. The Setters and Pointers, consisting of Irish Setters, English Setters, Gordon Setters and Pointers are one class. Spaniels — English Springers, Welsh Springers, Field, Clumber, Cocker, Sussex and Irish Water Spaniels — are the second; retrievers such as the Labrador, Golden, Flatcoat, Curly-coat and Chesapeake Bay comprise the third. The fourth; the Hunt, Point and Retrieve breeds; are more recent imports from the continent and include German Shorthaired Pointers, German Wirehaired Pointers, Hungarian Vizslas, Weimaraners, Brittany Spaniels, Italian Spinones and Large Munsterlanders.

Those classifications are the subject of some debate. Is the Brittany a spaniel or an HPR? Should there be a distinction between the pointers and setters, all of which are perfectly capable of retrieving, and the HPR breeds? Does the Irish Water Spaniel really belong with the other spaniels or should it be classed with the retrievers? Tradition, a certain amount of snobbery and a great deal of vested interest means that such arguments will continue among those who are interested. If you aspire to run your dog in Field Trials then the internal politics of the Trial and Show fraternity may be of interest to you — if not you are probably only concerned with finding, training and working the right dog for you.

The choice of gundog for the rough shooter is necessarily a very subjective one. There is no one breed which can be said to be the ideal rough shooting dog, though devotees of quite a number of breeds will give you a good argument that their particular favourite is *the* breed to beat all others. For them it probably is; but the dog which is perfect for one man may be nothing but a burden to another. Much will depend on the ground which you will be working and the type of shooting you favour.

The 'finding' aspect of a gundog's work involves hunting out hidden game by using its nose. If rabbit, pheasant or partridge is sitting in plain view then you have no need of a gundog to find it for you — your eyes are probably better than those of your dog. It is the hidden game: the rabbit crouched under a bramble; grouse tucked into the heather; partridges clapped down among sugar-beet and pheasants in the undergrowth of the covert that your dog will hunt out for you. A dog's sense of smell is so superior to that of a human that it is difficult for us to imagine just how much information scent supplies to the dog's brain. A working gundog uses his eyes for navigation but it is the nose that locates the quarry.

When considering gundog work it is important to distinguish between air scent and ground scent. A dog is said to be using air scent when it finds game by winding the smell of the bird or animal coming directly from its body. Ground scent, or foot scent, is the residual smell left on the ground as the bird passes. In spite of the name it does not refer only to scent left on the ground by the feet of the quarry, though such foot scent will be part of the overall residual scent trace. Obviously for a bird to be found with air scent it has to actually be there, somewhere upwind of the dog so that the scent can be carried to the dog on the breeze. Foot scent can linger long after the game has gone, which makes it possible for dogs to hunt out the line of a running bird or animal and track it down.

Irish Setters — boundless energy and a rollicking sense of fun make them superb companions for shooting grouse on the open hill.

A grouse found and retrieved by a young Labrador.

The two are not mutually exclusive. Grouse, pheasant, partridge, blackgame and many other gamebirds will often choose to run before they will fly. Imagine your dog has picked up the air scent from a bird which responds to the threat of the dog by running away across the line of the wind. Once it moves the invisible link of scent molecules from bird to dog is broken. By dropping the head and picking up the foot scent the dog can track the bird down as it runs. Equally, it may be residual scent from a feeding line that first alerts the dog to the presence of game somewhere close by. Then, either by tracking the foot scent or by casting across the wind, the dog will locate the exact position of the birds and raise them for the gun to shoot.

Always, always remember, whatever type of gundog you are working, that it is scent which is important to the dog, and that scent is carried on the breeze. If a bird or animal is downwind of the dog then the dog will not find it. Whether you are hunting for grouse on the open hill or sending the dog to retrieve a pheasant from cover, you should always consider the wind direction and try to get your dog downwind of its quarry.

Handlers of pointing dogs will sometimes refuse to work their dogs at all unless they are going directly into the wind. This may be all right at a field trial, though it is wasteful of both time and ground under practical shooting conditions, but it does illustrate the importance that handlers give to reading and working the wind correctly.

Flushing Dogs

These are the breeds which hunt out their game and force it to fly or run as soon as they find it. If they are working for a man with a gun then it is obviously important — you might say imperative – that they work well within gunshot. A bird which is flushed out of range is a bird lost, unless you are exceptionally lucky and it happens to fly towards you. There are times; working as a beater's dog, or moving birds out of a particular piece of cover into another; when you may be happy for your dog to flush game at a distance, but these are the exceptions, not the rule.

A flushing dog must be trained to work within thirty or so yards of his handler, and to flush the game that he finds within that distance. There is something of a dichotomy in this, as the dog must be controlled enough to regulate its work into a very small area yet have the aggression to push sometimes reluctant birds into the air, not allowing them to run ahead until they are out of range of the gun. At the same time the aggression should not be such that birds are pegged before they have a chance to rise. I should say at this point that it is not unknown for birds to be pegged or for dogs to roam out of range even in the best shooting circles.

When pheasants or rabbits are tucked down tightly among thick cover they are naturally reluctant to break out and take to their legs or wings. A dog which skirts the outside of the the brambles, nettles, thorn scrub or whatever is no threat to the quarry crouching within, and within is where the quarry is likely to stay. Only when the dog pushes itself through the thorns and briars does the danger of staying put begin to outweigh the threat posed by breaking cover. It takes both keenness and bravery for a dog to spend the day facing thorns and brambles, nettles and thistles, tangled roots and barbed wire. A thick coat helps; there are no thornproof jackets and leggings for dogs.

The spaniels are the specialist hunting and flushing dogs. With their thick coats, relatively short legs and bustling style they have been selectively bred over hundreds, and possibly thousands, of years to hunt game, face cover and water fearlessly, and produce that game for the hunter. Originally they would have been used to find game for falcons, greyhounds or hunters with nets; now they do the same job for the shooting man, with the added task of retrieving the game after it has been shot.

The most common of the working spaniels is the English Springer; a breed that is sometimes described as 'the rough shooting man's dog'. Certainly in terms of field trial success English Springers far out-reach all the other spaniel breeds combined, and in the shooting field too they are the most common spaniel by a long, long way. Brave, willing and strong, a good springer will hunt with tireless enthusiasm and a bouncing, tail-wagging zest that is a joy to watch. There is, however, a fine dividing line between tireless enthusiasm and headstrong stubbornness, and it is all too easy for the inexperienced trainer to lose control, particularly over the high paced, thrusting type of Springer favoured in competition. If you can handle such a dog it can make a superb shooting companion, but if the dog once begins to dominate the handler then the partnership is doomed.

Next to the English Springer, numerically at least, is the Cocker Spaniel. Smaller and lighter, the Cocker is said to be a more sensitive animal than its larger cousin, though there is common ancestry for both breeds. They were originally used to hunt woodcock, and it is from this that the name is derived. Their size is no handicap to their working ability, though a full grown hare will certainly test their strength if it has to be carried any distance.

In the field there is little to choose between a good Springer and a good Cocker — a remark that will probably annoy the devotees of both breeds unless I qualify it further. Both will hunt and find game in practically any cover, both will flush it out for the gun and both will retrieve. The differences, and they are certainly important to the handlers and trainers of the breeds, are mainly in the style of working and the type of training and handling that they require. If you have a great preference for one breed over the other then a good worker of that breed will be more satisfying, for you, than even a slightly better

going dog of the other type. If you have no preference then you will probably find a wider choice among Springers than Cockers. This may mean that you have more chance of finding a good one, though logically it also means more chance of doing the opposite.

Compared with Springers and Cockers the other spaniel breeds are, numerically, miles adrift. The combined annual Kennel Club registrations of Welsh Springers, Clumbers, Field, Sussex and Irish Water Spaniels amount to about a tenth of those for Springers and Cockers. In terms of field trial success the ratio is even lower, though this is not necessarily a condemnation of their working ability. Some, particularly the heavily built Clumber, have a slower, more relaxed attitude to life which is unlikely to catch the eye of a trial Judge when seen alongside the pace and bustle of Springers or Cockers. Remember though, that in a rough shooting dog stamina may be more important than pace; ease of handling a greater boon than thrust and style.

Pointing Dogs

There is something of an artificial divide between the British and the Continental breeds of pointing dog. The continentals are classified as Hunt, Point and Retrieve breeds, and that title neatly sums up the work they are required to carry out. The native Pointers and Setters are, in the eyes of the Kennel Club, hunters and pointers but not retrievers.

The HPR breeds were first introduced from the continent in the years after the second world war, and originally were classified with the pointers and setters, and took part in field trials with them. However, pointer and setter trials in Britain test only the hunting and pointing ability of the participants. They generally take place out of season and no birds are shot, therefore no retrieve is required. In 1962 the Kennel Club granted permission for separate trials to be arranged for the HPR breeds which include retrieving from land and water. There are now two completely separate sets of trials; HPR breeds can no longer run in pointer and setter trials and, naturally, HPR trials are not open to the native pointing breeds. On the continent though, all the pointing breeds are expected to retrieve, and there is competition between the British and the continental breeds.

Prior to the introduction of specialist retrieving breeds at the end of the last century the native pointers and setters would have been expected to retrieve as well as hunt and point game. Two things conspired to alter this. The introduction of field trials around 1860 saw handlers and their dogs gathering for competitions prior to the opening of the shooting season. This choice of dates was in part caused by the lack, in those day, of swift and reliable transport. The dogs and their handlers would be required on moors all over the north of England and Scotland once the shooting season began, therefore out of season trials, with no shooting and of course no retrieving, were organised.

At the same time the growing popularity of driven shooting saw the pure retrieving breeds increasing in numbers, and many owners wanted their Flatcoats, Goldens and Labradors to deal with the retrieves rather than their pointing dogs. It has since become fashionable to regard pointers and setters as non-retrievers, but this is a fallacy. Their retrieving ability may well have suffered over the years as many kennels no longer breed with that trait in mind, but if you want a pointing retriever then do not dismiss the native pointers and setters out of hand. They are just as capable of doing the job as any of the continental HPR group.

But it is their pointing ability that separates these dogs from the flushing breeds. When they scent game they stop and point; and they should hold that point until their handler orders them to move in and flush the birds. Only then will they hunt out and lift the game for the guns. There is one big advantage in this. Because they do not flush game as and when they find it they can be allowed to continue hunting even when they are out of gunshot of the handler. Indeed, they can be worked even when they are completely out of sight. This means that, instead of working thirty yards to either side of the gun and covering a beat sixty or so yards in width, they can be allowed fifty yards; a hundred

Yellow Labrador retrieving a rabbit.

Pointers can retrieve too — and bring their birds back alive.

yards; even a quarter of a mile away from the guns. If there is game to be found they should find it; point it; and stay patiently until the guns reach them.

If you are shooting in thick woodland, with dense undergrowth which is well populated with game, then there is little point in a dog which works several hundred yards away, comes on point somewhere completely out of sight and stands staunchly while you spend the rest of the day trying to find it. Under certain circumstances a pointing dog is more a liability than an asset. But let us imagine a different scenario. Suppose you have ten thousand acres of poor quality heather moorland. And suppose that, scattered over that ten thousand acres are a couple of hundred grouse: some single cocks, a few barren pairs and perhaps twenty coveys of six to ten birds. You have five day's shooting and permission to take twenty-five brace. How are you going to find them?

Ten thousand acres cover an area of about sixteen square miles; say a patch four miles square. If you can walk eight miles over moorland in the course of a shooting day you will be doing enough to be more than ready for your bath come evening. Some simple arithmetic will show you that a spaniel, working ahead of you on a sixty yards beat will cover about two hundred acres by the end of the day. That is about a fiftieth of the ground. If you find a fiftieth of the grouse, and shoot well enough, you might reasonably expect to have one brace at the end of the day.

But suppose you had pointing dogs which would work three hundred yards out to either side of your line of march. Now you can cover not two hundred but two thousand acres per day. In theory at least you can work the whole moor in the course of your five day's shooting. And that, quite simply, is the great advantage that pointing dogs have over the other breeds — when the conditions are right.

The author's old Pointer Charlie. Retired now, but we spent many hours on the hill together hunting grouse and woodcock, as well as working on pheasant and partridge on low ground shoots.

Let us do a little more mathematics. You are going to walk eight miles per day. Your dog though, in order to cover a six hundred yard beat, is going to have to run a great deal further than that — probably eight to ten times as far. And he or she is going to have to keep up a lively pace to cover that wide a beat while advancing at your walking pace. What you need is the canine equivalent of a long distance runner — a long-legged, lightly built dog with enormous reserves of stamina, an easy, energy saving pace, and the necessary drive to keep going even when there is no scent to spur it along. What you need is a pointer or a setter, or a wide ranging HPR.

Actually you will need more than one if you plan to work a six hour day in the heat of summer. The old handlers would take six or eight brace of dogs to the hill, though the chances were that the old handlers also took a dog boy or two to lead the spare dogs, a pony to carry the lunches and the shot birds, and a ponyman to lead the pony. If you are going to the hill with just your dog for company then you will obviously not cover the same amount of ground as you could with a whole rake of dogs working shifts around the clock. Provided you take your time, rest your dog when he or she needs it and head for home when one or both of you is tired you should enjoy the day just as much as if you were out on the hill with the full entourage. Me; I would enjoy the day more with just the dog for company.

The pointing breeds are at their best when there is plenty of space for them to run. Autumn stubbles, open moorland, wide East Anglian root fields, snipe bogs and marshes are the places where they are seen to the greatest advantage. Confine them in a thick, brambly covert and a good spaniel will beat the pants off them. Work them in thick woodland and you are likely to spend half your day hunting for a dog which is firmly on point somewhere out of sight. Most of the pointing breeds have quite thin coats and this alone puts them at a severe disadvantage when there are nettles and brambles to be faced — the Brittany Spaniel, German Wire-Haired Pointer and Italian Spinone are obvious exceptions to this.

The native pointing breeds — Pointers, Irish, English and Gordon Setters, and the recently revived Irish Red and White Setters — are unsurpassed when it comes to working open moorland and autumn stubbles. They have been selectively bred to do just that sort of work, and there is nothing to beat them. For the rough shooter though, unless his shooting is largely over the type of ground which suits pointers and setters, they are somewhat restricting. You can get a lively Irish Setter to sit beside you while you wait for driven birds, but it will not be a happy Irish Setter — I know, I have done it. You can send a thinly coated pointer into a bramble patch to flush pheasants, but few pointers will relish the experience. If you want an all rounder — a dog that will range widely on the grouse moors yet still work thick cover on the pheasant shoot; sit at a peg while you shoot driven birds or plunge into an icy estuary to retrieve wildfowl — then you might consider one of the HPR breeds instead.

Although they are known under the blanket classification of HPR breeds there is a considerable difference in temperament and style of work between the various types. They were developed by landowners on the continent to suit the particular circumstances of their shooting estates — the terrain, the type of game and the variety of work required. Nearly all have docked tails to protect them from damage when working dense cover. At the time of writing there are seven HPR breeds established as working dogs in Britain, but the number is likely to increase as further varieties are imported from across the Channel.

The German Shorthaired Pointer (GSP) is the most established working breed and has dominated HPR trials since their inception. Strong, powerful dogs, they can work the open hill almost as well as the native Pointer, though their greater weight and the 'rocking horse' action which is all too common may lead to hip and shoulder injuries on rough ground. Their short coats offer only limited protection in thick cover, though this will not discourage a good one from forcing its way through brambles and thorns. Some, particularly dogs as opposed to bitches, can display a Teutonic thrawnness which will defeat all but the most determined trainers and handlers, though I have also seen many which were biddable, gentle family pets as well as working dogs.

The German Wire-Haired Pointer with its thick, harsh outer coat and dense under-coat is probably better suited to withstand both severe cold and dense cover, though it lags far behind the GSP in popularity at least in so far as numbers are concerned. It is not just a long-haired version of the GSP, despite the similarity in size and build, but a separate breed altogether. There are undoubtedly common ancestors, but the same could be said of all gundog breeds if the family tree were traced back far enough.

Hungarian Vizslas were bred to hunt the wide open plains of their native Hungary and if bred to type should have the speed and stamina which such open ground work would demand. A much gentler, softer dog than their German cousins, they often seem more eager to please their master than to please themselves. It is important that this softness does not manifest as a lack of drive and a reluctance to get out and hunt, though selecting a pup from proven working stock should go a long way to ensuring that this does not happen. Handsome and lithe with their russet brown coat, they are a delight to watch in action and generally soft mouthed and good in water.

The lean, grey Weimaraner is a strikingly handsome dog, first bred in the Weimar Republic from which it takes its name. They have a tendency to become very much a 'one man' dog and may be extremely possessive of their owners. While this is no handicap to the lone shot it can become a problem if they are worked with other guns and their dogs.

The Brittany Spaniel (called simply the Brittany by the Kennel Club in order that it should not be confused with the spaniel breeds) is one of the more recent imports, and one that is growing rapidly in popularity. Built like a long-legged spaniel, but with the

Hungarian Vizsla pointing pheasant.

pointing instinct of the rest of the HPR breeds, they represent a potentially winning compromise between the flushing dogs and the pointers. That said there are as yet not a great many working Brittanys in the country, though the numbers are increasing every year, and any judgement of the breed as a whole should be reserved until a larger cross section is available for inspection.

The Italian Spinone with its thick coat is another recent import. Heavier and slower than the other HPRs, it is said to have great reserves of stamina which, allied to its trotting pace, should allow it to work day in and day out, though such a pace is unlikely to endear it to the devotees of hard running trialling dogs. Finally, the Large Munsterlander, which looks somewhat like an English Setter, also has a thick coat to protect it in cover and the long legs and athletic build of the pointers and setters.

All the Hunt, Point and Retrieve breeds are, primarily, hunting dogs which will also retrieve. Retrieving, though obviously important, is not their main function, and to use any of them just as a retriever is a double waste — you fail to take advantage of the dog's greatest strength while asking it to do a job that any of the specialist retrieving breeds would do far better. Similarly, if you want a dog to hunt solely within shooting range then a good spaniel will do the job better. But if you have some wide open spaces to hunt and you enjoy shooting over your dog alone, or with one friend, then one of the pointing dogs may be just the thing for you.

Retrievers

Although the Labrador, Golden Retriever, Flatcoat, Curly-coated Retriever and Chesapeake Bay Retriever are all classed as retrievers this is something of a misnomer. All of them can, and will, hunt live game and flush it for the gun as well as retrieving dead and wounded game. Some, Flatcoats particularly, will even point game and hold their point almost as well as a 'proper' pointer. Being generally more placid than the spaniels they have the edge when it comes to sitting patiently at a drive or in a pigeon hide. While a spaniel is bursting with energy and itching to be up and doing a Labrador is more likely to curl up and go to sleep.

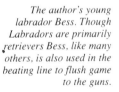

The author's young labrador Bess. Though Labradors are primarily retrievers Bess, like many others, is also used in the beating line to flush game to the guns.

That said, the retrievers can hunt along with the best. All have thick coats which will help to protect them in heavy cover, all have the nose and the hunting instinct. As retrievers they have the advantage of being bigger and stronger than the spaniels which may be important if you are shooting several hundred pheasants or hares at a time. The average rough shooter, who is going to have to carry what he shoots is less likely to test his dog's stamina with the weight of birds it is asked to retrieve.

There are times when a retriever is all that will be required. Flighting duck, decoying woodpigeon, roost shooting, or standing at a drive do not call for hunting ability from the dog. If your type of shooting does not need a pointing or flushing dog then one of the specialist retrievers will be the obvious choice. Most of us though are looking for all-round ability in a rough shooting dog — and that all round ability can be found in the retrieving breeds just as well as in the other gundogs.

The Labrador is a familiar sight at everywhere that fieldsports enthusiasts gather. The most common, numerically, of all the gundog breeds they are familiar as workers and as family pets, and very often as both. Strong, willing and easily trained, they can be used as hunting and flushing dogs or non-slip retrievers. The thick coat protects them from cold and wet as well as thorns and brambles and they are quick to mature and easily trained. If the English Springer is the rough shooter's dog then the Labrador must run it damn close second.

Almost as many Golden Retrievers as Labradors are registered with the Kennel Club each year, but in the shooting field they are nowhere near as common. Popular as pets and show dogs, this popularity has, to a certain extent, undermined their working ability. Nevertheless, a good Golden Retriever from working stock can hold its own in the shooting field with any other breed. Their long coats do tend to attract more than their fair share of twigs, burrs, brambles and mud, and they are said to be slower to mature than the Labradors.

The same is said of the Flatcoat Retriever. Once very popular with gamekeepers they were largely superseded by the Labrador in the first quarter of the century. Fast, strong and very determined, they can make superb rough shooting dogs for trainers who have the time and the patience to persevere with them.

The Curly-coated Retriever is another of the old breeds that has declined as a working breed. With its tightly curled coat it is a quite distinctive dog and is said to be excellent in water and brave in cover. Finally, the Chesapeake Bay Retriever is a relative newcomer to Britain though they have been popular for many years in North America. Bred to work in freezing water it is likely to grow in popularity, particularly as a wildfowler's dog.

Choosing a Dog

So which of the twenty or so breeds working in Britain is the right one for the rough shooter? I suppose if you were completely objective in your choice you would pick either a Springer Spaniel or a Labrador. Look at the advantages — both are well proven, rough shooting breeds; there are any amount of them to pick from; the working lines are well known and well established. No-one is going to raise an eyebrow if you turn up at the start of the season with a Springer or a Lab in tow. And because they are so common you should be able to find a kennel with good, solid working lines somewhere near you,

Irresistible, but is it the right choice for you? Hungarian Vizsla puppy.

wherever you live. You can meet the owner and perhaps see the sire and dam in action before you settle on a pup. But who among us is completely objective?

Many years ago I was sitting at my desk when a long, lean red dog bounced into the office, grinned at me, examined the place in some detail and then swept off down the corridor. He was an Irish Setter, belonged to someone across the street from where I worked, and as far as I can remember he never visited the office again, in which matter he showed excellent taste. But I was so taken with this happy, handsome, athletic dog that I went out a few months later and bought one of my own. There have been setters and pointers around the house ever since.

You may have your own reasons for favouring one breed above all others, or you may have a completely open mind about the whole business. If you want to be rational, take a look at the kind of shooting you expect to be doing over the next ten years or so, and ask yourself what kind of dog is best suited to the work. Then, provided you like the answer you come up with, get one of those. On the other hand, if the answer is a quiet, steady Labrador, but what you really fancy is a hard running, independently minded Irish Setter, then I suggest you start looking for the setter.

Whatever breed you choose there is one thing you must remember above all others. Your dog must come from working lines. Don't be fooled by those advertisements which specify 'show, work or pet'. You want a working dog, and it is from working stock that you must select it. Some breeds, in particular some of the HPR breeds, are truly dual purpose — they have working dogs which can win in the show ring and show dogs which can do a good day's work — but they are the exception. The majority of breeds are divided into two distinct strains. There are big, beautiful show dogs which have had all their drive and working instinct bred out of them in favour of pretty looks and quiet temperaments, and there are dedicated workers which are bred for what they can do, not for how they look.

Sadly, some working strains have been bred with too little consideration for conformation, resulting in ugly, under-sized specimens which do the breed no favours despite their working ability. That said, a dog that can work, however ugly, is infinitely preferable to some canine Adonis which can only stand around and look lovely. Best of all is the dog which has genuine working ability yet still looks the part. And if you take the time and trouble you should be able to find one, whatever your chosen breed. Remember though: it must be from working lines.

Training

Whatever breed you decide upon your new dog is going to have to be trained, and there are three routes open to you. You can train it yourself, you can get someone else to train it for you, or you can buy a trained dog.

Buying a trained dog is the low risk option. You are getting the finished product rather than a kit of parts, so you can actually go and see the dog at work; judge its drive and enthusiasm, its courage and steadiness, its handle-ability and obedience before you part with your money. There are risks in starting out with an eight-week-old puppy — it may turn out to be hard-mouthed or gunshy or frightened of water — and someone else has taken those risks on your behalf. Someone else has spent months teaching the pup to heel and to sit, to come when called and retrieve a dummy, not to chase rabbits and not to run in and to do, or not do, all the other things that a good gundog should do. Or not do. It all takes time, and someone is going to have to pay for that time. You are.

That alone will put the purchase of a trained dog out of the reach of many aspiring owners. If you can afford it, and if you lack the time or the interest to train a dog yourself, then buying one ready-made is the short cut to getting a working dog. A couple of words of warning though. Dogs are not machines that can be programmed to behave in a particular way and then just left to carry on *ad infinitum*. Once the dog is yours you will have to handle it. You have to replace the trainer as the master in the dog's own mind, and then maintain that position. If you let the dog take control then all the training in the world can quickly be forgotten. Take the dog back to its original trainer and it will probably behave perfectly. Even the best trained dog will still require proper handling if it is to maintain its discipline in the shooting field.

Getting a Vizsla onto live game. The handler has the drop whistle ready and has positioned herself ahead of the dog for better control.

But you may prefer to start out with a pup and see it grow up rather than buying a trained adult. In this case you either train it yourself or you deliver it up for professional training once it is ready to start. This can cost as much as buying a trained dog, but the payments will be spread out over a period instead of going in a lump sum. And of course, you take the risk that the pup will turn out to be lacking in some vital aspect when it grows up. You also need to take care in your choice of trainer — actual ability to train dogs is not a requirement when setting up a dog training business. Make sure you have seen some of the graduates and talked to a couple of satisfied customers before you hand over little Fido and a wad of cash.

The Halti collar: a useful device for the dog which insists on pulling at its lead.

Finally you can train the brute yourself. You may even find, as so many others before you, that training, and then working the dog that you have trained, is as much if not more fun than the actual shooting. There is enormous satisfaction in seeing your protégé out there in the field doing the job he was born and trained to do. In fairness I must add that there can also be a certain amount of frustration, not to mention hair tearing fury, when he does all the things you have trained him not to do, and does them in front of a crowd of your friends and shooting partners. But if you have the time and the temperament, then there are few things better than watching a gangly pup turn into a confident, competent, working dog and knowing that you helped him to do it.

People often say they haven't the time to train a dog. Actual training takes very little time — ten minutes a day will be ample for most dogs and far better than a couple of hours once a fortnight. Rather more time will be needed to feed and exercise it, keep its kennel clean and generally look after it. Dogs, particularly young puppies, need human attention if they are to turn into the right sort of working partners. You cannot expect a pup, locked in the kennel on its own for twenty-three and three-quarter hours every day, to grow into a responsive and reliable adult.

Training can be as easy or as difficult as you choose to make it. There are any number of books around telling you how to train dogs; how to train gundogs; how to train particular breeds of gundog; how to understand canine psychology; how to deal with problem dogs . . . Take your pick from hundreds. Beware of books which give you a timetable to follow. At eight weeks the pup should be doing this, at six months that, at one year the other. That is dangerous advice. Pups, even pups from the same litter, develop at different speeds, and one of the surest ways to ruin a dog is to rush its training and get it into the field before it is ready. Proceed with caution and never worry if you think things are taking too long. Far better to take ample time than to spoil the dog with a rush of false confidence engendered when things seem to be going too well.

As far as training goes, if you can get your pup to sit on command, wherever it is and whatever it is doing, to walk to heel and to come when it is called, even if there is something else more interesting to do, then you are well on the way to having a trained dog. The more interesting things like dropping to shot or to flush; hunting within a reasonable distance; learning not to chase fur or feather; retrieving from land and water, all follow on from those first, basic lessons. If you are lucky enough to have access to proper training ground within easy reach of home then so much the better, but the determined dog trainer can overcome most odds. I know of one man who trained setters in the middle of London, and damn good dogs they were too. It helps if you have plenty of ground with adequate game stocks, a rabbit pen, somewhere to practice water retrieves and plenty of free time, but it isn't essential.

Beating, Picking-Up, Tests and Trials

If you have a good dog and some free time there is usually work to be had during the season. A steady, well controlled spaniel is a real asset in the beating line, provided that it really is steady and well controlled. Picking up behind the guns at driven shoots will keep you and your retriever busy, again provided the dog is properly under control and soft-mouthed. No-one is going to thank you if your dog rampages through the next drive or turns every bird it picks into pheasant pâté. Given a half decent dog though, and a bit of free time, you should be able to find work for the pair of you throughout the shooting season with the added bonus of a few pounds to cover your expenses each day plus the possibility of shooting on the keeper's days at the end of the season.

If you like competing there are working tests and field trials which will match you and your dog against other trainers and their pupils. Working tests, until quite recently, were fun events arranged informally by breed clubs, dog training classes and country fair organisers. They have now come under the control of the Kennel Club, which is something of a mixed blessing as competitors may start taking them too seriously.

A working test is an attempt to simulate gundog work by a series of exercises such as sending the dogs to find and retrieve dummies. Often they are timed and the fastest dog declared the winner. There may be cups, medals and even cash for the winners, and a well-run working test can be an enjoyable day out for master and dog. Remember though that a working test is just a bit of fun, and the fact that a dog can win a working test does not necessarily mean that same dog will be a winner in the shooting field.

Field Trials are an altogether more serious business. Here the aim is to test dogs under actual shooting conditions, or as near to them as can be arranged. Originally the trials were set up to test the best working dogs against one another, though now, for many trainers and handlers, Field Trials are more important than proper work. There is some logic in this, since success at the trials can give a considerable boost to puppy prices and stud fees from the winners.

Field Trials are open to anyone, provided that their dog is registered with the Kennel Club. If you have a hankering to enter a trial but are not familiar with the procedures, I would suggest that you attend a few trials as a spectator before you fill in your first entry form. Be warned though, that trialling is an expensive and time-consuming bug to catch, albeit a very satisfying pastime for those who take part. The most successful trialling dogs may not necessarily be the best shooting dogs, though according to the rules the judges should be assessing the entrants from a shooting point of view.

In order to win a trial, a dog has to make an impression on the judges in the few minutes which it is allowed to run before them. At a spaniel stake with a dozen dogs

Teamwork — a rabbit found, shot and brought to hand.

A Gordon Setter puppy – bred to hunt game well out of gunshot, then point it and hold the point until the guns are in position.

Springer Spaniel – often called 'the roughshooter's dog' for its all-round ability as hunter and retriever.

German Shorthaired Pointer – the best known of the Hunt, Point and Retrieve breeds; they combine the work of the pointing breeds, the flushing dogs and the retrievers.

Yellow Labrador – primarily a retriever, but many are also used to hunt and flush game for the guns to shoot.

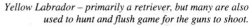

Shooting pheasants on a fine late autumn day in Dumfriesshire.

Teamwork – pointer and handler, gun and Labrador moving in to grouse.

entered an individual may have half an hour in front of the judges; at a pointer and setter stake with forty or so dogs to be judged the winner is going to have to catch the judges' eyes in a matter of minutes. This has led to an emphasis — perhaps an over-emphasis — on pace and style, at the expense of stamina and brains. Think carefully, particularly if you are new to dog training, before you acquire a hard running, field trial bred puppy to train. The very drive and pace that catches the judges' eye may make that pup an extremely difficult proposition for the novice handler.

Dogs and rough shooting are practically inseparable. You can shoot without a dog but half the fun of rough shooting is lost. When I was learning to shoot I saw the dog as a useful adjunct to the gun, hunting out game and retrieving it, but basically as a shooting accessory. Age and experience have altered my views somewhat. Now I would rather work the dog for someone else and leave my own gun at home than go shooting myself without a dog. This over-riding interest in gundogs and dog work has altered my whole life — the type of work I do, the place I live and the balance in my bank account. I wouldn't have it any other way,

You have been warned!

10 Learning to Shoot

It took me a long, long time to learn to shoot. It was not that I lacked advice — indeed, it was almost certainly the advice which I received that caused my shooting education to be so long drawn out a process. Had I been better advised I would undoubtedly be a better shot than I am today. And I can assure you there is no trace of false modesty when I say that there is plenty of scope for improvement.

I grew up in a village where most of the men were farm workers and most of the farm workers owned a gun. Living as I did in the village pub I was given advice on how to shoot by a dozen or so of the keenest shooting men. Unfortunately, what the advice gained in volume it lost in consistency. When I set out to shoot pigeons or rabbits I was thoroughly confused, which was much to the advantage of the pigeons and the rabbits.

I had been using air rifles for years before I got my first shotgun and the habit of aiming at a stationary target was deeply ingrained into me. Given a shotgun my natural reaction was to use it like an air rifle and aim at whatever I was hoping to hit. But now the target was moving. And I knew that the way to hit a moving target was to shoot in front of it — to lead it. What I didn't know was by how much it should be led, and it was here that all that conflicting advice came in. Let me give you a few samples.

'Lead a pigeon by the length of a five-bar gate.'

'If a hare is running away from you, aim between the tips of its ears.'

'Follow up an imaginary smoke trail and shoot when you're twenty feet in front.' Or ten feet, or twenty-five feet, or thirty feet, or . . .

'If you miss you must have been behind it.'

'However hard you try you will never miss a bird in front.'

There was lots more: I listened to it all, remembered it all, and when I was out shooting I tried to put it all into practice at the same time. Think about what I was doing. I was aiming my gun like a rifle, and trying, consciously to aim at a spot a specified distance in front of the pigeon. It was usually pigeons in those days. Depending on whom I had last listened to, that spot was ten feet, twenty feet, thirty feet or perhaps the length of a five-bar gate in front of the pigeon. And every time I missed, which was most of the time, I tried to shoot a little further in front the next time. Lots of people have shot at one bird in a flock and killed the one behind it. I have shot at one particular pigeon and killed one three birds ahead. And even then I didn't learn any better.

The problem is this. Shoot at a target with a rifle and you can usually see exactly where, and by how much, you have missed. Shoot at a moving target with a shotgun and all you know is that you have either hit it or you have not. And if not, you have no way of knowing if you were ahead or behind, above or below, or possibly a combination — behind and below, ahead and above etc. So if, like me, you keep missing, and are sure that you are missing behind because everyone told me that was where I would miss, you aim further and further in front. Eventually I was shooting at them almost before they had cleared the horizon. And still missing.

I could, of course, have used a little elementary mathematics to work out the necessary lead to give a crossing pigeon. Take a bird thirty yards away flying across your front at fifty miles per hour. Assume a muzzle velocity of 1,100 feet per second. Ignore any fancy bits about deceleration of the shot or differential velocities throughout the shot string. What have we got? The shot will take about eight hundredths of a second to cover thirty yards, during which time the bird will have flown nearly six feet. *Ergo*; shoot six feet ahead of the bird and it will fall down dead every time. Provided only that it really is exactly thirty yards away, flying directly across at right angles to you at precisely fifty miles an hour.

Of course, if it is forty yards away and travelling at sixty miles an hour you will miss. Behind. By about four feet. And if it is not travelling exactly at right-angles to you, but quartering towards you, or away from you, the calculations change again and begin to require a knowledge of basic trigonometry. You may be able to (a) estimate speed, angle and distance with sufficient precision, and (b) do the calculations quickly enough to work out where to shoot before the bird is out of range, but I beg leave to doubt it. And even if you can, you still have the problem of actually firing the gun at exactly the moment when it is pointing a precise distance ahead of a moving object, bearing in mind your own reaction times, and the mechanical delay between pulling the trigger and the cartridge actually firing. You may think you can do it; I know from long experience that you cannot.

Compare shooting a flying or running target with batting in a cricket match. You could try to calculate the speed of the ball, the height of its release, the angle at which it is descending, the angle at which it is approaching you, the arc through which it may be swinging and the direction in which it will bounce bearing in mind any spin which the bowler may have imparted. Then you could consider the plane through which you must swing your bat, the speed and the timing of that swing and the angle at which to incline the face of the bat. You could calculate all that and then try to use

Mounting the gun while ʲatching the quarry over the ends of the barrels.

The gun is brought into the shoulder and fired in one movement.

the result to cut the bowler to the square leg boundary: but only if he was a very slow bowler and you were extremely quick at mental arithmetic. Otherwise you would do what the rest of us do and swing the bat instinctively. It works on a cricket pitch, and not surprisingly, it also works out shooting.

Of course, there is more to batting than just an instinctive swing of the bat. Good batting requires good technique: the correct footwork, the right grip on the bat, a good eye for the ball, correct timing of the swing and plenty of practice. Substitute 'gun' for 'bat and 'target' for 'ball' and you will have a pretty fair recipe for becoming a good shot. Just how good you may become will depend on the soundness of your technique, the amount of shooting you do and on your natural ability. Anyone can learn to shoot properly, but the very best shots have an in-born ability that is denied to the rest of us. Anyone can learn to bat well enough to make the village cricket team, but if you want to open for England you need to be born with the ability. And then work hard on it.

Shooting is largely a matter of hand/eye co-ordination; of seeing the target, assessing its speed and direction, mounting the gun smoothly and firing as it beds into the shoulder. A good shot makes the whole business look ridiculously simple, just as a top class batsmen will drive a fast bowler to the boundary with nonchalant ease. When you are that good it is easy; but it takes a certain amount of coaching and a lot of hard practice to get there. So exactly how can the novice shot learn the basis of a sound technique that can be built up with practice until he or she is at least competent and safe with a gun?

Note that I say competent and safe. Of the two safety is unquestionably the more important. Far better an indifferent shot who handles his gun safely than any idiot, however brilliant his shooting may be, who takes risks with a gun. Guns are made to kill, and they don't care who or what are their victims. One dangerous shot fired in a careless instant can haunt you for the rest of your life. Learning to handle a gun should be synonymous with learning to handle a gun safely.

The best way to learn the basics of shotgun handling is to visit a shooting school and take lessons from a professional shooting instructor. The best time to visit the school is right at the beginning, before any bad habits have had the chance to become ingrained.

Indeed, you can go along the the school before you buy your first gun and they will advise you as to the correct fit for someone of your particular age, build and athletic ability. A try-gun — one in which the stock can be adjusted for length, drop, cast-off and comb height — will enable them to put theory into practice. Then, when you do choose your new gun, you can have it adjusted to fit you properly. And a properly fitted gun will go a long, long way towards helping you to become a competent shot.

A good instructor will not only show you the right way to handle a gun, but will also be able to identify and correct your faults as you are making them. Because your targets are clay pigeons and not live game there can be many repetitions of each target. A fault can be corrected, the instructor can demonstrate to proper way to deal with a particular clay, then coach the pupil until he or she gets it right. There is nothing like a little bit of success to encourage a beginner at any sport, and if your instructor can have you breaking a few clays during your first lesson you will quickly gain confidence — and confidence is vital to every sportsman.

One lesson is better than none, and if your pocket can stand it a course of lessons is better still. If there is no shooting school within reasonable range of your home, or if professional coaching is beyond your means, then you must find an alternative.

If you have a friend who is an experienced shot, a clay pigeon trap, and access to ground where it is safe to shoot clays, then you may be able to arrange for some private lessons. Remember though, that the fact that your friend is a competent shot does not guarantee that he/she is also a competent teacher.

Clay shooting clubs sometimes have beginners courses, or informal shooting days when there are no competitions to be won, and your local club may offer advice and instruction on an individual basis. Beware of learning some of the habits of competition clay shots, particularly the down-the-line style of shooting where the gun is mounted to the shoulder before each bird is called. This is fine for DTL shooting when the gunner knows exactly when, from where and in what direction his next target will fly, but it is no earthly use to the rough shot walking up pheasants in a bramble thicket.

Clay pigeons offer many advantages to the novice shot. They can be thrown at whatever height, speed and direction is required, and that trajectory can be repeated time after time. They are cheap and always available — there is no close season for clays. Best of all, they allow the novice to learn the rudiments of safety and straight shooting in a controlled environment where there are no beaters, no gundogs and no game to be put at risk. In the end though, they are still just clay pigeons.

They start off quickly and then slow down, they are released when *you* decide, and they take a pre-determined and generally straight course. Live game behaves a little differently. Now, though I would strongly suggest that any real novice starts out with clays before tackling live game, not everyone is going to have the facilities or the desire to do that. Lots of people learn their gun handling in the field, and will continue to do so unless our masters decide to legislate fieldsports out of existence. You may be one of those people.

Ideally you would go out with one experienced friend who would be there to advise and instruct you. He would thus pay attention to what you were doing rather than carrying a gun himself. The trouble with this sort of arrangement is that chances of a shot on a rough shoot are often sudden and unpredictable. A rabbit bolting from a patch of nettles or a pheasant rocketing out a bramble will have to be taken quickly or not at all.

If you have to wait for instructions then the chance will be gone. While the place to learn is most definitely not at a peg on a formal driven day, such a situation might be acceptable if your tutor was standing behind you advising which birds to shoot and which to leave alone. Perhaps a pigeon hide with a pattern of decoys is the best place for this kind of one-to-one instruction, somewhere well away from beaters, stops and neighbouring guns. In the end you will have to make the best of whatever opportunities are available to you. Remember though, that safety should always be your first consideration.

Some Thoughts on Safety

Until you put a cartridge into the breech, a gun is just a lump of wood and metal, dangerous only if used as a club. And it isn't even a very efficient club, having a tendency to fracture at the neck of the stock if you are so foolish as to whack anything with it. An empty gun is a safe gun. Put a cartridge into the breech and it becomes a lethal weapon.

Try a little test if you are unsure of just how dangerous a shotgun can be. Take a large turnip and imagine it is a human head. Place it on the ground, somewhere out in the open, and fire one barrel of your shotgun into it at a range of a couple of yards. The result is pretty much what it would be if you did the same thing to a real human head. A shotgun is not a toy. All it takes is one silly mistake; one moment of carelessness; and your best friend's head can look just like that turnip. The only difference is that the turnip can be replaced.

The only time your gun should be loaded is when you are expecting a shot. At all other times it should be empty. And just so you know that it really is empty, and so that anyone else can see that it is empty, you might as well carry it with the breech open and the empty chambers there for the world to see. Better still, put it into a gunslip. After first checking to see that it is empty.

You should not be expecting a shot when you are standing around talking before the start of the shoot: when you are walking between drives: when you are lugging your

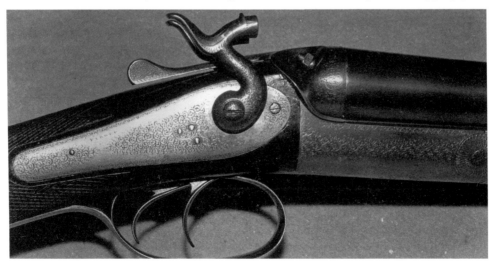

A beautiful Purdey hammer gun ready to fire. It may look dangerous but remember that hammerless guns are cocked all the time.

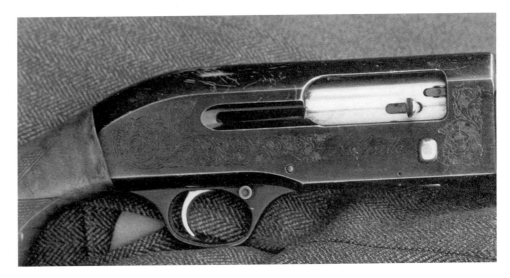

Automatic shotgun action. No way to tell if this gun is loaded or empty.

decoys and camouflage nets out to where the pigeon have been feeding on laid corn. If you are working pointers out on the grouse moors you needn't expect a shot until one of the dogs is actually on point. Keep the gun empty until then. You cannot shoot anyone with an empty gun.

Never take a loaded gun into a vehicle. Never take a loaded gun into a house. Never put a loaded gun into a gunslip. Never lean a loaded gun against a wall, a fence or a tree; never lay it on the ground. If the gun is leaving your hands for any reason at all take the cartridges out first. The only time a gun should ever be loaded is when you are holding it in your hands and expecting a shot.

Remember that a hammerless gun is cocked and ready to fire whenever it has a live cartridge in the breech. A jerk, a fall or quite a light blow can jog the sear enough to let the tumblers fall. All the safety catch does, on most guns, is to lock the triggers. Safety catches do not make guns safe — they simply prevent the triggers being pulled. Take a loaded gun into a car and a bump in the road could be enough to set it off. If you are lucky it will just blow a hole through the car roof. Or perhaps you lean the gun against the wall and someone's Labrador blunders into and knocks it over. It could well go off as it hits the ground. If you are lucky your legs won't be in the line of fire. Nor will anyone else's. If you are lucky.

Suppose you are climbing a fence with your gun in your hand and your foot slips on the top rail. You and the gun crash to the ground and the impact sets it off. If you are lucky the muzzles won't be directly in line with your head, or your legs, or your stomach, or someone else's head, legs or stomach. If you are lucky. Of course, you may not be lucky. You may be blinded, crippled or dead. And all because you kept the gun loaded when you were not expecting a shot.

Crossing a fence, a wall or a ditch is simple. If you are on your own you take the cartridges out of the gun and put them in your pocket; stand the empty gun down; cross the fence and then pick the gun up again. If you are with a friend you take the cartridges out of your gun; show your friend the empty chambers and give him the gun to hold while you cross the fence. Then your friend passes your gun and his own empty gun

But his boxlock is clearly empty — and safe.

across to you while he crosses the fence. When you, your friend, your dogs and all your other equipment are safely over you can both load up again. Assuming that you are expecting a shot.

Incidentally, whenever you are handed a gun you should open it and check that it is not loaded. It doesn't matter that the man who handed it to you said 'It's empty.' as he passed it across: it is not empty until you have personally satisfied yourself that there are no cartridges in the chambers. Then you may regard it as empty. If you form the habit of always opening a gun as soon as you pick it up — even if you have just taken it out of the gun cabinet, or taken it out of its slip — then you will never find yourself telling a coroner that 'I didn't know it was loaded'. An awful lot of people get shot with 'empty' guns.

But let us consider the handling of a gun after it has been loaded. You have slipped two cartridges into the breech, closed the gun and checked that the safety catch is on. When you closed it you brought the stock up to close the breech while keeping the barrels pointed down into the ground. You are standing at a peg or crouching in a muddy gutter out on the estuary: waiting tensely in a butt for the first sign of grouse or following a hunting spaniel along a tangled hedgerow. You are holding the gun ready to use as soon as your quarry runs or flies into range. What of safety now?

You must always be aware of where your muzzles are pointing. And unless they are pointing at your quarry they should be pointing up into the air or down into the ground. Your fingers should be outside the trigger guard, your thumb clear of the safety catch. You can rest the gun across your forearm, pointing downwards, or with the barrels on your shoulder pointing straight up. You can hold it with the butt on your hip and your right hand round the neck of the stock or you can hold it in both hands with the muzzles pointing upwards. Be very wary of carrying a gun in the half port position, held across the body. If your left hand drops just a fraction the muzzles will be pointing directly at whoever or whatever is standing on your left.

The secret of holding a loaded gun safely is to be constantly aware of the muzzles and where they are pointing. Never, ever point a gun at any man, dog, bird or beast unless you intend to shoot it. Always handle a loaded gun as if it might go off, spontaneously, at any moment. And always handle an empty gun as if it were loaded. If you do that at all times you will quickly get into the habit of handling a gun safely. At the same time you have to learn to shoot safely.

We looked at the range of shotguns in an earlier chapter and decided that somewhere about fifty yards was the maximum effective range at which you should expect to kill your quarry. Fifty yards is not very far, but we were considering the maximum distance at which the pattern and penetration of our shot charge would still be sufficient to ensure a clean kill — if we shot straight. When we consider safety though we must extend that distance way beyond fifty yards.

A shot charge may lack the pattern and penetration to kill a pheasant, but an individual pellet can still have sufficient striking energy to blind a man at some hundreds of yards from where the shot was fired. It happens rarely, but it is possible for the shot charge to ball together into a single lump which is potentially lethal at a couple of hundred yards. Safe shooting means being aware not only of the immediate vicinity of your quarry, but of the full trajectory of your shot charge. Even though they will do no physical damage, a load of spent pellets rattling against the windows of someone's bungalow is hardly good for the image of fieldsports. A careless shot like that could lead to the loss of your shotgun certificate; perhaps to the cancellation of your shooting lease.

Whether you are stationary at a butt or a peg, or walking up across farmland or moorland, you should always be aware of your safe angles of fire. Don't just watch the few yards ahead of you where you expect your quarry to rise; keep an eye on the other guns, the beaters, the dogs, and most of all the ground in the middle distance. Has your walking brought you near to a public road, to a house, to someone working in the fields? Are there other guns, hikers, picnickers, farm-workers, bird-watchers or fishermen sharing the countryside with you. It is up to you, as a responsible gun, to see them and to make sure that you do not endanger them. It is not their responsibility to warn you of their presence, though it is certainly a good idea if they do.

And finally, what about the shot itself? It is all too easy to be concentrating fully on the rabbit running, the grouse skimming the heather, the woodcock floating through the trees, and to miss what is immediately behind it. Obviously you will never fire into a bush unless you know what is behind that bush; you will never fire a low shot through a wood if there are beaters and stops ahead of you. You will never follow a grouse through the line without taking the gun off your shoulder and pointing the muzzles at the sky. You will never shoot at ground game unless you know exactly where all the dogs are working; you will never shoot low across water if there is any chance of the pellets ricocheting off the water (they do) and striking someone on the other side of the pond. You won't do any of those things, because you will have thought ahead, and considered safe angles of fire and possible dangers *before* the rabbit started running, the grouse or the woodcock flying.

At least; I hope you will never do any of those things. Too many people do: they do them all the time, and mostly they get away with them. Mostly there isn't anyone in line of fire; there isn't a dog in the bush behind the rabbit; there isn't another gunner crouched among the reeds on the other side of the pond. Except one day there is. And everyone says what a tragedy; what a terrible accident; what bad luck; could have happened to anyone. And it can happen to anyone. However careful you are there is always the

The gun is empty and open, but the sight is hardly one to inspire confidence.

chance that some day you will fire a dangerous shot and not get away with it. Until then you should do everything you can to minimise the chance of it happening — and if you are very careful, and very lucky, perhaps it never will.

Shooting

As we have already seen, the problem in shooting a moving target is to direct your shot charge to that point in space which your quarry will have reached when the shot charge arrives there. Broadly, there are four ways in which you may achieve this. You can aim directly at a fixed point ahead of your target. You can swing the gun at the same speed as, and at a constant distance ahead of, the target. You can start swinging the gun from behind the target, accelerate the gun as you follow its track, and fire as you overtake it. And you can follow the target with your muzzles before you mount the gun; bringing the gun into the shoulder and firing in a single movement.

The first method, aiming at a fixed point can be discounted. It should work in theory but it does not work in practice, except for anti-aircraft guns, and then only rarely. If you are going to have any success with a shotgun you have to learn to swing the gun onto a point the correct distance ahead of your target, fire it while swinging and keep on swinging after you have fired, otherwise you will simply poke at the target and miss behind. Stopping the swing is usually fatal: fatal for accuracy, not fatal for your quarry.

Which of the other methods will suit you best will depend on the mental image which you have of your muzzles in relation to your quarry. You do not aim a shotgun in the sense that a rifle shot consciously aligns sights and target. Shooting a rifle is like playing snooker — a conscious and deliberate alignment of backsight — the cue — foresight — the white ball — and target — the point on the coloured ball which you want the white to strike. A shotgun should be more akin to a cricket bat or a tennis racquet. You do not look at the bat or the racquet when playing ball games: you watch the ball. In exactly the same way you should not be looking at the foresight when you use a gun, you should be concentrating on your target. Which is why good gun-fitting and consistent gun-mounting are so vital to good shooting.

If your gun fits you correctly, and you have mounted it to your shoulder correctly, then the gun will be pointing wherever you are looking. You should not have to aim the gun at all. You will undoubtedly be aware of the muzzles at the lower edge of your vision, but your concentration should be on your target. Aligning the gun on the target should be automatic and sub-conscious. If the gun fits you correctly.

If not, then you have two choices. You get the gun adjusted to fit you, or you adjust your gun mounting to compensate for the error. In order to compensate you must obviously become aware of the alignment of the gun in relation to the target — in other words you must begin to aim the gun along the lines of a rifle. If you use the gun enough this compensation may become automatic, so that you eventually adapt your gun mounting to cancel out the errors in gun fit. It works: many thousands of shooters buy a gun 'off the peg' and do just that: but it is far, far better to start off with a gun that fits you properly. Any good gunsmith or shooting school can advise, and most guns can be adjusted within reasonable limits. The time to get it right is in the beginning *before* you have learned to compensate for the errors, or you will have to re-learn in order to get it right once the gun does fit properly.

But back to that mental image of gun and target. I once watched three good shots breaking clays which were being thrown towards them and high above their heads. One said he was leading them by twenty feet. The second said he was swinging the gun through them and firing as soon it got ahead. The third one claimed to be just putting the gun up and shooting straight at them. Mental images: that is what each one thought he was doing. Actually, none of them was right.

The clays were about sixty feet up, travelling at about sixty miles per hour. Assuming a muzzle velocity of 1,100 feet per second all three were actually firing at the moment when their muzzles were pointing around five feet ahead of the clay. The spread of the pattern and the stringing of the shot give a foot or two of leeway, but that is about all. If the clay broke, and most of them were being broken, then the actual lead given was around five feet.

But we need not be concerned with the true amount of lead: only with the perceived lead — the mental image formed by each shot. Only practice and experience can tell you what mental picture you will form when you are shooting successfully, but once you have got that mental picture you should not try to change it. If you are hitting the target consistently when you think you are shooting straight at it; or twenty feet in front of it; or by shooting as you overtake it; then keep on doing just that and don't worry that it is a ballistic impossibility.

There are books which will try to persuade their readers that one particular style of shooting is the correct one to the exclusion of all others. I am inclined to disagree. For some guns it may be best to shoot high birds by giving them a constant lead, take fast-crossers by swinging through them and kill walked up grouse by mounting with the bird and shooting straight at it. If they have found by trial and error that such a variation (or any any other combination of styles) works for them then they would be well advised to stick with what they know and damn all authors.

Of the three methods I would suggest that the use of constant lead is probably the hardest to learn. The quarry is observed and a judgement made as to the amount of lead that is required, bearing in mind its speed, distance and angle of approach. The gun is then mounted and swung so that the required lead is given to the quarry, the swing is continued with the lead being maintained as the trigger is pulled and for a moment afterwards. If it is done correctly the quarry will be killed.

But there are difficulties, particularly for the novice shot. Most obvious is the problem of estimating the correct distance to lead the quarry when you have little previous experience to guide you. It is no use asking someone to tell you the correct distance because their judgement of distance will almost certainly be different to your own. And of course, the correct distance will vary as the speed of the quarry varies, as the range varies and as the angle of approach varies. A grouse flying directly towards you, or away from you needs, at least in theory, no lead at all — a fast crossing bird at extreme range may need as much as twenty feet. Somewhere between the two will lie the appropriate lead for just about every shot you are likely to encounter.

In practice you have to watch the quarry while selecting the point ahead of it that you judge to represent the correct degree of lead. You mount the gun, and when that mental picture looks right you fire. You are most likely to be successful if the 'correct' picture forms quickly. I have always found that any attempt to make in-flight adjustments to the picture is likely to signal a miss; particularly if I think I am too far ahead and try to slow the swing to let the bird catch up. Then I end up slowing down, speeding up again and eventually expending an ounce of lead on the empty sky. Despite trying to learn to shoot by this method I have never found any degree of success with it, but it may work for you.

Swinging through your quarry, or following up an imaginary smoke trail as it is often described, is easier to understand. The gun is mounted behind the quarry and the swing accelerated along the line of flight until the muzzles have overtaken it. Then, depending on your personal interpretation of the method, the trigger is either pulled as the muzzles are passing the bird's head, or the muzzles are swung on beyond the bird until the desired lead is reached, and the triggers are pulled at that point.

Again, the 'mental picture' seen by the individual shot will control which method suits them, since in either case, if the quarry is to be killed, the actual lead will be the same. I suspect that guns who shoot as soon as they register that the muzzles have passed the bird's head are probably swinging their guns faster than those who continue their swing until a certain amount of lead is observed. It may well be that some guns shoot with a combination of this method and the sustained lead method, i.e. they accelerate the gun until it is a fixed distance ahead of the quarry, and then maintain that distance for a short time until the trigger is pulled.

Both variations have the advantage that the speed of the swing is largely dictated by the speed, distance and direction of travel of the quarry. Thus a crossing bird will need a fast swing to accelerate the gun sufficiently to overtake it whereas one quartering towards the gun will be overtaken with a much lesser swing. So, particularly for the 'fire as you pass the beak' school of thought, it is the apparent speed of the quarry which determines the amount of lead rather than any conscious decision on the part of the gunner.

I never had any success with the sustained lead method of shooting, but I could hit crossing birds by swinging through them and firing as I passed the beak. The problem, for me, came with going away shots; grouse or pheasants which got up in front of the dogs and were flying more or less directly away from me.

These require little or no lead; therefore little or no swing of the gun. Being conditioned to start the gun behind the bird and accelerate through it meant that I tended to start the gun to one side of them and swing across; the result being a miss to the opposite side. The easier the shot looked — that is the less deflection there was — the more likely I was to miss it. And missing a steady stream of 'easy' shots is very bad for the confidence of the gunner.

The third method relies on the natural co-ordination between hand and eye which we use to hit a ball with a bat. You watch the ball and swing the bat, and your brain automatically allows for the speed and angle of the ball approaching and the speed and direction of the swing of the bat. If the brain gets it right you score four runs: wrong and you start the walk back to the pavilion. You can do much the same thing with a gun.

You pick up your target over the muzzles of the gun. Keep the stock down below your shoulder but lay the muzzles on your target and keep them there until you are ready to shoot. Then bring the butt up into your shoulder with the muzzles still on the target and fire as soon as the gun is mounted. If you have done it correctly your target should be hit.

It is not at all the same thing as simply poking the gun at the quarry and firing, which is a certain recipe for a miss. The important thing is that the muzzles are laid on the target and kept there; that the gun is mounted only at the moment you are ready to fire, and the trigger is pulled as soon as the gun is at the shoulder. You might compare it to our cricketer, watching a slow ball in flight (picking up the quarry) with the bat lifted and ready (the muzzles laid on the bird). Then, only when the ball reaches him does he swing the bat and follow through (mount the gun and pull the trigger). The stroke, when it is played is a continuous swing of the bat. He does not start the swing, slow it down, speed it up again and still hit the ball. Similarly you cannot mount the gun and then try to adjust your swing. This instinctive style of shooting relies on a natural rhythm of mounting and firing the gun for its success.

It is vital that your gun is a proper fit, or that your gun mounting position is automatically adapted to compensate for any short-comings in fit. Because you are firing the gun the moment it is mounted there is no time to adjust your aim to correct any errors in mounting. The action of tracking the quarry with the muzzles has got the gun swinging at the correct speed relative to the quarry. Mounting and firing in one movement allows your natural hand/eye co-ordination to accelerate the swing to bring the muzzles ahead of the target, and the necessary lead is given automatically. At least, that's the theory.

How well it works will depend very much on how good your hand/eye co-ordination is. If you were a permanent member of the Extra B Eleven at school, can't put bat to ball unless the ball is (a) large and (b) stationary, then it is unlikely that this method of shooting will be a great success for you. Even so it is worth a try, especially if you have tested the other methods and found them wanting.

It may seem that, having blamed my early shooting failures on contradicting advice, I have simply produced a chapter of contradicting advice to confuse you. Confusion was never my intention.

You can no more learn to shoot by reading a book than you can learn to play cricket or tennis or golf without handling a bat, racquet or club. Books can give you advice, and an idea of technique, but shooting skills can only be acquired by practice. Practice though will only be of real value if you practice while using the correct technique. Practice alone will not remedy a golfer's slice: he must correct his swing and then practice. The same thing applies to the shotgun marksman.

First you should find a gun that fits you. Then you need someone to show you how to handle it correctly. Then you need practice to hone your skills and program your muscles to react automatically when you pick up your target, mount the gun and fire.

The advice I have given may appear to be contradictory. Mount and fire automatically, constant lead, swing through, fire at the bird's beak, fire six feet ahead . . . different techniques certainly, but only because there is no one right way to shoot with a shotgun. You have to find the method that works for you; practice it, and have faith in it even when it goes wrong from time to time. And it will. There may not even be one right method: you may need to use the follow through method for fast crossing birds but the mount and fire method for going away shots. As long as it works it doesn't matter to anyone but you and whatever you are shooting at.

But never, ever forget about safety.

Never load a gun unless you are expecting a shot.

Always handle a gun as if it was loaded.

11 Licences and the Law

I bought my first gun licence when I was eleven. They came from the Post Office in those days, and I can still remember what the man behind the counter said when I asked him how old I had to be to buy a gun licence. 'Old enough to have ten shillings,' he said and wrote out a small, green piece of paper for me in exchange for a slightly smaller brown piece. Some of you will no doubt still remember ten shilling notes. Once obtained, the gun licence permitted the holder to carry a gun in public — there was no need for a licence as long as you stayed on private land but you needed it as soon as you set foot on the road — and offered some useful advice on the effective range of shotguns, and following up wounded game. Things were much simpler in those days.

Today you must obtain a form from the police station, fill it in and get it signed by someone like a lawyer, doctor or magistrate who will vouch for your character, add four passport-sized photographs of yourself (one also signed by your character witness to say it is a good likeness of you) and return it to the police station with the appropriate fee. The police will probably want to visit your home and inspect the security arrangements you have made for the safe keeping of your gun — in practice this means you need a proper steel cabinet, bolted to a wall — and may ask you to satisfy them as to your reasons for wanting the gun and where you intend to use it. Then, provided you do not have a criminal record, you should get your shotgun certificate. You must take it with you when you buy cartridges, and if you buy or sell a gun you must enter the details on the certificate and notify the police within seven days. And the cost, for three years, is currently very near to fifty pounds instead of the fifty pence I paid for my first licence.

Strictly speaking you are entitled to hold a shotgun certificate unless the police can show reason why you should not be granted one. This is a subtle difference from the position with firearms certificates (for rifles) where the onus is on the applicant to satisfy the police that there is good reason for the certificate to be issued. In practice some police forces will try to apply this same vetting procedure to shotgun certificate applicants. If you are feeling militant you can refuse to tell them why you want the gun and where you intend to use it, though such a lack of co-operation will hardly enhance the likelihood of a certificate being issued. In practice it is probably better to co-operate willingly, within reason. If your certificate is refused without good grounds there is an appeals procedure. If you are a member of the BASC (*see* Chapter 12) they will probably help with the legal aspects.

A Game Licence is still obtained over the counter at your local post office. You may wonder why you should be required to pay the government six pounds before you may legally shoot any of the pheasants which you have bought, reared and released onto your shoot, but that is what the law demands. In America a great deal of the money raised in permits and licences is ploughed back into the sport, but our game licence simply provides an excuse for the Chancellor to pick your pocket every year. Nevertheless, the law is the law, and if you plan to shoot pheasant, partridge, grouse, blackgame, ptarmigan, capercaillie, woodcock, snipe or hares then you should obtain one, and renew it annually.

Purchasing a game licence does not confer the right to shoot anything. Shooting permission must be obtained from the landowner, the holder of the shooting rights or some other authorised person before you may legally take a gun on to private property. It is important to be quite certain that the person giving you (or selling you) permission to shoot actually has the authority to do so. The transfer of shooting rights is not always a straightforward matter.

Consider a great estate, somewhere near you. Formerly owned by the Dukes of Somewhereland, it is now a charitable trust administered by a committee of trustees. The land is managed by a firm of land agents who rent the farms to thirty different tenant farmers. Part of the shooting is retained by the old Duke, the rest is let out to shooting syndicates. The Duke employs a head keeper and four beat keepers, some of the syndicates employ professional keepers, some are keepered part-time by syndicate members and one has no keeper at all, though the estate keepers try to hold down the vermin. You would like to shoot rabbits on one of the farms on this last shoot. Who do you ask for permission?

There is the Duke himself or one of the trustees, the land agent, the estate keepering staff, the head of the syndicate hiring the shooting rights, any other member of the syndicate, and the farmer whose crops are being eaten. One or more of them probably does have the authority to transfer shooting rights to you, but only the details of their

Pheasant family — you must have a Game Licence to shoot pheasants, and then only from 1 October to 1 February.

*Red-legged Partridge —
their season opens on
1 September.*

various leases can tell you which ones. The farmer is almost certainly allowed to control rabbits, but he may not be entitled to give someone else permission to shoot them. Even the Duke and his land agent, having assigned the shooting rights to the syndicate, may not be able to give you permission to shoot.

Always make sure that you are asking the right person for permission, and if possible get it in writing. Then, if it turns out that the friendly farmer who invited you to shoot his rabbits didn't actually have any authority to give you permission, you will have some evidence that you were acting in good faith. Be particularly wary of 'third party' shooting rights. Your friend may have sought and been granted permission to shoot over a particular area, but it does not follow that he can pass on permission to you without first consulting the owner, farmer or keeper etc..

Once permission to shoot has been satisfactorily sorted out you should consider what you may and may not shoot, and when. The first thing to do is to make sure that you know what species are included and excluded in the terms of your shooting rights. Being given permission to flight pigeons into a wood does not mean that you may also shoot rabbits in there, though it may be that you are welcome to do so. Local rules may offer voluntary protection to particular species such as partridges, hares, blackgame or to hen pheasants after the end of December. Check first, and if you are not sure then don't shoot. If you have a shooting lease make sure that you have read, and understood, the small print; if you are a guest you should ask your host if there are any special exceptions. If there are not, then the law is quite specific about what may be shot and when.

There is a tendency to think that certain species such as hawks and falcons are protected by the law. In fact, *all* birds are protected except those which are specifically excluded from protection in the legislation. Some, including the birds of prey, are afforded special protection, which in practice means bigger fines or longer prison sentences for anyone killing them or damaging their eggs, nests or young. Provided you obey the law and shoot only those species which you are allowed to shoot, at the times you are allowed to shoot them, there is no need to concern yourself with the details of the Wildlife and Countryside Act's special protection provisions. If it is not included in the following lists then you may not shoot it, irrespective of whether or not it has special protection status.

The following birds can be shot at any time:

Great Black-backed Gull	Feral Pigeon
Lesser Black-backed Gull	Rook
Herring Gull	House Sparrow
Jackdaw	Starling
Jay	Carrion Crow
Magpie	Hooded Crow
Wood Pigeon	Collared Dove

The following may be shot during the specified season:
1 September to 31 January
(Ducks and geese below the high water mark 1 September to 20 February)

Coot	Moorhen
Gadwall	Pintail
Goldeneye	Golden Plover
Canada Goose	Pochard
Greylag Goose	Shoveler
Pinkfooted Goose	Teal
White Fronted Goose (Not in Scotland)	Wigeon
Mallard	

1 September to 1 February
Partridge

1 October to 31 January
Capercaillie
Woodcock (except Scotland, 1 September to 31 January)
1 October to 1 February
Pheasant

12 August to 10 December
Red Grouse
Ptarmigan (Scotland only)

12 August to 31 January
Common Snipe

It is a bit of a muddle, though not so complicated as it might seem at first glance. Grouse, ptarmigan and snipe come into season on 12 August followed by blackgame, eight days later on Twentieth. 1 September sees the start of shooting for partridge, ducks and geese, woodcock in Scotland, and all the other seasonally protected birds except for pheasant, capercaillie and woodcock (outside Scotland) which start on 1 October.

The season closes on 10 December for grouse, ptarmigan and blackgame, and on 31 January for everything else except pheasant and partridge which can be shot on 1 February. Finally, there is an extension of the shooting season to 20 February for ducks and geese shot below the high water mark.

Under the provisions of the Wildlife and Countryside Act certain species may be killed under special licence where they are causing serious damage to crops, livestock, fruit, growing timber and so forth. These include brent and barnacle geese, cormorants, goosanders and the like. The Act specifies serious damage, so it is no use hoping to be granted a licence just because half a dozen brent geese have taken to grazing on part of your shoot.

In times of very severe weather the Secretary of State for the Environment can suspend shooting of wildfowl and waders. If this happens it is usually a blanket ban over the whole country which can mean that your shoot is subjected to a severe weather restriction while basking in balmy, spring-like weather. If so then you are unlucky, but still subject to the law.

Trespass and Poaching

Trespassing is not a criminal offence: despite the threatening notices trespassers can NOT be prosecuted. They can be sued in the civil courts for damages, if any damage has been caused, and in the case of persistent trespass the landowner or occupier can ask the courts for an injunction instructing the trespasser not to repeat the trespass. Failure to obey the injunction places the trespasser in contempt of court, and a further application to the court could result in a fine or a prison sentence. Preventing trespass through the courts is a long, slow and expensive process.

If you are troubled by trespassers you can order them to leave your property and, if they refuse, use reasonable force to eject them. The interpretation which the courts put on that phrase 'reasonable force' has changed considerably over the years, and the type of behaviour which was common among keepers fifty or more years ago is deemed quite unacceptable now. Any keeper taking a stick to a passing hiker is likely to find himself in serious trouble, facing charges of assault and possibly grievous bodily harm.

Trespassing in pursuit of game — poaching — is a criminal offence. If a poacher is caught by the landowner, occupier, gamekeeper or the holder of the shooting rights, then they may confiscate any game he has taken, order him to give his full name and address and to leave the land immediately. If he refuses to give name and address, or to leave, then he may be arrested.

That is the law, and that is what you may do in theory. Whether you will be able to extract names and addresses from half a dozen armed louts and subsequently effect a citizen's arrest when you are all alone and miles from the nearest help is another matter. Common sense is vital when dealing with poachers. Since poaching is a criminal rather than a civil offence you should be able to enlist the help of the police if you suspect that poachers are operating on your shoot, and it is wise to keep the local police informed if you are instigating poacher patrols and night watches.

The extent to which poaching is likely to be a problem will depend on where your shoot is situated, how easy access is for the poachers and on the potential profit which they may make. A thousand pheasants concentrated in a release pen are a far more tempting target than the same number of grouse spread across ten thousand acres of moorland. The best deterrent to poachers is for someone — keeper, farmer, member of the shooting syndicate, — to be around and about the shoot as often as possible and preferably at irregular times. Lamping for foxes is doubly useful: it lets the poachers know that someone is about and it also helps keep the fox population in check.

Poisons, Traps and Predators

The law is quite specific about what is and is not permitted when controlling predators. In general the use of poison is banned except for use against rats and mice, moles and, under certain circumstances, grey squirrels. Poison gas (Cymag) may only be used against animals which live in holes — foxes, rabbits, rats and moles. It is illegal to set poison baits in the open. You may intend the bait to kill crows or foxes but poison is not selective. It will kill buzzards and eagles, badgers and pet dogs just as effectively. It can also result in a very heavy fine or a prison sentence for the person responsible. Worse: every time a case of illegal poisoning comes to light it provides ammunition for the antis who would like to see the end of fieldsports. To play into their hands in this way is stupid and irresponsible as well as being against the law. Don't do it.

Gin traps and pole traps are illegal. Those traps — Fenn, Juby, Imbra, Sawyer and Lloyd — which are legal for use against rabbits, weasels, stoats, rats and squirrels may only be set under cover in tunnels, boxes or burrows and not out in the open.

Self-locking snares are illegal.

All hawks, falcons, eagles and owls are protected as are otters, pine martens, bats, red squirrels, wildcats and badgers. Your feelings on the rights and wrongs of the legislation are not important. The law is the law, and to flout it is to invite prosecution, a fine or a spell in prison, the certain loss of your shotgun and firearms certificate and probably a page of half truths in the tabloid press. If you are a professional keeper it may well mean the loss of your job into the bargain. Don't do it.

There is no doubt that we are being increasingly hemmed in with legislation; from our own parliament and from Europe; and that some, if not most, is ill-conceived, badly written and an unwelcome interference with the freedom of the individual citizen. All too often our legislators set out to solve one problem and succeed only in creating three new ones. Nevertheless, we elected them, the law is the law, and should be obeyed. If you disagree with the law as it stands then the way to show your disapproval is through the ballot box. If you want to do more then become a member of one or more of the organisations which are working to protect fieldsports in Britain. There are several to choose from, and we will look at them in some detail in the next chapter.

12 Clubs and Organisations

Although rough shooting can be a solitary pastime there are quite a few clubs and organisations which work for and on behalf of shooting and other fieldsports enthusiasts. At a national level organisations such as the Game Conservancy and the British Association for Shooting and Conservation (the BASC) have membership lists running to thousands, and at the other end of the scale there are local wildfowling clubs, which may consist of only a dozen or twenty members.

They fulfil a variety of roles for their members. There are pressures on fieldsports from all sides. Loss of habitat; the decline in certain species such as grouse, partridge and blackgame; attacks by anti-fieldsports campaigners; attempts by local and national government to introduce legislation to ban shooting, hunting, coursing and other fieldsports and the increasingly restrictive shotgun and firearms certificate laws all pick at the fabric of fieldsports in Britain. By undertaking research, lobbying Parliament, organising Shows and Exhibitions, presenting the case for fieldsports at schools and in the media, providing legal assistance and advice, offering an advisory service to shoot organisers and in a dozen other ways the various clubs and organisations help to preserve and enhance the quality of shooting and other sports in Britain today.

They are very much a twentieth century phenomenon, but so are most of the problems which they are tackling. The decline in grouse and partridge numbers which has been seen over the past fifty years would have been unthinkable at the end of the last century. Even though there have always been people opposed to fieldsports the chances of Parliament introducing a ban on hunting and shooting were infinitesimal — then. You would not get very long odds against it happening today, and it is the work of the British Field Sports Society, the BASC, and others which represents our best bulwark against the unthinkable becoming a reality.

It is not expensive to become a member of any of the fieldsports organisations, though the cost will certainly mount up if you decide to join them all. For those who like to get involved there is usually plenty of scope for active participation: for the more retiring types it is enough simply to meet your subscriptions which will go towards promoting the future of the sport, and perhaps to help by selling a few draw tickets once or twice a year.

Inactive membership may be less welcome if you decide to join one of the local clubs. Often they originated with a group of wildfowlers getting together to bid for the shooting rights on a particular stretch of foreshore. Membership confers the right to shoot on the foreshore, but it may also mean that you will be expected to get actively involved in other ways. Almost any club will consist of two sorts of members — those who are prepared to work and those who are prepared to let them. If you plan to join and enjoy the benefits of membership it is only fair that you should be ready to get involved with some of the graft as well.

You can probably get details of what local clubs are in your area by asking at your nearest gun shop. As for deciding which of the national organisations to join, the choice is yours. You don't *have* to join any of them. Remember though, that without the efforts of the Game Conservancy, the BASC, the BFSS and the rest you might not be able to own a shotgun at all; you might not have any game to shoot or worse; shooting, hunting, coursing and fishing might all be made illegal. Take your pick from among them; join several if you can afford it, but do join at least one. You will be helping to ensure the whole future of the sport when you do so.

The Game Conservancy

The Game Conservancy is actually two organisations. One, the Game Conservancy Trust, is a registered charity which undertakes scientific research into game and its habitat: the other is a limited company, Game Conservancy Limited, which offers advice to shoot and fishery managers, runs day and residential courses on topics such as gamekeeping, grouse moor management, pheasant rearing and predator control, publishes advisory booklets and research findings and runs a trading operation selling a range of clothing, shooting and fishing equipment and accessories.

The research is primarily directed towards the future of game species, though any changes in land management or farming practices which take place as a result are likely to benefit a whole range of birds and animals besides those which are the direct objects of the work. By undertaking proper, scientifically controlled studies the staff of the Game Conservancy produce reports that are backed by hard evidence. At times it may seem to the outsider that many months of study have done no more than confirm the obvious — as for example the experiment on Salisbury Plain which proved conclusively that partridge populations benefit when predators are controlled — but by obtaining statistically valid evidence and presenting it scientifically they bring an objective view to what are often emotive issues. Thus when an opponent of hunting or shooting claims that foxes do little or no damage to game birds the Game Conservancy can produce incontrovertible proof that they do.

The Advisory Service operates at both a general and a specific level. There is a great deal of general advice available in the form of books, pamphlets and research results, and advice specific to your shoot can be obtained by arranging a visit from one of the experts employed by the Advisory Service.

The Game Conservancy organise courses for shoot managers and keepers and produced a Code of Good Shooting Practice which went some way to curbing the worst of the excesses which had begun to creep into the sport during the late Eighties. Of all the fieldsports organisations the Game Conservancy, through its dual roles as a research and an advisory body, probably does more than any other to ensure that there is a future in Britain for both the fieldsportsman and his quarry

BASC

The British Association for Shooting and Conservation (the BASC) began life as WAGBI, (the Wildfowlers' Association of Great Britain and Ireland), which somewhat

Pheasant over the gun . . .

simpler to pronounce title served from its inception in 1908 until it was changed to the BASC in 1981. Founded by a wildfowler called Stanley Duncan, the association was originally formed to combat threats to wildfowl and wildfowl habitats. A growing membership, and a widening of interests to include all live shooting led to the change of name; a change that was not met with universal approval at the time, though it is now established and accepted.

The BASC promotes and protects the interests of its members in a number of ways. Research studies, particularly involving wildfowl and waders are undertaken, such as the duck wing and woodcock wing studies. Members are asked to send one wing from each duck or woodcock shot to the BASC in order that statistics can be prepared showing such details of the woodcock and wintering duck populations as their age, sex and geographical distribution.

The BASC sets great store by education and training, and has produced a series of Codes of Practice to guide newcomers to the sport, and has introduced a proficiency award scheme which covers both the theory and practice of good, safe shooting. They work hard in taking the message to schools and are a familiar sight at country fairs, game shows and agricultural shows.

Besides seeking to educate the general public the BASC has a strong political lobby which will defend the sport against attacks from the anti-fieldsports activists who seek to discredit shooting through the media and eventually to bring in legislation which would ban it altogether. Closer to home, they will assist members who have trouble obtaining shotgun certificates or who are subjected to undue pressure from an over zealous police firearms department.

. . . cleanly killed and falling.

Their message always advocates sporting shooting, responsibly carried out, and to this end they will ban any member convicted of poaching or similar offences. This is not an empty threat, since membership of the BASC confers one particular benefit which is not obtainable elsewhere. Much of the foreshore in England, Wales and Northern Ireland is owned by the Crown. The BASC has an agreement with the Crown Estate Commissioners which authorises its members to be on Crown controlled foreshore with a shotgun. In effect, membership of the BASC makes wildfowling available to the members. It is important to understand that by no means all foreshore is controlled by the Crown: much is in private ownership or subject to management agreements by conservation bodies, wildfowling clubs, harbour authorities and the like. It is up to you to establish who controls what, and to establish it *before* you set out with your gun. Ignorance is no defence, in this as in any other aspect of law.

Members of the BASC are automatically covered by Third Party Insurance when shooting. This alone is probably worth the membership fees. One careless shot, an unfortunate ricochet, a faulty cartridge which allows the shot to ball and fly beyond its normal range: any of these could see you facing a civil law suit for damages which might run into hundreds of thousands of pounds. You can, of course, organise your own insurance, but joining the BASC will make it unnecessary.

The British Field Sports Society

The British Field Sports Society (BFSS) represents the interests of all sportsmen and women who follow or participate in fieldsports. Shooting, hunting, coursing, fishing, falconry and stalking all fall within their remit, and they maintain links with other clubs and organisations such as the BASC, the Game Conservancy, the National Anglers Council and the Captive Hawk Board.

While the charitable status of organisations such as the Game Conservancy forbids them to take part in political activity the BFSS operates under no such restraint. Much of the society's work is just that: working to ensure that fieldsports are properly represented in Parliament, and not banned at the whim of a collection of politicians, many of whom, knowing nothing of the true nature of the sports, nor their importance to the countryside, see them only as a means to capture votes.

All the fieldsports organisations — and there are many — will rally to the cause when there is a specific threat, but it is the BFSS that works at all times to anticipate threats before they become a reality and to organise the opposition when, as with the Macnamara Bill of 1992, there is a real and present danger to shooting, hunting or fishing. The society has a specialist political staff which maintains contact with the various ministries and parliamentary committees which might damage or ban outright any of the legitimate country sports which may be enjoyed in Britain today.

The threat is far wider than the head-on attacks which would make shooting, hunting, coursing and fishing illegal. Loss of habitat, pollution, poisoning by agricultural chemicals, and ill-conceived conservation plans can all represent a serious threat to fieldsports, both nationally and locally. Co-ordination of the work of the various fieldsports organisations is sometimes necessary, and the BFSS was a founder member and organiser of the Campaign for Country Sports which, as the title implies, was formed to defend, and to educate the public about, the role of country sports.

Other Organisations

There are dozens of other clubs and organisation involved with shooting, stalking, hunting, fishing, coursing and falconry. Some are purely local, such as the wildfowlers clubs which exist all over the country, many of which do a great deal of conservation work as well as promoting the image of wildfowling in their particular area. Then there are the national organisations: the British Falconers Club, The Muzzle Loaders Association of Great Britain, the Coursing Supporters Club, the Masters of Foxhounds Association, the Masters of Deerhounds, Draghounds, Minkhounds, Basset Hounds etc. Associations, the British Deer Society, the St Hubert Club of Great Britain and many, many others.

Gundog enthusiasts will find clubs and societies established for all the recognised breeds with some breeds having several clubs devoted to them. Field trials are run by these breed clubs as well as by the Kennel Club, and preferred entry is usually given to club members. Regular field trial competitors may be members of a dozen or more breed clubs. Fortunately the membership fees are generally modest, and entry fees to the trials are usually lower for members than for non-members, so some, at least, of the outlay can be recouped.

Joining one of the major fieldsports organisations is a way of putting something back into the sport, and a means by which we can all help to ensure that our sport has a future. Pressure on shooting comes in a number of ways; through the loss and degradation of habitat; through the decline of quarry species; through direct attacks which seek to ban the sport by legislation and through indirect attacks such as increasingly restrictive firearms controls.

Defences in the form of research, education and political lobbying are provided by the Game Conservancy, the BASC and the BFSS. The Game Conservancy is the most committed to pure research and the BFSS to political action, with the BASC somewhere between the two, and perhaps more aligned with the wildfowler and rough shooter. Ideally you should join all three, finances permitting, but every fieldsportsman should be a member of at least one. That way there may still be fieldsports to be enjoyed in ten, twenty and fifty years from now. If we fail to defend this part of our heritage it could be lost at any time; and once lost it will never be restored. Against such a background the cost of membership is a bargain.

13 Game Handling and Storing

Imagine an autumn landscape; leaves turning to red and gold, a touch of frost in the air and the urgent rustling as a busy spaniel hunts through the bracken. The rattle of wings, a raucous alarm call and then, suddenly, a cock pheasant hurls itself into the air. You bring the gun to your shoulder and fire. There is a thump as the pheasant crumples to the ground, a few golden brown feathers drift back towards you on the breeze accompanied by that evocative scent of gunsmoke. The dog waits, tail thumping eagerly until you click it on for the retrieve. A few moments later you are holding your first pheasant of the season.

The head is an iridescent bottle green broken by the scarlet wattle, by the fading gold of the eye, and terminating in the white ring of the collar. The copper and gold of the breast and back, is spotted with black and tinged with green on the rump and culminates in the long, bronze and black barred tail. Gaudy perhaps; a stranger to these shores, brought here by an invading army a couple of thousand years ago; but a cock pheasant in all his finery is a thing of beauty. So what do you do with it now?

All too often it will be slung into the back of a Land-Rover, kicked to one side by the muddy boots of the guns and the beaters, trampled underfoot by spaniels and Labradors and left there with the rest of the day's bag, in a bloody, crumpled heap, until the end of the day's shooting. An ignoble end for the birds and animals without which there would be no rough shooting. On a strictly practical note, such careless handling can also ruin the game for the table. And in the end, all the game we shoot is destined for a table somewhere — our own, that of our friends, or perhaps, via the game dealer, for the customers of the butcher. Proper handling will ensure that it reaches the table in the best possible condition.

In some European countries it is the custom, at the end of the day, to lay out the game in ordered rows in a square of evergreen boughs; to line up the guns, beaters and keepers and to sound a fanfare over the creatures that have made the day's sport possible. I am not suggesting that you should carry a bugle in your gamebag so that you can blow a salute over three woodpigeons, two rabbits and snipe while your spaniel stands to attention and tries not to giggle, but I do say that we should treat our quarry with respect, when it is dead as well as when it is alive.

Game can spoil very quickly, especially in hot or thundery weather. Once killed it needs to cool as quickly as is practical. This may not be such a problem during a January blizzard as when grouse shooting under a blazing August sun, but the principles of good game-handling remain the same.

Ideally game should be hung up, by the neck in the case of birds and the hind legs for rabbits and hares, as soon as possible after being shot. There should be free circulation of air around the carcases, and in summer flies should be excluded if possible. All of which is simple, obvious, and at times, totally impractical. If you are walking-up with just your dog for company then you are just going to have to carry whatever you shoot along with you by the best means at your disposal.

A gamebag is the usual solution, and has the advantage of doubling as a carrier for your lunch, waterproof clothing, spare cartridges, extra sweater and whatever else you may be lugging along. Most gamebags are equipped with a net, and if the weather is warm you should put your quarry in this rather than inside the bag itself. This will allow the air to circulate around it and cool it much faster than if it is crushed into the sweaty, waterproof lining of the interior. It will also keep any blood, fleas, ticks and urine being transferred from their late host to your lunch, spare sweater, waterproof clothing etc . . .

An alternative to the gamebag is a game carrier: a leather strap that hangs over the shoulder with a metal slide at either end into which birds are hung by their necks. It has the advantage of lightness, will fit in the pocket until needed, and obviously keeps the game out in the open where it will cool quickly. On the minus side it is useful only as a game carrier and cannot serve the gamebag's dual function as game carrier and general holdall.

Rabbits and hares can be hocked — that is have the skin behind one Achilles tendon slit with a knife and the other hind leg hooked through the slit — and then strung along a stick which can be carried over the shoulder. This is useful for carrying them home but only of limited value if you are walking along hoping for a shot as well as transporting your bag. And if you are coming back the way you set out it may be possible to cache your game somewhere along the route and collect it later. Always remember to squeeze the bladder to remove the urine before putting a hare or rabbit into the gamebag, or coat pocket, or even hanging it on the stick.

When you stop for lunch take the game out of the bag and spread it out to continue cooling. Keep it away from the dogs (or the dogs away from it) in case any disputes over ownership should arise, and after lunch make sure that you collect up the same number of bodies as you laid down before it. It may sound obvious, but it is all too easy to miss the odd bird, especially grouse laid out on a heather bank. Incidentally, the lunch break gives

A simple game-cart will keep birds safe from dogs and trampling feet.

A Labrador should fetch game to hand undamaged. Make sure that you treat it with respect thereafter.

you an opportunity to spread the load evenly if you happen to be carrying more than your fair share of the morning's bag, though if you have shot three hares you may well find that those three hares will be yours to carry — all day long.

If possible, when game is to be carried in a vehicle, it should be hung up rather than laid on the floor. If no hanging arrangement can be devised then try and spread it out rather than dumping it in a heap, and get it hung up as soon as possible. A proper game larder is ideal, with fly-proof gauze covering the windows, and plenty of air circulating around the birds, but you may not be lucky enough to have such a facility. A garage or outside shed will do, provided that it is cool. Do not make the mistake that a friend of mine once made and leave a couple of brace of pheasants hanging above your central heating boiler for a week. He only did it once.

If you are anything of a home handyman you should be able to build yourself a game larder without too much difficulty. A wooden frame with slatted doors and 'windows' covered by zinc gauze, built on stilts to keep rats, cats and dogs from breaking in, and with plenty of hooks to hang your game is all that is required. If you are a stalker as well as a rough shooter you may decide to make something a little bigger, or there are ready made larders on the market which can be erected inside a garage or outhouse and will keep carcases free from flies and wasps.

Rabbits should be paunched before they are hung; hares are usually hung with the guts left in, as is all feathered quarry. And there, depending on the weather, you can leave them to hang until they are ready for skinning or plucking, then cooking or consigning to the freezer. Your next decision is, how long should you leave game to hang?

You will undoubtedly have heard the stories of pheasants shot in January and left to hang until Easter; of game so ripe that it was almost ready to walk out of the larder on its own. If you happen to like your game that way then fine, but it is a matter of choice, not a strict rule. An awful lot depends on the weather as well as on your own taste. If it is sultry, muggy and thundery then game seems to spoil much quicker than when it is cold, bright and breezy. Birds which have been badly shot, fallen heavily onto stones or frozen ground, or been chewed by a hard-mouthed dog will spoil much more quickly than relatively undamaged ones.

Young grouse can be roasted and eaten on the day they are shot: old birds need a couple of days to hang unless they are being cooked slowly in a stew or a pie. Grouse can spoil very quickly if the weather in August is thundery, or they have been badly handled, so keep a sharp eye on your game larder and be prepared for an impromptu plucking party if they show signs of deteriorating. Your nose will warn you of the impending problem.

Snipe and woodcock can be eaten after a minimum of hanging time, but most birds benefit from at least a few days between the shot and the oven. I don't care for very gamey meat, and reckon to hang pheasants, ducks or geese for about a week before dressing them for the table, but you must make up your own mind as to what suits you best. Once the hanging time is over, be it Saturday to Monday or Christmas to Easter, it is up to you to get your quarry ready to eat.

There is nothing difficult about plucking game. You take a pinch of feathers between finger and thumb and you pull them out. Repeat the procedure until no more feathers remain to be pulled. That's it. Larger birds such as geese are best hung up by a string round their necks but most game is easier to handle if you sit down with the bird on your knees and pluck it into a box or open bag on the floor at your feet. Pigeon and woodcock are a delight to pluck; the feathers coming away easily to leave a clean, oven-ready finish. Wildfowl and particularly geese are hard work. First you have to remove all the feathers, then you virtually start over again with the down, and end up having to singe the carcase to get it properly clean. Pheasants need to be handled with care when plucking the breasts and the insides of the thighs or else the skin will rip away and spoil the appearance of the finished bird. The best way to learn is to practice.

I start with the breast, pluck down to the neck, turn the bird over and clean the back, legs and tail before tackling the wings. The flight feathers can be really hard work with the bigger birds so it is worth asking yourself how much of the wing you are likely to eat, and stopping plucking when you reach that point. I rarely get beyond the first joint before reaching for the knife and discarding the rest.

Once the birds are plucked they must be drawn. Use a sharp knife to slit along the skin at the back of the neck, then cut through the neck where it joins the body. The knife will do this easily with small game, particularly if you find the gap between two vertebrae, but for geese you may find a pair of secateurs more convenient. Cut the neck free just below the head and save it if you have a taste for giblet gravy. Cut the head off, leaving a flap of skin and remove the crop, gullet and windpipe. Then cut round the vent and carefully remove the guts, liver and gizzard, then reach right up into the chest cavity to remove the heart and lungs. Rinse, or wipe the inside of the bird with a damp cloth; add the liver, heart and gizzard to the neck and discard the rest. Result, one oven-ready bird.

If you are going to use the birds in a pie or a stew then it is quicker to skin them instead of plucking them. Pigeons, of which only the breasts provide much meat, are often skinned, as are old grouse which are destined for grouse pie. Lay the bird on its back on a table. Pinch up a flap of skin at the base of the breast bone and insert the point of your knife, sharp edge upwards, and cut forwards towards the neck, slicing up through the skin but not cutting into the flesh. You should then be able to ease the skin and feathers back from the meat.

Use a sharp knife to cut down on one side of the breastbone and follow the curve of the ribs around to ease the flesh away from the carcase, then repeat on the other side. You should now have two fillets ready for the pot or the freezer. Use your thumbs to ease the skin back clear of the thighs and drumsticks, and then sever the legs from the body at the hip joints. The rest: bones, feathers, skin, guts, feet, head and neck can be discarded.

Skinning hares and rabbits takes a little longer than skinning a pigeon, but the principle is the same. Start by slitting the skin from belly to neck, then pull it away from the body, using the tip of the knife to free the stubborn bits along the breast bone. Once the neck is exposed it can be severed, as can the four feet, leaving them attached to the skin unless you plan to dry and cure it. Remove the liver and heart, and the carcase is ready to be jointed. The hind legs can be severed at the hip joints and the front legs sliced away from the rib cage, then the body cut into joints across the backbone. One hare or rabbit, ready for the pot. I assume the same procedure works for grey squirrels which I am told are excellent eating, though I have yet to try one myself.

You may not want to go to the bother of dressing out your own game, and if you have an aged retainer, a friendly butcher, a wife, husband or child who can be persuaded, bribed or coerced into doing the job for you then you may not have to. But you should know how it is done, and be prepared to do it yourself if necessary. After all, if you are prepared to kill it and to eat it you should also be prepared to deal with the bit in between.

14 Further Reading

In attempting to cover a wide range of topics I have, of necessity, dealt with many in only the briefest manner. My aim has been to paint a broad canvas showing a little of the variety, the pleasure and the skills involved in rough shooting. Those of you who want more detail or an alternative view of the sport should find yourselves well catered for at your local library or book shop.

The sporting writer of today joins a long and (sometimes) distinguished company of authors stretching back to the very earliest days of the printing press. A comprehensive list of the works dealing with firearms, shooting, game management, and dog training would form a book in itself. Many of the older works are now collector's items and priced accordingly and there are a number of secondhand booksellers who deal exclusively in shooting, hunting and fishing works.

With such a breadth of choice any list of further reading can only be subjective, and for every book I recommend there will be a least a score of others equally deserving of mention. Some are included for no more reason than that I have read them myself at some time and enjoyed the writer's style, knowledge or perhaps sense of humour. I have categorised my choice broadly into instructional books and those which seek primarily to entertain, though the distinction is not always clear cut.

Guns and Cartridges

You may find the study of ballistics an absorbing and fascinating subject: then again, you may be bored to distraction by the whole business of chokes and bore sizes, muzzle velocities and shot stringing, breech pressures and recoil energies. Knowing how your gun works may help you to shoot better, but there is no guarantee. Point it in the wrong direction and you will still miss, no matter how much of a ballistics expert you may be. Provided you can handle your gun safely there is no real need to know what happens after it goes bang, though the genuine 'gun nut' will be almost as happy reading about guns and their performance as he will be when he is out shooting them.

Major-General Burrard produced what is probably the standard work on shotguns and shotgun ballistics with *The Modern Shotgun* and conducted a fascinating series of experiments to prove his theories. It is not light reading though, running to three thick volumes, and if you prefer something a little more reader friendly then any of the books by Gough Thomas, for many years a regular contributor to the *Shooting Times*, should meet the mark. *Gough Thomas's Gun Book*; *Gough Thomas's Second Gun Book*; and *Shooting Facts and Fancies* are all excellent, easy to read and understand but nevertheless quite technical works.

Gamekeeping

Keepering, gamebird rearing and the general running of a rough shoot are quite well catered for, though beware of the methods of vermin control advocated in some older books. I have a copy of *Shooting by Moor, Field and Stream*; part of the excellent Lonsdale Library series; in which one of the contributors says, of the Little Owl, 'It is a crafty little creature, and I think the country would be well rid of it.' There is much more in the same vein, but it must be read in the context of its time — in this case 1929. That said, it contains some first class advice on gundogs, gamebird rearing, shooting, field trials and a host of other subjects. Just beware of taking some of that advice too literally.

There are several recent publications dealing with keepering and shoot management. *Managing a Shoot* by M. Roberts; *A Modern Guide to Professional Gamekeeping* by Jill Mason; *The Moorland Gamekeeper* by J. Spottiswoode and *Partridge for Sport* by Geoffrey Nightingale have all found their way onto my bookshelf and all of them have been useful at one time or another. If you want a view of things as they once were, then the classic *The Gamekeeper At Home* by Richard Jefferies is available as a reprint and gives a fascinating picture of the life of a keeper in a previous century; as indeed does *The Banville Diaries* — the journal of a Norfolk gamekeeper in the early part of the nineteenth century. Banville was largely responsible for the re-introduction of the capercaillie to Britain, and his account of his travels in Sweden in search of these birds makes fascinating reading. You might also like to reflect on Banville's introduction to grouse shooting. When his employer was off to shoot grouse, Banville was ordered to make his own way from London to Yorkshire: in effect to walk (complete with dogs) to the moors. The journey was nearly three hundred miles and took a full week. Presumably both Banville and the dogs were fit by the time they got there.

Gundogs

There are literally hundreds of gundog books to choose from: books about training, breeding, working, showing or simply keeping gundogs as pets. Beware of training books that are too specific with their instructions. You cannot train a gundog on a strict timetable. It is not just the various breeds which differ in their learning curves; there are considerable differences between individuals of the same breed. The good trainer must treat each dog as an individual and tailor the learning process to that particular dog's ability to absorb and apply each lesson.

Some of the very early books are worth reading if only to see how things were done in past centuries. I particularly liked the advice in one book which said: 'A young dog, going to the moors for the first time, will benefit from a couple of hours roadwork before setting out. Your man can do this while you breakfast.'

Some of the early gundog books are now considered as classics, and may be priced accordingly, though many are also available as contemporary reprints. *The Dog in Health and Disease* by 'Stonehenge', Hutchinson's *Dogbreaking* and *The Pointer and His Predecessors* by Arkwright are three which spring to mind, but there are plenty of others. *Hounds and Dogs* from the Lonsdale Library is a an excellent guide to working dogs: the chapter on Field Trials could have been written today instead of fifty years ago and would still be just as controversial (and just as true).

A good modern introduction to the various breeds of gundog, their history and their ability is *Gundogs — Their History, Breeding & Training* by Louise Petrie-Hay. For birddog enthusiasts the recently published *Pointers and Setters* by Derry Argue will tell you everything you want to know about our native pointing breeds, and perhaps a few facts which you might prefer to ignore.

There is no shortage of books dealing with the training of dogs for the shooting field. Indeed, most dog books will include at least a chapter or two on training, though in some cases the advice given is best forgotten. Of the books which are primarily devoted to the training of gundogs my favourites are *Gundogs — Their Learning Chain* by Joe Irving and *Gundog Training* by Keith Erlandson.

A couple of other, recent books on gundogs: *The Dog and the Gun* by Crawford Little and *A Dog at Heel* by Veronica Heath deal more with the pleasure of owning and working gundogs and make good reading for a winter evening

The Law

The recent publication *Fair Game* by Charlie Parkes and John Thornley deals in some detail with the law affecting shooting and fieldsports in general. Clear and concise, as well as being easy to read and understand, it is a valuable reference book in these times when the law is increasingly invoked to curb and curtail the freedom of the individual to carry on their traditional country sports.

General Shooting Books

These are what I call fireside books: works to be enjoyed on a winter evening when the wind is howling outside and I am sitting with a glass in my hand, a fire in the grate and a dog or two sleeping at my feet. Some are old, some quite recent, but they all have one thing in common. They can take me out, away from the fire and back into the woods and the hedgerows, the moor or the foreshore, and recreate that rush of adrenalin as the dog swings onto point, the pheasant bursts from the covert or the whicker of pinions announces the arrival in the darkness of the first goose of the season. You will no doubt have your own favourites already: some of them may well be here.

Perhaps my all-time favourite fieldsports book is *The Old Man & the Boy* by Robert Ruark; long since out of print but a real treasure if you should come across a copy in a secondhand book shop. It tells the story of the young Ruark growing up in America between the wars and being introduced by his grandfather to shooting, fishing and the other important things in life such as hunting, boat-building and training a goat to pull a cart. Don't ask: just try and find a copy of the book.

Colonel J. K. Stanford was both a sportsman and an ornithologist and wrote several shooting novels which, though they may not rate as great literature, provide an interesting and evocative picture of sport in the early part of this century as well as a fascinating insight into social attitudes of the time. *The Twelfth and After*, *Guns Wanted* and *A Keeper's Country* are all well worth searching for in the original editions, and are also available as recent reprints.

Denys Watkins-Pitchford, writing under his familiar pen name of 'BB' was a regular contributor to the *Shooting Times* for many years, writing particularly of geese and ducks, of freezing nights out on the foreshore and epic journeys to the northern firths in the depths of winter. *The Autumn Road to the Isles*; his account of a caravan trip through Scotland in the late fifties; awoke a longing in me that was not satisfied until, many years later, I moved home and family seven hundred miles northwards to work on a stalking estate in Sutherland. Never under-estimate the power of the written word.

Dark Estuary and *Tide's Ending* are probably the best known of BB's many books and paint a superb picture of the way that coastal fowling was in the days before modern transport and an abundance of leisure time made our estuaries and foreshores the over-crowded, and sometimes over-shot, places that they are today. Indeed, perhaps at least a part of the blame for this should be laid at the door of writers such as 'BB' who could, by their skill in painting a mental picture, inspire others to follow in their tracks.

John Buchan; a fine writer, now condemned as 'racist' by those miserable killjoys the 'politically correct', was himself a keen sportsman. *John Macnab*, though not strictly concerned with shooting, is a cracking story as well as being the origin of the title 'a Macnab' for the feat of shooting a grouse, stalking a stag and landing a salmon, all on the same day — something, incidentally, that the John Macnab of the title never attempted.

There are hundreds, thousands even, of other shooting, fishing, stalking and wildfowling books: some old and some new; some enthralling and some just plain boring. They will give you both good and bad advice about every possible aspect of shooting, of dog training, of game-keeping and shoot management. I have only mentioned a few of the hundreds which I have bought, begged and borrowed over the years; not necessarily the best, nor even the best known; just those that spring to mind.

It does not take long to think of other books that I have enjoyed or found useful in some way. *A Veteran Sportsman's Diary* by Charles Ackroyd; *The Complete Shot* by G. T. Teasdale-Buckell; *Pigeon Shooting* by Richard Arnold; Colin Willock's *Landscape With Solitary Figure* . . . The list is endless. Some are read once and then forgotten, others I have read many times and I hope I will read again in the future. By the fire, with a glass in my hand and a dog or two at my feet.

15 Afterthoughts

At the beginning of this book I asked what was meant by rough shooting. Now, as we are nearing the end I hope that you will understand what I mean by rough shooting. It is certainly not a universal definition and I have no doubt that are plenty of experienced shots who will feel that I have been too wide, or perhaps not wide enough, in setting my boundaries. I make no apologies for this.

I will accept that there is a lack of depth in my coverage of many of the aspects of rough shooting, but a book which sets out to cover such a wide range can only scratch the surface. Gundog training, keepering, shotgun ballistics, shooting skills, fieldcraft: it would be possible to devote the whole book to any of these and other topics, and still leave much unsaid. There must be enough books on dog training alone to fill a fair sized bookcase, and more are appearing every year. Even here there are degrees of specialisation. I have books which deal with dog training — all dogs — with training for the gundog breeds only; with training for particular breeds of gundog, and with training particular breeds of gundog to compete in field trials. Like a Russian doll, the more layers you peel off the more there is to find.

But my objective was to give a flavour of the sport that I consider as rough shooting, and some advice, particularly for the novice rough shooter, as to how he or she might make a start in the sport. I suspect that most aspiring shooters start with an interest in shooting in general rather than rough shooting in particular and then may gradually gravitate to one or other branch of the sport.

All of us retain at least a vestige of the hunting instinct that once ensured our ancestors' survival in the thousands of years before the hunter/gatherers settled down and became farmers. That instinct may be subliminated, or modified in the way it finds its outlet, but it is still there, somewhere below the surface, in all of us. They might hate the suggestion, but it is that same hunting instinct that drives the most militant of the anti-fieldsports demonstrators — the only difference being that their 'fox' wears a pink coat and is seated on a horse.

Even those of us who find an outlet for their hunting instinct by shooting find different ways to approach the sport. You may like the formality and social structure of a driven day or the bleak solitude of wildfowling on a winter foreshore: the stealthy ambush from a pigeon hide or a rattle around the boundary ditches with a hard driving spaniel. However you choose to shoot, unless you are one of those unfortunates who see shooting only as a social duty that has to be endured, you are simply obeying one of the oldest and most basic instincts known to man. And of all the forms of shooting, rough shooting is probably the one that gets closest to our basic hunting instincts.

Fieldsports today are under attack as never before. At one end of the spectrum

Members of Parliament try to introduce legislation which would make hunting, shooting and fishing illegal and Local Authorities pass byelaws which will deny hounds access to land which they control. This is the open, honest and usually ill-informed opposition. Far removed from them in moral and legal terms, but closely allied in their aims, are the thugs who fire-bomb magazine offices, injure hounds and horses and physically attack those engaged in hunting and shooting. In between these extremes are the conservation bodies who use their powers to enforce local bans on hunting and shooting; the writers, broadcasters and producers who attack us in the press, on radio and on television, the various associations which exist solely to oppose fieldsports and the teachers who try to impose their anti-fieldsports views on their pupils.

Everyone is, of course, entitled to their own opinion. If they are implacably opposed to country sports then they are at liberty to campaign against them; just as we are entitled to counter their arguments and to pursue our sport as long as it remains legitimate. I accept that some people are, and will always be, totally opposed to the taking the life of any bird or animal in the pursuit of sport, and I respect their views, even though I do not share them. For the Marxists, the Trotskyists, the Whateverists who attack fieldsports because they see it as part of some great class struggle I have no time at all. As for the rest; the largely town based population who are 'anti' fieldsports despite knowing nothing about them; I can only hope that they will take the trouble to learn exactly what they are opposing before they combine to legislate us out of existence.

Fieldsports, properly conducted, are good for the countryside, good for the environment and above all, good for the quarry. No sportsman wants to eliminate the very birds and animals which he hunts or shoots. If there is no quarry there can be no sport. That much is self-evident. What is perhaps less obvious, though no less true, is the fact that, in many cases, if there were no fieldsports there would be no quarry.

Partridge, grouse and blackgame have all seen a serious decline in their numbers during the past fifty years. The causes of these declines, though still the subject of a great deal of expensive research (funded, incidentally, by fieldsports enthusiasts), are likely to turn out to be pollution, changes in agricultural practices and loss of habitat. That these trends may be — are being — reversed is largely due to the efforts of fieldsports enthusiasts who wish to preserve their quarry so that their sport can continue. Other moorland and farmland species from skylarks to sawflies will also benefit, but it is primarily to preserve the quarry species that research is financed, changes implemented and harmful practices banned.

Copses and woodlands planted to harbour foxes or pheasants enhance the countryside. Where gamebirds are reared and released predator control raises the breeding success of other species; feed hoppers support more than just the gamebirds they are intended to sustain and the presence of keepers polices the area. Game cover strips and conservation headlands harbour songbirds, butterflies, wild flowers and bumble bees as well as the gamebirds they are meant to encourage. Flight ponds provide wetland habitat for a whole range of plants, insects, amphibians, animals and birds besides the ducks which drop in to feed each evening. Conservation bodies undoubtedly do a great deal of good work in the countryside, but for every pound spent by the conservation enthusiasts I guarantee twenty or more are spent on conservation by the proponents of country sports. Country sport *is* conservation: the two are inseparable.

It is wrong for those of us who support and take part in fieldsports to view the main body of conservation enthusiasts as a danger to our activities. Rather we should be trying, by education and example, to demonstrate that our objectives and their objectives are broadly the same. A countryside rich in variety; farming practices which are sympathetic to wild plants and animals; minimal use of herbicides and pesticides and a determined effort by industry and government to combat pollution would do wonders for most of our threatened quarry species. It would also find favour with practically the whole of the conservation movement.

Banning fieldsports would do nothing but harm to the ecology of Britain. Our aim is to create an environment that will produce and support a sustainable surplus of the birds and animals which we pursue in order that we may take an annual crop from them. In creating the conditions which will allow that surplus to accumulate we are also creating the conditions which will benefit a myriad of other species. And in cropping the surplus we are simply playing our part in the food chain. If, by rearing and releasing, by heather burning, by feeding, planting cover crops and controlling predators we try to increase the surplus we not only enhance our own sport but we improve the prospects for many other creatures which form links along the chain.

All sports should be fun to take part in, and fieldsports are no different. I shoot because I enjoy shooting; the joy of watching my dogs working; the pleasure of time spent in the open air among the woods, moors and fields; the challenge of a difficult shot as an old cock grouse curves away on the wind. At times I may be soaked or frozen, bone weary and frustrated by my poor shooting or a recalcitrant dog, but such is the lure of rough shooting that I keep coming back for more. And I hope to keep doing so for many years to come.

Index

SILVER AND SOCIETY IN LATE ANTIQUITY

Silver and Society in Late Antiquity

Functions and Meanings of Silver Plate in the
Fourth to Seventh Centuries

Ruth E. Leader-Newby

ASHGATE

© Ruth E. Leader-Newby 2004

Published by

Ashgate Publishing Limited
Gower House, Croft Road
Aldershot, Hants
GU11 3HR
England

Ashgate Publishing Limited
Suite 420
101 Cherry Street
Burlington, VT 05401–4405
USA

Ashgate website: http://www.ashgate.com

British Library Cataloguing in Publication Data
Leader-Newby, Ruth E.
    Silver and society in late antiquity : functions and
    meanings of silver plate in the fourth to seventh centuries
    1. Silverware–Europe–History–To 1500. 2. Art and society
    –Europe–History–To 1500. 2.
    I. Title
    739.2' 383' 094' 09015

US Library of Congress Cataloging in Publication Data
Leader-Newby, Ruth E., 1970–
    Silver and society in late antiquity : functions and meanings of
    silver plate in the fourth to seventh centuries/Ruth E. Leader-Newby
        p.cm.
    Includes bibliographical references (alk. paper)
    1. Silverwork–Rome. 2. Silverwork, Early Christian–Rome.
    3. Silverwork–Social aspects–Rome. I. Title
    NK7107.3L43 2003
    739.2' 737–dc21   2003045152

ISBN 0 7546 0728 3

Typeset in Palatino by Pat FitzGerald

Printed and bound in Great Britain by Biddles Ltd, Kings Lynn

Contents

List of figures

Acknowledgements

During writing and researching this book I have had the good fortune to enjoy the support of a number of institutions and individuals, and I am pleased to be able to give them the acknowledgement they deserve. Jaś Elsner oversaw this book's original incarnation in the form of my PhD thesis, providing astute criticism and advice, combined with unfailing support and encouragement. It was he who first encouraged me to explore the art of late antiquity in general and silver in particular. David Buckton and Christopher Kelly, as examiners of that thesis, have offered welcome guidance in transforming my work into book form. Their enthusiastic support for my approach to late antique silver has been much appreciated. Anthony Cutler offered helpful comments on sections of the first and final chapters. John Hanson kindly made sections of his PhD thesis available to me and has allowed me to cite his work in Chapter 4. Naturally, none of those named should be held responsible for any remaining errors of fact or judgement.

Financial support for my research was provided in the first instance by the Student Awards Agency for Scotland, who supported my studies with a Major Scottish Studentship, and provided funds for research travel. Subsequently the British Academy generously granted me a Postdoctoral Research Fellowship at King's College London which enabled me to complete this book. I would like to thank both funding bodies, and also to extend my thanks to my colleagues in the Department of Classics at King's for providing such a congenial enviroment in which to work. My research would not have been possible without the resources of the libraries of the Institute of Classical Studies and the Warburg Institute, and I thank their staff for their help on numerous occasions. I am also grateful to the Roman Society's Hugh Last and Donald Atkinson Funds, and the Dr M. Aylwin Cotton Foundation for two generous grants towards the cost of illustrations.

Examples of late antique silver can be found in museums, church treasuries and private collections around the world. Among these are the following institutions where staff kindly allowed me to examine objects in their care, or otherwise assisted me: the British Museum (David Buckton and Chris Entwistle); the Louvre (Catherine Metzger); the Cabinet des Médailles of the Bibliothèque Nationale (Mathilde Avisseau-Broustet); Cathedral of St Euphemia, Grado; Bibliotheca Malatestiana, Cesena. George Ortiz graciously allowed me to view examples of early Byzantine silverware in his collection. David Mitten and Valerie Huet assisted me in arranging visits to Mr Ortiz and the museums in Paris respectively. I am also grateful to the many individuals who have helped me (directly or indirectly) to acquire the numerous photographs required to illustrate this book. While there is not space to name them individually here, they should see their institutions acknowledged in the photo credits in the List of Figures.

Finally, thanks are due above all to my family. My parents have always provided unwavering support and understanding throughout my academic career, as well as helping with proofreading and technical aspects of word-processing. During the time I have worked on this book, I met and married my husband, and gained another set of parents and a sister. Their support has been equally extensive and sincere, and I am deeply grateful for it. This book is dedicated to the memory of my grandfather, who took a great interest in my studies of silver, but sadly did not live to see them completed.

Abbreviations

The following journal abbreviations are used:

AJA	*American Journal of Archaeology*
AA	*Archäologischer Anzeiger*
BABesch	*Bulletin Antieke Beschaving*
CA	*Cahiers Archéologiques*
CQ	*Classical Quarterly*
DOP	*Dumbarton Oaks Papers*
Mon. Piot	*Fondation Eugène Piot: Monuments et Memoires*
GRBS	*Greek, Roman and Byzantine Studies*
JdI	*Jahrbuch des deutschen archäologischen Instituts*
JbAC	*Jahrbuch für Antike und Christentum*
JRA	*Journal of Roman Archaeology*
JRS	*Journal of Roman Studies*
RM	*Römische Mitteilungen*

Introduction: the significance of silver

Hec Sevso tibi durent per saecula multa
Posteris ut prosint vascula digna tuis

May these, O Sevso, yours for many ages be
Small vessels fit to serve your offspring worthily

The elegiac couplet which encircles the central medallion of the great Hunting Dish of the Sevso Treasure (Fig. I.1) has come to carry a prophetic tone quite unintended by the anonymous craftsman who worked it in niello-filled impressions on the vessel's surface. While Sevso and his descendants have disappeared forever, leaving no trace of their identity, their ironically described 'vascula' or 'small vessels' – in this case a plate 70 cm in diameter and weighing nearly 9 kg – have survived them by more 'saecula' than they could possibly have imagined. The Sevso Treasure, a hoard of 14 large and richly decorated silver vessels dating from the late fourth and early fifth centuries AD, is only the latest in a long line of modern discoveries of late Roman and early Byzantine silverware, which have made this medium increasingly prominent in our view of artistic production and consumption in late antiquity.

In this book I investigate the rich body of artistic material that these discoveries have provided, in the belief that it can offer invaluable perspectives on many facets of late antique culture. My aim is to show that silverware evokes a wide and significant range of aspects of late antique cultural history, thereby establishing its importance for an understanding of late antique art which is grounded in the role of visual culture in this society. Why, however, privilege silver as a starting point for understanding late antique culture and society through its art? Does this medium offer a better insight than the many other rich resources of artistic material surviving from this period, including mosaics or ivories, both of which also cross the boundaries between domestic, religious and imperial art? Naturally it would be absurd to claim that silver is intrinsically more meaningful than other art forms of the period. However, there are a number of factors which make it particularly suitable for a study such as this. In practical terms, the corpus of surviving late antique silver is of a sufficient size to allow a representative study, yet not so large as to make an overview of the range of its functions in both halves of the empire impossible, as would be the case with the huge corpus of mosaics, which demands regional and typological specialization. We also have a reasonable record in our written sources – even if they are not as full or specific as scholars would

I.1 Great Hunting Dish, Sevso Treasure, private collection: detail of central medallion (courtesy of the Trustees of the Marquess of Northampton 1987 Settlement)

like them to be – of late antique attitudes towards silverware, and ways in which it was used. This is not the case for other types of late antique luxury arts, such as ivory diptychs (especially the non-consular examples, like the magnificent diptych of the Symmachi and Nicomachi now divided between the Victoria and Albert Museum and the Musée de Cluny). Such artforms are by no means absent from this study, however, and serve to place silverware in the context of other artistic production of the time.

The prominence of silver in our sources must surely be due in part to the fact that silverware had a very concrete financial value for its owner, which only jewellery shared in this period. Silver's basic value was as bullion, reflected in the weight inscriptions incised on the underside of many examples. Thus the weight of silver owned – and perhaps displayed prominently at public events, such as banquets, in the owner's house – could reflect an individual's overall wealth.[1] At the same time, it represented a cash reserve, which could be converted in times of need, or, in the context of late antique Christian piety, disposed of to charitable ends – as Palladius relates of the fourth-century aristocratic ascetic Melania the Elder, who took her movable wealth with her when she left Rome for Egypt and there presented the Egyptian abbot Pambo with 300 Roman pounds of silver (approximately 90 kg) in a silver casket, which he immediately ordered to be distributed among the monasteries of Nubia.[2] That this aspect of silver tends to be reflected in written sources, not the significance of its decoration, helps to explain the scarcity of discussion of other forms of artistic production. While silver was one of many forms of visual communication available to the late antique patron, its material value added extra dimensions to its significance. The status of silver in the late Roman world presents a marked contrast to the way that, until recently, scholars of Roman art have tended to marginalize its importance, through following aesthetic hierarchies developed in the eighteenth and nineteenth centuries, which branded it a 'minor' or 'decorative' art.

Silver's intrinsic value is also responsible for the particular way in which the majority of surviving pieces have been preserved – as hoards, concealed in times of perceived danger for safekeeping, and not recovered by their owners.[3] Such hoards are usually discovered accidentally, since they are frequently buried away from areas of habitation and are thus unlikely to be found as part of an archaeological excavation.[4] Although individual pieces and hoards have been found since the seventeenth century, the latter half of the twentieth century has seen a considerable increase in the number of late antique hoards discovered, a result of modern agricultural methods such as deep-ploughing, and the technology of metal detectors.[5] Not all hoards discovered in earlier centuries survive today. In 1628, a vast hoard (weighing almost 115 kg) of what seem from descriptions to have been fourth- or early fifth-century Roman silver vessels was discovered in the grounds of a Jesuit monastery in Trier. Shortly afterwards it was melted down to realize its financial value for its ecclesiastical owners – an example of how silver plate's intrinsic worth as bullion has always made it vulnerable to recycling.[6] This surely must have been the fate of many other unrecorded hoards, from the middle ages up to the nineteenth century when the foundation of national museums, the concept of artistic patrimony and the growth of the antiquities market placed a value on the artefacts themselves, not just the metal which they contained.

The chance finding of hoards has meant that even in recent times there have been few opportunities for professional archaeologists to excavate them, since a hoard tends to be removed from the ground before the finders report its discovery to the relevant authorities. Such discoveries are in any case by no means always promptly reported (as was the case with the Mildenhall, Thetford and Kaiseraugst Treasures), and on occasions have even been deliberately concealed from the authorities in order that the finders might sell them on the international art market (as happened with the two Cyprus Treasures around the beginning of this century, the Sion or Kumluca Treasure in Turkey in the 1960s and most recently the Sevso Treasure, which unlike the previous two is completely unprovenanced).[7] While these instances are obviously to be much regretted, at the same time it can be argued that there are limits to what excavation can tell us about such hoards. On the positive side, if a hoard is excavated archaeologically, as in the case of the Hoxne Treasure – whose finder did not try to dig it out himself, but reported it to the local archaeological service – much can be learnt about the way the hoard was packed before it was buried, even to the extent of recovering minute fragments of the containers it was placed in; fragile objects can be safely recovered without further damage; and one can be sure that no pieces of the hoard are left in the ground.[8]

However, there is much even controlled excavation cannot tell us: unless the hoard contains coins, or is buried in some type of building, which is rarely the case, archaeology will not provide a date for its deposition to serve as a *terminus ante quem* for its contents. Moreover, the location where a hoard is found provides little help in determining where the pieces were actually made. A good example is the Kaiseraugst Treasure, found in a fort on the Rhine frontier in Switzerland, which contains items inscribed on the reverse with the name 'Pausylypos of Thessalonike'.[9] These components are thus likely to have been made in this imperial capital, and purchased there by its owner, perhaps a military official, who was later transferred to Kaiseraugst. Since silver was such an important sign of status, the elite would carry their tableware around with them, whether on military campaign or travelling from one property to another. But such convenient labelling is rare and can be hard to interpret correctly. Originally only a single plate in the hoard – the so-called 'Achilles Plate', one of the most ornate with sophisticated figural decoration – was known to carry this inscription, leading scholars to believe that this was a rare instance of an artist's signature on silver. However the recent rediscovery of further pieces of the Kaiseraugst hoard has revealed that the same 'signature' occurs on some small undecorated bowls as well, prompting the suggestion that Pausylypos was as likely to have been an official controlling the production of silver as a craftsman.[10] The centres of silver production and the mechanisms by which craftsmen and workshops operated are a dark area, shrouded by the longstanding indifference of the ancient writers to those individuals who created works of art.[11] The tragedy of the Sevso Treasure is that it is futile to attempt a guess at its provenance. Although comparable pieces have been found, mainly in the Western provinces of the empire, this may mean no more than that conditions there led to more hoards being buried or surviving in the ground until the present day. But it is interesting to note that the countries which rumour has associated with the Sevso Treasure, and which tried to claim possession of the hoard in the New York court case held to establish its ownership (Hungary, Croatia and Lebanon) have no record of similar material being found on their soil previously. In fact, any one of the Roman Empire's many provinces could have been the home of the treasure.

Despite the limitations of field archaeology for increasing our understanding of late antique silverware, recent trends in the scholarship of this material have been heavily influenced by archaeology. This is reflected in a review article, published by the *Journal of Roman Archaeology* in 1990, on the subject of 'Research on Roman Silver Plate'.[12] Its author is Catherine Johns, a curator at the British Museum, who has been involved in the publication of several recent finds of late Roman silver from Britain. She noted that since 1966, when Donald Strong published his classic survey of ancient silverware *Greek and Roman Gold and Silver Plate*, publications on silver had become increasingly 'archaeological' in character, a development which she welcomed.[13] She argued that in the past silver had been seen as the province of the art historian, to be studied in 'aesthetic isolation', an approach which in her opinion had 'achieved little in creating any sound framework for the study of this material', and she praised those publications which employed 'methods customary in the publication of pottery and other finds rather than the style traditionally favoured for art-objects from antiquity'.[14] This is a clear reference to works like the catalogues of Kaiseraugst Treasure (1984) or the Thetford Treasure (1983), the latter of which Johns co-authored, with their vessel profiles, line-drawings, and scientific and technical analyses.[15] The continuing appeal of this approach can be seen most recently in the use of these methods in the first part of the Sevso Treasure catalogue (1994).[16]

This book attempts to offer an alternative both to a strictly archaeological approach and to art history's traditional stylistic one. There is a need to synthesize the range of approaches to silver which have previously been deployed in isolation. Without the tremendous labour which has gone into the production of catalogues and monographs of silver over the past 30 years, this book would stand on far less solid ground. At the same time, the point has come to move beyond a simple history of artefacts to one which seeks to determine their role in the wider sphere of visual culture and allows questions about the relative significance of individual forms of artistic production, and their relationship with each other.

Each the four chapters which follow this introduction is devoted to a different key function of silverware between 300 and 650 AD. They are not comprehensive accounts of all known examples of these chosen categories, nor are they structured as a chronological progression (although my first chapter includes much fourth-century material, and the last chapter concentrates on the problem of the 'end of late antiquity' in the seventh century). Instead, I adopt a selective approach, using case studies and close analyses of significant, often canonical, examples to focus on broader issues for the artistic and cultural history of this period. Among the most prominent of these are the use of the imperial image, the visual construction of the sacred in Christianity, the cohesive social role of elite intellectual culture, and the Christianization of the domestic sphere. To present a multi-dimensional picture of late antique society through its use of and attitudes to silverware, this study has three parts. This is a consequence of what I perceive to be the three main spheres of use for silver in the late antique period: as imperial largesse, for the adornment of the Christian church, and for display and use in the domestic sphere. Each of these spheres requires a different approach to bring out the most interesting and significant aspects of the artistic material. For this reason, there are few explicit links between the first two chapters, or between them and Chapters 3 and 4, which can be seen as a single section, since these last two chapters share the common theme of the use of mythological imagery on domestic silver. That this subject should require two chapters is a result of two factors. First, the topic of *paideia* – elite education and culture – through which I examine the late antique use of classical mythology and its Christianization, is itself a large one with implications beyond this particular study. Second, the principal use of silverware throughout the Hellenistic and Roman periods had been domestic and remained so into the late antique period. The continuity with earlier domestic silver is reflected in the decoration and style of surviving late antique examples, which show a preference for mythological themes executed in a classicizing style that lasts into the seventh century.[17] The use of silver in the imperial and the Christian sphere should, in my view, be seen as a late antique innovation, which to some extent depended on the 'normative' domestic use of silver for its meaning. This is not to underestimate the significance of this innovation or extension in the use of silver: in fact, it is crucial for this study, since it means that silver intersected with three key areas of late antique culture, namely the emperor, the Church, and elite culture. I have chosen to place the chapters on imperial and sacred uses of silver before those on its domestic uses, with the aim of introducing the reader to the ways in which the use of silver was transformed in late antiquity, before dealing with the in many ways more complex issue of subtle change masked by apparent continuity, which is one of the most fascinating aspects of late antique culture.

This book compares silver with a wide range of other forms of artistic production: ivories, mosaics (on both walls and floors), sculpture, textiles, illustrated manuscripts, glass and pottery. These comparisons balance stylistic perspectives with the iconographic and functional ties between silver and other artistic media. But while iconographic analysis plays a prominent role throughout, it is used as a tool to establish links between silver and other media, or to reflect upon function and meaning, not as an end in itself. In this context ivories, like silver, are not just a means of tracing stylistic change, but enter the arena of official art and its iconography for the first time in late antiquity. Liturgical vessels were only one part of a network of images and rituals which articulated the space of the late antique church. A richly decorated silver plate and a floor mosaic may share a similar classicizing style, and even depict some of the same mythological themes, but crucially they played complementary roles in the dining room of an upper class villa, as signs of their owner's membership of an elite culture based on a common education in Hellenism.[18] In Chapter 4, the set of plates depicting the early life of the Old Testament king, David, are compared with illustrated biblical manuscripts, not in traditional terms of iconographic parallels, but as two forms of Christian luxury art.[19]

Although silver's value as a source for social and cultural history has not gone unacknowledged, there is still a need for subtle explorations of the ways in which silver can serve as material evidence for a range of social and cultural practices, which are given visual and symbolic expression in this medium.[20] These range from the articulation of social status and political hierarchy to the construction of the sacred in the Christian church. The wealth of references to silver in written sources, to which I referred earlier, can be a valuable tool here, although in the past such passages have often been read as straightforward documentary evidence of objects and practices associated with them, without sufficient attention being paid to the genre of writing where the reference occurs. Instead of collecting 'facts' about silver, I have tried to use texts to trace the range of late antique society's attitudes towards the use of silver. This is especially productive in understanding the role of silver in early Christianity, while texts which are not directly concerned with silver can offer interpretative models for late antique viewing of silver. However, visual media themselves can be a valid historical source, offering evidence for aspects of a culture which cannot adequately be traced in surviving texts, a situation which is especially relevant for the silver of the early seventh century and its use of classical iconography.

Ownership of silverware was part of the social fabric of the world of the late Roman elite. The fact that late antique emperors and the Church both put silverware to their own uses – in one case projecting an idealized image of themselves, in the other transforming silver's worldly meanings into new sacred ones – is confirmation of the centrality of this medium to late antique life. The central medallion of the Sevso Great Hunting Dish, with which I opened this introduction, offers a powerful image of the role of silver in elite self-perception. Its scenes of a hunt on a country estate combined with an outdoor banquet represent an idealized image of the owner and his lifestyle, while the encircling inscription makes a direct connection between family continuity and the preservation of their silver plate ('may these small vessels, Sevso, last you for many ages, so that they may be worthy of and benefit your descendants'). Since the social ritual of dining, which it depicts, was the prime sphere for the use and display of such elaborately decorated silverware, a layer of self-reflexivity is added to its message. The small yet elegantly formed chi-rho symbol in a wreath that marks the juncture between the beginning and end of the inscription adds another layer to the identity expressed there: Sevso and his family advertise (albeit discreetly) their Christianity, or at least show their belief in the apotropaic, luck-bringing power of Christian symbols, which may account for their use in contexts like these. Here we have the image of a member of the late antique ruling class which can be linked, more or less directly, to the three key aspects of silver which this book explores. The invocation of Christianity through the chi-rho sign on domestic silver such as this was the first stage in the Christianization of the domestic sphere, and at the same time reminds us of the many other uses which the Christian church found for silver, as I discuss in Chapter 2. While Sevso's identity as a member of the elite is expressed on this plate through the activities of dining and hunting, other items in the Sevso Treasure, such as the Achilles and Meleager plates discussed in Chapter 3, reflect an equally important way in which membership of this group was defined, namely through education and culture. However, the Great Hunting Dish medallion crucially defines Sevso's identity through an idealized, iconic image which tells us not about the reality of his life, but how he chose to imagine it. It is this aspect of the plate which has perhaps unexpected resonances with the imperial *largitio* plates and their representations of the emperor which I discuss in Chapter 1. For these, in common with many late antique images of the emperor, offer not the portrait of an individual (with individual strengths and weaknesses) but the image of the office of emperor, replete with the connotations of sacred power and majesty which it had by then come to embody, regardless of the personality or talents of the holder. Although clearly the emperor's image had wider-reaching implications for the inhabitants of the Roman Empire than the elite's shared self-image, both are premised on the projection of an unchanging ideal, which lies at the heart of the social effectiveness of this type of image in late antique art. I shall now turn to this very issue of the emperor's image in late antiquity and silver's role in creating and propagating it, in the first of four chapters which explore in greater detail the multiple uses and meanings of late antique silver.

Notes

1. Weight inscriptions on silver are discussed by M. Martin in H.A. Cahn, A. Kaufmann-Heinimann, et al., *Der spätrömische Silberschatz von Kaiseraugst*, Baseler Beiträge zur Ur- und Frühgeschichte 9 (Derendingen, 1984), 382–93, and M.M. Mango & A. Bennet, *The Sevso Treasure: Part I, Art Historical Descriptions and Inscriptions, Methods of Manufacture and Scientific Analyses*, JRA Supplementary Series 12.1 (Ann Arbor, MI, 1994), 38–44. Although slightly earlier, Lucian, *Saturnalia* 33 writes of letting guests examine the weight of silver drinking cups.

2. Palladius, *Lausiac History*, 10.2–4. See also the discussion in P. Brown, *The Body and Society: Men, Women & Sexual Renunciation in Early Christianity* (London, 1988), 280.

3. Recent scholarship has emphasized that the motivations for hoarding in the Roman period, as at other times, could be complex and varied: see the discussion in R. Duncan-Jones, *Structure and Scale in the Roman Economy* (Cambridge, 1990), 38–42, and the articles by C. Johns, 'The Classification and Interpretation of Romano-British Treasures', *Britannia* 27 (1996), 1–16, and K.S. Painter and E. Künzl, 'Two Documented Hoards of Treasure', *Antiquaries Journal* 77 (1997), 291–325.

4. Exceptions include the Daphne Treasure (M.C. Ross, 'A Silver Treasure Found at Daphne Harbiye', *Archaeology* 6 [1953], 39–41), and the third-century Vienne Treasure (F. Baratte, et al., *Le Trésor de la Place Camille-Jouffray à Vienne [Isère]*, Gallia Supplement 50 (Paris, 1990). The Esquiline Treasure is unusual in being found in an ancient urban area, though it was not excavated archaeologically: see K. Shelton, *The Esquiline Treasure* (London, 1981), 13–17.

5. These early discoveries are recorded in a number of antiquarian studies, the most important of which are: J. Spon, *Recherches des antiquités et curiosités de la ville de Lyon* (Lyon, 1673), 185 and 'Sur un Bouclier antique d'argent appellé par les Latins CLYPEUS VOTIVUS qui se voit à Lyon dans le Cabinet de M. Octavio Mey', in *Recherches curieuses d'antiquité: contennues en plusieurs dissertations, sur des médailles, bas reliefs, statues, mosaiques et inscriptions antiques* (Lyon, 1683), 3–32 [the so-called 'Shield of Scipio']; W. Stukeley, *An Account of a Large Silver Plate of antique basso rielievo,*

Roman Workmanship, found in Derbyshire, 1729 (London, 1736) [the Risley Park Lanx];
D.A. Bracci, *Dissertazione sopra un clipeo votivo, spettante alla famiglia Ardaburia trovato l'anno 1769, nelle vicinazo d'Orbetello ora esisente nel museo di S.A.R. Pietro Leopoldo* (Lucca, 1771) [the Missorium of Ardabur Aspar]; E.Q. Visconti, *Lettera di Ennio Quirino Visconti intorno ad una antica supelletile d'argento scoperta in Roma nell' anno 1793*, ed. P.P. Montagnani-Mirabili (Rome, 1827) [the Esquiline Treasure]. There is a good discussion of French antiquarians in the seventeenth and eighteenth centuries and their interest in silver in F. Baratte, *La vaiselle d'argent en Gaule dans l'antiquité tardive* (Paris, 1993), 9–14.

6. W. Binsfield, 'Der 1628 in Trier gefundene römische Silberschatz', *Trierer Zeitschrift* 42 (1979), 113–27; Baratte, *La vaiselle d'argent en Gaule*, 197–204. The same factor accounts for the relatively low survival rate of silver plate from antiquity as a whole, especially earlier periods such as Classical and Hellenistic Greece: see M. Vickers & D. Gill, *Artful Crafts: Ancient Greek Silverware and Pottery* (Oxford, 1994), 53–76, esp. 73–76.

7. Mildenhall: K.S. Painter, *The Mildenhall Treasure: Roman Silver from East Anglia* (London, 1977), 11; Thetford: C. Johns & T. Potter, *The Thetford Treasure: Roman Jewellery and Silver* (London, 1983), 13–15; Kaiseraugst: Cahn, Kaufmann-Heinimann et al., *Der spätrömische Silberschatz*, 31–39; Cyprus Treasures: A. and J. Stylianou, *The Treasures of Lambousa* (Lapethos, 1969), preface ix–x; Sion: N. Firatli, 'Un trésor du VIe siècle trouvé à Kumluca en Lycie', in *Akten des VII Internationalen Kongress für Christliche Archäologie*, 2 vols (Vatican City, 1969), vol. 1, 523–25, S.A. Boyd & M.M. Mango, *Ecclesiastical Silver Plate in Sixth Century Byzantium* (Washington DC, 1992), 5; Sevso: Bennet and Mango, *The Sevso Treasure*, 11.

8. C. Johns & R. Bland, 'The Hoxne Late Roman Treasure', *Britannia* 25 (1994), 165.

9. Cahn, Kaufmann-Heinimann et al., *Der spätrömische Silberschatz*; A. Kaufmann-Heinimann, 'Eighteen new pieces from the late Roman silver treasure of Kaiseraugst: first notice', *JRA* 12 (1999), 333–41.

10. Kaufmann-Heinimann, 'Eighteen new pieces', 340.

11. This has not prevented some scholars speculating on regional schools centred in the imperial capitals. For an incisive critique of the problems involved in regional stylistic attribution of silver, see B. Kiilerich, *Late Fourth Century Classicism in the Plastic Arts: Studies in the So-Called Theodosian Renaissance* (Odense, 1993), 198–201.

12. C. Johns, 'Research on Roman Silver Plate', *JRA* 3 (1990), 28–43. A more recent summary of the state of research by François Baratte, in a volume of the journal *Antiquite Tardive*, which featured a number of papers on late antique silver delivered at a conference in the British Museum in 1995, differs little from Johns in its emphases. See F. Baratte, 'La vaisselle d'argent dans le monde romain: bilan et perspectives', *Antiquité Tardive* 5 (1997), 25–28.

13. D.E. Strong, *Greek and Roman Gold and Silver Plate* (London, 1966). This pioneering book is still the only comprehensive survey of classical silverware. Although his discussion of the late antique material has suffered from being overtaken by recent discoveries, his focus on typologies of vessel and decoration has the advantage of allowing the reader to assimilate new finds to those already known.

14. Johns, 'Research', 28, 40–41.

15. Johns and Potter, *The Thetford Treasure*; Cahn, Kaufmann-Heinimann et al., *Der spätrömische Silberschatz*.

16. Mango and Bennet, *The Sevso Treasure*.

17. For discussion of classicism in late antique silver see L.A. Matzulewitsch, *Byzantinische Antike: Studien auf Grund der Silbergefässe der Ermitage* (Berlin, 1929); E. Kitzinger, *Byzantine Art in the Making: Main Lines of Stylistic Development in Mediterranean Art, 3rd–7th Century* (London, 1977); Kiilerich, *Late Fourth Century Classicism.*

18. Cf. S.P. Ellis, 'Power, Architecture and Decor: How the Late Roman Aristocrat Appeared to his Guests', in E.K. Gazda ed., *Roman Art in the Private Sphere* (Ann Arbor, 1991), 117–34; idem., 'Late-Antique Dining: Architecture, Furnishings and Behaviour', in R. Laurence & A. Wallace-Hadrill, *Domestic Space in the Roman World: Pompeii and Beyond, JRA* Supplement 22 (Portsmouth, RI, 1997), 41–51.

19. Cf. A. Cutler, 'Uses of Luxury: on the Functions of Consumption and Symbolic Capital in Byzantine Culture', in A. Guillou and J. Durand eds, *Byzance et les images* (Paris, 1994), 287–328.

20. Johns, 'Research', 41–43; Baratte, 'Bilan et perspectives', 27. Most work in this area has been relatively unsophisticated and dominated by a positivist standpoint, for example K.S. Painter's 'Roman Silver Hoards: Ownership and Status', in Baratte ed., *Argenterie romaine et byzantine* (Paris, 1988), 97–111, to which A. Cameron, 'Observations on the Distribution and Ownership of Late Roman Silver Plate', *JRA* 5 (1992), 176–85, is an essential corrective. A notable exception is Baratte, 'Vaisselle d'argent, souvenirs littéraires et manières de table: l'example des cuillers de Lampsaque', *CA* 40 (1992), 5–20.

1

The emperor's gifts: the Missorium of Theodosius and imperial largitio

The Missorium of Theodosius (Fig. 1.1), a silver plate measuring 74 cm in diameter and weighing 15.35 kg, preserved in the Real Academia de la Historia, Madrid, is a spectacular surviving example of silver plate issued as largitio, that is as a ceremonial gift given by the emperor to a civic or military official. It is perhaps the most iconographically elaborate (and certainly the largest and heaviest) of the 19 largitio vessels which have survived from the Roman world. The Missorium is exceptional, both within the history of officially issued silver plate and within the history of late Roman and early Byzantine art, standing at the centre of a complex network of art-historical narratives relating to the way in which the emperors of this period shaped and distributed their official images. It is included in most general handbooks and surveys of this period, both in stylistic narratives as a securely dated example of late fourth century classicism (often called the 'Theodosian renaissance'), and in iconographic narratives as a stage in a crucial transitional period for the development of the Byzantine imperial image.[1] This lends it a prominence in the literature which is exceptional for silver plate. For these reasons, the Missorium of Theodosius is the focus of this first chapter's case study of imperial largitio silver of the fourth century. Through it, three central aspects of largitio silver will be analysed, namely its role in economic history, its place in the development of iconic modes of imperial representation in late antiquity, and its relationship with largitio outside the imperial sphere, and in other media. My aim is to shed light on the role that silver played in the discourses surrounding the image of the emperor in the late antique and early Byzantine period, discourses that in turn shape our understanding of the structure of late antique society.

The Missorium was discovered by a labourer in 1847 near Almandralejo, about 11 km from Mérida (ancient Augusta Emerita) in southern Spain. Shortly after its discovery it was acquired by the Real Academia in Madrid, and an account of it was published in 1849 by A. Delgado y Hernandez.[2] In this he makes a brief reference to two small silver cups 'of simple form' allegedly found with Missorium.[3] These are not illustrated and do not seem to have been acquired by the Real Academia. It is unfortunate that these were not preserved, since they might have helped in establishing the date

1.1   Missorium of Theodosius, Madrid, Real Academia de la Historia (P. Witte/Deutsches Archäologisches Institut, Madrid, neg. R 50–76–11)

of the plate's burial. The generally good condition of the dish is marred by a diagonal break running from upper left to lower right. The dish was found folded in half along this line, and was divided in two pieces in an attempt to unfold it immediately after its discovery.[4] At some point in antiquity before the dish's burial an unsuccessful attempt may have been made to hack the plate diagonally in half along the line of the fold. The jagged line left by the tool used in the attempt to divide the dish closely resembles the broken edges of the fragments of another late antique largitio plate, stylistically very close to the Missorium, which formed part of the Groß Bodungen hoard of scrap silver (Fig. 1.2).[5] This suggests that by the time of burial (which is uncertain) the Missorium may have been destined for the melting pot, a possibility whose significance I will discuss in a later section of this chapter.

1.2   Groß Bodungen largitio plate fragments, Halle, Landesmuseum für Vorgeschichte (Landesamt für Archäologie, Sachsen-Anhalt)

1.3   Munich Treasure, Munich, Archäologische Staatsammlung, Museum für Vor- und Frühgeschichte

Fortunately the break in the plate has done little to obscure the legibility of its design, while the fact that it was folded inwards during burial has done much to preserve the surface detail.[6] The plate shows Theodosius I enthroned between his two co-emperors, Valentinian II and Arcadius, beneath an arcaded pediment.[7] The imperial group is flanked by a pair of guards on each side, recognizable as members of the German imperial body guard by their hair, shields and torques. Theodosius presents a codicil of appointment to an official on his right, who holds out his hands veiled in the folds of his chlamys to receive it. He is shown on a much smaller scale than the three emperors; their ranks too are indicated by size, with Theodosius considerably the largest, followed by Valentinian, and finally Arcadius, Theodosius' son who was only 11 years old in 388 AD. All three are nimbed. In the exergue beneath the ground line of the main scene is a reclining female figure with a cornucopia, usually identified as Tellus, and three putti who hold up offerings of fruit to the imperial trio above. They are matched by two similar fruit-bearing putti in either corner of the pediment. An inscription around the edge of the plate reveals that it was presented on the occasion of the decennalia, or tenth anniversary of rule, of Theodosius I (379–95 AD), which was celebrated on the 19th of January 388.[8] On the underside, the foot-ring bears an inscription recording an original weight of 50 Roman pounds (16.13 kg). The relief surface is worked with chasing and punching to show the details of the elaborately embroidered 'segmenta' which adorn the emperors' tunics and chlamydes, their jewelled fibulae and diadems, their footstools, the designs of the guards' shields, and the hem of the robe of Tellus. Altogether it represents a high standard of late fourth-century craftsmanship, which deliberately draws on the classical tradition of preceding centuries for the style of the figural representations, and for the inclusion of the personification of Tellus in the composition.[9]

The Missorium of Theodosius is one of 19 known examples of silver plate issued as imperial largitio. All date to the fourth century AD, the Missorium with its date of around 388 being possibly the latest of the series. This poses the difficult question of whether this group is an accident of survival, or whether the practice of giving largitio in the form of plate was solely a fourth-century phenomenon.[10] The issue is further complicated by the distribution of the surviving items among the emperors of the fourth century, and the varying sizes, weights, and levels of craftsmanship represented among them. Of the 19 emperors (excluding usurpers) who ruled during the fourth century, dishes issued by Licinius, Constans, Constantius II, Valentinian I or II and Theodosius I survive. And of these, ten dishes were issued by Licinius (three on behalf of his infant son, Licinius II, nominated caesar in 317). These are relatively small, light bowls with minimal decoration. Only three – the dish showing the mounted Constantine II from Kerch, now in the Hermitage, the Groß Bodungen fragment, and the dish of Valentinian I or II in Geneva – come close to the Missorium of Theodosius in their complexity of figural design, if not in size or weight.

History, archaeology, economics

It has been traditional in discussions of the Missorium of Theodosius and other largitio silver plate to incorporate an excursus on the institution of largitio, its operation, administration and function. Although this helps to frame a context in which to understand the artefacts in question, it should be borne in mind that the sources of the information cited are limited and our understanding of the practice of imperial largitio is by no means complete, as debates in recent work of numismatic and economic historians make clear.[11] Key sources of information are the Theodosian and Justianic law codes, the Notitia Dignitatum, an early fifth-century list of civil and military officials, and a range of literary sources, from the highly problematic Historia Augusta to the letters of Symmachus and the panegyric of Corippus.[12] I will present the historical facts as concisely as possible, focusing on those aspects of the institution of largitio which relate directly to our understanding of the place of silver plate in imperial donatives.

The production of silver plate to be distributed by the emperor on ceremonial occasions came under the control of an official called the *Comes Sacrarum Largitionum*, whose office was created as part of Constantine's administrative reforms, replacing the earlier *Rationales Summarum*. His primary responsibility, however, was the issue and striking of coinage generally.[13] Plate was probably not the predominant form of imperial largitio, which was far more likely to have been coins, especially gold solidi which could be minted in multiples for such occasions. Ingots and luxury clothing were also presented.[14] Largitio in some form was given on a range of imperial occasions, such as regnal anniversaries (held every five or ten years), but also on the emperor's ascension, at a victory or before a battle, or at New Year in those years when the emperor assumed the consulship. While this list of potential occasions for the giving of largitio is large, the plates bearing inscriptions (which excludes only the Kerch dish with a mounted emperor and the Groß Bodungen fragment) all indicate that they were made for regnal anniversaries. The recipients of largitio were both military and civilian, though this distinction is perhaps less clear-cut than it seems, since imperial officials (such as the *Comes Sacrarum Largitionum*) received military pay and rations. For soldiers, largitio was an institutionalized bonus from the time of Diocletian (and perhaps earlier), and from at least 360 AD consisted of a minimum of five gold solidi and a pound of silver on an imperial accession, and five solidi alone on quinquennial anniversaries.[15] This would suggest that largitio is closely connected with the increased importance of the army to the emperor in the fourth century.

While the known examples of largitio silver are all from the fourth century, the institution of largitio was current from at least that century until the reign of Justinian in the sixth, seeming to die out in the seventh.[16] The most common explanation proposed by economic historians for the disappearance of largitio silver plate after the fourth century links it to the disappearance of silver coins produced for general circulation.[17] Yet the fact that the rare silver coinages of the fifth and sixth centuries were probably minted for ceremonial occasions complicates the issue slightly, since this would not seem to rule out similar occasional productions of plate. There are dangers in placing too much weight on an argument *ex silentio*, yet by analogy with the silver coinage if largitio plate was produced in the fifth and sixth centuries perhaps it was in similarly reduced quantities, which would make its total loss less surprising.[18]

While the above discussion makes it clear that imperial largitio in general, including silver plate, plays a significant role in late Roman economic history, I do not want to lose sight of the individual items of surviving largitio silver as well as the recipients of these items. Although they cannot be identified as individuals, they should be considered nevertheless, since they formed the main audience for the imperial imagery on largitio silver. Receiving this largitio was a financial bonus for them, as well as an affirmation of their place in the imperial hierarchy and their relationship with the emperor. What did largitio mean to its recipients, and how is this reflected in the treatment of the surviving examples? In an attempt to answer these questions, I present a descriptive survey of the known items of imperial largitio silver and the archaeological contexts of their discovery, to the extent that these are recoverable. This will be followed by a comparison between the roles of silver plate and coins as forms of largitio, which raises some wider issues of the uses and perception of wealth in late antiquity.

The 19 known pieces of largitio silver break down into a number of discrete groups. The earliest of these is the group of three hoards associated with Licinius I, Constantine's co-emperor from 313 to 324. The largest of these in terms of the number of vessels it contains is the so-called Munich Treasure (Fig. 1.3), consisting of a total of nine bowls, five of which were definitely given as imperial largito, as well as a hollow silver repoussé bust of Licinius.[19] The bowls comprise first, three shallow bowls with coin-like portrait medallions stamped in their centres of Licinius and his infant son, Licinius II, who had been appointed junior emperor (caesar) in 317. The busts are enclosed by legends indicating that the bowls were issued for the quinquennalia in 321–22 AD of Licinius II.[20] Secondly, there are two inscribed bowls issued by one and two (unnamed) caesars, respectively, commemorating the making of vows for a decennalia.[21] The inscriptions, which run around the midpoint of the interior wall, form the bowls' only decoration. These bowls too were probably made around in 321–2, and their inscriptions are thought to refer to Licinius II and Constantine's two sons, Crispus and Constantine II, who were also caesars.[22] The first three bowls each weigh about one Roman pound, whereas the second two weigh about one and a half Roman pounds.[23] The rest of the hoard is made up of four undecorated silver bowls, only two of which weigh a pound or more. The findspot of the hoard was (allegedly) in the eastern part of the empire. Several bowls have stamps or punched inscriptions indicating manufacture in Nicomedia, Antioch and Naissus.[24]

If we assume that this group was the possession of one individual, what can this tell us about him and the silver plate? The five pieces of largitio silver are made in different parts of the empire, but around the same time. Three definitely (and probably a fourth) commemorate the quinquennalia of the caesar Licinius II, while one possibly commemorates the quinquennalia of Crispus and Constantine II, which was celebrated in the same year. The five bowls fall into two groups, each of which weighs 3 pounds, and it is tempting to suggest from this that they were given on two separate occasions during the quinquennalia year 321–22.[25] The amount given per donativum would have depended on the owner's rank, which is unlikely to have changed in this short period. But it is also possible that a donativum could be made up of a number of different types of vessel, just as it might include a number of different coin types. Despite their similarities, the two caesar bowls seem to have been made in two separate workshops, which suggests the homogeneity of imperial largitio at this time, and that several different workshops (like several different mints) might provide silver for a donativum. The imperial bust – not a standard largitio offering – also suggests a military context, as its construction resembles similar imperial busts that are thought to have decorated military standards.[26]

We do not know the rank of the owner of the Munich Treasure, yet one would guess it was not especially high, both on account of the weight of the silver, six times the minimum largitio donativum of 1 pound of silver, and the quality of the workmanship. This is not especially skilful and the use of lathe turning and die stamping suggests production in large numbers.[27] There is also the evidence of the remaining four pieces of plate in the hoard. Three of these are identical bowls of decreasing sizes with broad projecting rims, which are edged with beading in the two larger ones. This shape and decoration are extremely characteristic of fourth-century domestic silver plate, a close parallel being found in the Kaiseraugst Treasure.[28] The fourth bowl has a flat base with a simple rosette in the centre and a vertical fluted edge. It belongs to a type which spanned the second half of the third century and the first half of the fourth.[29] There is no evidence that these bowls were given as largitio, and given their domestic parallels it seems likely that the owner acquired them privately. This does not necessarily imply great wealth on his part, since the bowls are small (their combined total weight is 597g, under 2 Roman pounds) and without any decoration beyond beading.

There is also the question of the reason for the burial of the Munich Treasure. It has usually been suggested that the most likely date is around the year 324 when Licinius was defeated by Constantine. Yet in suggesting that the date of the burial coincides with Licinius' defeat, one must confront the question, not often asked in this context, of how politically charged were these and other largitio vessels? Is it plausible to suggest that these bowls could have been hidden to conceal support of Licinius? Or does defeat simply provide a context of unrest and uncertainty when someone might (conceivably) have concealed his valuables? After all, these constituted not only items of plate which he had received as imperial largitio, but also a few pieces of domestic silver which together with the largitio could have served as a financial reserve. However, the bust of Licinius associated with the hoard was crushed before its burial, suggesting the deliberate destruction of the image of a now discredited emperor (perhaps with the intention of reclaiming the metal as scrap once a safe period of time had passed). Since there are two other groups of largitio silver plate issued by Licinius surviving (making him the emperor most represented in this corpus), we cannot dismiss the political question entirely. Are we dealing with an accident of survival, and if so was this survival a result of his defeat, which led to greater numbers of his supporters burying the wealth they had accrued in his service? Or did Licinius produce unusually large numbers of largitio bowls?

The remaining vessels that bear Licinius' name are earlier than those in the Munich Treasure, since they commemorate his decennalia in 317 AD. A group of five near-identical bowls was found at Niš, former Yugoslavia, in 1901. It was dispersed among several museums, including the British Museum which acquired one bowl (Fig. 1.4). The bowls have a laurel wreath engraved in the centre with the legend SIC X, SIC XX (as ten, so twenty). Around the edge of the bowl the legend LICINI AUGUSTE SEMPER VINCAS (Emperor Licinius, may you always conquer) is stamped with letter punches between incised parallel lines. Perhaps the most interesting point about these bowls is that they are each stamped NAISS, an abbreviation of Naissus, the ancient name for Niš, and thus are highly unusual among silver plate for being found in the place where they were made. The third group of plate issued by Licinius was found in Červenbreg, Bulgaria, in 1952, and consists of two flat dishes with vertical fluted rims (the same shape as the rosette dish in the Munich Treasure), in the centre of each of which is a stamped medallion showing a profile bust of Licinius, encircled by the legend LICINIUS INVICT AUG

1.4   Largitio bowl of Licinius I from Niš, London, British Museum (© The British Museum)

OB DIEM X SUORUM (Licinius, unconquered emperor, on the occasion of his tenth anniversary).[30] These dishes are the heaviest among all the groups discussed, weighing 620 g and 635 g, about 2 Roman pounds each, and were found together with a silver plate (with a rosette in the centre and narrow projecting rim decorated with vertical lines and beading) 40 cm in diameter, weighing 1.260 kg, slightly under 4 pounds. This brings the total weight of the hoard to just under 8 pounds, which is the same as the Munich hoard, though achieved with fewer pieces. Thus, overall, the level of wealth of the two owners was perhaps not so different. The British Museum Niš bowl (the only one whose weight has been published) weighs just under 1 Roman pound at 304g. Its four companions in the hoard are of similar diameter, and probably therefore weigh about the same, which would bring the weight of this hoard to 5 pounds.[31] The three hoards seem to be relatively homogenous in their composition and the style of the items, despite the geographical distances between their findspots and places of manufacture (as far as these are known).

A further degree of homogeneity is found in iconography of the Munich, Niš and Červenbreg Treasures, which has close links with coin types. This parallel is most striking in the stamped portrait medallions of Licinius I and II found in the centre of three vessels in the Munich hoard and two vessels in the Červenbreg hoard (Fig. 1.5). The portraits in the Munich hoard (one of Licinius I and two of Licinius II, distinguished principally by the presence or absence of facial hair) are frontal, whereas those on the Červenbreg plates (both of Licinius I) are in profile. These medallions resemble coins both in their method of production (die stamping) and in the portraits themselves with their surrounding legends, which can be matched with coin types (Fig. 1.6).[32] The portraits on the Munich Treasure are particularly interesting in this context, since they represent a rare early example of frontality in coin portraits, which – despite the trend towards frontality in other types of imperial portraiture – remain, for the most part, profile busts throughout the fourth century. Although the methods of coin production are not replicated as directly in the other vessels in the three hoards associated with Licinius, the Niš bowls have stamped inscriptions and echo numismatic legends and iconography. Their design of a central laurel wreath with the decennalia vows inscribed inside it is identical to a common type of coin reverse for commemorating such anniversaries, in use since the Tetrarchy. The language of the inscriptions on these bowls, and on the caesar bowls from the Munich Treasure, closely resembles that of coin legends in its use of conventional and abbreviated honorific formulas. What are the implications of these numismatic parallels? They certainly reinforce the point that largitio silver should be seen as developing in a military context as an extension of the practice of distributing commemorative coinage, especially multiples, on special occasions. If – and this is by no means certain – largitio silver is principally a fourth-century phenomenon, and the vessels issued by Licinius are an early stage in its formation, it would seem that the craftsmen commissioned to produce it extended some of the simpler features of coin design to their work.

1.5   Munich Treasure, detail of stamped medallion portrait on largitio bowl of Licinius II, Munich, Archäologische Staatsammlung, Museum für Vor- und Frühgeschichte

1.6   Aureus of Licinius I commemorating the quinquennalia of Licinius II (© The British Museum)

Among the other surviving examples of largitio silver, there is another 'grouping' of finds analogous to that of the Licinius dishes: the three Kerch dishes, issued by Constantius II and found in graves in Kerch, ancient Panticapaeum, on the north coast of the Black Sea, which was the capital of the Bosporan kingdom.[33] The precise nature of the links between the Bosporan kingdom and the Roman Empire is not known, but there seem to have been fairly friendly relations between the two states, with artistic interchange attested. In 362 the Bosporans asked the emperor, Julian, Constantius' successor, for protection of their lands in return for tribute. Whether they received this is not known, but in around 370 their kingdom collapsed under attack from the Huns.[34] The three plates were found with other examples of fourth-century Roman silver plate in richly furnished graves of Bosporan

nobles. Discovered in 1891 and 1904 through a mixture of looting and controlled excavation, the graves have been dated through coin finds to the latter half of the fourth century.[35] Two of the dishes have a similar, if rather unusual, design executed in engraving, niello and gilding. In the centre of each is an engraved medallion with a profile bust of Constantius II. These busts bear some resemblance to the portrait medallions in the Munich and Červenbreg Treasures discussed above, but are engraved into the surface of the dishes rather than stamped. They evoke coins to the extent that the craftsman seems to have used a coin portrait as his model when he carved them. But the numismatic analogy is limited here, since around this medallion on each bowl are three separate zones of decoration: a frieze of vine leaves, followed by the inscription VOTIS XX D N CONSTANTI AUGUSTI ('On the occasion

1.7   Largitio bowl of Constantius II from Kerch 'with arcading', St Petersburg, Hermitage Museum

1.8   Largitio bowl with mounted emperor from Kerch, St Petersburg, Hermitage Museum

of the vicennalia of our lord the emperor Constantius'), followed by an engraved wave decoration. One of the bowls has a fourth zone of decoration, an arcade with twisted columns and arches, with garlands hanging between the columns (Fig. 1.7). Despite this difference, the bowls have approximately the same diameter: 23.3 cm and 24.5 cm, the slightly smaller one has the extra zone of decoration. Their weights are also identical, and are inscribed on the underside: '1 pound, 11 ounces, 8 scruples', just under two (Roman) pounds.[36] The bowl without arcading was only one of a number of Roman silver vessels in the pair of adjoining graves where it was found: two silver jugs with ovoid bodies, and a bowl with a projecting beaded rim (like those in the Munich Treasure) were found with it.[37] The third largitio bowl is the best known of the finds from Kerch, being like the Missorium of Theodosius an important example of early Byzantine art (Fig. 1.8). It is engraved with the image of a mounted emperor dressed in military costume, nimbed, flanked on the left by a foot soldier whose shield is decorated with a chi-rho, and on the right by a Nike, who holds a wreath in one hand, a palm branch in the other. Although this dish has no inscription naming the emperor represented on it, he has long been identified as Constantius II – not improbable given the presence of the other two plates with his portrait in the same cemetery.[38] This dish too was found with a hemispherical bowl with beaded rim, almost identical to that found with the bowl without arcading.[39]

The findspot of these plates outside the borders of the Roman Empire raises a different set of issues about the function of such vessels. The three testify to relations between the Roman Empire and the Bosporans in the reign of Constantius II that are not otherwise known from historical sources. It was once suggested that they were local productions, a somewhat dubious hypothesis based on the idea that the flatness and frontality of the mounted emperor must be the work of 'barbarian' artists.[40] Such a theory does not attempt to explain the function of these pieces – why the emperor's anniversary should be commemorated outside the empire – and isolates them from the other surviving imperial largitio. The alternative to a theory of local production, is to assume that the plates were given to one or more important individuals in the Bosporan kingdom. If so, did they receive them through serving in the Roman army (suggesting that they were brought to Kerch by their recipient, who was presented with them in Roman territory), or as a form of tribute (recognizing the role of their kingdom as a buffer state protecting the frontiers of the empire)? And how were the non-official jugs and bowls acquired? Since these could quite possibly be later than the largitio plates, we have evidence of relations between the Romans and the Bosporans in the second half of the fourth century which included the consumption of luxury goods. The presence of these in graves of the elite of this kingdom indicates that they were valued possessions, though whether this is related to the links with the Roman world to which they testify is uncertain, a tantalizing possibility.[41]

Two other largitio plates have figural decoration comparable to that of the Missorium of Theodosius, and the Kerch rider plate. The largitio plate of Valentinian is a lone find which was discovered in the vicinity of the river Arve, near Geneva in 1721 (Fig. 1.9).[42] Despite its very worn surface, the inscription LARGITAS DN VALENTINIANI AUGUSTI (Largesse of our lord, the emperor Valentinian) can be read around the upper rim of the plate. The relief scene on the plate shows the emperor in military costume, flanked by three soldiers on either side, with a collection of weapons in the exergue. The fragmentary Groß Bodungen largitio plate forms part of a so-called 'Hacksilber' hoard of assorted silver fragments, coins and an ingot.[43] Seven pieces join to form the lower part of a plate 26 cm in diameter, on which can be seen the legs of a figure covered by a chlamys with a segmentum, seated on a cushioned throne, flanked on one side by a pair of feet protruding from beneath a large oval shields, like those of the guards on the Missorium of Theodosius (Fig. 1.2). The shoulder of the seated figure and parts of two

1.9 Largitio plate of Valentinian I or II, Geneva, Musée d'Art et d'Histoire (J.M. Yersin/© Musée d'Art et d'Histoire, Ville de Genève, inv. no. C 1241)

more shields are also visible. Neither the head of the emperor nor any part of an inscription survive, making close identification impossible, but the close iconographic, stylistic and technical parallels to the Missorium of Theodosius suggest it is most likely contemporary. The hoard as a whole comprises material from the second half of the fourth century, and was probably deposited in the early fifth.[44] Like the other items in the hoard, it represents only a small portion of the original vessel, which must therefore have been chopped up and divided before the formation of the hoard. It is often assumed that hoards like that from Groß Bodungen, found outside the borders of the empire, represent barbarian loot, broken up before being melted down. Yet this does not explain why only a few fragments of the Groß Bodungen largitio plate survive. Grünhagen, in his study of the Groß Bodungen hoard, argues

The emperor's gifts   25

that the combination of silver fragments, coins and ingots, typical of scrap silver hoards of this period, suggests that the silver fragments measured by weight served as a form of currency both inside and outside the empire.[45] Thus such hoards need not necessarily have been looted (or might have been looted in the form of scrap), and the vessels could well have been broken up within the Roman Empire.

I have already suggested that the treatment of the Missorium of Theodosius before its burial indicates that at this point it was considered as bullion, which raises the possibility that the person who buried it was not the person to whom it was originally given.[46] Likewise the Groß Bodungen plate appears not to have remained in the possession of its original recipient and at the time of burial its bullion value had clearly superseded its status value as an imperial gift. It seems more likely that the three hoards of Licinius' largitio and the three Constantius II plates from Kerch were deposited by their original owners, and that their status value played a role in this, although non-Roman cultural practices caused the Kerch plates to be buried as grave goods rather than concealed for security. In none of these cases were largitio dishes hoarded with coins, which is interesting because the recipients of largitio were likely to have received coins as well as plate. The Kaiseraugst Treasure, however, presents an example of a mixed hoard of coins and plate, which includes a largitio plate issued by Constans and silver ingots given as largitio by the usurper Magnentius.[47] It contains 183 silver coins, including 17 multiples, which date to the years 330–49 AD and are in mint condition. They include a significant number issued to commemorate the regnal anniversaries of Constantius II and Constans in the years 338 and 343.[48] The largitio plate, like some of the multiples, commemorates the decennalia of Constans, with a central medallion encircled by the inscription: AUGUSTUS CONSTANS DAT LAETA DECENNIA VICTOR/ SPONDENS OM[I]NIBUS TER TRICENNALIA FAUSTIS ('Augustus Constans, victorius, celebrates ten years of prosperity, promising solemnly, after having had auspicious omens three times, to celebrate his thirty years' jubilee').[49] This is the most sophisticated largitio inscription encountered so far, as it is written in two hexameters rather than prose. The plate itself, while not featuring any major figural decoration, is skilfully decorated with inlaid geometric designs in niello, partially gilded, in the central medallion and around the rim, where they are interspersed with generic busts of young men. It is also large, measuring around 55 cm and weighing almost 3 kg, making it nearest to the Missorium of Theodosius in size of all the known largitio plates. Given the findspot of the treasure within the ruins of a late Roman fort, a military owner seems likely, presumably one of relatively high status.

Was the motive for hoarding *donativa* in the form of coins and multiples financial prudence or commemoration? And can that tell us anything about the way that largitio silver plate was perceived by its recipients? There is a substantial amount of evidence that coins, especially the multiple issues of solidi ('medallions'), were preserved in ways outside their role of currency. Gold jewellery which uses coins in elaborate settings of pierced open-work (*opus interrasile*) is one manifestation of the 'non-financial' attitudes to coined money in late antiquity. This type of jewellery becomes increasingly common from the third century AD onwards, and whereas some examples favour aurei of the second century, others incorporate multiples.[50] One of the most elaborate examples of the latter is a set of four pendants (findspot unknown) which would have been hung from a necklace, now divided among Dumbarton Oaks, the Louvre and the British Museum. Each contains a gold double solidus of Constantine I, in three cases dating to 321 AD, and in one case to 324 AD, commemorating the consulship of his sons Crispus and Constantine II in those years. This is set to show the obverse profile portrait of Constantine I with a radiate crown, and surrounded by elaborate *opus interrasile* scrollwork into which are set six miniature busts in tondos, probably of mythological figures.[51] Another example is a fragment of a girdle or gorget in the Walters Art Gallery, which preserves a 9-solidus multiple of Constantius II minted in Nicomedia, in an *opus interrasile* setting.[52] A woman's body chain from the Hoxne Treasure is decorated with a solidus of Gratian set in an octagonal border.[53]

All these pieces, and others like them, have a dual function of display: of wealth and of the emperor's image (the obverse is invariably the side of the coin visible from the front of the jewellery, although the settings do not conceal the reverse, which can be seen from the underside). These same functions arguably operate in largitio silver plate; indeed the concrete display of wealth is a key factor in the ownership of any silver plate. However, when coins are used in jewellery they are *de facto* taken out of circulation. While a nine-solidus multiple would never have had a wide circulation, the mounting of multiples corresponds to the use of coinage in the Roman and Byzantine world in ways which are distinctly alien to modern economic thought.[54] These included the tendency not to see the facilitation of commerce as the prime function of coinage. Hendy comments on this in discussing a fifth century formula preserved in Cassiodorus' *Variae* for appointing someone to the *comitiva sacrarum largitionum:* 'here the acknowledged end of coining is the circulation of the imperial portrait, and ... the means only are provided by the operation of commerce: the relative emphasis is not at all untypical'.[55]

Ambiguous or unexpected attitudes to the use of coinage also occur in Hendy's discussion of private wealth in the *Byzantine Monetary Economy*. Although this is primarily an account of Middle Byzantine attitudes, drawing predominately on 11th century sources, a certain degree of continuity with the Early Byzantine period can be observed. His statement that, for private individuals, '[money] was not necessarily desirable beyond a certain measure. It could not be gainfully employed or invested in any large quantity in a society where trade, industry and credit played a very restricted role', seems to correspond to Finley's assessment of the character of the Roman economy.[56] In the wills, dowries and assorted anecdotes which Hendy uses as his sources, wealth is expressed in buildings, land, livestock and movable possessions, frequently luxury items such as jewellery, plate and clothing. Coinage, he argues, is absent from such accounts, since: 'It did not easily and obviously express either status or even the possession of wealth itself – in other words, it could not be used, worn or otherwise publicly and successfully exhibited.'[57] Incorporating coins into jewellery in this earlier period was perhaps one way of overcoming the 'undisplayability' of coins. Although there is plenty of archaeological evidence for the amassment of large hoards of coins in the later Roman period, this may be a phenomenon that occurred at a relatively lower level in the social scale. The wealthiest individuals (both in the fourth and the eleventh centuries) found it preferable that coins should be converted into concrete, material wealth, such as land, houses, luxury clothing, jewellery, tableware. These were not so much *signs of* wealth, as they are perceived today, but wealth itself. The sign and the signified were the same thing, and silver plate was the perfect medium for this ontological blurring.

Largitio silver and imperial iconography

Let us return now to the Missorium of Theodosius and examine the second aspect of largitio silver which contributes to its significance for our understanding of late antique society and culture. What role do the Missorium, and the other largitio plates discussed above, play in the formulation of imperial iconography in a period when that iconography was undergoing a radical development, away from the forms it had taken for the previous three centuries towards those which it would assume for as many as ten centuries in Byzantium? I will begin by looking at the iconography of the Missorium in detail, focusing especially on its relation to imperial iconography in other media.

The interpretation of the iconography of the Missorium has never been subject to any real controversy. A few minor debates have arisen: are the two co-emperors Valentinian II and Arcadius or Honorius and Arcadius?[58] Who exactly is the female personification?[59] Can the official be identified with any particular individual or position?[60] Do the five putti represent five years (each or singly), five dioceses in the eastern half of the empire, the *gaudium publicum*, or simply the attributes of Tellus?[61] The relatively minor nature of such quibbles is revealed by the fact that whatever position is taken on these issues, it makes little difference to the overall 'meaning' of the plate, which it is agreed is to glorify the emperor through the hierarchical image of enthronement and through the female personification, which suggests the abundance and fecundity of Theodosius' reign.[62] Yet this 'uncomplicated' interpretation suppresses the more exceptional aspects of Missorium. Its greatest interest lies not with *what* it says, but with *how*, visually, it says it. The circular surface of the plate is divided into two fields: the main field with the representation of the three emperors enthroned beneath a pediment, which occupies about two-thirds of the surface, and the exergue with the reclining figure of Tellus, which fills the remaining third. This 'split', marked by the multiple horizontal lines of the podium upon which the imperial group and their guards stand, in addition to being a convenient compositional device to fill the picture surface represents a deeper division between two iconographic traditions of imperial imagery in the Roman Empire. Janus-like, it places back to back prospective and retrospective modes of representing the emperor and his power. The retrospective mode is exemplified by the classicizing figure of Tellus in the exergue; the prospective by the frontal, hierarchical figures of Theodosius, his co-regents, and their bodyguards. Before examining the way this juxtaposition works, I want to analyse the nature of the pro- and retrospective elements more closely.

First, the retrospective. The figure of Tellus, suggesting the fecundity and prosperity of the emperor's reign, has a distinguished pedigree going back to the earliest imperial art in the reign of Augustus. While the most frequently cited parallel in Augustan art for the Theodosian figure is the relief panel on the south-east side of the Ara Pacis (the so-called Tellus relief), perhaps the closest parallel is the figure on the lowest part of the cuirass of the Prima Porta Augustus (Fig. 1.10). This figure, more unequivocally identifiable as Tellus (or a related earth goddess) than that on the Ara Pacis, reclines on the ground, supporting herself on one arm. She has a cornucopia filled with fruit and grain, and two children nestle by her. Like the figure on the Missorium she wears a wreath, and her gaze is directed upwards, towards the complex assemblage of figures arranged on the cuirass which together articulate the concept of the divinely guaranteed victory of Augustus' reign.[63] A highly naturalistic, classicizing style is employed in both the Ara Pacis and the Prima Porta statue, which is echoed in the classicism of the Tellus figure on the Missorium.

Imagery of fertility and abundance was a vital part of the Augustan imperial ideology of the rebirth of Rome and the anticipation of a golden age under Augustus.[64] Like many aspects of Augustan imperial iconography, Tellus continued to be used by subsequent emperors. Following the model of the Prima Porta Augustus, she appears on both Flavian and Antonine cuirassed imperial statues.[65] She is particularly popular under Hadrian, where coins with a reclining figure of Tellus and the legend TELLUS STABILITA are issued to commemorate the renewal of peace and prosperity in the empire under his reign.[66] Domitian and Septimius Severus also place her on coins to commemorate the Ludi Saeculares held in their reigns.[67] Tellus is not just a personification of the earth's abundance, but also appears in imperial iconography in a cosmological context, paired with Oceanus to represent the earth and the sea. This is how she is shown on a relief on the Arch of Galerius at Thessalonike (Fig. 1.11), which shows the four tetrarchs, flanked by Mars and Roma and other mythological and allegorical figures, while Tellus and Oceanus recline in respective corners (the heavens are represented by the two sky gods which support the seated figures of the augusti). Yet apart from this example Tellus is not common in the imperial iconography of the fourth century, nor was she much used in the third.[68] What impact, therefore, did the inclusion of Tellus in the scene on the Missorium have on its viewers? Does Tellus simply represent abundance as guaranteed by Theodosius' reign and his dominion of the *oikoumene*, or does the image at the same time carry historic resonances which associate Theodosius with the peaceful prosperity

1.10 Statue of Augustus from Prima Porta, Rome, Vatican Museums: detail of Tellus on cuirass (Moscioni/ Deutsches Archäologisches Institut, Rome, neg. 62.1794)

1.11 Arch of Galerius, Thessalonike, southwest pillar: enthroned tetrarchs with Oceanus and Tellus (Magni/Deutsches Archäologisches Institut, Rome, neg. 79.464)

of the earlier empire? The classicism of the representation encourages this idea, and certainly Tellus stands out in the imperial iconography of the late empire by her association with peace rather than war and victory. Yet there are differences between this image and the earlier Augustan or Hadrianic images. The putti of the Missorium are not the passively nurtured children of the Augustan reliefs, and while Hadrianic coin types show Tellus with four children representing the seasons, on the Missorium the putti present the fruits of the earth directly to the emperor, holding them in respectfully veiled hands, just as the official on the Missorium covers his hands to receive his codicillary diptych.[69] Despite being predominately retrospective in character, the exergue of the Missorium has been adapted to the late antique ceremonial with which it is paired.

This brings us to the prospective elements of the Missorium's style and iconography. The main scene of enthronement and investiture is characterized above all by extreme symmetry and frontality, which are easily recognizable as characteristics of the transformation of classical art into mediaeval art, the beginnings of which are conventionally associated with the Tetrarchy at the end of the third and the beginning of the fourth century. Can the Missorium help us to understand why frontality became the favoured mode of imperial representation in late antiquity and beyond? To answer this question, one needs to look backwards as well as forwards, since by the end of the fourth century when the Missorium was made, its 'prospective' composition and iconography already had a history which is significant for their understanding. The image of the emperor has rightly been pinpointed by art historians as the area where the transformation of the classical modes of representing the human figure first occurred.[70] The art of the Tetrarchy is perhaps the first point at which frontality was combined with 'non-classical' proportions, and a linear style of carving which produced sharp contrasts between light and shade, as in the porphyry statues of the four tetrarchs re-used in St Mark's, Venice. However, the frontal representation of the emperor can be traced back to monuments from the end of the second century AD.

The Column of Marcus Aurelius (180–92 AD) is perhaps the first major imperial monument where a significant proportion of the representations of the emperor are frontal. The contrast is particularly noticeable in comparison to the Column of Trajan, the prototype of the historiated column, erected around 70 years earlier (110–13 AD).[71] The scene of *adlocutio*, or the emperor addressing his troops – a frequent event within these campaign narratives – is one where the change first makes itself felt. On Trajan's column such scenes tend to be shown laterally, so that the emperor speaking from a podium occupies one side of the composition and his audience the other. He is shown either in profile or three-quarters view. In contrast, the adlocutio scenes of the column of Marcus Aurelius tend to move the podium from which he speaks to the centre of the composition, so that it is flanked by soldiers on either side, who turn their heads towards the centre. The viewer is presented with the back view of those soldiers standing directly in front of the platform. The emperor is no longer shown from the side, but from the front. Ernst Kitzinger has written that here 'the imperial person, rather than turning to his listeners, is in effect presented ceremonially to us, the beholders'.[72] Yet this is not entirely true: rather the viewer's position is aligned with that of the front row of soldiers, whose backs they see as though they stood behind them, so that the viewer becomes the subject of empire. The move towards symmetry from contraposto can be seen both in the centralized podium and the tendency for the emperor to be flanked by an equal number of supporting figures on either side (usually two, sometimes four), who are of course shown slightly shorter.[73] Frontality is only one of the modes used on the column of Marcus Aurelius to depict the emperor, who is represented many times in the whole frieze of the column. Other Aurelian monuments, such as the panels from a triumphal arch preserved on the Arch of Constantine and in the Palazzo dei Conservatori, show the emperor's adlocutio in the old mode. But the use of frontality on the column is significant because it is not a new style which comes into being to serve a new function (as one might argue is the case with the porphyry tetrarchic representations), but represents a deliberate change in a scene for which a 'formula' already exists. Moreover the new formula was persuasive, as its reoccurrence on the panels of the Arches of Septimius Severus (203 AD) in the Roman Forum and Leptis Magna, as well as the Severan Arch of the Argentarii in Rome, shows.[74]

The next significant change in the use of frontal compositions is the expansion in the range of scenes for which they are used. Our key evidence is again triumphal arches, those of Galerius at Thessalonike and of Constantine in Rome (300 and 312–15 AD respectively, so about 100 years after the monuments in which we see frontal representations enter the imperial iconographic repertoire). In these we see the development of the frontal enthronement, where the emperor is acting less within a narrative, than being 'presented ceremonially' in Kitzinger's words, which are more applicable here. Thus the Four Emperor relief on the Arch of Galerius (Fig. 1.11) shows the two senior members of the tetrarchy seated side by side in its centre, flanked by the standing figures of the two junior members and a series of conceptually juxtaposed gods and personifications (of which Tellus and Oceanus are two). The key factors shaping this composition are frontality and symmetry, with the traditional imperial narrative of war and victory conspicuously absent. Although the Constantinian reliefs on the Arch of Constantine show him performing traditional actions of the emperor in Rome – speaking to the people, distributing largesse – at the same time they enthrone the emperor in the very centre of the composition (Fig. 1.12). He stands on a podium or sits on a raised throne, but unlike the reliefs on the column of Marcus Aurelius, no spectators are shown standing in front of it; the emperor is at the front of the picture plane, which is thereby reduced to the depth of a single figure.

These developments allow us to see how the Missorium's image of Theodosius forms part of a trend in imperial iconography which had been developing over the two centuries since the creation of Trajan's column.[75] This development takes place in monumental sculpture; the Missorium, on the other hand, is silver plate, not – so far as we can tell from the surviving

1.12 Arch of Constantine, Rome, north side: Constantine distributing largesse (Deutsches Archäologisches Institut, Rome, neg. 1546)

evidence – a traditional medium for imperial representation in the earlier empire.[76] How does the Missorium relate to the earlier monumental images? Its composition and theme derive from the scenes of enthronement such as we saw on the Arches of Constantine and Galerius, rather than the long-standing schemata of historical relief. Although Theodosius is shown presenting a codicillary diptych to an official, this action – as has often been recognized – is subordinated within the composition to the exhibition of his own splendour.[77] The spectators in front of the emperor in the Aurelian relief and the crowds of onlookers of the Constantinian version are excluded, creating a simplified iconic image instead of a narrative one. Here links with numismatic imagery are visible, especially the coins of Constantine's sons, which often show the three brothers enthroned together.[78] Yet the plate's surface allows for a greater elaboration of detail than on a coin die. Indeed the details of costume and regalia, which are a noticeable feature of this plate, contribute significantly to the iconic character of the image. The status of Theodosius, Valentinian and Arcadius as augusti can be recognized by their jewelled diadems and their circular jewelled fibulae. Their tunics and chlamydes are decorated with elaborate segmenta (in real life probably made with gold thread).[79] This forms a pointed contrast to the costume of the official, who although he wears the same type of clothes as the augusti, fastens his chlamys with a crossbow fibula, and has less elaborate, smaller segmenta. These distinctions play an important role in early Byzantine representations of the emperor, as a comparison with the emperor Justinian and his attendants in the mid-sixth-century mosaic in S. Vitale, Ravenna shows (Fig. 1.13). There the richness of Justinian's purple chlamys with a gold segmentum, fastened by a fibula decorated with pearls

around a ruby, and his jewelled diadem contrast with the white chlamydes with purple segmenta, secured by crossbow fibulae, worn by his bare-headed attendants. The imperial bodyguards in both cases also have their appropriate regalia of torques and large oval shields. Although imperial costume was significant in the earlier Roman Empire, it was less concerned with articulating distinctions in rank.[80]

1.13 Sanctuary mosaic, San Vitale, Ravenna: Justinian with Bishop Maximian and their retinue (Bartl/Deutsches Archäologisches Institut, Rome, neg. 57.1744)

Another feature of the Missorium which is absent both from monumental reliefs and coin images is the use of architectural elements to form a frame which accentuates hierarchic frontality of the image. Above the heads of the three emperors is a triangular pediment, the lintel of which forms an arch in the centre. It is supported by four Corinthian columns, one at each end and one at either side of the arch. The spaces between these columns form three niches in each of which is the throne of an emperor. Theodosius is enframed by the central arch and his head rises into it, since he is represented on a larger scale. The other figures in the composition are carefully aligned with the columns, so as to detract as little as possible from the emphasis that the bays give to the three augusti. In fact, architectural frames are a common component of late antique design, especially in Christian sarcophagi where scenes from the Old and New Testament are separated from one another by the columns of a continuous colonnade across the front of the sarcophagus.[81] There, the columnar frame provides a means of unifying a series of episodes juxtaposed for their typological meanings. However the architectural element of the Missorium is designed to express the dominance of a single figure.

The architectural frame represented on the Missorium has caused much comment ever since the early twentieth-century publications of Diocletian's villa at Split drew attention to a very similar pediment there. This was placed over the entrance to the residential quarters of the complex, which was situated at one end of a narrow courtyard bordered on its long sides by the facades of a temple precinct and a mausoleum. This area was interpreted by some scholars as a type of open air atrium, enabling the pediment to be read as 'a gable of glorification' where 'the emperor appears to those gathered in the atrium'.[82] Thus Diocletian's villa was seen as a prototype for the palaces of Byzantium and their ceremonial, and the Missorium was used as support for this argument, since it was supposed that the image on the Missorium reflected actual palace architecture and court ceremonial connected with it. Indeed it is possible that the Missorium gave rise to this reconstruction of Diocletian's villa in the first place. The circularity of this argument is clear. More recent scholarship, aided by archaeological excavation in Split during the 1960s and 70s, has questioned whether it is correct to see the private residence of a retired emperor as a prototype of the Byzantine palace, and has criticized the theory that the pedimented entrance was used in any form of ceremonial connected to the courtyard outside.[83] Clearly, characterizing the function of the villa at Split is problematic, since Diocletian was the only emperor ever to retire (apart from his colleague Maximianus, whose retirement was both less whole-hearted and less permanent than Diocletian's), and thus the concept of a retirement villa is anomalous. Yet leaving aside the issue of the precise use of the Split pediment in its original context, its presence there establishes the form as one with symbolic resonance in late antique architecture, especially since the arched architrave reoccurs three times on the exterior facade of the seaward facing wall of the villa. The Missorium of Theodosius shows how well-suited this architectural structure is for emphasizing triangular, hierarchical arrangements of figures, whether or not it was used in this way at Split, and although it is unlikely that the Missorium is evoking any particular building, it does evoke monumental architecture in general.

I now want to return to my original observation about the 'divided' nature of the Missorium's iconography. We have seen how the exergue with the figure of Tellus and her attendant putti draws on a tradition of imperial iconography which goes back to Augustus, and enjoyed a revival under another 'classicizing' emperor, Hadrian. Although adapted to a certain extent within late antique conventions, this motif was chosen in part because of its history, to place Theodosius within an imperial tradition. Unlike the main scene of Theodosius and his co-emperors, which represent the beginning of the history of this type of image, the figures in the exergue stand near the end of their history. Why do we find these two images juxtaposed and what is their effect? The tetrarchic Luxor cult room, a now destroyed mural scheme recorded in nineteenth-century watercolour sketches, offers an important perspective on the transformation of the imperial image in late antiquity.[84] The most remarkable thing about this scheme seems to have been its representation of the tetrarchs in both naturalistic and frontal modes on different walls. Jaš Elsner has interpreted this double representation as a reaction to the tension implicit in naturalistic representations of the emperor which seek to embody both his human and divine status. The frontal portrayal of the tetrarchs in the cult niche places them in a context of 'divine otherness', whereas their representation among the procession of troops, which are shown moving towards the niche, places them in their secular context.[85] Here we have a split which we might parallel with that on the Missorium. Rather than being a split between the two natures of the emperor, it is between two ways of evoking his power. Yet why should such a split be required? Does Theodosius need to distance himself from the personification of Tellus in some way? Let us return to the issue of divinity. Theodosius was a Christian emperor whose reign is remembered for its anti-pagan legislation, although perhaps surprisingly there are no references to the Christianity of the empire on the plate. Elsner points out that Constantine's conversion was a crucial stage in the development of the imperial image, since it obliterated the problem of representing an emperor as both human and divine.[86] Instead the emperor imitates the divine image, just as, for his subjects, his rule is an imitation of the divine order where the emperor serves as a mediator between human and divine spheres.

To what extent does such a concept apply to Theodosius and his co-emperors on the Missorium? The scene of enthronement is redolent with divine connotations, both pagan and Christian. The throne is the seat both of gods (most famously Pheidias' Zeus at Olympia), and of emperors, who adopted it from divine imagery to offer intimations of their own divinity (albeit most often in a backless form like that on the Missorium).[87] A little-known late antique example which shows this particularly well is a headless porphyry statue of an emperor, probably Diocletian, sitting in a jewelled throne.[88] The image of Christ as Cosmocrator or universal emperor clearly borrows (pace Thomas Mathews) from such divine images of the emperor. The three imperial figures on the Missorium are nimbed – a representation of sacred radiance – and Valentinian and Honorius hold globes, while Valentinian also holds a sceptre. Both these items have a divine origin, as well as a long tradition of use as imperial insignia.[89] The context of this image's production in a Christian empire suggests that the pagan origin of such insignia is subsumed within their imperial connotations, and that the references to divinity should be read out from the image of emperor to that of Christ whom he imitates (despite the historical illogicality of such a move in modern eyes). The problem with this reading is the lack of any explicit Christian imagery or symbols on the Missorium. Could this be in any way connected to the presence of Tellus? Personifications are not highly charged religious figures, nevertheless it might have been thought inappropriate to combine an explicitly Christian image of the emperor with an iconographic motif intended to evoke the pre-Christian empire. It is worth noting that in San Vitale in Ravenna, the vault of the apse is framed by a band of stylized intertwined cornucopiae: in the sixth century the abundance of the earth is symbolized not by the image of the earth herself, but by her more neutral attribute. Another way of understanding the situation would be to say that the designer of the plate was acknowledging the conceptual divide between the iconic enthronement image and the naturalistic embodiment of the empire's prosperity.

The question of how to understand the image of a Christian emperor in a context which is not specifically Christian, is a complex one. It complicates Elsner's model of the transformation of the emperor's image in late antiquity, since his two case studies which enclose the period of the late empire, the Luxor cult room and the mosaics of San Vitale, are both drawn from the religious sphere. Other examples of silver imperial largitio, however, are more easily accommodated into his model. The Kerch plate with a mounted emperor (Fig. 1.8) and the largitio plate of Valentinian (Fig. 1.9) have explicit references to Christianity as the imperial religion. The nimbus around the head of Valentinian has a chi-rho superimposed on it, and the shield of the imperial bodyguard on the Kerch dish is decorated with a large chi-rho, like those on the shields of Justinian's bodyguards in San Vitale. These two largitio dishes come closer to the Missorium of Theodosius than any of the other surviving examples in the complexity of the images which they bear. Their subject matter, however, is more typical of imperial art of the fourth century than that of the Missorium: both plates represent the concept of imperial victory. In this context their use of the Christian symbol, the chi-rho, acknowledges the role of Christ as an enabler of that victory, and the victorious emperor as a model of Christ. At the same time, this evokes Constantine's Christian vision and victory at the Battle of the Milvian Bridge in 312 AD, highlighting the importance of Constantine as a pattern for all subsequent Christian emperors.[90]

Although the iconography of these two plates differs from that of the Missorium of Theodosius, their style can be described as prospective like that of the Missorium, dramatically more so in the case of the Kerch rider dish. Its representation of a mounted emperor – unnamed but generally identified as Constantius II – flanked by a Victory and a member of the imperial guard, shows a flattening of the picture plane, which is accentuated by the technique used to execute the image, namely engraving, with niello inlays and gilding. This produces a more dramatic impression of flatness than the low relief technique used in the Missorium. At the centre of the composition is the image of the emperor, whose upper body is presented frontally, although the horse on which he is mounted is shown in profile. As on the Missorium, the emperor's costume is represented in detail: he wears a short tunic decorated with segmenta, a decorated sword-belt, shoes and leggings. His horse's harness is similarly ornate. On his head, which is nimbed, is a jewelled diadem. Behind his horse is a soldier on foot, whose costume and regalia suggest he is an imperial bodyguard like those on the Missorium and the San Vitale mosaics.[91] In front of him stands a Victory, who holds a crown in her right hand (that nearest the emperor) and a palm in her left. A shield lies beneath the horse's hooves, a symbol of the defeated enemy. The scene on Valentinian's largitio

1.14 36-solidus multiple of Justinian (electrotype copy), London, British Museum: reverse (© The British Museum)

plate is both hierarchical and frontal – the emperor is flanked on either side by three soldiers. He is a little taller than them and raised slightly on a small platform. He wears a cuirass and chlamys (of which only the fibula is now visible, owing to the very worn state of the plate's surface), and holds a labarum in his left hand and a globe with a crown-bearing victory on the right. He is bareheaded, with a nimbus enclosing a chi-rho as described above. His soldiers wear crested helmets and carry large round shields with traces of animal emblems on them. In the exergue lie a shield, a sword and a helmet.[92]

It has generally been agreed that such images represent the concept of imperial victory in the abstract, as an imperial prerogative, rather than in reference to a specific victory.[93] Thus like the Missorium, the interpretation of these largitio plates has been straightforward. Again their art historical importance lies with the manner in which they present their subject, rather than what that subject represents, although these two cannot be completely separated here, since by creating an iconic image of the victorious emperor, the artist is contributing to an increasingly iconic concept of victory as an eternal attribute of the emperor, rather than attached to specific events. Such presentations of imperial victory are especially common in coin types, but also in other media between the fourth and sixth centuries. The iconography of the Kerch dish is echoed on the reverse of a gold solidus of Constantius II minted between 347 and 355, which shows the mounted emperor in profile greeted by a female personification of the Roman state.[94] Stylistically, however, the resemblance between this and the Kerch dish is slight. A much closer parallel is the 36-solidus multiple of Justinian (Fig. 1.14) from between 527 and 538 (once in the Cabinet des Médailles, now surviving only in an electrotype copy in the British Museum). It also depicts the emperor mounted carrying a spear, while a Victory with a palm and a trophy walks before his horse. The posture of Justinian on his horse mirrors that of Constantius on the Kerch dish: the lower part of the body is in profile together with the horse, while the upper half is turned frontally towards the viewer. The obverse is essentially a detail of Justinian's face from the reverse: nimbed, with exaggeratedly large eyes. Although his costume differs from that of Constantius on the Kerch plate (he wears full battle regalia), there is otherwise remarkably little difference between the two representations, and it is perhaps understandable that early scholars of the Kerch plate dated it to the sixth rather than the fourth century, since its links with the art of that period are so much more obvious.

The largitio plate of Valentinian also finds numismatic analogies, at least for the figure of the emperor who usually features alone on such issues.[95] Significant parallels exist in other media, however, for example the cuirassed figures of Honorius and Arcadius on the south side of their column base, who hold sceptres in one hand and victories in the other. Even closer is the figure of Honorius on the ivory diptych issued by the consul Probus (Fig. 1.15). On the left hand leaf he is represented cuirassed, diademed and nimbate, with a labarum in his right hand and a Victory with wreath and palm on a globe in his left. The Probus diptych makes the role of Christ in the emperor's victory yet more explicit: the labarum which Honorius holds is topped with a chi-rho, and bears the inscription IN NOMINE XPI VINCAS SEMPER (In the name of Christ, may you always be victorious). Thus the most striking parallels for the iconic images of the emperor that appear on Valentinian's and Constantius II's largitio plates are found in other media and postdate them.

I asked at the beginning of this section what role the largitio silver of the fourth century played in the formulation of imperial iconography in a key stage of that iconography's development. Having surveyed the iconography of the silver from a variety of different angles, I am now in a position to be able to answer this question, at least provisionally. We already saw in the first section of this chapter that the group of silver vessels associated with Licinius (and to a lesser extent the two medallion bowls from Kerch) have close links with coinage, but not with other media. In this second section it has become clear that those pieces of silver plate with more complex scenes generally appear to be at the forefront of the development of an iconic image of the emperor in the fourth century, much more so than coinage, although there are iconographic links between the two media. Overall, links exist not just between largitio plates and other metallic media such as coinage, but with the whole range of media used for imperial representation, from large-scale monumental sculpture, to mosaic and ivory. Taken altogether, these observations suggest a more important role for silver plate than that usually attributed to the 'minor arts'. Anne Kuttner's study of the Boscoreale cups, the only surviving examples of Augustan silverware with imperial iconography, has argued that they represent a small-scale copy of the relief sculpture of a lost Augustan monument.[96] I have shown that for fourth-century silver with imperial iconography, a very different set of circumstances are at work.

1.15 Probus
Diptych, Aosta,
Cathedral
Treasury
(Alinari)

While I have pointed to their parallels with monumental sculpture, there is
no reason for believing that the Missorium of Theodosius, the Kerch dish
or the largitio plate of Valentinian, copy any surviving or lost work directly.
Rather they share in a *koine* of imperial iconography, and in making use of it,
they look forward to the Byzantine era when monumental sculpture lost the
prestigious position which it had occupied in the imperial commissions of the
Roman Empire.[97]

1.16 Clementinus Diptych, Liverpool Museum (The Board of Trustees of the National Museums and Galleries on Merseyside)

Emperors and consuls

I have compared the image of the emperor on Valentinian's largitio plate
to that of Honorius on an ivory diptych. The two images are remarkably
similar: the emperors wear the same type of clothing and are shown with
the same attributes. Although in different media, both images are executed
in low relief. But the inscriptions on each reveal an important difference: that
on the silver plate tells us that it is the largitio of the emperor Valentinian,
whereas an inscription along the bottom edge of the diptych tells us that it
was commissioned by a consul, Probus.[98] This serves to remind us that the
emperors were not alone in using the applied arts in late antiquity for their
self-promotion, and that images of the emperor could be produced in spheres
beyond his direct authority. In this section I would like to examine both these
phenomena, namely the imitation of the imperial practice of largitio by those
further down the social scale, and the function of imperial images which are
not commissioned by the emperor.

The Probus diptych is one of many such ivory diptychs commissioned
by consuls which survive from late antiquity.[99] Although the dates of these
consular diptychs run from the beginning of the fifth century to the middle
of the sixth, making them consecutive to rather than contemporary with
surviving silver imperial largitio, the diptychs offer the opportunity to
investigate to what extent imperial patronage of luxury art for self-promotion
was copied by the senatorial elite. Consular diptychs consist of two rectangular
panels of ivory hinged together on one side, with relief carving on the
exterior which is visible when the diptych is folded. The decoration varies in
elaborateness: some examples have simple medallions with inscriptions or the
consul's portrait, while others have the entire surface carved, often showing
the consul presiding over games which he has sponsored to inaugurate his
consulship.[100] Diptychs were presented as gifts by new consuls and other
senatorial magistrates to their circle of acquaintance when they assumed
office. The letters of the fourth century Roman aristocrat Symmachus provide
a good insight into this custom. Among his voluminous correspondence are
several letters accompanying gifts of ivory diptychs and silver bowls which
he distributed on the occasion of his son's quaestorship. The following, with
its elegant formal language, is a good reflection of the ceremonial nature of
this practice and gives an idea of the type of people who received such gifts.

It is a solemn and delightful obligation for quaestors *canditati* to present the
customary gifts to people of consequence (*potissimis*) and close friends (*amicissimis*), in
which number you are naturally included. So I offer you an ivory diptych and a small
silver bowl (*canistellum argenteum*) weighing 2 pounds in my son's name, and I beg
you to accept this token of respect with pleasure.[101]

The number and range of Symmachus' correspondents preserved in his letters
suggests that, for him, the total of 'friends and people of consequence' would
be quite large. In this context it is worth noting that in the case of each gift
the weight of the silver is very small (about 600 g) compared to that of the

Missorium of Theodosius, weighing over 15 kg. The aim of such largitio was to spend a large amount giving small presents to many.

The passage of Symmachus suggests that diptychs were produced for distribution by senatorial magistrates in the fourth century, despite our lack of surviving examples. The earliest mention of them is in a law of 384 AD, issued by Theodosius I, which restricted the distribution of ivory diptychs to the consuls alone, and by implication the emperor too.[102] However, diptychs were only one part of the programme of senatorial largesse. As well as the distribution of these among their peers, consuls and other senatorial magistrates were also expected to put on staged wild beast hunts and chariot racing, where they offered generous prizes for competitors and threw money to the people. These were the major item of expenditure for holders of senatorial magistracies. The law of 384 (actually titled *de expensis ludorum*: 'concerning expenditure on games') also regulates the distribution of money and other gifts to the people at senatorial games – no-one had the right to give silk clothing (which was presumably reserved for imperial munificence); only consuls (and again, presumably the emperor too) might give gold coins; those lower in rank must distribute small silver coins. The existence of this law offers evidence that there were attempts by the senatorial elite to imitate, perhaps to compete with, the emperor in munificence. By imposing restrictions on the type and value of gifts which could be given by senators lower than consular rank, the emperor reserves direct emulation of his own largesse to no more than two men per year, whom he himself would select (and who would often include himself, or one of his relatives). Subsequent laws in the fifth and sixth century imposing restrictions on consuls also indicate that the emperor was increasingly concerned to distinguish his largesse from that any member of the elite.[103]

Nevertheless, the extent to which the senatorial elite could emulate the emperor was diminished by the different audiences for their largitio. Not only were there more occasions when the emperor presented largitio (most notably regnal anniversaries, with which surviving silver largitio is most often associated), but the emperor also presented it to the widest audience, comprising both the army and court officials, as well as the senatorial aristocracy. In the poet Corippus' description of the emperor Justin II's assumption of the consulship, Justin personally presents gold coins in silver bowls to the senators, and then to the Palatine guard.[104] Indeed there is no evidence that senators were the recipients of his largitio except when the emperor assumed the consulship (only one of the occasions for the distribution of imperial largitio), although some senators held army or court posts, so might receive largitio on other occasions in that capacity.[105] But the opportunities for senators to distribute largitio occurred only in their capacity as holders of senatorial magistracies. In this context, the role of emperors and senators as givers of largitio overlapped. The law of Theodosius tried to force a distinction between imperial and senatorial largitio by limiting the value of the latter. However the consulship was exceptional, since it was an office held both by emperors and members of the elite, and for this reason perhaps was exempted from these controls. It was possibly the only time in late antiquity when the emperor maintained any semblance of being *primus inter pares*.

It is in that slightly ambiguous context that we can best try to understand the representations of the emperor on diptychs. For although it is unusual for the emperor to form the sole subject of the representation, as he does on the Probus diptych, his image usually appears somewhere in the composition. The diptych of Clementinus (Liverpool Museum), made in Constantinople in 513, is typical in this respect.[106] On each of the two identical leaves of the diptych we see the seated consul, dressed in a triumphal toga, flanked by personifications of Rome and Constantinople (Fig. 1.16). In front of him two boys are shown emptying sacks of coins onto the ground, where they are shown mixed with ingots, plates and palms. In Clementinus' left hand is a sceptre, surmounted with a bust of the emperor Anastasius, and above his head, over the tabula which records his name and titles, are clipeate portraits of Anastasius and his empress Ariadne with a cross between them. The role played by these imperial portraits within the composition as a whole is not one of narrative involvement in the *sparsio* at the games over which Clementinus is presiding. Rather they seem to represent – together with the Christian cross – the ultimate authority sanctioning Clementinus' actions. Here he is anxious to acknowledge (despite his temporarily elevated position) that he recognizes the emperor's superiority.

But what of those diptychs which represent only the emperor? As well as the Probus diptych, there is the well-known Barberini ivory, often assumed to be a diptych-leaf.[107] Like the Probus diptych, its iconography is that of the victorious emperor sanctioned by Christ. Both are classed by Delbrueck at the top of his hierarchy of diptychs as 'emperor diptychs', which he assumes to have been unique one-offs, presented by the consul to the emperor. He supports this theory with a reference to a passage in a letter of Symmachus, where he writes that he has sent the emperor a special diptych framed in gold, although no mention is made of the subject represented on the diptych.[108] In fact, the Barberini ivory may not be a diptych leaf at all, nor is its consular character proven; the figure carrying a victory to the left of the central plaque cannot be securely identified as a consul, as many (including Delbrueck) have claimed.[109] However, it is interesting to look at the idea underlying Delbrueck's hypothesis of the 'emperor diptych', namely that if the imperial image does not emanate from the emperor (as in the case of largitio plates or coinage), it must be directed towards him. But need this always have been the case? Or did members of the senatorial elite represent the emperor's image on objects for themselves, their peers and those of lower social status, without the direct involvement of the emperor? We saw how the Clementinus diptych combined the portraits of the emperor and empress with the image of the consul in a visual reminder of the political structure of the empire. It is also possible to imagine the Probus diptych being produced in this context: Probus chooses not to represent himself, but the emperor through whose agency he holds his power. A good analogy for this can be found in the conventions of the *gratiarum actio*, the speech of thanks to the emperor which a consul

1.17 Fragment of glass largitio plate, Rome, Antiquario Communale

delivered on taking office, focusing on the emperor's virtues rather than his own.[110] However, the later diptychs suggest that such a 'modest' strategy was unusual in the visual sphere, and did not become the favoured mode of consular self-representation.

Another strategy for non-imperial largitio was the use of a less valuable material, which was advocated in Theodosius' law on expenditure on games. A fragment of the upper rim of an engraved glass plate, approximately 21 cm in diameter, which was found during excavations in the Roman Forum in 1882–84, shows part of a pediment supported by four columns, with the heads of three male figures in the centre and right-flanking column bays (Fig. 1.17).[111] The hierarchy of the figures is indicated by their respective sizes and positions, the one in the centre being the largest. Above his head in the pediment are two flying victories, who support a wreath inscribed 'VOTA XX, MULTA XXX', a formula which celebrates an emperor's twentieth regnal anniversary. The corner of the pediment shows a seated male and a reclining female figure, probably personifications. The resemblance of the composition to the Missorium of Theodosius is striking. Although the figure in the central bay does not appear to wear a diadem, and the fragment does not preserve the emperor's name, the inscription makes it highly likely that an emperor is represented, who has been identified as either Constantine I or Constantius II.[112] The plate thus seems to imitate those silver largitio plates presented on the occasion of the emperor's anniversaries. Who would receive glass plates like this one – for presumably our fragment is merely the survivor of multiple examples – and from whom?

It has been argued that the name SEBERUS, inscribed above the head of the outermost figure of the group, can be matched with that of the city prefect of Rome at the time of Constantine's twentieth anniversary, a man named Acilius

Severus. It is to him that the commissioning of the bowl has been ascribed, which by this interpretation would show the emperor in the company of the city prefect.[113] While the identification and dating of the portraits has been contested, this argument remains attractive because it places the bowl in the urban context in which it was found, and suggests analogies between this plate and the later consular diptychs where the representation of the consul is accompanied by imperial portraits. The position of city prefect was one usually occupied by the senatorial aristocracy in Rome, which would place patronage of this plate outside the emperor's immediate circle, but among people who felt it necessary and desirable to exhibit their loyalty to the emperor by commemorating his vicennalia. Indeed it has been argued that the emperor and imperial festivals retained considerable importance for the urban elite in late antiquity, which would support this reading of the plate's manufacture.[114]

Glass does not have intrinsic financial value, unlike the gold and silver of other largitio, although its craftsmanship can bestow a certain value, and modern scholars have commented favourably on the high standard of engraving this fragment displays in comparison to other examples of fourth-century glass.[115] Nevertheless, to receive a glass plate is clearly less prestigious than receiving a silver one. It seems likely therefore that these glass plates would have been intended for a wider – and less socially distinguished – audience than the friends and 'people of consequence' to whom Symmachus sent gifts on his son's behalf. But in what context would they have been distributed? We know that the spectacles in the amphitheatre and the circus which consuls and other magistrates hosted as the main duty of their office were an occasion not just for scattering coins to the audience (*sparsio*) but for distributing other gifts to them, which are known in our sources by the collective term *missilia*.[116] Thus, this glass fragment could have been part of one of many plates distributed at games held to celebrate the *vicennalia* which the pediment inscription refers to. By having these glass plates made, Acilius Severus – or some other fourth-century aristocrat, for the social level is surely right, if not the name – was offering those further down the social scale an imitation of the silver largitio plates that more important individuals (like himself) would receive from the emperor, made in a lower grade of applied art with an iconography closely related to that of the emperor's own gifts. Although this mode of imitation is not mentioned in written sources, it seems to have been practised in other contexts. Fragments of at least six African sigillata plates have been found which show consuls or other officials with their insignia of office or presiding over games, clearly imitating the form and iconography of the ivory consular diptychs.[117] The bronze contorniate medallions of the fourth and fifth centuries offer another parallel. Produced by the late antique urban aristocracy at Rome, their iconography is closely related to that of commemorative imperial medallions in gold or silver, as well as being linked with the circus and games where it is thought they were probably distributed. They first appear when the emperor ceased to strike bronze medallions, thereby making it an acceptable material for the aristocratic imitation imperial medallions.[118]

1.18 Missorium
of Ardabur
Aspar, Florence,
Museo
Archeologico
(Hirmer Verlag,
Munich)

A different strategy of imitation of imperial practice is found in our only
surviving example of consular largitio silver, the Missorium of Ardabur
Aspar – consul in the West in 434 – found in 1750 near Florence, and now
in the Archaeological Museum there (Fig. 1.18).[119] This little known silver
plate presents an interesting example of intersection between the form of the
fourth-century largitio plates and the iconography of the consular diptychs.
The plate measures 42 cm in diameter, and originally had a high foot-ring and
a raised edge, both of which are now lost. Within this rim is a band with an
inscription reading FL[avius] ARDABUR ASPAR VIR INLUSTRIS COM[es]
ET MAG[ister] MILITIUM ET CONSUL ORDINARIIUS. In the centre of the
plate Aspar is shown togate, seated on a sella curulis, holding a mappa and
sceptre with imperial busts on it. To his left stands his young son, also togate

and holding a mappa, with his name and title, ARDABUR IUNIOR PRETOR, inscribed above him. These two are flanked by personifications of Rome and Constantinople, and below their feet are several large plates and some palms, either prizes for the games over which they preside or largitio. Above the central group are two clipeate portraits of togate men with sceptres, labelled ARDABUR and PLINTA, identified as Ardabur Aspar's father and father-in-law who were consuls in 427 and 419 respectively. These portraits represent the only major difference between this plate's iconography and that of the standard consular diptychs, such as the Clementinus diptych, since they show not the reigning emperor but Arbabur's relations who have already held the post of consul. This plate is a unique survival, but as we have seen from the letter of Symmachus quoted above, it was not unique in its time and we should presumably imagine such objects being produced in similar quantities to the diptychs for the same circle of recipients. While the diptychs survive in relatively large quantities, this is probably because their financial value was not as easily converted into hard cash as that of silver.[120] That we have only one consular silver largitio plate, and nineteen imperial examples, may suggest that the latter were produced in substantially greater quantities, or that their owners were less willing to destroy an object with the emperor's image, but as my earlier survey of imperial largitio plates showed, even some of the surviving examples seem to have been deliberately damaged.

Why, however, are there no examples of largitio given by the emperor as *consul*, either in the form of plate or ivory diptychs? This may be an accident of survival, since the sixth-century poet Corippus describes how Justin II presented the senators in Constantinople with gold coins in silver vessels decorated with figures and inscriptions ('*pressum titulis sculptumque figuris*'), which presumably would have represented the emperor.[121] It is also possible that the Barberini ivory could have been a gift from the emperor, but it is not possible to connect it with an imperial consulship, since the surviving leaf of this diptych bears no allusion to the holding of that office. Part of the answer lies in coinage, which regularly commemorated imperial consulships in late antiquity, with images of the emperor in his consular robes and insignia. The emperor alone had access to this mode of commemoration as consul: other consuls could distribute coins, but only the emperor could represent himself as consul on them. Largitio legislation highlights the emperor's control of coinage, and is quite specific about the types and weights of coin that may or may not be distributed.[122]

The Missorium of Theodosius re-visited

I have shown some of the different ways in which the emperor's use of luxury art in a political context set a pattern for the late Roman elite in positions of authority under him. Their emulation of imperial largesse was, at times at least, carefully nuanced to avoid the appearance of direct competition with the emperor. Sometimes the distinction lay in the use of a less precious material, sometime in an iconography which focused on the officials' obligation to provide games for the people. The imperial image is rarely absent altogether from any of the surviving largitio which was produced by members of the elite, but sometimes (as in the case of Probus) it is the dominant image. This should not be considered too surprising: the emperor's image had never been merely a personal portrait. Rather, from the time of Augustus it had served as a symbol of the Roman Empire and its well-being.[123] Thus it would be wrong to imagine that the emperor had a monopoly on the use of his own image, and that any use of it should be traced directly back to him.[124] Bearing this in mind, I would like to return to the starting point of this chapter, the Missorium of Theodosius, to suggest an alternative reading that focuses on perhaps the most overlooked figure in the whole composition: the official who receives his codicillary diptych of office from the emperor. Only André Grabar, trying to categorize this image, recognized how unusual such a scene of investiture is in imperial iconography.[125] But even he did not ask why this scene should be found on a plate ostensibly commemorating the emperor's decennalia. It has been suggested that the recipient of the plate was the official whom it represents.[126] However, the inscription mentions only Theodosius' decennalia, and there is no evidence that personal investitures by the emperor were associated with anniversary celebrations. Grabar described the act of investiture as the emperor transferring some of his supreme power to a high dignitary. Might the representation of such an act not be of more interest to the dignitary than to the emperor? In other words, can we be so sure that the Missorium was an imperial commission, as this chapter has assumed until now? My discussion of the varied use of the emperor's image in the context of consular largitio raises the possibility that a recently appointed official had it made to commemorate the two separate events of his own investiture and Theodosius' decennalia, in an act which both displayed his loyalty to Theodosius and promoted his own position. Although there is never likely to be sufficient evidence to make this more than a hypothesis, as such it should at least be entertained, because it suggests that the luxury applied arts used for late antique largitio may have offered a greater degree of flexibility in the use of the imperial image – if not in the form or meanings of that image – than the monumental art of the period.[127]

The imperial largitio silver of the fourth century represents a highly significant departure for late antique silver plate. Its representation of the emperor means that it becomes part of the discourse about the emperor in late antiquity, a position which – beyond the exceptional Boscoreale cups – there is no surviving evidence of silver plate occupying in the earlier imperial period. Thus we seem to be dealing with a domestic, 'private' artform acquiring, possibly for the first time, the language of the public sphere, both written and visual. Yet is it right to consider largitio a fully public art? Rather the materials which it uses – silver, gold, ivory – are those of 'private' art, and in becoming the property of those to whom they are given are reincorporated into the domestic sphere. Just as the gold multiples were mounted as personal jewellery, we should perhaps imagine silver largitio vessels displayed proudly together with the rest of their owners' silver tableware. In this way, one might argue, the emperor was integrated into the lives of his subjects, as he had been through the imperial cult.[128] The Missorium of Theodosius, whether a gift of the emperor or an act of homage to him, is important evidence of how those subjects saw the emperor, not just in the ceremonial of the palace but in their own homes.

Notes

1. Important stylistic discussions include R. Bianchi Bandinelli, *Rome: The Late Empire AD 200–400* (New York, 1971), 357–60; Kitzinger, *Byzantine Art in the Making*, 31–32; Kiilerich, *Late Fourth Century Classicism*, 19–26. Among the major iconographic discussions are R. Delbrueck, *Die Consulardiptychen und verwandte Denkmäler* 2 vols. (Berlin and Leipzig, 1929), 235–42; A. Grabar, *L'empereur dans l'art byzantin* (Paris, 1936), 88–89; S. MacCormack, *Art and Ceremony in Late Antiquity* (Berkeley, CA, 1981), 214–221. M. Almagro-Gorbea, J.M. Alvarez Martinez, J.M. Blazquez Martinez and S. Rovira eds, *El Disco de Teodosio* (Madrid, 2000), a collection of essays relating to the history, manufacture and interpretation of the Missorium, was published after this chapter had been completed, and it has not been possible to include detailed references to this useful work.

2. A. Delgado y Hernandez, *Memoria historico-critica sobre el gran disco de Theodosio, encontrado en Almendralejo* (Madrid, 1849). It should be noted that the designation 'missorium' is a modern one, extrapolated from the use of this term in ancient texts to describe large flat plates. See W. Hilgers, *Lateinische Gefässnamen. Bezeichnungen, Funktion und Form römische Gefässe nach den antiken Schriftquellen* (Beihefter Bonner Jahrbuch 31., Dusseldörf, 1969). Delgado (60–81) identified the plate as a votive shield, a designation which antiquarians had applied to large silver plates with decorated surfaces since the seventeenth century: cf. Bracci, *Dissertazione sopra un clipeo votivo*; J. Spon, 'Sur un Bouclier antique d'argent'.

3. Delgado, *Memoria historico-critica*, 5: 'dos pequeñas tazas del mismo metal, de forma sencilla'.

4. Delgado, *Memoria historico-critica*, 7, 12. See also S.D. Martinez, 'Tratamiento de Restauración del Disco de Teodosio', in Almagro-Gorbea et al., *El Disco de Teododosio*, 151–58.

5. W. Grünhagen, *Der Schatzfund von Groß Bodungen*. Römisch-Germanische Forschungen 21 (Berlin, 1954), 15–38.

6. The main damage is to the head of Valentinian, the head and hands of the official, Theodosius' knees, and one of the cupids in the exergue.

7. Many nineteenth-century scholars (including Delgado) identified the flanking emperors as Honorius and Arcadius. However, this seems unlikely since all three figures are identified as augusti by their diadems, and Honorius was not made an augustus until 393. See Kiilerich (n. 1 supra) 22, n. 52 for bibliography. Most recently, J. Meischner, 'Das Missorium des Theodosius in Madrid', *JdI* 111 (1996), 389–432, has tried to identify the three as Theodosius II with Honorius and Valentinian III. She argues that the plate was made as a tool of dynastic propaganda by Constantius III and his wife Galla Placida on behalf of their son Valentinian III, to promote his acceptance as Augustus and Honorius' heir by Theodosius II, an overly complex and not entirely convincing argument necessitated by her claim that the Missorium must be considered a product of the early fifth century on stylistic grounds.

8.   D[OMINUS] N[OSTER] THEODOSIUS PERPET[UUS] AUG[USTUS] OB DIEM
     FELICISSIMUM X (our lord Theodosius, emperor for ever, on the most happy
     occasion of his decennalia).

9.   The technical study by M. Jesús Sánchez Beltrán in Almagro-Gorbea et al., *El Disco de
     Teododosio*, 111–37 suggests that the Missorium was cast and then further elaborated
     with chasing and punching. This concurs with the overview of M. Hughes, J. Lang,
     S. La Niece and A. Oddy in F. Baratte and K. Painter, eds, *Trésors d'orfèvrerie gallo-
     romains* (Paris, 1989), 21–28, and the comments by F. Baratte in the same book on the
     manufacture of the so-called 'Shield of Scipio' (no. 235, 269), which suggest that only
     the 'blanks' for large plates were cast, and were further shaped by hammering, with
     the relief ornament executed entirely through chasing.

10. Scholars have sometimes argued that surviving Julio-Claudian silverware with
     imperial representations indicates that silver was given as largitio in this early period.
     However, the only examples with securely identifiable imperial representations, the
     Boscoreale Cups, are arguably exceptional pieces: cf. A. Kuttner, *Dynasty and Empire
     in the Age of Augustus: the Case of The Boscoreale Cups* [Berkeley, CA (1995)], 1–6. Other
     imperial identifications, such as the 'portrait' of a Julio-Claudian prince or emperor on
     a silver plate found at Aquileia, now in the Kunsthistorisches Museum, Vienna, that
     shows Triptolemos sacrificing to Demeter in an allegorical scene in the Hellenistic/
     Alexandrian tradition have been shown to be unlikely: see C. Wölfel, 'Der Teller von
     Aquileia', in H.-H. von Pritwitz und Gaffron and H. Mielsch, eds, *Das Haus lacht vor
     Silber: die Prunkplatte von Bizerta und das römische Tafelgeschirr* (Cologne, 1997), 149–52.

11. Detailed discussions of the practice of largitio in the context of economic
     administration in late antiquity include R. Delmaire, 'Les largesses impériales et
     l'émission d'argenterie du IVe au VIe siècle', in F. Baratte, ed., *Argenterie romaine et
     byzantine: actes de la table ronde, Paris 11–13 octobre 1983* (Paris, 1988), 113–22; idem,
     *Largesses sacrées et res privata: l'aerarium impériale et son administration du IVe au VIe
     siècle* (Paris, 1989); M.F. Hendy, *Studies in the Byzantine Monetary Economy c. 300–1450*
     (Cambridge, 1985), 175–78, 192–201; idem, 'The Administration of Mints and
     Treasuries, Fourth to Seventh Centuries, with an Appendix on the Production of Silver
     Plate' in *The Economy, Fiscal Administration and Coinage of Byzantium* (Northampton,
     1989), VI, 1–18.

12. For the main literary sources see R. MacMullen, 'The Emperor's Largesses', *Latomus* 21
     (1962), 159–66. On the Notitia Dignitatum, see the entry by A. Kazhdan in the *Oxford
     Dictionary of Byzantium* (Oxford, 1991), vol. 3, 1496.

13. Delmaire, 'Largesses impériales', 113; Hendy, 'The Administration of Mints and
     Treasuries', 1–2.

14. Three silver three-pound ingots stamped with the portrait of the emperor Magnentius
     found in the Kaiseraugst Treasure can be identified as largitio: Cahn, Kaufmann-
     Heinimann et al., *Der spätrömische Silberschatz*, 324–26. Luxury clothing: a law issued
     under Theodosius (*CTh* xv.9.i) restricts the right to give silk garments to the emperor
     alone and is discussed in Hendy, *Byzantine Monetary Economy*, 193–94. In the broader
     category of imperial gifts (which I would not term largitio in the strictest sense) are the
     fibulae and buckles in precious metals that were given as badges of office to military
     and bureaucratic personnel: see I.M. Johansen, 'Rings, Fibulae and Buckles with
     Imperial Portraits and Inscriptions', *JRA* 7 (1994), 223–42.

15. The distinction between accessional and quinquennial donatives is made by Hendy,
     Byzantine Monetary Economy, 177. However Delmaire, 'Largesses impériales', 115,
     cites five solidi and a pound of silver as the minimum donative on all occasions. The
     official exchange rate valued a pound of silver at four or five solidi (Hendy, *ibid.*).

16. Baratte refers briefly to an unpublished example of largitio silver that may date to the mid-third century in *La vaiselle d'argent en Gaule*, 213 and n. 964. The decline of largitio has been explored by R. Delmaire, in 'Largesses impériales', and 'Le déclin des largesses sacrées' in C. Morrisson and J. Lefort, eds, *Hommes et Richesses dans l'Empire Byzantin I: IVe–VIIe siècle* (Paris, 1989,) 265–77.

17. Hendy, 'The Administration of Mints and Treasuries', 17. For more on the absence of silver coinage in the fifth and sixth centuries see P. Grierson, 'The Role of Silver in the Early Byzantine Economy', in Boyd and Mango, eds, *Ecclesiastical Silver Plate*, 137–46.

18. Hendy's suggestion in 'Administration of Mints and Treasuries', 14–18, that some Byzantine silver plate with control stamps from the fifth and sixth centuries decorated with non-imperial imagery might have been given as public largesse seems implausible. The problem of identifying largitio silver plate after the fourth century is discussed further in Chapter 4.

19. B. Overbeck, *Argentum Romanum: Ein Schatzfund von spätrömischen Prunkgeschirr* (Munich, 1973); J. Garbsch and B. Overbeck, *Spätantike zwischen Heidentum und Christentum* (Munich, 1989), 58–64. The hoard is owned by the Bayerisches Hypotheken- und Weschselbank, Munich, which acquired the bowls in 1972 and the bust subsequently (Garbsch and Overbeck, 58). Also see the discussion in J.P.C. Kent and K.S. Painter, *The Wealth of the Roman World: Gold and Silver AD 300–700* (London, 1977), 20–22.

20. One of the three bowls has a bust of Licinius I and the legend LICINIUS AUG OB D V LICINI FILI (The emperor Licinius for the fifth regnal anniversary of his son Licinius); the other two have busts of Licinius II with the legend LICINIUS CAES OB D V SUORUM (Licinius caesar for his fifth regnal anniversary).

21. The inscriptions read VOTIS X CAESS NN and VOTIS X CAESARIS NOSTRI (On the occasion of vows for a decennalia by our caesars/caesar). These vows would have been made at the quinquennalia celebration of the caesars, one function of such occasions being to declare the vows made five years earlier fulfilled, and make vows for the five subsequent years.

22. Overbeck, *Argentum Romanum*, 47.

23. Weights are given by Overbeck, *Argentum Romanum*. A Roman pound is between 317g and 326g. All subsequent uses of the term 'pound' here should be understood as denoting the Roman measure; modern equivalents will be give in grams.

24. Nos 1 and 2 in Overbeck's catalogue (the Licinius I bowl and one of the Licinius II bowls) have a stamp of Nicomedia. No. 3 (the other Licinius II bowl) has a stamp of Antioch. No. 4 (the bowl mentioning two caesars) has a pointillé inscription of Naissus; and no. 5 (the bowl mentioning one caesar) has a fragmentary pointillé inscription XIAS which Overbeck restores as Antioch.

25. One of the bowls has lost part of its rim, so that its present weight of 421g is less than its original weight. Its companion weighs 470g, around one and a half Roman pounds, so it is possible that this was also the original weight of the other.

26. For example, the silver bust of Lucius Verus from the Marengo Treasure. For further discussion of the function of the Munich bust, see Garbsch and Overbeck, *Spätantike zwischen Heidentum und Christentum*, 63.

27. For example, the letters on the two caesar bowls are rather clumsy and written between two incised lines, with an equally clumsy hedera separating the first and last letters.

28. Cahn, Kaufmann-Heinimann et al., *Der spätrömische Silberschatz*, 155–58, for a set of four small bowls in this shape without beading on the rims. More elaborate examples of this shape with figural and geometric decoration are represented in the Mildenhall Treasure. See Painter, *The Mildenhall Treasure*, 27–29.

29. The earliest example of this type is found in the mid-3rd century Maçon Treasure; closer are two further largitio dishes of Licinius from Červenbreg, Bulgaria (discussed below). See the entry on the Maçon Treasure in Baratte and Painter, eds, *Trésors d'orfèvrerie gallo-romains*, 185–87.

30. L. Ognenova, 'Plats en argent du décennaire de l'empereur Licinius', *Bulletin d'Institut Archéologique Bulgare 19* (1955), 233–43.

31. D. Buckton, ed., *Byzantium: Treasures of Byzantine Art and Culture from British Collections* (London 1994) no. 1, 25.

32. Overbeck, *Argentum Romanum* compares the Munich bowls to coins issued on the same occasion, namely the quinquennalia of Licinius II in 322. The coin type has a reverse with Jupiter enthroned, and appears with two obverses, the portraits of the elder and younger Licinius respectively, which bear a close resemblance to the portrait types of the bowls. In the case of the elder Licinius, the coin type and the bowl feature the same legend (LICINIUS AUG OB D V FILII SUI).

33. A. Effenberger et al., *Spätantike und früh-byzantinische Silbergefässe aus der Staatlichen Ermitage, Leningrad* (Berlin, 1978), Kat.-Nr. 2, 82–84, Dok.-Nr. 1, 132–34.

34. See Effenberger et al., *Spätantike und früh-byzantinische Silbergefässe*, 30–32. For further historical background, V.F. Gajdukerič, *Das Bosporanische Reich* (Berlin/Amsterdam, 1971).

35. On the circumstances of the find see Effenberger et al., *Spätantike und früh-byzantinische Silbergefässe*, 30–32. The coins date from the end of Constantius II's reign to that of Valentinian II.

36. A Roman pound=12 ounces=24 scruples. Thus the bowls are both two-thirds of an ounce short of two pounds.

37. Effenberger et al., *Spätantike und früh-byzantinische Silbergefässe*, Kat.-Nr. 4, 85–86; Dok.-Nr. 2, 134; Dok.-Nr. 3, 135. Since these objects were looted from two graves and later recovered by the authorities, it is not possible to say which item was found in which grave. The jugs, like the bowl, are types well represented in hoards of the fourth and early fifth century, such as the Sevso Treasure, which contains parallels for Kat.-Nr. 4. A jug found near Beneventum, now in the Cabinet des Médailles of the Bibliothèque Nationale, resembles Dok.-Nr. 3 (illustrated in Kent and Painter, *Wealth of the Roman World*, no. 104, 54).

38. Early tentative identification as Constantius II, Grabar, *L'empereur*, 48.

39. Effenberger et al., *Spätantike und früh-byzantinische Silbergefässe*, Kat.-Nr. 3, 84.

40. Matzulewitsch, *Byzantinische Antike*, 95–100.

41. The late Roman silver vessels found at Kerch are only a few of the many (attested by the wealth of late Roman and early Byzantine silver in the Hermitage Museum) that made their way into the geographical area of Russia and the Ukraine in the late Roman and early Byzantine period and were preserved in graves. See Matzulewitsch, *Byzantinische Antike*; Effenberger et al., *Spätantike und früh-byzantinische Silbergefässe*.

42. B. de Montfaucon, 'Dissertation sur une antique ou disque d'argent trouvé près de Geneve en 1721', in *Supplément au livre d'antiquité expliquée et représentée en figures* (Paris, 1724), vol. 4, 51–65; W. Déonna, 'Notes d'archéologie suisse VI. Le missorium de Valentinien', *Anzeiger für Schweizerische Altertumskunde*, neue Folge 22 (1920), 18–32, 92–104.

43. Grünhagen, *Der Schatzfund von Groß Bodungen*.

44. These dates are established by the coins included in the hoard, which run from Magnentius to Constantine III, with issues of Honorius being the most numerous. The other fragment of silver with figural decoration in the hoard would also support this dating. See Grünhagen, *Der Schatzfund von Groß Bodungen*.

45. Grünhagen, *Der Schatzfund von Groß Bodungen*, 58–70. His suggestions are repeated in Kent and Painter, *Wealth of the Roman World*, 123.

46. The possible relevance of the findspot in Spain is discussed in Kiilerich, *Late Fourth Century Classicism*, 22–24.

47. Cahn, Kaufmann-Heinimann et al., *Der spätrömische Silberschatz*; Kaufmann-Heinimann, 'Eighteen New Pieces', 333–41.

48. Cahn, Kaufmann-Heinimann et al., *Der spätrömische Silberschatz*, 322–59; 405–07. Cf. the coin hoard from Beaurains, northern France, which comprises coins of 285–315, most of which seem to have been issued on the occassion of *donativa*: P. Bastien and C. Metzger, *Le trésor de Beaurains (dit D'Arras)* (Wettern, 1977), 193–213. The hoard also included some gold jewellery in known third century styles and a few pieces of domestic silver plate. These seem to be family possessions of the hoard's owner rather than official gifts.

49. Kaufmann-Heinimann, 'Eighteen new pieces', 339.

50. J.A. Bruhn, *Coins and Costume in Late Antiquity*, Dumbarton Oaks Byzantine Collection Publications no. 9 (Washington DC, 1993), 1–34. Also see H. Maguire, 'Magic and Money in the Early Middle Ages', *Speculum* 72 (1997), 1037–54.

51. Buckton, *Byzantium*, no. 2, 26–27 with bibliography. For the Dumbarton Oaks examples, Bruhn, *Coins and Costume*, nos 4–5, 40–41.

52. Bruhn, *Coins and Costume*, no. 7, 43–44.

53. Johns and Bland, 'The Hoxne Late Roman Treasure', 170; C. Johns, *The Jewellery of Roman Britain: Celtic and Classical Traditions* (London, 1996), 96, Fig. 5.9.

54. On the difficulty of understanding the operation of the ancient economy within modern concepts of economic behaviour, see the *locus classicus*, M.I. Finley, *The Ancient Economy* 2nd edn (London, 1985).

55. Hendy, 'Administration of Mints and Treasuries', 2. Cf. Finley's comment that the production of coins of an artistically high standard in classical Greece was inspired not by a desire to facilitate trading, but for political advertisement on the part of city states, whereas the civilizations of the ancient Near East did not use coins despite their trading successes, *The Ancient Economy*, 166–67.

56. Hendy, *Byzantine Monetary Economy*, 218.

57. Hendy, *Byzantine Monetary Economy*, 219.

58. See the bibliography in n. 7 supra.

59. Ceres, Annonia Publica, Hispania and Abundantia have been suggested as well as Tellus/Terra: Kiilerich, *Late Fourth Century Classicism*, 23, n. 60 with bibliography.

60. Kiilerich, *Late Fourth Century Classicism*, 22, n. 53 with bibliography.

61. Kiilerich, *Late Fourth Century Classicism*, 24, n. 65 with bibliography.

62. Kiilerich, *Late Fourth Century Classicism*, 22–23 with bibliography.

63. For Tellus on the Prima Porta cuirass see P. Zanker, *The Power of Images in the Age of Augustus* (Ann Arbor, MI, 1988), 175, Fig. 137; for the imagery of the cuirass as a whole and its meaning, *ibid*. 188–92.

64. Zanker, *The Power of Images*, 167–83. Also see D. Castriota, *The Ara Pacis Augustae and the Imagery of Abundance in Later Greek and Roman Imperial Art* (Princeton, NJ, 1995), esp. 3–12, 124–69; K. Galinsky, *Augustan Culture: an Interpretative Introduction* (Princeton, NJ, 1996), 90–121.

65. See K. Stemmer, *Untersuchungen zur Typologie, Chronologie und Ikonographie der Panzerstatuen* (Berlin, 1978,) 34–35 (no. III 7, pl. 19.2–4); 61 (no. V 9, pl. 37.1–4); 85 (no. VII 19, pl. 59.2).

66. J.C.M. Toynbee, *The Hadrianic School: a Chapter in the History of Greek Art* (Cambridge, 1934), 140–43.

67. E. Ghisellini, 'Tellus', *LIMC* VII (Zurich, 1994), 888; Toynbee, *The Hadrianic School*, 140, n. 4.

68. She appears frequently, however, in the domestic art of the fourth and fifth century. Good examples have been found at Antioch, where she was called by her Greek name Ge, as in the late third/early fourth-century mosaic of Ge and the Karpoi from Bath E, the fifth-century mosaic from the House of Ge and the Seasons, and a small mosaic in the fifth-century House of the Worcester Hunt. See D. Levi, *Antioch Mosaic Pavements* (Princeton, NJ, 1947), 263–69, 346–47, 365.

69. Their gesture recalls the figures of barbarians making offerings to the emperor on the obelisk base of Theodosius or the Barberini Ivory, cf. Grabar, *L'empereur*, 54–55, pls IV, XII, 2.

70. H.P. L'Orange's essay *Art Forms and Civic Life in the Late Roman Empire* (Princeton, NJ, 1965) takes this idea to its furthest extreme, by drawing parallels between the political changes in the administration of the empire in late antiquity and the changes in the visual arts.

71. As noted in D.E.E. Kleiner, *Roman Sculpture* (Yale and New Haven, 1992), 289–301. But see J. Elsner, 'Frontality in the Column of Marcus Aurelius', in V. Huet and J. Scheidt, eds, *La Colonne Aurélienne: autour de la Colonne Aurélienne. Geste et image sur la colonne de Marc Aurèle à Rome* (Brussels, 2000), 251–64. for some problems implicit in constructing this monument as a prototype of late antique style.

72. Kitzinger, *Byzantine Art in the Making*, 14. On the development of imperial adlocutio representations cf. P.G. Hamberg, *Studies in Roman Imperial Art, with special reference to the State Reliefs of the Second Century* (Uppsala, 1945), 135–49; R. Brilliant, *Gesture and Rank in Roman Art: Use of Gestures to Denote Status in Roman Sculpture and Coinage* (New Haven, 1963), 165–70.

73. For further examples of frontal presentations of the emperor see C. Caprino, *La Colonna di Marco Aurelio* (Rome, 1955), figs 11, 15, 16, 101, 106, 120.

74. R. Brilliant, *The Arch of Septimius Severus in the Roman Forum*. Memoirs of the American Academy in Rome 29 (Rome, 1967), e.g. pl. 80c; D.E.L. Haynes and P.E.D. Hirst, *Porta Argentariorum* (London, 1939), pl. VI, VII.

75. There are even instances of what one might describe as proto-frontality in Trajan's Column. See C. Cichorius, *Die Reliefs der Traianssäule* 2 vols (Berlin, 1896–1900), pls XII, XX, XXXIX. These show the emperor on the ramparts of a fort, flanked by two attendants. In pl. XX the frontal position of Trajan is accentuated by his being aligned with the corner of the wall viewed end-on. The case for seeing Trajan's Column as the beginning of late antique art has been made by K. Lehmann-Hartleben, *Die Trajanssäule: ein römisches Kunstwerk zu Beginn der Spätantike* (Berlin and Leipzig, 1926), esp. 47 (discussion of frontality in scenes XII and XX), 152–54.

76. See n. 10 supra.

77. Grabar, *L'empereur*, 89; Kiilerich, *Late Fourth Century Classicism*, 22.

78. J.P.C. Kent, *The Roman Imperial Coinage VIII: the Family of Constantine I AD 337–364* (London, 1981), 350, 352, 403, 406. These issues date from 337–40 AD, and were minted at Siscia and Thessalonike. They bear the reverse legend FELICITAS PERPETUA, and VOT V either on the base of the central emperor's throne or in the exergue.

79. A. Alföldi, *Die monarchische Repräsentation im römischen Kaiserreiche* (Darmstadt, 1970), 187.

80. Alföldi's comprehensive study of Roman imperial costume and insignia traces the forms of official imperial clothing back to their republican origins, but stresses at the same time the changes in their use from the time of the Dominate. *Die monarchische Repräsentation*, 127–85.

81. This type derives from the so-called 'Asiatic sarcophagi', produced in Asia Minor from the second century AD onwards. See further M. Lawrence, 'Columnar Sarcophagi in the Latin West: Ateliers, Chronology, Style', *Art Bulletin* 14 (1932), 103–85; G. Rodenwaldt, 'Säulensarcophage', *RM* 38/39 (1923–24), 1–40.

82. L'Orange, *Art Forms and Civic Life*, 74.

83. This was first argued by N. Duval, in 'La place de Split dans l'architecture antique du bas-empire', *Urbs* 4 (1961–2), 67–95; the issue of interpretation is conveniently summarized by J.J. Wilkes, *Diocletian's Palace, Split: Residence of a Retired Roman Emperor* (Sheffield, 1986), 65–82.

84. See J.G. Deckers, 'Die Wandmalerei im Kaiserkultraum von Luxor', *JdI* 94 (1979), 600–52 with bibl., and the discussion in J. Elsner, *Art and the Roman Viewer: the Transformation of Art from the Pagan World to Christianity* (Cambridge, 1995), 159–89.

85. Elsner, *Art and the Roman Viewer*, 173–76.

86. Elsner, *Art and the Roman Viewer*, 176.

87. On the throne as a seat for emperors, see Alföldi, *Die monarchische Repräsentation*, 242–57. T. Mathews has claimed that the emperors were usually depicted on a sella curulis (consular seat), and almost never on a throne, rejecting instances such as that below as 'exceptions'. In doing so he surely underestimates the conflation of imperial

and divine imagery which had taken place since the early years of the Roman Empire. See *The Clash of Gods* (Princeton, NJ, 1993), 103–09, and the reviews by D. Kinney in *Studies in Iconography* 16 (1994), 237–42, and P. Brown, *Art Bulletin* 77 (1995), 499–502.

88. R. Delbrueck, *Antike Porphyrwerke* (Berlin, 1932), 96–98, pls 40–41.

89. Alföldi, *Die monarchische Repräsentation*, 234–38. For a late antique representation of the Olympian gods with these attributes, see the illustration of the Council of the Gods in the Virgilius Romanus manuscript (f. 234v), reproduced in E. Rosenthal, *The Illuminations of the Vergilius Romanus (Cod. Vat. Lat. 3867). A Stylistic and Iconographic Analysis* (Zurich 1972) pl. VI.

90. See further P. Magdalino, ed., *New Constantines: The Rhythm of Imperial Renewal in Byzantium, 4th–13th Centuries* (Aldershot, 1994), introduction 1–9; M. Whitby, 'Images for Emperors in Late Antiquity: a Search for a New Constantine', 83–93.

91. He wears a torque, carries a large shield (round rather than oval) decorated with a chi-rho enclosed in geometric border, his hair is chin-length with a long fringe, and he wears a tunic and leggings, a simplified version of the emperor's clothes, which are in fact standard military uniform in peacetime, called by Alföldi 'militärische Friedenstracht' or 'Dienstcostume' (*Die monarchische Repräsentation*, 175–84).

92. For a detailed discussion of individual iconographic elements, see Déonna, 'Le missorium de Valentinien'.

93. Matzulewitsch, *Byzantinische Antike*, 97; Grabar, *L'empereur*, 45–46, 129–31.

94. Kent and Painter, *Wealth of the Roman World*, no. 459, 170.

95. For example Kent and Painter, *Wealth of the Roman World*, no 493, 172, a silver milarensis of Valentinian II from 378–83, whose reverse shows the emperor with a shield and labarum standard to illustrate VIRTUS EXERCITUS.

96. Kuttner, *Dynasty and Empire*. Unfortunately she does not explore the broader methodological implications of this argument for an understanding of the relationship between the 'major' and 'minor' arts.

97. Cf. Grabar's comments on the disappearance of monumental sculpture in Byzantium: *L'empereur*, 126.

98. LARGITAS DN VALENTINIANI AUGUSTI; PROBUS FAMULUS V[IR] C[LARISSIMUS] CONS[UL] ORD[INARIUS].

99. The standard corpus is still Delbrueck, *Die Consulardiptychen*. Also valuable is W.F. Volbach, *Elfenbeinarbeiten der Spätantike und des frühen Mittelalters*, 2nd edn (Mainz, 1952).

100. Delbrueck's suggestion (*Die Consulardiptychen*, 15–16) that the less elaborate diptychs were gifts for less important people and his tentative hierarchy of recipients for the different types of diptychs are reaffirmed by A. Cutler, 'The Making of the Justinian Diptychs', *Byzantion* 54 (1984), 104–12. Three varieties of diptych made for the eastern consul Areobindus survive, and two for Philoxenus, another eastern consul (Delbrueck, *Die Consulardiptychen*, 9–12, 13–14, 30, 31). Only one group of diptychs, however, records the recipient's status, the three identical surviving diptychs presented by Justinian to senators in 521 (Delbrueck, *Die Consulardiptychen*, nos 26–28), for which see Cutler, *ibid*. 75–115.

101. Symmachus, *Ep.* 7.76. Translation from Cameron, 'Distribution and Ownership', 180. Symmachus is one of our few written sources for the distribution of senatorial largitio: see also *Ep.* 2.81, 5.56.

102. The full text reads: 'No private person shall be permitted to distribute any silk vestments as gifts at any exhibition of games. We also confirm by this constitution that, with the exception of consuls ordinary, no one else shall have the right to give presents of gold or ivory tablets. When public spectacles are celebrated, the present shall be a coin of silver and the tablets shall be made of other materials than ivory. Nor shall it be allowed to expend a greater silver coin than that which is customarily formed when one pound is divided into sixty pieces of silver. If any person should wish to give less, he is not only free to do so, but We also permit this to be an honourable action.' *CTh* xv.9.i. trans. C. Pharr (Princeton, NJ, 1952). Alan Camron has argued that this law applied only to the Senate in Constantinople, where its chief purpose was to 'reduce the expenses of the praetors by removing one of their obligations': see 'Consular Diptychs in their Social Context: New Eastern Evidence', *JRA* 11 (1998), 399–400.

103. A law issued under Marcian in 452 withdrew the right of non-imperial consuls to perform the sparsio in processions, *CJ* xii.3.2. This right was restored under Justinian (*Novel* CV), but they were restricted to using silver coins only. For further discussion see Hendy, *Byzantine Monetary Economy*, 192–95 and Cutler, 'The Making of the Justinian Diptychs', on Justinian's fear of being outshone as consul by a private citizen.

104. Corippus, *In Laudem Iustini Augusti Minoris*, ed. with trans. and commentary by A. Cameron (London, 1976), 4, 142–47.

105. It should be remembered that late antique holders of senatorial magistracies did not belong to a single social class, but rather comprised several elite classes: the traditional senatorial aristocracy, court officials, and military commanders. Members of latter two groups often had less distinguished social origins than the first, but also had a closer relationship with the imperial court and were more likely to be appointed consul. See J. Matthews, 'The Letters of Symmachus', in J.W. Binns, ed., *Latin Literature of the Fourth Century* (London, 1974), 68–70; idem, *Western Aristocracies and the Imperial Court, AD 364–425* (Oxford, 1975), 1–55.

106. Delbrueck, *Die Consulardiptychen*, no. 16, 117–21; Volbach, *Elfenbeinarbeiten der Spätantike*, no. 15, 26–27; M. Gibson, *The Liverpool Ivories: Late Antique and Medieval Ivory and Bone Carving in Liverpool Museum and the Walker Art Gallery* (London, 1994), no 8, 19–22.

107. Its date is greatly disputed, but is possibly Justinianic. Volbach, *Elfenbeinarbeiten der Spätantike*, 36–37; K. Wessel, 'Das Diptychon Barberini', *Akten des XI Internationalen Byzantinistenkongress* (Munich, 1960), 665–70.

108. Symmachus, *Ep.* 2. 81.2.

109. A. Cutler, 'Barberiana: Notes on the Making, Content and Provenance of Louvre OA 9063', in *Tesserae. Festschrift für J. Engemann*. JbAC Ergänzungsband 18 (Münster, 1991), 329–39.

110. For a late antique example see Claudius Mamertinus' speech of thanks to Julian delivered on the first day of 362: *XII Panegyrici Latini*, 3 with the trans. and commentary by C.E.V. Nixon and B.S. Rogers, *In Praise of Later Roman Emperors: the Panegyrici Latini* (Berkeley, CA, 1994), 386–436.

111. H. Fuhrmann, 'Studien zu den Consulardiptychen verwandten Denkmälern I. Eine Glasschale von der Vicennalienfeier Constantins des Grossen zu Rom im Jahre 326 nach Chr.', *RM* 54 (1939), 161–75; D.B. Harden, ed., *Glass of the Caesars* (Milan, 1987), no. 124, 223–24; K. Painter, 'A Fragment of a Glass Dish in the Antiquarium Comunale, Rome', *Kölner Jahrbuch für Vor- und Frühgeschichte* 22 (1989), 87–98.

112. Fuhrmann, 'Studien zu den Consulardiptychen', identified him as Constantine I. Constantius II was suggested by K. Kraft, 'Eine spätantike Glaspaste', *Jahrbuch für Numismatik und Geldgeschichte* 2 (1950–51), 36–42, and supported by J.W. Salomonson, 'Kunstgeschichtliche und ikonographische Untersuchungen zu einem Tonfragment der Sammlung Benaki in Athen', *BABesch* 47 (1973), 3–82, but the identification of unnamed late antique representations of emperors is notoriously difficult.

113. Fuhrmann, 'Studien zu den Consulardiptychen'.

114. M.R. Salzman, *On Roman Time: The Codex-Calendar of 354 and the Rhythms of Urban Life in Late Antiquity* (Berkeley, CA, 1990). This luxury manuscript (known through three Renaissance copies of a Carolingian copy) was produced for the private consumption of an aristocrat in Rome outside the circle of the imperial court, but contains images of the emperor Constantius II and his junior colleague Gallus as consuls for the year 354 and the dedication 'Salvis Augustis, Felix Valentinus' (Under safe Augusti, may Valentinus [the manuscript's owner] prosper). See also H. Stern, *Le Calendrier de 354: étude sur son texte et ses illustrations* (Paris, 1953).

115. Salomonson, 'Kunstgeschichtliche und ikonographische Untersuchungen', 52.

116. Delbrueck, *Die Consulardiptychen*, 68–73.

117. H. Fuhrmann, 'Studien zu den Consulardiptychen verwandten Denkmälern II: Tönerne Missoria aus der Zeit der Tetrarchie' *RM* 55 (1940), 92–99 [a fragment from Ephesus in Vienna, Kunsthistorisches Museum]; J.W. Salomonson 'Spätrömische rote Tonware mit Reliefverzierung aus Nordafrikanischen Werkstätten: entwicklungseschichtliche Untersuchungen zur reliefgeschmückten Terra Sigillata Chiara "C"', *BABesch* 44 (1969), 4–109, Fig. 7 [Carthage Museum], 14 [Athens, Benaki Coll.]; idem. 'Kunstgeschichtliche und ikonographische Untersuchungen' [a second fragment in the Benaki Coll.]; Garbsch and Overbeck, *Spätantike zwischen Heidentum und Christentum*, no. 28, 85; no. 258, 195–96 [both in Munich, Prähistorische Staatssammlung]. On the imitation of more precious materials in pottery see M. Vickers and D. Gill, *Artful Crafts: Ancient Greek Silverware and Pottery* (Oxford, 1994).

118. Salzman, *On Roman Time*, 193–231. Cf. the standard corpus by A. Alföldi, E. Alföldi and C.L. Clay *Die Kontorniat-Medallions* 3 vols (Berlin, 1976–90).

119. Bracci, *Dissertazione sopra un clipeo votivo*; Delbrueck, *Die Consulardiptychen*, no. 35, 154–56; K.S. Painter, 'The Silver Dish of Ardabur Aspar', in E. Herring, R. Whitehouse and J. Wikins, eds, *Paper of the Fourth Conference of Italian Archaeology 2: The Archaeology of Power, part 2* (London, 1991), 74–79.

120. However, ivory diptychs were subject to recarving and reuse, especially in the Carolingian period. See P. Lasko, *Ars Sacra 800–1200*, 2nd edn (New Haven and London, 1994), 17; Delbrueck (n. 1 supra), 22, K. Weitzmann, 'The Heracles Plaques of St. Peter's Cathedra', *Art Bulletin* 55 (1973), 25–29.

121. Corippus, *In Laud. Iust.* 4.110.

122. For example, Justinian, Novel CV (536/7 AD) emphasizes the emperor's exclusive right to give gold 'whether small in form or – and more particularly – large, whether

of medium size either struck or simply weighed [i.e. ingots]', trans. in Hendy, *Byzantine Monetary Economy*, 194.

123. Cf. K. Hopkins, *Conquerors and Slaves*, Sociological Studies in Roman History vol. 1 (Cambridge, 1978), 197–242, esp. 215–31.

124. This point has been made most influentially by Zanker, *The Power of Images*, esp. 265–95, although for some important reservations see A. Wallace-Hadrill, 'Rome's Cultural Revolution' *JRS* 79 (1989), 157–64.

125. Grabar, *L'empereur*, 88.

126. Kiilerich, *Late Fourth Century Classicism*, 22. Meischner, 'Das Missorium des Theodosius', 419 identifies him as Constantius III.

127. This hypothesis does not intend to challenge the established readings of the iconography of the enthroned emperor and Tellus, whose meanings I see as part of the established language of imperial iconography shared by the emperor and his subjects, that structured communication between them.

128. On the continued vitality of the imperial cult in the fourth century, purged of those aspects offensive to Christians such as animal sacrifice, see Salzman, *On Roman Time*, 142.

2

Sacred silver: from patera to paten

In [Pope Silvester's] time, the Emperor Constantine built these churches and adorned them:
The Constantinian Basilica, where he placed these gifts:

> *A hammered silver fastigium … weighing 2025 lb of burnished silver;*
> *the apse vault of finest gold; and hanging beneath the fastigium, a light of finest*
> *gold with 50 dolphins [ornamental wick-holders], of finest gold weighing 50 lb, with*
> *chains weighing 25 lb;*
> *4 crowns of finest gold with 20 dolphins, each weighing 15lb;*
> *the apse-vault of the basilica, of gold-foil in both directions, 500 lb;*
> *7 altars of finest silver each weighing 200 lb;*
> *7 gold patens each weighing 30 lb;*
> *16 silver patens each weighing 30 lb;*
> *7 scyphi [large chalices] of finest gold each weighing 10 lb;*
> *a special scyphus of hard coral, adorned on all sides with prase and jacinth jewels,*
> *inlaid with gold, weighing in all its parts 23 lb 3 oz;*
> *20 silver scyphi each weighing 15 lb.*

The above quotation is a short extract from a list of Constantine's lavish endowments to the church that would later be known as the Lateran Basilica.[1] It appears in the Liber Pontificalis, a history of the Church in Rome told through a series of short biographies of the popes, from St Peter onwards. A notable feature of this text is its listing of the donations made both by individual popes, and by emperors – above all Constantine – to the major churches in Rome. Liturgical vessels and revetments of silver, gold and other precious materials feature heavily in these lists, of which the extract above is typical. I have chosen to begin this chapter on 'sacred silver' with the donation lists of the Liber Pontificalis for a number of reasons. The Lateran Basilica, to which the quotation refers, was probably Constantine's first church foundation in Rome following his victory at the Milvian Bridge, and his resulting adoption of Christianity.[2] Official recognition of Christianity brought reparation for confiscations of property during persecution, tax privileges for clerics and church property, and extensive imperial patronage both in Rome and in the Holy Land.[3] The Church therefore began to accumulate considerable wealth. These changes in the status of the Church inevitably affected its relationship with wealth in the private sphere.[4] While the Christian ideal of renouncing one's personal wealth and distributing it among the poor was still widely advocated, imperial patronage of church buildings and furnishings provided another model for pious disposal of wealth, which could be seen as a middle ground between hoarding one's wealth and using it exclusively for charity.[5] This strategy revived pre-Christian models of building-dedication where the benefits for the donor and the recipient were well established.[6] Thus Constantine's conversion, and his embarkation on a major programme of church building arguably transformed the role of silver, as an important means of measuring and displaying wealth, within the Church.

It is that transformation, 'from patera to paten', that this chapter shall attempt to trace, through a range of texts relating to the three centuries after Constantine's conversion, and in the surviving silver artefacts from the same period. While for the most part less elaborate and less costly that those listed in the Liber Pontificalis, the surviving liturgical silver nevertheless offers us valuable insights into the ways that the Church made this medium a sacred one, and distinguished it from domestic silverware. Although gold is as important as silver in Constantine's donations, this should be seen as a measure of the exceptional richness of the imperial endowments; for the majority of churches in the Roman Empire, silver (albeit sometimes gilded) was the norm, just as most affluent householders used silver rather than gold tableware. While Christian uses of silver represent a significant late antique innovation, it should not be forgotten that the use of silver (and other precious metals) in sacred contexts was as much a feature of the classical world as it was of the late antique one. The role of temples and sanctuaries as storehouses of wealth, public or private, in the ancient world is well known. While the Parthenon served as a repository for the financial resources of Athens (even possessing an emergency reserve in the gold cladding of its cult statue of Athena), Panhellenic sanctuaries like Delphi grew rich on the dedications of states and individuals.[7] For this reason, a discussion of the few surviving hoards of Roman silver dedicated to pagan deities is included in this chapter. Indeed the inventory-like quality of the donation lists in the Liber Pontificalis finds clear echoes in such pre-Christian temple inventories, as well as resembling (albeit on a much grander scale) actual inventories of church possessions, written on materials which have survived in the dry climate of Egypt, or copied in later manuscripts.[8] Although continuities with pagan practices cannot be ignored, the use of silver in the service in the church did substantially transform the way it was perceived in the world of late antiquity, not least because of Christianity's traditional, even fundamental, problematization of the ownership of wealth. This created inherent contradictions in the position of the Church as the recipient of lavish imperial patronage from the fourth century. By studying its use of and attitudes to silver we can gain valuable insights into how Christians strove to come to terms with these contradictions.

Popes, emperors and patronage

The Liber Pontificalis in its current form was composed towards the middle of the sixth century, and subsequently added to, life by papal life, from

the mid-seventh century until the latter half of the ninth century.[9] Much
of its historical material, at least until the late fifth century, is of dubious
veracity. However, the details which it contains of church foundations and
endowments from the time of Constantine onwards are generally considered
to be authentic and reliable. The possibility of its being a sixth-century forgery
seems ruled out, above all by the inclusion of information which someone
in the sixth century was unlikely to have been aware of, for example that
Egypt in the fourth century was included in the diocese of the East (specified
in one of Constantine's land bequests to St Peter's).[10] The lists of donations
were therefore probably excerpted from documents in the papal archives
recording such bequests, and it is possible that the sixth-century compiler
and his continuators were relatively junior clerical officials working for the
Roman church.[11] As well as recording the building of many of the churches
in Rome which survive to this day – albeit often concealed by later alterations
– this valuable work also records the wealth of movable and non-movable
furnishings in gold and silver which adorned these buildings, all of which
has now vanished without trace. For this reason, those parts of the Liber
Pontificalis which discuss building activity have received the most attention
from art historians, since it is possible to compare what is recorded with
what survives.[12] Discussions of individual details of the lists of liturgical
vessels and other fittings are rare, and for this reason I want to concentrate
almost exclusively on such details here, although they are only one aspect of
patronage presented in the Liber Pontificalis

So what does the Liber Pontificalis tell us about the silver and other precious
metals which decorated Rome's churches? Although it does not offer a detailed
description, it does allow as to define the different ways precious metals were
used in churches. The lists divide into movable and non-movable fittings,
the former category comprising liturgical vessels, baptismal equipment and
lamps, the latter comprising metal revetments for a variety of structures, such
as altars, tombs, arches and fonts. Within the category of movable fittings,
a fairly small and standardized vocabulary is used throughout to denote
the different type of object. The decoration of individual vessels is seldom
recorded, and then only in a general way (for example, 'a silver scyphus
decorated in relief'),[13] but the type of metal and its weight are always noted.
This is in keeping with the original purpose of recording such donations when
they were made, to note the value of each individual item. The same strategy
can be seen in the lists of land endowments, which record their revenue in
solidi. Thus the Liber Pontificalis is not a literary work (at least where the
records of donations are concerned) and from the outset, the Church's use
of silver is simply recorded, not problematized, justified or mystified. The
compilers (both of the Liber Pontificalis, and the documentation on which it
drew) are concerned with numbers, weights and types of items donated – in
short with their value in material terms.[14] They are also concerned with the
donors themselves. The activities of the popes as patrons from the time of
Constantine onwards play a significant role in the Liber Pontificalis, which
can be read simultaneously as a history of the See of Rome, and of papal

patronage within that See. To understand why patronage plays such an important part in the lives of the Liber Pontificalis, we must turn briefly to the history of the papacy in late antique Rome.

This history is, broadly speaking, one of gradually increasing independence and political power for the papacy, as Rome was transformed from an imperial to an ecclesiastical capital. As Robert Markus succinctly states:

> In the course of the hundred years from the pontificate of Damasus (366–84) to that of Leo I (440–61) the physical aspect of the City had altered: it had become a fitting backdrop for the exercise of a new kind of authority by its bishop. The ecclesiastical claims elaborated by the popes during this period found a counterpart in the municipal authority gradually taken over by them.[15]

The 'new kind of authority' developed by the popes from the late fourth century includes the take-over of the emperor's role as the most important patron in Rome, which can be explored through the records of ecclesiastical and imperial patronage in the Liber Pontificalis. We should begin by considering the first and longest list of donations in the Liber Pontificalis: those donations attributed to Constantine (in reality perhaps representing the munificence of the Constantinian dynasty, down to the reign of Constantius II).[16]

It is significant that while the first records of church building and endowment in the Liber Pontificalis are imperial, after Constantine no emperor or other secular ruler gives on anywhere near the same scale.[17] This is closely connected to the fact that it was Constantine who decided to abandon Rome as an imperial capital, and thus as the prime location of major imperial patronage. Thus, his list of donations serves less as an imperial model than a model to be imitated by subsequent popes.[18] However, major papal patronage does not really begin until the fifth century. Between Silvester (314–335) and Xystus (or Sixtus) III (432–440), there are five lists of donations of liturgical vessels by popes. Two of these, for Mark (336) and Damasus (366–384) are quite short, representing about 100 lbs of silver each.[19] Innocentius (401/402–417) presents almost 500 lbs to the basilica of Gervasius and Protasius, but this seems to have been bought with funds left in the will of the wealthy widow Vestina, who had specified that money be raised to build the basilica by selling her jewellery, so is really an example of lay rather than ecclesiastical patronage.[20] Boniface (418–422) gives almost 100 lbs of silver to the oratory of St Felicity, while his successor Celestine (422–432) presents the much larger amount of 1286 lbs to one of the five basilicas of Julius, and the basilicas of St Peter and St Paul.[21] The generosity of Celestine can in part be explained by the need to refurbish Rome's major churches after the Gothic sack of 410: unlike his predecessors, his attention is not directed at new foundations. He can also be seen as heralding a new era of papal patronage, which develops fully under Xystus III, when we see a clear papal imitation of Constantinian patronage. This was recognized by Krautheimer, who pointed out that Xystus' donations of plate and estates to his foundation of S. Maria Maggiore were deliberately intended to rival imperial donations to St Peter's and St Paul's, just as his church to the Virgin was intended to rival those of the apostles as a major sacred site in Rome.[22] This idea is strengthened by a closer analysis of the items in the list of donations. Altogether there are 998 lbs of silver, and 14 lbs of gold, the first gold items recorded in the Liber Pontificalis since Constantine's donations.[23] Three hundred pounds of this silver are expended on an altar, another item listed in Constantinian inventories but not in those of the intervening period (the Constantinian altars weigh between 200 and 350 lbs). Xystus' other recorded donations are similarly lavish: vessels weighing a total of 459 lbs of silver are given to his foundations of S. Lorenzo in Lucia, as well as 'a special gold scyphus adorned with pearls, weighing 10 lb' and a gold lamp of equal weight.

The Liber Pontificalis records Xystus' relationship with present as well as past emperors, in this case the emperor of the West, Valentinian III. The latter made three substantial donations to the Roman church during his reign: a gold and jewelled image of Christ and the apostles for St Peter's, a replacement for Constantine's silver fastigium in the Lateran which had been plundered by the Goths, and a silver confessio for St Paul's.[24] These gifts are presented, unlike those of Constantine, as being orchestrated by the pope, rather than merely occurring during his time in office. Whether this represents the actual mechanism behind these donations we cannot tell, but it is surely significant that the emperor is presented as complying with the pope's request. That Valentinian's gifts are all to Constantinian foundations is not surprising, in part because they represented some of the most important holy sites in Rome, but also because the propaganda value of (re-)embellishing some of his illustrious predecessor's buildings must have been clear. The Liber Pontificalis continues to record votive gifts from the various rulers of the former Roman Empire to the churches of the two apostles into the sixth century. During the pontificate of Hormisdas (514–523), King Clovis of the Franks sends a votive crown with jewels to St Peter while the Gothic king, Theodoric, sends two silver candlesticks with a combined weight of 70 lb. But the most lavish gifts come from the Byzantine emperor Justin I, who sends gospel covers, liturgical vessels, and pallia; the first two being mostly gold with jewels, and the latter purple cloth embroidered with gold.[25] Similar gifts were presented by the same emperor in the pontificate of John I (523–526), and by Justinian in that of John II (533–535). In each case, St Peter's was the recipient, although it shared Justin's second donation with St Paul's, St Mary's and St Laurence's.[26] The gifts of the Byzantine emperors are distinguished by the lavishness of individual items and the inclusion of liturgical robes of luxury fabrics, which do not appear in the Liber Pontificalis until this point.

But if secular rulers concentrated their attentions on the Constantinian foundations, they also were extensively embellished and re-embellished by the popes. Xystus himself gave 400 lb of silver for the confessio of St Peter's (twice the weight of Valentinian's confessio at St Paul's), and redecorated the confessio of St Laurence's with porphyry columns and 550 lbs of silver (though this is just over half of the 1000 lbs of silver which Constantine gave to this church, all or some of which may have been stolen by the Goths).[27] Hilarius (461–468) did very little actual building work, but concentrated on endowing the Lateran, St Peter's, St Paul's, and St Laurence's with liturgical vessels and lighting equipment, which were probably needed to make good losses in the Vandal sack of Rome in 455.[28] His gifts, like those of Xystus, are lavish: 16 lbs of gold and 350 lbs of silver at the Lateran; 9 lbs of gold and 156 lbs of silver at St Peter's; 10 lbs of gold and 64 lbs of silver at St Paul's; and 22 lbs of gold and 333 lbs of silver at the tomb of St Laurence. In some cases the gold items are described as jewelled. This pattern continues into the sixth and seventh centuries: at St Peter's, Gregory the Great (590–604) 'built a canopy over the altar with four columns of fine silver, provided a purple-dyed cloth to go above the apostle's body, and decorated it with the finest gold, weighing 100 lbs', while Honorius (625–638) 'renewed all the sacred vessels at St Peter's', covered the apostle's confessio with 187 lbs silver, the main doors of the church with 975 lbs silver and placed two 62 lb candlesticks in front the apostle's body.[29]

This pattern of refurbishment and renewal in the originally Constantinian foundations must have had the effect of slowly obliterating the original signs of imperial patronage with those of the new rulers of Rome, the popes. It is questionable how many of Constantine's original gifts of liturgical vessels, lighting equipment and other less movable furnishings remained by the beginning of the seventh century. The barbarian sacks of Rome must have been responsible for a large part of their loss, as must such events as the sack of the Lateran by the Byzantine exarch of Italy, Isaac, in 640, described in the life of Pope Severinus. Constantine, as ruler of the Roman Empire, stood at the end of the line of emperors whose prestige was enhanced by building projects carried out in Rome. In transforming Rome into the sacred centre of the West, the popes usurped the emperors' role as the most important patron in the city. Though votive gifts from rulers of the West and the East continued to be sent to Rome, these gifts served to acknowledge the city's role as a potent sacred centre rather than assert their donor's authority there. Indicative of this transformation is the inscription in the mosaics of the triumphal arch in S. Maria Maggiore, which reads: 'BISHOP XYSTUS TO THE PEOPLE OF GOD'.[30] The citizens of Rome have become the people of God, and their prime earthly benefactor is their bishop.

Saints and silver

The attitudes towards the use of silver in a sacred context which the Liber Pontificalis reveals are very different from those encountered in the hagiography and homilies of the sixth and seventh centuries. There are several works of this type which mention liturgical vessels and the furnishing of churches. Since these sources are for the most part much more self-consciously literary works than the Liber Pontificalis, they need careful interpretation, with attention to genre and the use of topoi, but can be among the most interesting for understanding the complexities of the discourse surrounding silver and other luxury materials in the late antique church. The key texts here are in Greek and Syriac, thus the focus will be on the Church in the East of the empire. It has been suggested that social conditions in the East – population increases, natural disasters and resultant famine – created more pressure on the financial reserves of the Church there than in the West, where surpluses were more common.[31] It may be for this reason that issues of sacred and secular wealth are prominent in the Eastern texts; that the tension between the traditions of Christian poverty and the status of the Church as a wealthy member of early Byzantine society was more marked. Overall, the texts attest to anxieties on this subject, which manifest themselves in a variety of different ways.

In the Life of St Theodore of Sykeon, written in Greek in the early seventh century and describing the life of an ascetic monastic saint who lived in central Anatolia in the latter half of the sixth century, there are signs of anxiety about the way in which the church's use of silver exposes it to the pollution of secular life.[32] This work describes how, as the monastery which Theodore had founded increased in size, he sent his archdeacon to Constantinople to purchase a silver chalice and paten set (42.5: διοκοποτήριον) to replace the marble ones then in use.[33] The archdeacon accomplished his task, returned to the monastery, and showed the vessels to Theodore, who immediately declared that they were defiled. When the archdeacon protested, and stressed the craftsmanship, and the imperial control stamped on the vessels, Theodore invited him to celebrate mass with these vessels, in the course of which, through Theodore's prayers, they turned black. The archdeacon returned the vessels to Constantinople, and it was discovered that they had been made from the chamber pot of a prostitute (42.34: σίτλας τινὸς ἑταιρίδος)! New vessels were provided, and everyone was happy.

In the context of the study of early Byzantine silver, this seemingly extraordinary story has most often been valued for the details it provides of sixth-century silver-working practice: the relatively long journey made by the archdeacon to the capital to purchase silver vessels, the rare mention of the early Byzantine practice of marking silver vessels with five imperial control stamps (42.17–18: τήν τε πεντασφάγιστον αὐτῶν δοκιμήν).[34] The central incident of the story – how the silver from which the chalice and paten were made had been contaminated by a previous use – has aroused less interest. However, in its way it is equally important for understanding early Byzantine attitudes to silver. In this text silver forms the centre of a discourse about purity, a discourse which is articulated through several topoi. First of these is the silver chamber pot, which has a long history as a paradigm of senseless, immoral extravagance.[35] As such, it makes a prime example of a prostitute's tainted wealth: her immoral earnings are spent on an object which is polluted by its function, while the prostitute herself is an extreme example of worldly sin.[36]

The central theme of this story – the transfer of a silver item, polluted in a secular context, into the sphere of the sacred and the consequences thereof – appears elsewhere in contemporary Byzantine literature. The historian Theophylact Simocatta tells the tale of a magician in Constantinople who sells a silver bowl, which he has used in his magic rites, to some traders, who resell it to the bishop of Heracleia, Perinthos. He uses this bowl to collect the miraculous ointment which flows from the bones of the martyr Glyceria in his church, for which purpose a bronze bowl had previously been used. However, with the silver bowl in place, the flow of ointment – and of miracles – ceases. After much prayer and lamenting on the bishop's part, the past history of the silver bowl is revealed to him in a dream. The bronze bowl is brought back, the ointment flows again, the bishop returns to the city, and contacts both the traders and the Patriarch, who has the magician arrested and executed.[37] Despite the differences between the two stories – the source of the pollution in Theophylact is different (more severe, since the practice of magic was viewed as apostasy), the bowl is bought second-hand rather than recycled to form a new vessel, and the defect is not perceived immediately by the bishop, but has to be revealed in a dream by God – the same central anxiety is present in both texts. Buying silver in the secular sphere for use in a sacred context lays that context open to the danger of pollution. But this is not presented as a reason to reject the use of silver in the church.[38] Rather, distinctions must be made between visible/worldly and invisible/sacred purity, a task which requires divine insight, such as that of a holy man.

This is articulated in the conversation between Theodore and his archdeacon after the latter's return from Constantinople. The vessels which the archdeacon bought are described as 'pure and well-finished, as far as the quality of the silver and the workmanship was concerned' (42.7–9: καθαρὸν καὶ εὐκατασκέαστον ἔργον, ὅσον κατὰ τὴν τοῦ ἀργύρου δοκιμὴν καὶ τοῦ τεχνίτον τὴν ἐργασίαν). The saint, on being shown the vessels, recognizes through his 'clear-sighted eye' (42.13: τῷ διορατικῷ ὀφθαλμῷ) 'their manner of use and their defect'. As the archdeacon stresses the purity of the vessels in the conventions of the secular world (repeating the terms of craftsmanship used in ll 7–9), we are told that he 'looked at the appearance, and not that which was hidden' (42.15–16: οὐ πρὸς τὸ κρυπτόμενον ἀλλὰ πρὸς τὸ φαινόμενον ἀποβλέποντος), and this difference is made explicit in Theodore's reply to him: 'in appearance (42.20: τὸ φαινόμενον) this is a most beautiful specimen … but another hidden (42.23: ἄφανης) cause is spoiling it'. Finally, after the silver turns black, 'the brothers … glorified God who made invisible things visible at the hands of his servant' (42:28–29: οἱ ἀδελφοὶ ἐδόξασαν τὸν θεὸν τὸν τὰ ἄδηλα ποιοῦντα ἔκδηλα διὰ τοῦ δούλου αὐτοῦ). Theodore's status as a holy man is confirmed by his ability to perceive those things which are invisible or hidden, and to know that material objects cannot be judged by their outward appearance. This is forcefully presented in the text by the use of the opposing terms 'φαινόμενον–κρυπτόμενον/ἄφανης' and 'ἄδηλα–ἔκδηγα'. In this story, and that of Theophylact Simocatta, the quality of silver vessels for church use is shown to be subject to different criteria from those which operate for silver vessels in the secular sphere. We may ask whether this was really the case in sixth-century Byzantium? I would suggest that this was not literally so. On the contrary, it seems more likely that stories like this one arose from anxieties that the silver used in the church was judged on the same criteria – craftsmanship, control stamps, weight – as silver used in the secular sphere. We should see here an attempt to differentiate between the two.

A text which raises issues closely related to those in the *Life of St Theodore*, is the story of Sosiana and John, one of John of Ephesus' *Lives of Eastern Saints*.[39] This Syriac work is a collection of lives of holy men and women in the Monophysite church, mainly set during its persecution in the sixth century. It is a work characterized by its historical and individual detail, unlike some of the collections of saints' lives written at the same time, which rely more on didactic stereotypes.[40] The *Life* of Sosiana and John exemplifies the individualistic character of John of Ephesus' work, being the story of an unusual woman who performs an unusual act of donation to the church. Sosiana and John are a pious couple who are chamberlains to a patrician woman, Caesaria (whose ascetic withdrawal is described in the previous *Life*).[41] Following her husband's death, Sosiana gives his and her own costly silk garments to be made into liturgical cloths and distributed to churches and monasteries. John of Ephesus and other church officials feel that a more correct action would be to sell the clothes (which are worth a pound of gold each) and give the proceeds to the poor, however Sosiana is adamant that the conditions of her donation are equally acceptable to God. She defends her decision to leave herself only 'cheap, ordinary clothes', by proclaiming that she will not live more than a year, and if she were to spare any of her fine clothes, they might fall into the hands of a prostitute 'and I on my part shall be called to account for them'. After this, 'she brought her silver, which amounted to many pounds, and it was given up and chalices and patens were made, and many dishes and spoons'. Both clothes and silver are recycled from their secular forms to produce sacred objects: the silver is melted down, while the clothes are cut up and embroidered with the names of John and Sosiana in gold. This points to the important parallels between silk textiles and silver vessels as types of luxury items which were used both in sacred and secular contexts.[42] The altar cloths and chalice veils made from the couple's silk clothes occupy the same ritual space as the liturgical vessels made from their household silver. Sosiana dies within the year, as she had predicted, and is thus recognized as a saint.

Sosiana's story should be seen against the background of ascetic renunciation and concern for the welfare of the poor which characterizes so many of the lives described by John of Ephesus. Why does Sosiana adopt a different strategy from, for example, her mistress Caesaria, who gives away some of her wealth and uses the rest to found a monastery? Her chief concern appears to be her fear that her worldly goods might be subject to worldly pollution after her death. It is as if her and her husband's silk robes and silver plate – which would have been required by their position in the patrician Caesaria's household – had been already semi-sacralized by their ownership, and so the obvious way to protect that status is to transform these goods into consecrated church possessions.[43] Sosiana claims that were one of her robes to fall into the hand of a prostitute, she would be held responsible by God for allowing such contamination to take place. This is the reverse of the episode in the *Life of St Theodore*, where the Church is shown to be in danger of pollution from the wealth of prostitutes. Here the Church acts to protect wealth from such pollution.

Another Syriac text, *Severus of Antioch's Homily 100*, delivered on the feast of the martyr St Drosis, exhibits a different attitude to the wealth of private individuals and the Church, which is less a product of anxiety and perhaps a more accurate reflection of the motives for donation to the Church by wealthy individuals.[44] The main body of the homily dwells at length on the rejection of worldly luxuries by Drosis (who is said to have been the daughter of the emperor Trajan) in favour of Christ. In the latter part of the homily however, Severus (the patriarch of Antioch) complains that, despite the favours granted to the people by the martyr, none of them give her any of their surplus wealth.[45] He appeals to the congregation to give sufficient silver to cover the dome of the ciborium in the church of St Drosis, saying that this could be achieved either if everyone in the congregation were to donate a pound of silver or if a single wealthy person were to give the whole quantity required.

In his attempt to persuade his congregation that they can easily afford to give silver towards Drosis' ciborium, Severus compares their use of silver in a secular context with their failure to give any to St Drosis. He envisages the person who could afford to pay for the revetment of the whole ciborium as 'one of those who lie on high couches and eat their meals from silver dishes'.[46] He describes women who are accompanied to the baths by silver vessels weighing many pounds, who ride in chairs adorned with silver, pulled by mules whose harnesses are also decorated with silver.[47] Although there is a certain degree of rhetorical sarcasm in these comments ('even the bits of the mules do not lack silver') women's toilet vessels, fittings for chairs and horse trappings are all represented in the fourth-century Esquiline Treasure, and there is no reason to suppose that such objects were not also found in sixth-century Antioch.[48] Finally Severus contrasts the eagerness of the women in his congregation to give wedding presents of gold jewellery and other expensive objects to imperial brides when they visit Antioch, to their neglect of St Drosis, who in conventional Byzantine hagiographic terminology is called 'the daughter of the King of Heaven' and the 'bride of Christ'.[49]

Thus Severus presents the act of giving to the church in terms of traditional patterns of giving in Antioch. Fully aware of the political motives behind the pattern of giving to figures such as the emperor's daughters, he spells out the benefits that the congregation will receive from Drosis' husband Christ if they give to her church, constructing the advantage to the donor in both material and spiritual terms.[50] Although in an earlier part of his homily, Severus had suggested imitation of the martyr's renunciation of marriage and worldly possessions, in this final section he advocates behaviour which is less disruptive of the social structure of the household.[51] The congregation is encouraged to extend the patterns of secular gift-giving to the church, which thereby becomes a participant – ideally the most prominent one – in a traditional social process. St Drosis is a worthier recipient of their gifts than the emperor's daughter, because she can provide benefits both in this life *and* the next.

The pragmatic, traditionalist approach adopted here by Severus, which appears to acknowledge that ascetic renunciation is something which the citizens of Antioch would rather hear about than practice themselves, seems far removed from the anxieties expressed in the *Life of St Theodore* or the *Lives of Eastern Saints*, despite its also being a product of the sixth century. If however we turn to Severus' reasons for wanting the ciborium to be covered in silver, we see a theological approach to church furnishings which has more in common with the attitude found in those texts discussed previously. To cover the ciborium with silver is, he states, not just an aesthetic issue but one of reverence (σέβας).[52] A theological value is implied in the decoration of the church, which is reinforced by the allegorical description of the ciborium that follows, where its dome is compared to the dome of heaven 'to show us who perform the priestly functions that we stand inside heaven, following the example of the incorporeal armies, and we celebrate mysteriously the holy rites'. The analogy between a dome and the heavens is commonplace in Byzantine thought, but the implication that the holiest part of the church should receive the most lavish decoration is interesting and can be paralleled elsewhere.[53] Procopius, in his description of Hagia Sophia uses a single example to allow the reader to gage the amount of precious metal which Justinian has bestowed upon the church: 'that part of the church which is especially sacred and accessible to priests only – it is called the sanctuary – exhibits forty thousand pounds of silver'.[54] Procopius' choice of example is surely inspired by the liturgical importance of the sanctuary within the church, as well as the vast amount of silver which embellished it. Or rather the two facts are intimately linked – the sanctity of the place and the value of its decoration.

Perhaps the most famous ciborium in the Byzantine world was that of St Demetrius at Thessalonike, which plays an important role in four of the stories contained in the seventh-century collection of the *Miracles of St Demetrius*.[55] This ciborium was unusual in that it housed the tomb of the saint, rather than the main altar, but (like Severus of Antioch hoped the ciborium of Drosis would be) it was completely covered in silver. The importance of its silver revetments is articulated in the sixth miracle, where the story is told of how, after a fire, not enough silver could be salvaged to re-cover the saint's ciborium entirely. The archbishop decides that the episcopal throne should be melted down to provide the extra metal needed, 'because the ciborium was said to contain the tomb of the martyr, and moreover, it was truly the most beautiful ornament in the whole church' (διότι καὶ τὸ ἡγιασμένον μνημεῖον τοῦ μάρτυρος λέγεται περιέχειν, ἄλλως δὲ καὶ τοῦ παντὸς οἴκου ἐτύγχανεν ὡς ἀληθῶς μεγίστη εὐπρέπεια).[56] Just as for Severus, the decoration of the martyr's ciborium is the top priority for the archbishop of Thessalonike. It is also shown to be a priority for the saint, who repeatedly warns the archbishop not to melt down the episcopal throne, and finally causes two donors to turn up and offer the necessary silver – 115 lb – between them. The active intervention of St Demetrius on behalf of his ciborium and on behalf of the archbishop's throne – as well as the city of Thessalonike as a whole – is a theme which runs through the other miracles involving that structure. In one, a visitor to the city for the first time has a vision in a dream of the ciborium (which is described in detail), where he sees St Demetrius sitting inside it, persuading the Lady Eutaxia or Good Order to stay within the city at a time of unrest in the empire.[57] In another, the saint reprimands a sacristan for replacing large candles offered by worshippers at his ciborium by small ones.[58] He is even not above causing a fire to destroy his own ciborium during the night, so that the city is up and alert when barbarians attack it.[59]

The *Miracles of St Demetrius* show an overwhelmingly positive attitude to the use of silver to decorate the most sacred places in the church. Not surprisingly, the saint is shown to approve of the embellishment of his shrine, and to provide material for its refurbishment without depriving other parts of the church of their adornment. However, within the individual descriptions of the parts of his ciborium in the tenth miracle we find the spiritual value of these furnishings emphasized as well as their material value. The cross which crowns the dome of the ciborium is described in these terms: 'At the very summit flashes forth the trophy that is victorious over death: by its silver composition it amazes our corporeal eyes, while by bringing Christ to mind, it illuminates with grace the eyes of the intellect – I mean the life-giving and venerable cross of God our Saviour.'[60] A metaphorical comparison between the material and spiritual value of the silver from which the cross (and indeed the whole ciborium) is made is articulated here. The 'eyes of the intellect' (τοὺς τῆς διανοίας ὀφθαλμοὺς) here recall the 'clear-sighted eye' (τῷ διορατκῷ ὀφθαλμῷ) of St Theodore of Sykeon with which he perceived the hidden impurity of his monastery's new chalice and paten. It is through the development of this type of 'seeing' that the late antique Church developed its own distinctive set of meanings for the silver and other types of precious materials which decorated its buildings. These meanings co-exist with, rather than replace, the secular and materialist attitudes towards the use of such media. It is arguable that the Church never abandoned those, since it continued to exist in a society where wealth and the exercise of power were closely linked. However its contribution lay in the way it sanctified and transformed material value, by removing it from the plane of the visible to that of the invisible.[61]

Material remains: pagan and Christian cult treasures

We now return to the visible plane to consider the most tangible evidence we have for the use of silver in the late antique Church, namely surviving hoards of liturgical silver. As indicated earlier, I will begin by considering the relationship between church and temple treasures, to see if pagan practice provided any antecedents for later ecclesiastical use of silver, and where any differences between the two types of hoard lie. The number of silver hoards which can be securely associated with pagan cults is small. The three known examples come exclusively from the western part of the empire, namely Britain and Gaul. Not unexpectedly, they are rather earlier than the surviving church treasures, which mainly belong to the sixth century. The two Gaulish finds, the Berthouville Treasure and the Notre-Dame-D'Allençon Treasure were both concealed in the late second/early third century AD, but contain many pieces from earlier in the second century, and even the first century.[62]

The Thetford Treasure, found in East Anglia, has been dated to the second half of the fourth century, with a suggested deposition date of the 380s or early 390s, and is thus both chronologically and geographically close to the earliest known Christian pieces.[63]

The objects in the Berthouville, Notre-Dame-D'Allençon and Thetford Treasures carry inscriptions dedicating them to Mercury, Minerva and Faunus respectively. The three hoards are not associated with large towns or well-known shrines, a characteristic they share with the church treasures. Being in Gaul and Britain, the cults may well have been Romanized versions of Celtic deities, but as we cannot associate the hoards with the remains of specific shrines, it is impossible to say what local peculiarities the cults may have incorporated.[64] At least in the case of the Gallic hoards, the practice of votive giving that they represent is typical of that known from literary sources for other parts of the Roman world, and the images of Mercury on pieces of the Berthouville Treasure use the standard Graeco-Roman iconography for that god (the case of the Thetford Treasure is more complicated and will be discussed in further detail below).[65]

The Berthouville (Bibliothèque Nationale, Cabinet des Médailles) and Notre-Dame-d'Allençon (Louvre) Treasures were both found in the 1830s in north-west France. The former consists of a total 93 items (some of which are small fragments and detached handles) with a total weight of 25 kg. Most of the items are bowls, cups and jugs, but there are also two statuettes of Mercury, and a bust of a female figure, perhaps his mother, Maia. Most of the pieces in the hoard date approximately to the late second/early third century, but there is a distinct sub-group of about 15 first-century vessels, similar to those recovered from Pompeii and probably of Italian manufacture, dedicated by one individual, Quintus Domitius Tutus. It seems likely that they were already old when he dedicated them, their financial value perhaps enhanced by their antiquity. The Notre-Dame d'Allençon hoard is somewhat smaller, and the vessels it contains are both lighter and less elaborate. As well as about 30 bowls and ladles, it consists of two silver 'masks' or front parts of female heads, presumably images of Minerva, and 20 or so miscellaneous handles, spoons and other small objects, possibly collected for their monetary value alone. A large number of the vessels in both treasures have dedicatory inscriptions to the deity of the shrine. Those in the Berthouville Treasure use neat pointillé letters and name the donor as well as the god; those on the Notre-Dame-d'Allençon Treasure, with the exception of three with pointillé inscriptions naming the donors, are scratched graffiti which read 'Minervae' or abbreviations thereof.

Do any of the vessels in these two hoards have a marked religious character? Clearly the statuettes in the Berthouville hoard, and the 'masks' in the Notre-Dame-d'Allençon hoard are suggestive of cult images.[66] However the majority of the bowls in the latter hoard have no figural imagery at all.[67] In the Berthouville Treasure there is a group of four bowls with emblemata which represent Mercury, in two cases in the setting of a rustic sanctuary. The group of first-century silver, although extremely rich and diverse iconographically, does not appear to have any connection with Mercury. The complexity of its imagery, and the depiction of epic and Dionysiac themes is typical of the domestic silver tableware found at Boscoreale and the House of the Menander, as is the predominance of drinking vessels. Another plate in the hoard has hunting scenes around its rim and in its centre and shows close links with similar plates in contemporary Gallic hoards of domestic dining plate, such as the Rethel Treasure.[68]

What was the function of the vessels in these two treasures? There are two basic possibilities. The first is that such objects mainly served a 'passive' function as a form of symbolic capital. Given by the worshipper to the god, they enriched the god's shrine and established a reciprocal relationship between the worshipper and the god (cf. the use of the dedicatory formula 'votum solvit libens merito' – abreviated to VSLM – on some of the Berthouville pieces). Such gifts were preserved in the shrine as symbols of the compact between the god and the donor, but also represented a financial asset for the shrine which could be liquidated if necessary. This latter aspect provides the most likely motivation for the concealment of both hoards. Such votive gifts might be something already in the donor's possession (like the offering of Quintus Domitius Tutus) or something bought for that purpose.[69] The second possibility is that such vessels were used in the cult rituals of the god. What did such rituals require? The standard sacrificial ritual, which we can assume would be offered to Minerva and Mercury, involved pouring a libation before the killing of the victim. The vessel which was used to pour the libation is represented in Roman art as an omphalos phiale, that is, a flat-bottomed shallow bowl with a hollow knob in the centre.[70] Sometimes this is associated with a jug, presumably to hold the wine used for the libation.[71] Of the two hoards, only the Berthouville contains any of the above vessels, and these (two jugs and a phiale) are part of the group of first-century vessels dedicated by Quintus Domitius Tutus. This complicates any assumption that they were necessarily used in sacrificial ritual. These types of vessel did not have an exclusively sacred function in the Graeco-Roman world, and their association in the Berthouville Treasure with other types of domestic drinking vessel argues against ritual use. The other cultic function which the tableware in the Berthouville and Notre-Dame-d'Allençon might have served was use in cult meals. Cult meals, which are a feature of Greek and Roman religion in both private and state cults, seem from the available evidence to have been festive occasions of communal dining where the meat of the sacrificed victim was consumed.[72] Although in some cases there is evidence for the existence of special rooms with couches for such meals in shrines and public buildings, neither the epigraphic nor the archaeological record offers any evidence for what type of tableware was used by the diners, nor whether such tableware would be owned by the cult or provided by the participants. It would be unwise therefore to claim that the contents of either hoard was used for such a purpose.

The fourth-century Thetford Treasure (British Museum) is both later than the Berthouville and Notre-Dame-d'Allençon hoards, and raises rather different issues. While its religious character is, like theirs, attested by dedicatory inscriptions on some of its pieces, its silver component consists of 33 spoons and 3 strainers (Figs 2.1–2.5), which were found together with a group of jewellery. Most of the spoons carry inscriptions dedicating them to Faunus, a rustic Italian god (sometimes identified with Pan), the existence of whose cult in Britain was unknown until the treasure's discovery.[73] The inscriptions use Celtic epithets for Faunus, suggesting that we may be dealing with an originally Celtic deity who has been conflated with Faunus. The hoard also contains two spoons, which in another context would be identified as Christian. Overall, the hoard raises problems of its function in its religious context. Why, for example, does it contain jewellery, spoons and strainers, but no larger silver vessels? What, if any, ritual function did its components serve in the cult of Faunus? How do we understand the presence of 'Christian' images and inscriptions in this 'pagan' hoard?

It has been argued that the jewellery represents the stock-in-trade of a merchant or craftsman, rather than a personal collection, because of the lack of wear on any of the items (as well as the presence of some unfinished pieces), and the stylistic and chronological homogeneity of the pieces.[74] It is also claimed that the jewellery was commissioned by the shrine as 'religious regalia', or else that the jewellery was placed by the merchant/craftsman in the temple of Faunus for safekeeping.[75] Both these suggestions are hypothetical, and I find neither especially convincing, in particular the 'regalia' theory, which rests on the supposed iconographic references to Faunus among the jewellery. As Johns and Potter mention, jewellery was a common votive gift at shrines of Romano-Celtic deities such as Sul Minerva in Bath. Although it seems more likely such pieces were given singly, unlike the Thetford jewellery, the possibility that the latter was a votive gift (without the function of regalia) should not be ruled out. If that is the case, then it must have been specially commissioned, rather than comprising pieces already in the donor's possession (unlike so many of the Berthouville pieces).

The spoons in the Thetford Treasure fall into a number of groups. Typologically there are 16 large-bowled, 'duck-handled' spoons, and 17 long-handled cochlearia. The inscriptions (which occur on both shape of spoon) fall into three groups: those with religious inscriptions (Figs 2.1, 2.3), those with personal names in the vocative or genitive, often including the word 'vivas' (Figs 2.2, 2.4), and mottoes (Fig. 2.1). Three of the spoons have figural decoration in the bowl: a panther, a triton and a fish are represented (Figs 2.3). The fish is often used in late antiquity as a Christian symbol, and the presence of this spoon, and another long-handled spoon with the inscription 'SILVIOLA VIVAS' followed by a Greek cross (Fig. 2.4), among a majority of spoons with dedications to a pagan deity is not easily explained or understood. How would a Christian of the fourth century have reacted to the knowledge that objects with Christian symbols had been dedicated to a pagan god? Would this amount to sacrilege, or would the Christian symbols be emptied of meaning when they were seen by non-believers?

Both Johns and Potter, who first published the hoard, and others subsequently have assumed that the spoons must have been used in a ritual

2.1   Thetford Treasure, London, British Museum: duck-handled spoons with dedications to Faunus (first three from top) and mottoes (© The British Museum)

of the cult of Faunus. The logic behind such assumptions seems to rest more on the idea that the spoon is a practical implement for use, rather than on evidence for such practices in the worship of Faunus and related gods.[76] In fact, the assumption that the spoons were used in some type of ritual feast ignores the evidence for the nature of cult meals in the Graeco-Roman world, which suggests that these differed little (externally at least) from non-sacred feasts and did not involve 'sacramental' practices.[77] There seems to be little to suggest that the spoons were not votive gifts in the same way that the objects in the Notre-Dame-d'Allençon and Berthouville Treasures were. To give a set of inscribed silver spoons to the god would represent the same in terms of weight as a silver bowl.[78] The possibility that larger silver vessels were also dedicated at the shrine should also be considered, as there is no way of knowing that the Thetford Hoard represents all the objects of value dedicated there. Much of the contents of the late fourth/early fifth-century Hoxne Treasure (which appears to be domestic) closely parallels the Thetford Treasure: it contains gold jewellery and a large number of spoons, ladles and other small table implements, but only five bowls, the largest of which is no more than 20 cm in diameter. It seems inconceivable that the owner of this rich hoard (which also contains almost 15 000 gold and silver coins dating from the latter half of the fourth through to the early fifth century) did not possess larger items of silver tableware, but these clearly were not concealed together with the smaller items of his household valuables.[79] The parallels between the near-contemporary Thetford and Hoxne Treasures further suggest that, apart from their inscriptions, the treasure of Faunus' shrine as it is represented in this hoard differed little from a private hoard of domestic silver and jewellery.

Another area of similarity between the Hoxne Treasure and the Thetford Treasure is the presence of Christian symbols in both. The Hoxne hoard has two spoons with the chi-rho, one with the inscription VIVAS IN DEO, and a set of ten ladles (Fig. 2.6) decorated with the monogram cross, a variant form of chi-rho, which also adorns a necklace clasp.[80] This is a typical feature of other hoards of fourth-century domestic silver plate, such as the Mildenhall and Kaiseraugst Treasures. The Mildenhall Treasure contains eight spoons, of which three are decorated with foliate ornament, three have a chi-rho flanked by an alpha and an omega in the bowl, and two are inscribed 'PAPITEDO VIVAS' and 'PASCENTIA VIVAS' (Fig. 2.7). Unlike the other groups, these last two are not identical and the inscriptions are by different hands. Neither the Mildenhall or Hoxne hoards contain strainers, but the Kaiseraugst Treasure contains 2 small strainers, as well as 22 long-handled cochlearia spoons, 14 duck-handled spoons, and 3 utensils each with a small spoon on one end and a flat, comma-shaped finial on the other, which on one is pierced with a chi-rho (Fig. 2.8). The comma-shaped finial also terminates one of the Kaiseraugst strainers and the smallest of the Thetford strainers (Fig. 2.5).[81]

Strainers and spoons continue to be present in the later sixth-century hoards of liturgical silver (such as the Kaper Koraon Treasure). The question of the the interpretation of the Christian symbols on the spoons in the Thetford Treasure, and the function of the Thetford spoons as a group, can be placed in a wider

2.2   Thetford Treasure, London, British Museum: long-handled spoon inscribed
AGRESTE VIVAS (© The British Museum)

2.3   Thetford Treasure, London, British Museum: duck-handled spoon with triton
engraved in bowl (top); long-handled spoon with panther engraved in bowl, inscribed
DEI FAUNI NARI on handle (centre); long-handled spoon with fish engraved in bowl
(bottom) (© The British Museum)

2.4   Thetford Treasure, London, British Museum: long-handled spoon inscripted
SILVIOLA VIVAS + (© The British Museum)

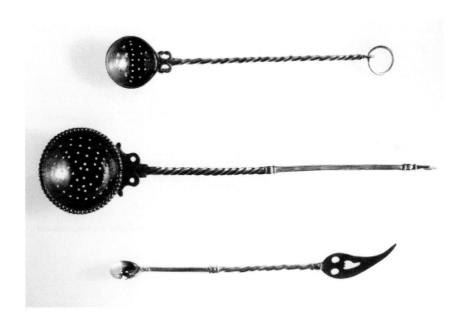

2.5   Thetford Treasure, London, British Museum: strainers (© The British Museum)

context if we compare them with similar spoons and related implements found in hoards of tableware with predominately pagan mythological imagery. Moreover the original context of spoons and strainers in domestic dining services is important in understanding their presence (and subsequent development of their function) in hoards of liturgical silver. It is generally considered that the use of Christian symbols in a domestic context is an expression of the owner's Christian affiliation without liturgical implications – the integration of Christianity into the cultural traditions of well-to-do Romans for whom owning a silver dining service was an essential articulation of their social status.[82] It is reasonable to assume that the two 'Christian' spoons in the Thetford Treasure may have been part of a dining service before being dedicated to the god's shrine. Whether they were dedicated by their original or subsequent owners, and whether they were dedicated to be used or for the value of the silver that they represented, we cannot know. It is likely that they were given by a subsequent, non-Christian owner, but we should leave open the possibility that the donor recognized the Christian imagery, and interpreted it in a way that made it seem appropriate to include these spoons in a dedication to Faunus without further inscriptions being added.

The use of domestic tableware as a votive dedication in a pagan sacred context has important implications for Christianity, since it allows us to see, by comparison, the extent to which the use of silverware in a sacred context is transformed by Christianity; from being one of many possible offerings to a god's shrine, it becomes a prime offering to God in the Church because of the centrality of sacralized eating and drinking to Christian ritual. For this reason, liturgical silver relates as much to the implements of dining as to the tradition of pagan votives. Although this is less visible in the shapes and decoration of the major liturgical vessels such as chalices and patens – which by the sixth century had developed their own distinctive forms – spoons and strainers retain traces of these links. This is well exemplified in the Syrian liturgical hoard, the Kaper Koraon Treasure, which contains five spoons (four of which have crosses on the bowls, and two of which have dedicatory inscriptions) (Fig. 2.9), three strainers (two similar in design and size to the Thetford strainers) and a second group of seven spoons with an Apostle's name and the personal monogram of someone called Domnos on each (Fig. 2.10).[83]

The precise way in which spoons and strainers were used in eucharistic ritual in the early Church is not attested in literary or visual sources. By analogy with later known practices in the West and the East it seems possible, though not certain, that spoons were used at times to administer communion; while strainers have an obvious function of straining wine, which was necessary whether in a domestic or a sacred context.[84] The first group of spoons in the Kaper Koraon hoard (those traditionally considered part of the Hama Treasure) seems to have been designed for eucharistic ritual: the spoons are decorated with a simple incised cross, as are several of the Kaper Koraon patens. The spoons' inscriptions name the donors ('in fulfilment of a vow of Heliodorus', '[gift] of John, Thomas, the sons of Theophilos') or the patron saint of the church ('[treasure of] St Sergius'), and are comparable to the

2.6   Hoxne Treasure, London, British Museum: ladle with monogram cross on handle
(© The British Museum)

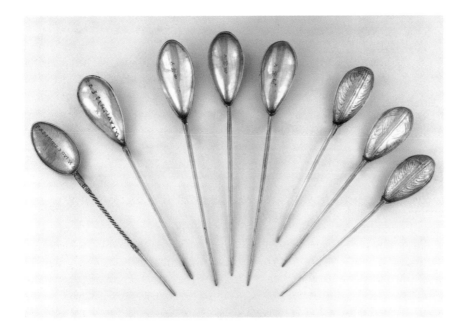

2.7   Mildenhall Treasure, London, British Museum: spoons (© The British Museum)

dedicatory inscriptions on other pieces of the treasure.[85] However the second group of spoons (associated with the Antioch Treasure), despite the apostles' names on them, can be argued to have been made originally for domestic use, a sixth-century version of the Christian spoons in the Mildenhall Treasure.[86] Marlia Mango has suggested they were donated to the church of St Sergius in Kaper Koraon primarily for their monetary value, rather than for their liturgical function. But can such a clear distinction be made between spoons made for donation to the church, and spoons made for private use and later donated to a church? What happens to the latter when they become part of church property? What is there to stop these spoons being used in the liturgy, since each one proclaims the blessing of an apostle on its handle (e.g. 'blessing of the holy Thomas')?[87] One could argue that their earlier profane use is sacralized by their transition to the church, and thus that they have a potential ritual use. The spoons in the Kaper Koraon Treasure allow us to measure the degree of transformation that has occurred over the two centuries since the fish spoon and the Silviola spoon were dedicated to Faunus. On the one hand what was previously a domestic implement has been incorporated into the vessels consecrated for the rite of the Christian Church. There is no evidence that this was the case in the fourth century, though here our evidence is so scanty that this perhaps does not mean much. On the other hand, the tradition of decorating tableware for private domestic use with Christian inscriptions and symbols continues in to the seventh century in the East, as I shall discuss in Chapter 4. The predominance of Christianity in public and private life makes possible the situation where domestic silver could enter the church treasury without having to be transformed by recycling and refashioning.[88] But as we have seen, the Antioch spoons are in many ways an exception. The texts discussed in the previous section show that the Church for the most part maintained a space between sacred and secular silver and was subject to a range of anxieties about that space.

Typologies of decoration on liturgical vessels

Having looked at some of the links between pagan temple treasures and Christian liturgical silver, I now want to examine more closely certain aspects of the liturgical hoards. There are seven surviving hoards of early Christian liturgical silver, as well as some significant individual items. Chronologically, all but one can be placed in the sixth century AD (with some items possibly reaching into the seventh century). The relative security of such dating is due not to controlled excavation (a weak point where these hoards are concerned), but to the presence of imperial control stamps on many of the pieces. The exception here is the Water Newton (Durobrivae) Treasure, found (like the Thetford Treasure) in East Anglia, which dates to the fourth century AD and is the earliest known hoard of liturgical silver.[89] It is also one of two hoards found in the western half of the empire, the other being the sixth-century Gallunianu Treasure from northern Italy.[90] The remaining five liturgical hoards are all

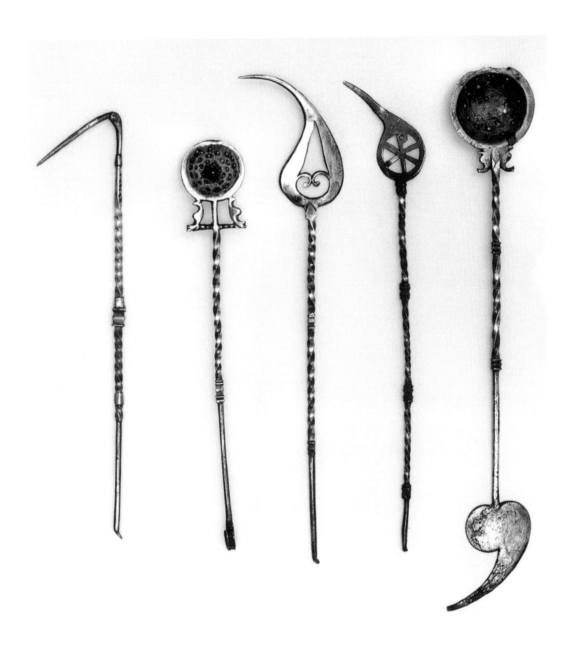

2.8   Kaiseraugst Treasure, Augst, Römermuseum: strainers and pointed utensils (G. Fittschen/Foto
Römerstadt Augusta Rarica)

2.9   Kaper Koraon Treasure: spoon from 'Hama Treasure', inscribed '[gift] of John, Thomas, the sons of Theophilos', Baltimore, The Walters Art Museum (The Walters Art Museum, Baltimore)

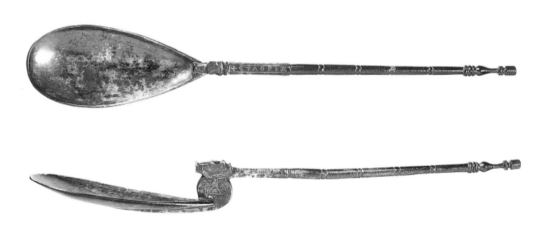

2.10 Kaper Koraon Treasure: spoon from 'Antioch Treasure', inscribed on handle 'blessing of St Matthew' and '[property] of Domnos' on disc, Washington DC, Dumbarton Oaks (Byzantine Photograph and Fieldwork Archive, Dumbarton Oaks, Washington DC)

from the eastern half of the empire. Of these, the two most significant are the Kaper Koraon Treasure (from Syria),[91] and the Sion or Kumluca Treasure (from Turkey).[92] Three much smaller hoards are also associated with Syria: the Beth Misona, Phela and Ma'aret en-Noman Treasures.[93] Finally there is the paten of Bishop Paternus which was found with the large and diverse Malaia Pereschepina Treasure found in the Poltova district of Russia, which is also of eastern (possibly Constantinopolitan) manufacture.[94] Within these hoards, there is considerable variation in the size, weight and craftsmanship of the vessels, and a number of decorative options can be identified. I shall focus here on the issue of decoration, viewed in the context of these other factors. Above all, I want to investigate whether the decoration of liturgical vessels helps to articulate their ritual function. Do different types of decoration reflect the range of ways in which a vessel's liturgical function could be enunciated? How does the decoration of liturgical vessels relate to other sacred art in the early Byzantine period?

To try to answer some of these questions I shall use a case study – the paten, the plate for the communion bread and therefore an essential liturgical vessel, which is represented by one or more examples in all seven liturgical hoards except the Ma'aret en-Noman Treasure. It therefore allows us to make a representative survey of the different decorative options which existed for liturgical vessels in our period. The paten is a vessel-type which has significantly transformed any domestic prototype which it might have had in serving plates, and thus forms a useful comparandum with the case of spoons in domestic and liturgical hoards discussed in the previous section. The typical shape of the paten from the fourth to the seventh century was a large, deep dish with a flat base (no ring foot in most examples), high sloping sides (generally between 3–5 cm in height) and a flat horizontal rim. This form differs significantly from that of the large dining plates of the same period, which typically have a flat surface with a high ring foot. In size and weight however there is considerable variety. The smallest surviving example is that from the Gallunianu Treasure, with a diameter of 20.3 cm, while the largest is from the Sion Treasure, with a diameter of 77.5 cm.[95] Weights are equally varied, and an interesting feature is the difference in weight between examples of similar dimensions: Mango cites the sixth-century Syrian Beth Misona paten, with a diameter of 32.4 cm and a weight of 542 g, against the fourth-century Water Newton paten, with a diameter of 33.5 cm and a weight of 1.305 kg.[96] The difference lies not in the elaborate decoration of one and the simplicity of the other, but in the thickness to which the silver has been worked in each case.

In fact the similarity in design between these two examples, separated by a considerable distance both chronologically and geographically, is striking. Both use the interior surface of the base as the field for decoration. The Water Newton paten (Fig. 2.11) has an incised chi-rho within a circular groove 11.2 cm in diameter. The Beth Misona paten (Fig. 2.12) has a similar incised circle of about the same proportions, inside which is an engraved cross with flaring arms. Around the edge of the circle is an inscription: 'Having vowed, Domnos

2.11 Water Newton Treasure, London, British Museum: paten (© The British Museum)

2.12 Beth Misona Treasure, Cleveland Museum of Art: paten (© The Cleveland Museum of Art, 2002, Purchase from the J.H. Wade Fund 1950.381)

2.13 Gallunianu Treasure, Colle di Val d'Elsa, Museo di Arte Sacra: paten (Ministero
per i Beni e le Attività Culturali / Soprintendenza per il Patrimonio storico artistico e
demo-etnoantropologico di Siena e Grosseto)

2.14 Kaper Koraon Treasure: paten from 'Hama Treasure', Baltimore, The Walters Art
Museum (The Walters Art Museum, Baltimore)

son of Zacheos has offered [this paten] to St Sergius of the village of Beth Misona'.[97] The chi-rho and the cross are arguably fourth- and sixth-century equivalents of the most basic symbol for Christ. The Water Newton paten does not have a dedicatory inscription, but other objects in the hoard do. A simple formula for the decoration of this type of liturgical vessel thus appears to have developed relatively early in the Church's history and to have persisted for several centuries.

This is borne out by the number of other patens with similar decorative schemes, consisting of engraved crosses and/or inscriptions. Among these we have the paten from the Gallunianu Treasure with a niello inscription on the rim (Fig. 2.13), and five patens from the Kaper Koraon Treasure, all of which have engraved crosses with flared arms surrounded by an inscription band (Fig. 2.14 shows one of these).[98] The paten in the Phela treasure is similar, though its central cross is elaborated by the addition of a hill with the four rivers of paradise on which it stands, the dove of the Holy Ghost above it, and an acrostic of the words ΦΩΣ (light) and ΖΩΗ (life) running vertically and horizontally along the arms. Within this decorative strategy there are differences in the quality of the decoration and the weight of individual pieces which (as with the two examples discussed in the paragraph above) do not correspond in the way that might be expected. In the Kaper Koraon Treasure, the two largest and heaviest patens of this type, Mango nos 6 and 39, have the simplest and least elegantly executed decoration, the former a small cross enclosed by an inscription with plain, unremarkable lettering (especially when compared to the accomplished serifed letters found on Mango no. 5), the latter only a cross. Here size and weight seem to be as important as decoration, and the decoration, while establishing the object as sacred, does not refer to its precise liturgical role.[99]

Part of the reason for the prevalence of such simple designs may be that these vessels were dedicated to village churches rather than urban establishments. However if we compare these hoards with the Sion Treasure, whose components overall are of a higher standard of craftsmanship than those of other surviving liturgical hoards, we can see the influence of the same basic compositional ideas, only executed in more elaborate form in the richer hoard. The Sion Treasure, although it belonged to a provincial monastery in the mountains of southern Lycia, is probably the nearest to urban church treasures.[100] Such monasteries, although remote, could attract rich patrons and pilgrims from urban centres, especially if they were the residence of a holy man. The Sion Treasure has been associated with the monastery of Holy Sion in Lycia, founded by St Nicholas of Sion, who lived during the first half of the sixth century, and whose contemporary *Life* survives.[101] Unfortunately the *Life* does not mention any cases of patronage of the monastery by individuals outside the local community, although the resources of the monastery are indicated in a couple of incidents: the restoration of the nearby sanctuary of St Daniel in Sabandos, paid for by the monastery at a cost of 88 and a half nomismata, with provisions for the workmen also supplied by the monastery and the building of the shrine of the Theotokos in Pinara funded by Nicholas while he was bishop

of this city, at a cost of 400 nomismata.[102] However, St Theodore of Sykeon – a sixth century contemporary of St Nicholas – whose monastery was in an equally remote and rural area, attracts patronage from high imperial officials and future emperors, and it seems possible that the Holy Sion monastery might equally have attracted outside patrons, such as the otherwise unknown Bishop Eutychianos who donated about half of the surviving hoard, even if the *Life of St Nicholas* does not choose to record them.[103]

The Sion Treasure contains six patens, which represent three different designs. The first type (of which there are three examples, all dedicated by Bishop Eutychianos, in Dumbarton Oaks, Antalya, and the Ortiz Collection in Geneva, Boyd nos 1, 2, 3 respectively) has a cusped border which is worked in relief with alternating palmettes and acanthus leaves (Fig. 2.16). The rim is decorated with a border of tongues. In the centre of the paten is a large gilded christogram with flaring ends and around the edge of the interior is an inscription in niello letters.[104] The second design (of which there are two examples in Dumbarton Oaks, Boyd nos 4, 5) has a concave fluted border with a large gilded Latin cross in the centre, surrounded by a niello inscription (Fig. 2.17). A second paten in Antalya (Boyd no. 6) has a large gilded Latin cross surrounded by a gold band, but straight sides like the Kaper Koraon patens. It too has an inscription, and is simultaneously the largest and the plainest of the Sion patens.

2.16 Sion Treasure: paten with cusped border, Washington DC, Dumbarton Oaks (Byzantine Photograph and Fieldwork Archive, Dumbarton Oaks, Washington DC)

Although the Sion patens, especially those with the cusped borders and exuberant floral ornament, represent a higher level of craftsmanship than the Syrian and Western examples so far described, the principal decoration on the interior field in each case is still a cross or chi-rho surrounded by a dedicatory inscription. This would suggest that we are not dealing here with a different conception of how a paten should be decorated, but that a different level of patronage is elaborating upon a basic concept of the decoration of such vessels. The closest parallel to the Sion patens is the early sixth century 'paten of Bishop Paternus' in the Hermitage (Fig. 2.18).[105] This has a large gilded chi-rho with alpha and omega in the centre, enclosed by a gilded inscription. Its sloping sides are left plain, but the horizontal rim is decorated in relief with a vine scroll inhabited by birds, animals and chalices. Like the patens in the

2.17 Sion Treasure: paten with fluted border, Washington DC, Dumbarton Oaks
(Byzantine Photograph and Fieldwork Archive, Dumbarton Oaks, Washington DC)

2.18 Paten of Bishop Paternus, St Petersburg, Hermitage Museum

Sion treasure, this vessel has a footring with a weight inscription on its inside (a feature found in the Sion patens with fluted borders). Paternus has been identified with an early sixth-century bishop of that name in the Black Sea town of Tomis (in present-day Romania), and while the paten's inscription is in Latin, it has Byzantine control stamps and seems most likely to have been made by Greek craftsmen, quite possibly in Constantinople, which was probably the nearest major artistic centre.[106] Unlike the floral imagery on the Sion paten borders, the vine scroll on the rim of the Paternus paten can be seen to have eucharistic connotations in the grapes and the chalices and broader soterific allusions in the sheep and the peacocks which inhabit the scroll. Such components have a long history of Christian use, especially in funerary contexts.[107] But one would not want to place too strong an interpretation on this aspect of the paten's decoration in defining its function, since in late antiquity the vine scroll is as generic a form of decoration as the Classical acanthus and palmette. The major sacralizing imagery here is still the chi-rho and the dedicatory inscription.

Two patens out of all those surviving in late antique liturgical hoards adopt a very different decorative strategy, which actively engages with the function of the vessel in the ritual of communion. These are the two 'Communion of the Apostles' patens in the Kaper Koraon Treasure (the so-called Stuma and Riha patens, in Istanbul Archaeological Museum and Dumbarton Oaks respectively) (Figs 2.19, 2.20). These plates are not identical: they are worked by different hands, differ in their border decoration and other details, and were donated by different people.[108] However, worked in relief on the surface of both plates is an image of Christ administering communion to the Apostles in the setting of a contemporary (that is sixth-century) church. Christ is shown twice, in mirror-image, standing behind an altar table and leaning to the right and left to offer a chalice or bread to the apostles, who are divided into two groups of six on either side. The details of the church setting varies: the Istanbul paten shows a domed ciborium with a hanging lamp in the background, while the Dumbarton Oaks paten shows a chancel beam, supported by two spiral columns, above which are standing lamps. In the centre a dome or niche is decorated with a scallop shell. A chalice, another footed vessel and two wineskins are shown on the altar table. In the foreground exergue is a washing set of a trulla and ewer. The sides of the Istanbul paten are decorated with egg-shaped indentations alternating with palmettes, while those of the Dumbarton Oaks vessel are undecorated. On each however an inlaid niello inscription runs around the projecting rim.

The scene of the Communion of the Apostles is not a straightforward representation of biblical narrative. Rather it represents a fusion of Christ's instructions to his apostles at the Last Supper, to eat and drink the bread and wine which represent his body and blood in his memory, with the church ritual of the eucharist in which the performance of these instructions – handed down by the apostles – is enshrined.[109] In this representation Christ and his apostles take the place of the sixth-century priest and his congregation at the altar. The scene is highly appropriate for a liturgical vessel, since it combines

2.19 Kaper Koraon Treasure: 'Stuma' Communion of the Apostles paten, Istanbul, Archaeological Museum (Hirmer Verlag, Munich)

an image of the ritual in which the paten will be used, with an image invoking the foundation of that ritual. Indeed the self-reflexive character of the images on the patens is highlighted by the prominence of other pieces of liturgical equipment in them, especially in the Dumbarton Oaks example. The patens themselves do not appear to be represented.[110]

Since the Communion of the Apostles seems so appropriate for a liturgical vessel, why is it found only on these two closely connected vessels from the Kaper Koraon Treasure? This could of course be an accident of survival, since the surviving liturgical hoards represent only a tiny proportion of all those that must have existed. However the scene is not especially common in the early Byzantine period in general.[111] More surprising perhaps is the absence of any liturgical vessels which depict the literal prototype of the Eucharist, the Last Supper. Again this might be chance, but overall there seems to be a reluctance to depict narrative scenes on liturgical vessels. The two Communion of the Apostles patens are among the few examples of this.[112] Individual figures of Christ, the apostles and evangelists are represented, as in the book covers in the Sion and Kaper Koraon Treasures (Mango nos 44–47, Boyd no. 23). When such individual figures appear in a different contemporary artistic context, as in decorative programmes of mosaics covering churches like those in Ravenna, their iconic representations would be incorporated in a larger exegetical scheme where they would be combined with narrative.[113] It is perhaps possible that liturgical vessels were conceived as components of the exegetical scheme of the church decoration as a whole, rather than independent bearers of meaning. Nevertheless, the lack of narrative episodes is significant.

The decoration of early Byzantine liturgical vessels goes against traditional artistic hierarchies of decoration which emphasize the elaborate over the simple, and figural narrative over non-figural ornament. The results of this survey seem to suggest the assumption that, the more important an object, the more likely it is to have elaborate figural ornament, is not really appropriate for understanding the decoration of early Byzantine liturgical vessels. Figural decoration was not automatically the choice of those who could afford to give the largest and most ostentatious vessels to their churches. The Communion of the Apostles patens, despite their exceptional decoration, are significantly smaller and lighter than any in the Sion Treasure.[114] The most common type of figural decoration for liturgical vessels (which does not however occur on any of the surviving patens) is the iconic clipeate portrait or the orant. Such representations are extremely standardized, with Christ, the Virgin, Peter and Paul being most frequently represented.[115] However equally common is a complete absence of figural decoration – sacred symbols, floral ornament and prominent inscriptions being chosen in its place. I have mentioned some of these inscriptions in passing, but to close this section I want to look at the role of inscriptions as decoration, rather than document.

The only patens without inscriptions are the Water Newton paten and one from the Kaper Koraon hoard (Mango no. 39). The remainder all bear inscriptions which employ a variety of formulae to indicate the donor(s), the reason for the dedication, and sometimes the recipient.[116] As such, inscriptions are an important sign of the consecrated status of these objects. However at the same time they form a major element of the decoration of these objects, and there is as much variation in the style and craftsmanship employed on the lettering as there is in the rest of the decoration. It is therefore worth asking what role lettering plays *as ornament* on these examples of liturgical silver. The most elaborate examples of lettering are to be found on the Sion patens, especially Boyd nos 1, 2, 4 and 5 (Figs 2.16, 2.17). On these the letters are engraved into the surface of the silver and filled in with niello. The strokes that make up the letters are broad and have elegant serifs. On patens nos 1 and 2 (Fig. 2.16), the central upright of the lunate omegas is bisected by a horizontal stroke to form a cross. On paten no. 3, the workmanship of which is of a lesser quality (possibly a locally made 'copy' of nos 1 and 2), the lower standard of craft can be seen in the letters too, which are made with narrower

2.20 Kaper Koraon Treasure: 'Riha' Communion of the Apostles paten, Washington
DC, Dumbarton Oaks (Byzantine Photograph and Fieldwork Archive, Dumbarton
Oaks, Washington DC)

2.21 Carved entablature inscription, St Polyeuktos, Istanbul (Byzantine Photograph
and Fieldwork Archive, Dumbarton Oaks, Washington DC)

lines and lack ornamental flourishes such as the crosses on the omegas. The two Communion of the Apostles patens (Figs 2.19, 2.20) also have inlaid niello lettering, which in line-width is closest to Sion paten no. 3, although the letter forms are rounder. Some of the letters have serifs, but these are often quite rudimentary. Paten no. 36 in the Kaper Koraon hoard also has lettering with niello inlay, similar to that of the Communion of the Apostles patens. The other patens in the Kaper Koraon hoard have simple incised lettering executed with varying degrees of skill. No. 5 (Fig. 2.14) is the most accomplished example: its lettering is serifed, regular, and well spaced. No. 4 has similar letter forms which are, however, somewhat unevenly written and less closely spaced. The lettering on no. 6, as I have already commented, is extremely cursorily executed and unserifed.

The lettering on the Bishop Paternus paten, although not as accomplished as that of the Sion patens, which this vessel in many ways resembles, is interesting for other reasons. The letters are engraved with a double outline on a gilded band around the edge of the paten's interior. As stated above, this is a Latin inscription which was executed by Greek craftsmen. We might at first be tempted to use this as an explanation of some of the unusual letter forms which it employs: M like an inverted omega, V with a hint of the stem of the upsilon, rhomboid O, with a tail tagged on to form Q. But explanation is not really sufficient, for after all the letter M exists as mu in Greek, and the upper case forms are identical, as are O and omicron. Although there certainly seems to be an element of a Greek craftsman interpreting Latin letter forms through a Greek alphabet which was more familiar to him, at the same time this inscription is an extreme example of the diversity of letter forms in early Byzantine inscriptions, which is well displayed on liturgical silver.

How should we understand this diversity? In this context some comments made by Charlotte Roueché on the change in the function and form of monumental epigraphy from the third century onwards, are helpful. She has suggested that as fewer inscriptions are erected, the reduced demand led to their being cut by sculptors rather than by professional epigraphic stone-cutters. This in part was responsible for the move away from uniformity in scripts, but changes in taste and in the function of inscriptions also played a role. Late Roman civic inscriptions prefer to offer idiosyncratic honours to individuals rather than conveying formal official information, a shift in function which Rouché sees as anticipating the decorative function assumed by inscriptions in Byzantium, as exemplified by those in Justinian's church of SS Sergius and Bacchus, and Anicia Juliana's church of St Polyeuktos.[117]

As far as we can tell from our surviving material, there never was a tradition of inscribing silver before the fourth century, so a professional class of metalworkers with epigraphic skills arguably never existed.[118] From the fourth century onwards, and especially in the liturgical silver of the eastern empire of the sixth century, inscriptions predominate as a form of decoration on otherwise very plain objects. This suggests that silver workers now had to include epigraphic skills among their abilities. Whether the same craftsman was responsible for both figural design and inscription we cannot tell (if not, the situation is the reverse of the stonecarvers, who become less rather than more specialized).[119] Bert Smith has questioned Rouché's link between the enscribed entablatures of early Byzantine churches, and the acceptability to late antique patrons of non-professional inscriptions in the civic sphere, and he is right to stress that the changed content of such inscriptions has more to do with the changing values of the period than a concept of the inscription as decoration (a viewpoint that Rouché's more recent work also reflects).[120] However it is arguable that the growth of inscriptions on silver, and the development of monumental stone inscriptions to use in the decoration of churches, are both a product of the same changes in the use of the inscription in early Byzantium. Indeed there are many parallels between the encircling inscriptions on the entablature of SS Sergius and Bacchus and similarly positioned frieze of St Polyeuktos, and the inscriptions which encircle the paten-rims (Fig. 2.21). The clear, elegant forms of the stone lettering are of a similar quality to those on the most elaborate of the Sion patens. Moreover unlike classical inscriptions, the letters are cut away from their background and stand in relief. In the fragments of the inscription from St Polyeuktos, traces of blue paint have been found on the background surface, suggesting a visual effect of white marble letters against a dark background, an opposite but analogous effect to black niello letters on a shining silver background. Like the paten inscriptions, those in the two churches are dedicatory inscriptions (although much longer, and in verse) which praise the respective donors for having built them, just as the patens recall the smaller gifts of their donors.[121] The church inscriptions are integrated into the architectural structure of the buildings, just as the inscriptions on the liturgical silver follow the shape of the vessel. In both cases legibility is compromised, yet the role of inscriptions as decoration in sixth-century Byzantium should not be seen as denigration of their meaning, but rather as an expansion of it, which made sense in a Christian society where the written word had far greater religious significance than it ever did in classical antiquity.

Silver reliquary caskets

In his *Glory of the Martyrs*, Gregory of Tours relates the following tale:

A count of Brittany suffered severely from pains in his feet, and spent a fortune on doctors. When he had no relief, one of his servants said to him: 'If one of the liturgical vessels that are on the altar would be brought to you from the church, and if you washed your feet in it, this could offer you a cure from your infliction.' These were silly and idle men who did not know that the vessels of God should not be adapted to human use. But the count quickly sent [men] to the church, took from the sacristy a silver paten [used] on the holy altar, and washed his feet in it. Immediately he suffered additional pains and was totally crippled; thereafter he was unable to walk.[122]

The events in this story construct a neat inversion of the numerous anecdotes in *Glory of the Martyrs* where sick individuals are cured through the power of the martyrs, transmitted through contact with their relics. This story of the 'silly and idle' count fits an equally recognizable type of tale in Gregory's collections of miracle stories: that of the ignorant or arrogant individual who refuses to recognize the power of the holy and receives fitting retribution. But the precise nature of the mistake made by the count of Brittany and his servant is of particular interest here. They were rash enough to presume that the healing power of saints' relics applied also to liturgical vessels, when as Gregory pointed out, their sanctity was of an altogether different order.

Their action was apparently not unique – Gregory tells us that 'a duke of the Lombards did the same thing' – and for a student of late antique silver, this unfortunate mistake may seem understandable, for as we have seen in the church of the sixth century, both cult at the altar and the cult of the saints provided opportunities for patrons to adorn the church building with this precious metal.

In this section, I want to examine the function and decoration of a type of silver object that is intimately linked to the cult of the saints and the healing power of their relics, the late antique reliquary casket, and to ask to what extent these were differentiated from silver liturgical vessels. Is Gregory's distinction articulated in the decoration of the two types of object? They have not, to my knowledge, been compared before, and indeed of the surprisingly large number of surviving silver 'reliquary' caskets, most are not very well known.[123] A typical example of the late antique reliquary casket is the silver hexagonal lidded pyxis (h. 12.3 cm) found in 1860 during excavations in the apse of the sixth-century cathedral of St Mary, in Pola, Istria (now in Croatia, but then part of the Austro-Hungarian empire, for which reason the find is preserved in the Kunsthistorische Museum in Vienna).[124] The silver casket is decorated with figures in relief, the figures of Christ and five of the apostles being distributed around the six sides; these same figures are repeated as half-length busts on the pointed lid (Fig. 2.22). It had been placed in a small marble sarcophagus in a stone chamber beneath the cathedral floor, under a marble slab. Inside the silver casket was a tiny gold box (1.6 × 2.3 × 1.9 cm) with acanthus decoration and a blue enamel cross on the lid, which contained two pieces of bone wrapped in yellow silk (Fig. 2.23). The archaeological context of this reliquary deposit is paralleled in a number of other finds, many of them in towns around the north Adriatic coast, all of which date between the end of the fourth and the beginning of the seventh centuries. In each case, the relic was enclosed in a series of containers (usually stone, silver, gold, as with the Pola deposit, and often with fabric wrapping too) placed inside each other and deposited in a chamber beneath the church floor, usually near the altar.[125] In such reliquary deposits, the silver caskets are usually the most elaborately decorated of the containers used to enclose the relic. The decoration of the caskets arguably represents a significant contrast with silver liturgical vessels. It is often figural (as we saw with the Pola casket), and sometimes depicts scenes from biblical narrative. A further element in the comparison between reliquary caskets and liturgical vessels is provided by the Palestinian lead pilgrim ampullae, the largest collections of which are preserved in the cathedral treasury at Monza, and the Basilica of St Columban in Bobbio.[126] These are made of a base metal, not silver, and thus are not strictly speaking

2.22 Silver pyxis found in cathedral of St Mary, Pola, Vienna, Kunsthistorisches
Museum

2.23 Gold and enamel box, found inside pyxis from Pola, Vienna, Kunsthistorisches
Museum

2.24 'Capsella Vaticana', Rome, Vatican Museums: top

2.25 'Capsella Vaticana', Rome, Vatican Museums: side

luxury objects. They are however, like the silver reliquaries, containers for holy matter and are decorated with a distinctive iconography. Moreover those ampullae from the Basilica of St Columban were buried in a casket in the crypt of that building, near the tombs of St Columban and other early seventh century abbots of his monastery, in a close parallel to those silver reliquaries which have been found concealed beneath altars. For these reasons, they provide a further dimension to this study.

The archaeological context in which late antique reliquaries have been found is a reminder that they are one piece of material evidence for the development of the cult of the saints, which took place from the late fourth century onwards.[127] As such, it is misleading to see them as isolated examples of purely iconographic interest. They stand within a larger network of rituals, worship and theology which constituted and defined the cult of the saints in this crucial period of its development. It has been argued that when fourth-century bishops such as Ambrose of Milan removed the remains of martyrs from cemeteries and buried them beneath the altars of churches, they were linking the cults which had begun to develop around these martyrs with the eucharistic liturgy as a way of regulating them and integrating them into the churches over which they presided.[128] The sacrifice of the martyrs is thus equated both theologically and spatially with the sacrifice of the eucharist. Such equations are of particular interest here because of the relationship which they suggest between the silver caskets containing the relics and the liturgical vessels used in the celebration of the eucharist.[129] This is as much a relationship of physical proximity, as a deployment of a material – silver – to highlight the sacred within the church. Perhaps the key difference here is between the visibility of the liturgical vessels and the invisibility of the reliquaries (for most of the year at least). In this respect the late antique reliquaries differ from later medieval examples in the West, which tended to enhance the visibility of the relics which they contained by providing a context for their display. Such relics were housed in treasuries and displayed on altars rather than vaults beneath the floor.[130]

The silver reliquary casket found at Pola has been dated (on stylistic criteria) to the fourth century, while the gold box which was found inside it has been dated to the sixth century.[131] If this dating is correct, it suggests that the function of the silver casket as a reliquary may have been a secondary use and raises questions about the purposes such silver caskets could serve and the uses to which 'antique' objects could be appropriated. Of the two reliquaries found together beneath the altar of the sixth-century basilica of St Euphemia in Grado (a small town on the north-western Adriatic coast of Istria), one can be dated on stylistic and epigraphic grounds to the late fourth/early fifth century, while the other for the same reason is most likely sixth century.[132] Another instance where the presumed date of the reliquary casket is earlier than that of its deposit is that of the 'Capsella Vaticana', which is dated to the first half of the seventh century (610-41) by Byzantine imperial control stamps on its underside (Figs 2.24, 2.25). This casket is part of the Sancta Sanctorum Treasure, which was rediscovered in 1905 in the altar of the Sancta Sanctorum chapel in the Lateran. Along with a hoard of other early medieval reliquaries, it was kept in a special cupboard enclosed within the altar, which was built by Pope Leo III (795–816).[133] Thus the casket, which contained fragments of bone, a small glass ampulla and various pieces of stone, must have been placed in the cupboard in the early ninth century, or even later, since the cupboard seems to have been accessible until the early sixteenth century, after which it remained locked until the early twentieth century.[134] The Capsella Vaticana is the closest parallel we have among silver reliquaries to the Monza ampullae which have formed part of the cathedral treasure there since the early seventh century. Such instances indicate that a certain amount of caution is desirable in assuming that the date of manufacture and the date of deposition is the same for each casket. This in turn means that we should consider alternative functions for these small silver caskets, such as containers for consecrated communion bread or incense.[135] A casket which had been used for one such sacred function might have later been chosen for use as a reliquary. Would the imagery which decorated the silver caskets have played a role in such appropriations?

While the function of the Palestinian ampullae as containers for holy matter is clearly marked by the inscription which they bear – 'oil of the wood of life [i.e. the cross] from the holy places of Christ' – and depictions of those holy places on them, the corresponding function of the silver caskets is by no means so clearly indicated. Moreover while the ampullae are of a uniform sixth-century date, the reliquary caskets range from the late fourth to the early seventh century and display a greater range of iconographic strategies. One such strategy is represented by two late fourth-century reliquaries: the casket found in San Nazaro Maggiore, Milan and the Thessalonike casket, found during the building of a road between Nea Heraklea and Chalkidike. Both are distinguished for the classicism and the high quality of their representations of biblical episodes, and are considered to be products of the so-called 'Theodosian renaissance'.[136] While both deploy similar iconographic strategies (depicting several episodes from the Old and New Testaments which stand in an exegetic relationship to one another) the choice of episodes, and the way in which they are depicted on each casket is rather different. The Thessalonike casket (Fig. 2.26) is by far the more 'conventional'. A rectangular box with a high lid, its four sides show three scenes from the Old Testament and one from the New: Moses receiving the law on Mount Sinai, Daniel in the Lions' Den, the Three Hebrews in the Fiery Furnace, and the *traditio legis* of Christ with Peter and Paul. The sides of the lid (badly damaged) are decorated with a vine scroll and the top of the lid bears a chi-rho flanked by an alpha and an omega. The biblical scenes represented on this casket are easily recognizable and familiar, above all from a late antique funerary context of sarcophagi and wall paintings in the catacombs. As in these contexts, an exegetical relationship between the different episodes can be established: Moses receives the old law from the hand of God, Christ gives the new law to Peter and Paul; both Daniel and the three Hebrews (who are here shown clothed identically) are precursors of the Christian martyrs who endure torments for their faith, types of Christ

2.26 Reliquary casket found at Nea Herakleia/Chalkidike, Thessalonike, Museum of Byzantine Culture (TAPA)

2.27 Reliquary from San Nazaro Maggiore, Milan, Cathedral Treasury (Hirmer Verlag, Munich)

himself, and paradigms of Christian faith in general. Their representation on this casket would certainly seem to make it an appropriate repository for relics (though we do not know for certain if it was used as such).

The San Nazaro casket (Fig. 2.27) is a cube-shaped box which, like the Thessalonike casket, has decoration on five sides. It even shares one scene with the Thessalonike casket, namely the Three Hebrews in the Fiery Furnace. Yet unlike the Thessalonike representation, here neither the structure of the oven nor the flames are represented and the unity of the group of the three Hebrews is split by the position of God's messenger in the centre right of the composition. The remaining four scenes on the box find far fewer parallels in the repertoire of late antique biblical scenes. Two of these four scenes are taken from the Old Testament: the Judgement of Solomon and the Judgement of the Elders by Daniel (both relatively uncommon scenes); the other two are from the New Testament and show Christ enthroned between the apostles and the Adoration of the Virgin and Child. Both of these scenes feature iconographical peculiarities. The scene of Christ and the apostles has its closest parallels with the representation of Christ as a philosopher teaching. However in the foreground of the image are five baskets filled with bread and six wine jars, allusions to the Multiplication of the Loaves and Fishes and the Marriage of Cana, integrated and juxtaposed into this scene most probably as a eucharistic allusion. Equally unusual is the representation of the Virgin and Child. This shows the Virgin and Child enthroned, and approached on either side by a man, dressed in a philosopher's pallium and holding a large oval plate in his hands. If this image depicts the Adoration of the Magi – the scene which it most resembles – why are the two men not dressed in the 'oriental' dress (trousers, Phrygian caps) by which the Magi are usually distinguished? It is sometimes called the Adoration of the Shepherds, but there seems little justification for this identification since no animals are shown, nor is the pallium typical shepherd's clothing.[137] The exegetic relationship between the scenes on this casket, especially as regards the scenes of Daniel and Solomon, is less clear than that between the scenes on the Thessalonike casket. While this is not the place for a detailed discussion of this complex object, it seems possible that these two scenes might allude to Christ's role as judge, complementing both the depiction of him as teacher and saviour on one panel of the casket and the image of his adoration as Son of God on another. The links between the different sides of the box are constructed formally through the choice of a frontal composition with an enthroned figure for four out of the five sides.

Although the San Nazaro casket itself offers no clues as to what relic was held in it, it is possible, given its late fourth-century date, that it held the relics of the apostles Peter and Paul which are referred to in a dedicatory inscription from this basilica which Ambrose founded in 382.[138] These would have been contact relics, the strips of cloth or *brandea* which had touched the graves of the apostles in Rome, since the popes are known to have been unwilling to disperse the bodies of the apostles. In this context, the absence of any reference in the casket's decoration to the individual apostles seems surprising. Here we have a marked contrast with the Palestinian ampullae, which as a group depict a series of scenes in the life of Christ – nativity, adoration, baptism, crucifixion, resurrection, ascension. These scenes, of which two or three are usually represented on each ampulla, relate to the contents of the ampullae in several ways. By representing Christ's life, in which his crucifixion played a pivotal role, they attest to the importance of the holy matter which they contain, which is a contact relic of the True Cross. It is no coincidence that the crucifixion and resurrection (usually depicted as pendants on a single side) are the most frequently represented scenes on the ampullae.[139] Moreover, each of the scenes represented relates to a pilgrimage site in the Holy Land, so that the act of pilgrimage and the Holy Land itself are represented for the pilgrim who collects these ampullae.[140] Thus the image of the Adoration on the ampullae (which like that on the San Nazaro casket is a frontal enthronement image, with the Virgin approached by Magi on one side and acclaimed by Shepherds on the other) arguably carries a more specific set of meanings in its context than that on the San Nazaro casket. How necessary was it therefore that the imagery on a reliquary refer at all to its function? Was in fact any valuable box with sacred images sufficient? Can the specificity of the iconography of the Palestinian ampullae be directly linked to their lack of material value?

There is one instance where the image of a martyr is represented on a reliquary casket, the so-called 'Capsella Africana' – a small oval box with a domed lid, now in the Vatican, which was discovered in the foundations of a possibly sixth-century church in Numidia (present-day Algeria) at a place called Aïn Zirara (Fig. 2.28).[141] On stylistic grounds it has been dated to the fifth century. The lid shows a standing youthful male figure who holds a wreath at the same time as being crowned with one by the hand of God.[142] The four rivers of paradise flow from beneath his feet, and he is flanked by two torches. On one side of the casket is the Lamb of God, flanked by three approaching sheep on either side, while on the other side are two deer which drink from a spring, above which is a chi-rho. The reliquary, unlike those from San Nazaro and Thessalonike, is decorated with a juxtaposition of allegorical rather than narrative representations. While this relationship may still be exegetic – for example the deer at the spring may refer to the first line of Psalm 42, 'as the hart panteth after the waterbrooks, so panteth my soul after thee, O God' – the sacred texts alluded to are themselves allegorical.[143] The martyr on the lid is not named, and may thus refer to a generic idea of martyrdom and its rewards (in the same way that the images of the Three Hebrews and Daniel in the Lions' Den can), rather than a specific individual whose relics the casket contained.

The Capsella Africana is not alone among late antique reliquary caskets in its use of iconic and allegorical modes of decoration. This can be seen in a group of three caskets, which all share a common decorative feature: clipeate portrait busts of Christ, apostles and saints arranged around their sides. These are the oval casket found in the basilica of St Euphemia in Grado, dated to the late fourth or early fifth century, and two caskets of eastern manufacture, the Chersonesus Casket in St Petersburg with control stamps dating to the

2.28 'Capsella Africana', Rome, Vatican Museums

2.29 Chersonesus reliquary, St Petersburg, Hermitage Museum

mid-sixth century (Fig. 2.29), and the Capsella Vaticana, with stamps dating to the first half of the seventh century (Fig. 2.25).[144] Two of them (the Grado casket and the Capsella Vaticana) also feature an adoration of the Cross on their lids (Fig. 2.24). On each casket with clipeate busts, Christ, Peter and Paul are portrayed in a group of three on one side of the casket. The choice of the remaining portraits varies, and without inscriptions it is often hard to name them, since individual features are not usually distinguished. The Capsella Vaticana seems to show four other apostles, who cannot be individually named. The Chersonesus Casket has the Virgin flanked by two angels, and two beardless male saints, possibly Demetrius and George or Cosmas and Damian. The Grado Casket, however, labels its portraits of four youths and an aristocratic woman with an elaborate head-dress and jewels as the saints Cantius, Cantianus, Cantilla, Quirinus and Latinus.[145] Without the inscription, these relatively obscure martyrs would be unidentifiable.

The caskets with clipeate busts have perhaps the closest relationship with the decoration of liturgical vessels. This can be observed especially in a comparison of the 'Homs vase', a sixth-century silver ewer in the Louvre, with the Chersonesus casket, also datable to the sixth century, and of eastern manufacture (Fig. 2.30).[146] Both have a total of eight portrait medallions, skilfully executed in a markedly classicizing style, six of which represent the same subjects: Christ, Peter, Paul, the Virgin and two angels (the remaining two on the Homs vase show John the Baptist and John the Evangelist). The portraits are arranged in corresponding fashion around the two objects: Christ, Peter and Paul forming one group, the angels with the Virgin another, and the two remaining saints each placed between an apostle and an angel. This comparison shows the degree of standardization which can be observed in the choice of clipeate portraits, along with small and subtle variations. Could such variations have depended on the patron saint of the church where the liturgical vessels were used, or the saints whose relics were enclosed in the caskets? There seems to be a case for this with the Grado casket, but in most other cases the evidence is insufficient to prove this.

The three reliquaries which I have just discussed combine the iconic imagery of the clipeate busts of sacred figures with the allegorical representation of Christ through the symbol of the Cross (the Chersonesus casket, although it does not feature an adoration of the cross like the other two, nevertheless has a cross on each side of its vaulted lid). Unlike the Palestinian ampullae, where the symbol of the cross – present on the neck of most ampullae, and forming the decoration of the side on some[147] – stands in direct relation to the holy matter contained within the ampullae and the place where this was obtained, the use of the cross on the silver reliquary caskets seems to evoke the sacred, in the person of Christ, in a more general way. This observation is applicable generally to reliquary caskets, whether their iconography is narrative or allegorical. Images of Christ and types of Christ in both modes mark the reliquary as sacred, but a highly specific iconography does not develop as it does for the pilgrim ampullae, although the two types of object clearly belong in the same context of the late antique patterns of relic collection and

2.30 Homs vase, Paris, Louvre (Photo RMN)

deployment. This presents a parallel with the way that the Last Supper does not appear on liturgical vessels.[148]

The surviving silver reliquaries span a longer period in time than the liturgical vessels, which cluster in the sixth and early seventh centuries. They thus allow a perspective on the quality of fourth- and fifth-century liturgical silver beyond that offered by the early fourth-century Water Newton hoard, which was the property of a small Christian community in Britain. The quality and character of the liturgical vessels in use in Ambrose's basilicas in Milan must surely have been analogous to that of the San Nazaro casket. Such comparisons are validated by the iconographical and stylistic similarities between sixth-century reliquaries and liturgical vessels, as the comparison of the Homs vase and the casket from Chersonesus showed. But the iconographical relationship between reliquaries and liturgical vessels should not be viewed in isolation. Both types of object are part of the same sacred space around the altar in the church, and repeat elements of the decoration that can also be found on the walls and ceilings of the church. Their decoration arguably articulates the way that their propriety for their function was perceived (or intended to be perceived) by those who used them.

Towards an *ars sacra*

While areas of broad continuity certainly exist between pagan and Christian sacred uses of silver, there are also significant discontinuities. We have seen in this chapter how the rituals of Christianity demanded the development of new types of sacred vessels, while the cult of the saints offered opportunities for innovation in the deployment of precious metals in tombs and reliquary caskets. The sacred status of such objects was articulated both by their material and by their decoration. Perhaps the greatest discontinuity was the complex attitude towards wealth which developed in the Christian Church. Although the use of precious metals for liturgical vessels and church decoration from the fourth century onwards shows that the Church did allow a connection to be established between value and the sacred, a variety of texts choose either to question or to reinforce this equation (sometimes both). Such texts have no parallel in pre-Christian writing and offer an especially rich dimension to the study of Christian silver.

Just as there was no single fixed attitude towards the use of silver in the sacred sphere in late antiquity, this chapter does not propose a single theory about its use. Rather I have tried to survey some of the different aspects of this, and some of the networks of meaning of which silver was a part. The use of silver and other precious substances by the Church after Constantine was indebted to secular forms of social communication, which used wealth to denote status. In the area of patronage, however, the sacred displaced and subsumed the secular, as we saw reflected in the accounts of the Liber Pontificalis. As a component part of church furnishing, silver shared in the images which decorated and helped define the meaning of that sacred space.

Yet at the same time, as the *Life of St Theodore* and John of Ephesus' account of the widow Sosiana reveal, the transition of silver between the sacred and secular realm could be a major source of concern, as could the possibilities of the former being polluted by the latter. In the end, the sacred use of silver was defined through its differentiation from secular uses. If the art of the early Middle Ages has been characterized as an *ars sacra*, by studying the sacred silver of Late Antiquity in all its aspects we can gain insight into an important stage in the development of this 'sacred art'.[149]

Notes

1. *The Book of Pontiffs* ed. and trans. R. Davis, Translated Texts for Historians, Latin Series V (Liverpool, 1989), 16. Constantine's donations form part of the *Life of Silvester*, pope between 314 and 335.

2. R. Krautheimer, S. Corbet, and W. Frankl, *Corpus Basilicarum Christianarum Romae: The Early Christian Basilicas of Rome (IV–IX centuries)* vol. 5 (Vatican City, 1977), 89.

3. A.M.H. Jones, *The Later Roman Empire 248–602. A Social, Administrative and Economic Survey*, 2 vols (Oxford, 1964), 894–99. For the Holy Land, see Eusebius, *Life of Constantine* 3.25–47.

4. This is explored in D. Janes, *God and Gold in Late Antiquity* (Cambridge, 1998), esp. 48–60.

5. As Jerome condescendingly admits in a letter to the Roman aristocrat Demetrias, although he prefers to council her to use her wealth for charitable purposes rather than building: Jerome, *Ep.* 130.14.

6. On this see B. Ward Perkins, *From Classical Antiquity to the Middle Ages: Urban Public Buildings in Northern and Central Italy, AD 300–700* (Oxford, 1984).

7. Athenian resources in the Parthenon: Thuc. II.13.2–5. The riches of Delphi are perhaps best evoked by Herodotus' description of the gold dedications given by Croesus, king of Lydia in the sixth century BC, I.50–51.

8. For temple inventories see D.M. Lewis, 'Temple Inventories in Ancient Greece', in M. Vickers, ed., *Pots and Pans: Proceedings of the Colloquium on Precious Metal and Ceramic in the Muslim, Chinese and Graeco-Roman Worlds* (Oxford, 1986), 71–81. Early church inventories include a Coptic list of lamps on an ostraka: D. Montserrat, 'Early Byzantine Church Lighting: A New Text', *Orientalia* 64 (1995), 430–44, with references to other known Egyptian inventories, 434–35. For lists preserved in later manuscripts see M.M. Mango, 'The Monetary Value of Silver Revetments and Objects Belonging to Churches', in Boyd and Mango eds, *Ecclesiastical Silver Plate*, 124, n.12.

9. *Book of Pontiffs*, ii–iii, xxxvii–xxxviii.

10. *Book of Pontiffs*, 19. For a full statement of the case for authenticity, see xix–xx.

11. *Book of Pontiffs*, v.

12. For example in Krautheimer, Corbett and Frankl, *Corpus Basilicarum Christianarum Romae*, and many of Krautheimer's other works. Also see Ward Perkins, *From Classical Antiquity to the Middle Ages*.

13. Given by Innocentius (401–17), *Book of Pontiffs*, 32.

14. Note the continuity in practice with pagan temple donations. In the bequest of C. Vibius Salutarius the weight and metal of each of the 29 statues is listed, together with their total weight. See G.M. Rogers, *The Sacred Identity of Ephesos: Foundation Myths of a Roman City* (London and New York, 1991), 159–65.

15. R.A. Markus, *The End of Ancient Christianity* (Cambridge, 1990), 126. 'Municipal authority' includes taking over areas of formerly civic patronage: by the seventh and eighth century popes in the Liber Pontificalis are recorded as organizing food supplies, building palaces, and repairing walls and aquaducts, as well as building churches, eg. Sabinian (604–606), Honorius (625–638), Sissinius (708), *Book of Pontiffs*, 62, 63, 89. Also see Ward Perkins, *From Classical Antiquity to the Middle Ages*, 77.

16. *Book of Pontiffs*, xix–xx, suggests that the document from which the list in the life of Silvester was taken was compiled near the end of Constantius II's reign (361), and includes donations made after both Constantine's and Silvester's deaths.

17. It should be noted, however, that the Liber Pontificalis does not give a full picture of imperial patronage in Rome in the fourth century: it omits, for example, the construction of S. Paulo fuori le mura by Theodosius and Honorius. The imperial foundation of this church is alluded to in Prudentius, *Peristephanon* 12.45–54: see M. Roberts, *Poetry and the Cult of the Martyrs: the Liber Peristephanon of Prudentius* (Ann Arbor, MI, 1993), 177–80.

18. The garbled account in the life of Silvester of the two tituli founded by him (possibly in fact one foundation) makes it unclear whether he or Constantine gave the liturgical vessels and land endowments. See *Book of Pontiffs*, xx, 14, 26.

19. *Book of Pontiffs*, 27, 30.

20. *Book of Pontiffs*, 31–32.

21. *Book of Pontiffs*, 33–35.

22. R. Krautheimer, 'The Architecture of Sixtus III: a fifth century renaissance?', in idem, *Studies in Early Christian, Medieval and Renaissance Art* (New York, 1969), 184–85.

23. *Book of Pontiffs*, 35–37.

24. *Book of Pontiffs*, 36.

25. *Book of Pontiffs*, 48.

26. *Book of Pontiffs*, 50, 52.

27. *Book of Pontiffs*, 36.

28. *Book of Pontiffs*, 39–40.

29. *Book of Pontiffs*, 61, 64.

30. XYSTVS EPISCPVS PLEBI DEI. G.B. De Rossi, *Inscriptiones Christianae Urbis Romae*, vol. II, part 1 (Rome, 1881), 435 no. 111.

31. P. Brown, *The Cult of the Saints: Its Rise and Function in Latin Christianity* (Chicago, 1981) 40, citing E. Patlagean, *Pauvreté économique et pauvreté sociale à Byzance, 4e–7e siècles* (Paris, 1977).

32. A.-J. Festugière ed. and trans., *La Vie de Théodore de Sykéon*, Subsidia Hagiographica 48, 2 vols (Brussels, 1970). English translations are adapted from E. Dawes and N.H. Baynes, *Three Byzantine Saints* (London and Oxford, 1948).

33. *Vie de Théodore*, 42.

34. E.C. Dodd, *Byzantine Silver Stamps. With an excursus on the Comes Sacrarum Largitionum by J.P.C. Kent*, Dumbarton Oaks Studies 7, Washington DC, 1961, 26–27; M.M. Mango, 'The Purpose and Places of Byzantine Silver Stamping', in Boyd and Mango, *Ecclesiastical Silver Plate*, 203.

35. Pliny the Elder, *NH*, 33.14.50 mentions a gold chamberpot; Trimalchio uses a silver one in Petronius, *Satyricon*, 27.3–6; John Chrysostom, *Homily VII on Colossians*, PG 62, cols. 349–52, complains about the use of silver ones.

36. On prostitutes in Byzantium see S. Leontsini, *Die Prostitution im frühen Byzanz* (Vienna, 1989). The prostitute is an important rhetorical figure in early Byzantine hagiography, while the reformed prostitute is used as a paradigm of salvation: see B. Ward, *Harlots of the Desert: a Study of Repentence in Early Monastic Sources* (London, 1987). The mother of St Theodore is herself a prostitute (*Vie de Théodore*, 3–4), which highlights Theodore's 'abnormality' and consequent potential for holiness (R. Cormack, *Writing in Gold: Byzantine Society and its Icons* [London, 1985], 40).

37. Cited and translated by Festugière in *Vie de Théodore*, vol. II, 196–98. A related theme of unclean wealth is found in chapter 10 of the seventh-century *Life of John the Almsgiver* by Leontius of Neapolis, where a ship's captain who is given money by John combines this with money from 'an evil source' and a ship acquired 'by unjust means', and comes to grief. See Dawes and Baynes, *Three Byzantine Saints*, 216–18.

38. As Cormack, *Writing in Gold*, 42, has pointed out, the acquisition of silver liturgical vessels by the monastery should not be seen in conflict with Theodore's personal asceticism, but as recognition of his status within the monastery as a holy man and the benefits this brought to the community and indeed the whole empire. Cf. the gift of a chalice and paten to the monastery by the emperor Maurice (54), and the gold cross presented by the imperial official Domniziolos (128).

39. John of Ephesus, *Lives of the Eastern Saints* 55, ed. and trans. by E.W. Brooks, Patrologia Orientalis 19, Paris, 1925, 191–96.

40. For example, Theodoret of Cyrhus, *Historia Religiosa*, John Moschus, *Pratum Sprituale*. For a full discussion of John's place in this genre, and the distinctive characteristics of his writing see S. Ashbrook Harvey, *Asceticism and Society in Crisis: John of Ephesus and 'The Lives of Eastern Saints'* (Berkeley and Los Angeles, CA, 1990), 29–42, 134–46.

41. John of Ephesus, *Lives* 54, 186–91.

42. Because of the highly perishable nature of textiles, there are no surviving examples of early Byzantine embroidered ecclesiastical textiles, though fragments recovered from tombs convey an idea of the woven patterns on some silks. See Buckton, *Byzantium* , cats. 49–50, 111, 137–39 for examples dating between the fifth and the ninth century. Two of these, 137 and 139 were used in Western saints' tombs. For a description of the splendours of early Byzantine embroidery, see Paulus Silentarius' ekphrasis of the altar cloth in Hagia Sophia, *Descriptio S. Sophia*, ll, 755–806.

43. Cf. the description of the 'double life' led by Sosiana and John during their time as chamberlains: during the day they perform their duties, but their nights are spent chastely praying, crying and sleeping on mats on the floor, 'without this becoming known to many'. John of Ephesus, *Lives* 55, 192.

44. Severus of Antioch, *Homiliae Cathedrales*, ed. and trans. I. Guidi, Patrologia Orientalis 22 (Paris, 1930), 230–48. The passages quoted in the text are my translation of Guidi's French.

45. Severus of Antioch, *Homiliae* 100, 246.

46. Severus of Antioch, *Homiliae* 100, 247.

47. Severus of Antioch, *Homiliae* 100, 247.

48. Shelton, *The Esquiline Treasure*, no. 1 (Project a casket); no. 2 (Muses casket); nos 30–34 (sedan chair fittings), nos 36–41 (horse trappings), 72–78, 86–91.

49. Severus of Antioch, *Homiliae* 100, 248.

50. The congregation is promised health and success for their children, 'honest gain' for themselves, blessings on their houses and goods during their lifetime, as well as the Kingdom of Heaven after death. Severus of Antioch, *Homiliae* 100, 248. Cf. Janes, *God and Gold*, 18–60.

51. Severus of Antioch, *Homiliae* 100, 243–45.

52. Severus of Antioch, *Homiliae* 100, 246.

53. On Christian dome-symbolism see K. Lehmann, 'The Dome of Heaven', *Art Bulletin* 27 (1945), 1–27.

54. ὁ γὰρ τοῦ ἱεροῦ τὰ μάλιστα χῶρος ἀβέβηλος, καὶ μόνοις ἱεροῦσι βατός, ὅνπερ καλοῦσι θυσιαστήριον, λιτρῶν ἀργύρου μυριάδας ἐπιφέρεται τέτταρας. Procopius, *Buildings* I.1.65. Translation from C. Mango, *The Art of the Byzantine Empire 312–1453. Sources and Documents* (Englewood Cliffs, NJ, 1972).

55. P. Lemerle, *Les plus ancients recueils des miracles de S. Démétrios*, 2 vols (Paris, 1979), 6th, 7th, 10th and 12th miracles. The fame of St Demetrius' ciborium is attested through a surviving middle-Byzantine reliquary in the Moscow State Museum which is a miniature representation of the saint's tomb/ciborium. See A. Grabar, 'Quelques reliquaires de Saint Démétrios et le martyrium du saint à Salonique', *DOP* 5 (1950), 18–28, figs 19–22.

56. *Miracles de S. Démétrios* I, Sixth Miracle, 55.

57. *Miracles de S. Démétrios* I, Tenth Miracle, 81–93.

58. *Miracles de S. Démétrios* I, Seventh Miracle, 62–67.

59. *Miracles de S. Démétrios* I, Twelfth Miracle, 100–115. Chronologically the events described in this narrative come before those in the sixth miracle.ˆ

60. *Miracles de S. Démétrios* I, Tenth Miracle, 87: ὦν πάντων ἐπάνω τὸ κατὰ τοῦ θανάτου πεπηγὸς τρόπαιον ἀκτινοβολεῖ, τῷ μὲν ἀργυρέῳ δημιουργήματι τὰς τοῦ σώματος ὄψεις ἐκπλήττεσθαι, τῇ δὲ τοῦ Χριστοῦ νοήσει τοὺς τῆς διανοίας ὀφθαλμοὺς τοῖς οὐρανίοις καταυγάζον χαρίσμασιν, ὁ ζωοποιός, φημί, καὶ τίμιος τοῦ θεοῦ καὶ σωτῆρος ἡμῶν σταυρός. The translation is from Mango, *Art of the Byzantine Empire*, 129.

61. Similar arguments have been convincingly proposed in Janes, *God and Gold*, 61–84, for the late antique Church's acceptance of the display of wealth in the West. He has argued that biblical exegesis provided a host of symbolic meanings (concentrating

around value and brightness/light) for precious metals which were used to justify their use in the church, and mask their relationship with secular forms of elite display.

62. E. Babelon, *Le Trésor d'argenterie de Berthouville près Bernay (Eure), conservé au Department des médailles et antiques de la Bibliothèque nationale* (Paris, 1916); F. Baratte, *Le Trésor d'argenterie gallo-romaine de Notre-Dame-d'Allençon*, Gallia supplement XL (Paris, 1981).

63. Johns and Potter, *The Thetford Treasure*, 71–72.

64. Excavations carried out near the findspot of the Berthouville Treasure in 1861–62 and 1896 revealed a theatre and shrine (fanum) in the area, the latter of which may be the site of the cult to which the treasure was dedicated. This only confirms that it does not come from a major cult site. See Babelon, *Le Trésor de Berthouville*. The site where the Notre-Dame-d'Allençon Treasure was found has never been excavated and no remains of any sanctuary are known in the vicinity, Baratte, *Notre-Dame-d'Allençon*, 20–21. On religion in Roman Gaul see: T. Derks, *Gods, Temple and Ritual Practices: the Transformation of Religious Ideas and Values in Roman Gaul* (Amsterdam, 1998); G. Woolf, *Becoming Roman: the Origins of Provincial Civilization in Gaul* (Cambridge, 1998).

65. Generally on temple treasures in the Roman period, and the aims of donors see F. Baratte, 'Les trésors de temples dans le monde romain: une expression particulière de la piété', in Boyd and Mango, *Ecclesiastical Silver Plate*, 111–21; E. Künzl, 'Römische Tempelschätze und Sakralinventare: Votive, Horte, Beute', *Antiquité Tardive* 5 (1997), 57–81.

66. Cf. the 29 silver processional statues dedicated to Artemis of Ephesus by C. Vibius Salutarius in 104 AD, which were kept in the pronaos of her temple there. Nine of these were statue-types of the goddess, while others represented Roman emperors, personifications of the Roman state and the city council of Ephesus, the Hellenistic king Lysimachus, and legendary founders of Ephesus. See Rogers, *The Sacred Identity of Ephesos*, 80–126.

67. A total of six items have figural representations: Babelon, *Le Trésor de Berthouville* , nos 5–6 (two detached emblemata for bowls, with relief images of Apollo, and a togate figure with a cornucopia and Victory on a globe, possibly the young Caracalla), nos 7–9 (bowls with lightly incised images of putti and a young man in their interiors), and no. 40 (a mirror with birds, baskets of fruit and dogs hunting rabbits incised on the back). Of these, only the Apollo emblemata seems to have any possible cultic significance, but has no relation to Minerva.

68. F. Baratte, F. Beck, et al., *Orfèvrerie gallo-romaine: le trésor de Rethel*, Paris, 1988, no. 2, 40–58.

69. Baratte, *Notre-Dame-d'Allençon*, 18, suggests that the homogenous group of simple bowls which form the core of this hoard may have been manufactured locally for sale at the shrine to worshippers.

70. For example, the representations of the emperor's piety where he is shown pouring a libation. See R. Gordon, 'The Veil of Power: Emperors, Sacrificers and Benefactors', in M. Beard and J. North, eds, *Pagan Priests: Religion and Power in the Ancient World* (London, 1990), 204, fig. 22, for this image on coins.

71. For example, on the Aeneas relief on west side of the Ara Pacis, where Aeneas pouring a libation is accompanied by an attendant with a jug and another phiale filled with fruit. See Zanker, *The Power of Images*, fig. 157.

72. See the useful overview of the cult meal in Greek and Roman religion by J.P. Kane, 'The Mithraic Meal in its Greek and Roman Environment' in J.R. Hinnells, ed., *Mithraic Studies: Proceedings of the First International Conference of Mithraic Studies*, 2 vols (Manchester, 1975), vol II, 321–43.

73. Johns and Potter, *The Thetford Treasure*, 49–52. They note that although Faunus is familiar in literary sources, 'archaeological evidence for the worship of Faunus, either at that time [late Republic/early Empire] or during the later Empire seems to be non-existent'.

74. Johns and Potter, *The Thetford Treasure*, 20–29.

75. Johns and Potter, *The Thetford Treasure*, 73–74.

76. Johns and Potter, *The Thetford Treasure*, 71. They admit that 'the nature of these rites and the way in which the spoons may have been used must of course remain obscure'. A more extreme position is taken by D. Watts, *Christians and Pagans in Roman Britain* (London and New York, 1991), 146–58, who argues that the Christian elements of the treasure indicate that the cult was formed by a group of lapsed Christians, thereby implying that the ritual in which the spoons were used incorporated a (per)version of the eucharist.

77. Kane, 'The Mithraic Meal'. This article is particularly relevant in context of the claims made by Watts for a cult of Faunus analogous to Dionysiac mystery cults, as Kane explores whether Mithraism included sacramental meals and if so, whether this was adopted from existing pagan practices. He concludes (343): 'contrary to opinions often expressed, there is very little evidence for sacramental ritual meals in the pagan environment of Mithraism'.

78. On the weight of spoons, Johns and Potter, *The Thetford Treasure*, 43. They believe that one workshop was responsible for the manufacture of all the spoons, although this makes the presence of the Christian symbols harder to explain.

79. The hoard was found in 1992 in Sussex. See Bland and Johns, 'The Hoxne Late Roman Treasure', 165–73.

80. Bland and Johns, 'The Hoxne Late Roman Treasure', 169–73.

81. Cahn, Kaufmann-Heinimann et al., *Der spätrömische Silberschatz*, 55–132, nos 1–21, 22–35, 36–40; Johns and Potter, *The Thetford Treasure*, no. 49, 107.

82. On the domestic use of Christian images and inscriptions see J. Engemann, 'Anmerkungen zu spätantiken Geräten des Alltagslebens mit Christlichen Bildern, Symbolen und Inschriften', *JbAC* 15 (1972), 154–173. Also Elsner, *Art and the Roman Viewer*, 252–260, who warns against neutralizing the implications of Christian images and symbols.

83. M.M. Mango, *Silver from Early Byzantium: the Kaper Koraon and Related Treasures* (Baltimore, 1986), nos 18–22, 24–26, 49–56. Spoon 21 and strainer 24 are now lost. The first group of spoons and strainers are from what was originally presented as the Hama Treasure, and are in the Walters Art Gallery; the second group of spoons are from the Antioch Treasure.

84. See V. Milojčić, 'Zu den spätkaiserzeitlichen und merowingischen Silberlöffeln', *Bericht der Römisch-Germanischen Kommission* 49 (1968), 111–33, and E. de Bhaldraithe in Watts, *Christians and Pagans*, 231–33 for later evidence (8th century onwards) for the use of these implements in the liturgy and its relevance to earlier practice. For practices in

the eastern church, now see R.F. Taft, 'Byzantine Communion Spoons: a Review of the Evidence', *DOP* 50 (1996), 207–38.

85. Mango, *Silver from Early Byzantium*, nos 18 (+ Ὑπὴρ εὐχῆς Ἡλιωδόρου), 19 (Ἰωάννου. Θωμᾶ. + τῶν Θεοφίλου [the first two names are written as cross monograms on either side of the disc of the spoon]), 26 (+ τοῦ ἁγίου Σεργίου). The names of the individuals who gave these spoons are found on other pieces of the hoard (idem, 120).

86. Another set of apostle spoons are found in the domestic Lampsacus Treasure: Mango, *Silver from Early Byzantium*, 216–18. See also F. Baratte, 'Vaisselle d'argent, souvenirs littéraires et manières de table: l'exemple des cuillers de Lampsaque', *CA*, 40 (1992), 5–20.

87. + Εὐλογία του ἁγίου Θωμᾶ: Mango, *Silver from Early Byzantium*, no. 49.

88. However, even in the fourth century, domestic silver donated to a church was not necessarily recyled, even if its decoration was decidedly secular: the Risley Park Lanx, which is decorated with hunting and pastoral scenes, carries an inscription recording that a certain bishop Exuperius gave it to the church of Bogiensis (possibly an estate-church in Britain). See C. Johns, 'The Risley Park Lanx: a Lost Antiquity from Roman Britain', *Antiquaries Journal* 61 (1981), 53–72; C. Johns and K. Painter, 'The Risley Park Lanx: Bauge, Bayeux, Buch or Britain?', in *Orbis Romanus Christianusque ab Diocletiani aetate usque ad Heraclium. Travaux sur l'Antiqué Tardive rassemblés autour des recherches de Noël Duval* (Paris, 1995), 175–87.

89. K.S. Painter, *The Water Newton Early Christian Silver*, London, 1977.

90. O. von Hessen, W. Kurze and C.A. Mastrelli, *Il tesoro di Galognano* (Florence, 1977). Another sixth-century Italian hoard, The Canoscio Treasure, was identified as liturgical on its discovery, but this has since been questioned. See D.E. Giovagnoli, 'Una collezione di vasi eucaristici scoperti a Canosca', *Rivista di Archeologia Cristiana* 12 (1935), 313–28, and J. Engemann, 'Anmerkungen zu spätantiken Geräten des Alltagslebens mit Christlichen Bildern, Symbolen und Inschriften', *JbAC* 15 (1972), 154–73.

91. This comprises the four hoards known respectively as the Riha, Stuma, Hama and Antioch Treasures. Their identification as a single hoard was proposed in Mango, *Silver from Early Byzantium* and has been accepted by many specialists in the field, although it has been contested by A. Effenberger, 'Bemerkungen zum "Kaper-Koraon-Schatz"', in *Tesserae. Festschrift für J. Engemann, JbAC* Ergänzungsband 18 (Münster, 1991), 241–77, and S.P. Hauser, *Spätantike und frühbyzantinische Silberlöffel: Bemerkungen zur Produktion von Luxusgütern im 5. bis 7. Jahrhundert, JbAC* Ergänzungsband 19 (Münster, 1992), 45–49.

92. This hoard remains unpublished, despite being known for over 30 years, because of the circumstances of its find, which led to a large part of the treasure being illegally removed from Turkey and sold to Dumbarton Oaks and private collectors, while the rest remained in Turkey. A provisional checklist and introduction is provided by S.A. Boyd, 'A "Metropolitan" Treasure from a Church in the Provinces: An Introduction to the Study of the Sion Treasure' in Boyd and Mango, *Ecclesiastical Silver Plate*, 5–38. This provides accurate information on the pieces in Dumbarton Oaks and private collections, and attempts to do the same for the pieces that remain in Turkey (in the Antalya Museum) relying on the accounts of those scholars who were able to examine them in the 1960s as Boyd herself has been unable to gain access.

93. Beth Misona: W.H. Milliken, 'The Cleveland Byzantine Silver Treasure', *Bulletin of the Cleveland Museum of Art* 38 (1951), 142–45, Mango, *Silver from Early Byzantium*,

228–30. Phela; M.C. Ross, *Catalogue of Byzantine and Early Medieval Antiquities in the Dumbarton Oaks Collection* I (Washington, DC, 1962); E. Dodd, *Byzantine Silver Treasures*, Monographien der Abegg Stiftung 9 (Bern, 1973); Mango, *Silver from Early Byzantium*, 232–36. Ma'aret en-Noman (also known as the 2nd Hama Treasure); M.C. Ross, 'A Second Byzantine Treasure From Hama', *Archaeology* 3 (1950), 162–63; Mango, *Silver from Early Byzantium*, 280–304. The Syrian findspots of all three treasures are conjectural. A recent addition to the Syrian ecclesiastical hoards, the Attarouthi Treasure, was acquired by the Metropolitan Museum of Art in 1986. It has yet to be published, and for that reason will not be discussed in this chapter.

94. L.A. Matzulewitsch, *Byzantinische Antike: Studien auf Grund der Silbergefässe der Ermitage* (Berlin and Leipzig, 1929), 101–07; J. Werner, *Der Grabfund von Malaia Perescepina und Kuvrat, Kagan der Bulgaren*, Bayrische Akademie der Wissenschaften, phil.-hist. Klasse, Abhandlungen, neue Folge, Heft 91, Munich, 1984.

95. Boyd, 'A "Metropolitan" Treasure', no. 6.

96. Mango, *Silver from Early Byzantium*, 13. Compare these dimensions and weights with those of the largest of the fourth-century domestic serving plates: Kaiseraugst Waterfront City Plate (Cahn, Kaufmann-Heinimann et al., *Der spätrömische Silberschatz*, no. 62) diameter 59 cm, weight 4749.9 g; Sevso Hunting Plate (Mango and Bennet, *The Sevso Treasure*, no. 1) d. 70.5 cm, weight 8.873 kg; Sevso Meleager Plate (idem. no. 2) diameter 69.4 cm, weight 8.606 kg; Sevso Achilles Plate (idem. no. 3) diameter 72 cm, weight 11.786 kg.

97. Εὐξόμενος Δόμνος υἱὸς Ζαχέου προσήνενκεν τῷ ἁγίῳ Σεργίῳ χω(ρίου) Βεθ Μισωυα.

98. Mango, *Silver from Early Byzantium*, cat. nos 4, 5, 6, 36, 39.

99. The inscriptions are similar in character to that already quoted for the Beth Misona paten. As well as fulfilling vows they also pray for the salvation (σωτερίας) and the repose (ἀναπαύσεως) of the donor and his or her relatives, the former term being applied to the living and the latter to the dead.

100. The donors were predominately high ranking clergy, a Bishop Eutychianos being responsible for the largest proportion of donations (29 out of 59). See also Boyd, 'A "Metropolitan" treasure', 16–18.

101. The cases for and against this identification are summarized by I. Ševčenko, 'The Sion Treasure: the Evidence of the Inscriptions', and H. Hellenkemper, 'Ecclesiastical Silver Hoards and Their Findspots: Implications for the Treasure found at Korydalla, Lycia', both in Boyd and Mango, *Ecclesiastical Silver Plate*, 49–52 and 65–70.

102. I. Ševčenko and N. Patterson Ševčenko, ed. and trans., *The Life of St Nicholas of Sion*, (Brookline, MA, 1984), 90–91, 102–03.

103 St Theodore's most distinguished patrons were the emperor Maurice (whose ascent to the throne he prophesied) and Domniziolos, nephew of the emperor Phocas and army commander in the Persian Wars. See *Vie de Théodore*, 54, 120, 128.

104. Despite the overall similarities between the three, they are not identical. The Antalya paten has only acanthus leaves, not palmettes, on its border and a cross superimposed on an X rather than a chi–rho; the Geneva paten has a smaller, less well-proportioned chi–rho. For a discussion of workshop practices which might be responsible for such differences, see Boyd, 'A "Metropolitan" treasure', 14–16.

105. So-called from its inscription which reads EX ANTIQUIS RENOVATUM EST PER PATERNUM REVERENTISS(imum) EPISC(opum) NOSTRUM AMEN. This vessel is comparable in size and weight to the Sion patens, which are all substantially larger and heavier than the Syrian examples. It has a diameter of 61 cm and weighs 6.224 kg. The diameters and weights of the Sion patens are as follows: no. 1: 60.5 cm, 5.2 kg; no. 2: 61 cm, weight not recorded; no. 3: 73.5 cm, weight not recorded; no. 4: 58 cm, 4.357 kg; no. 5: 58.5 cm, 4.234 kg; no. 6: 77.5 cm, weight not recorded (Boyd, 'A "Metropolitan" treasure', 19–20).

106. Cf. the distance of 400 km between Constantinople and Sykeon, which St Theodore of Sykeon's archdeacon travels to buy liturgical vessels in the capital. *Vie de Théodore*, 42.

107. Fourth-century examples include the vault mosaics in the mausoleum of S. Constanza and the wall paintings of the Peacock tomb in Nicea. The mosaic pavement of the Basilica of Justinian at Sabratha is a good sixth-century example in a church context. For further discussion of this type of imagery, see H. Maguire, *Earth and Ocean: The Terrestrial World in Early Byzantine Art* (University Park, PA, 1987).

108. Mango, *Silver from Early Byzantium*, nos 34 & 35, 159–70. She argues against the earlier view of Dodd, *Byzantine Silver Stamps*, 160–64 that they were made in different workshops.

109. The scriptural references for the Last Supper and institution of the eucharist are: Matthew 26:26–29, Mark 14:22–25, Luke 22:19–20, 1 Corinthians 11:23–26.

110. Mango, *Silver from Early Byzantium*, 164, 170, claims that patens are represented in each scene, but I am unconvinced, since the objects she appears to identify as patens bear no resemblance in shape or relative scale to the patens in the Kaper Koran hoard. Such resemblances can be detected in other liturgical vessels represented, such as the lamps and the chalices. Mango also discusses the possibility that these vessels are meant to represent other donations to the same church by the patens' donors, but such a literal reading is not necessary in my opinion.

111. It appears in the Rossano Gospels, and a lost monumental prototype of a mosaic or wall painting has been postulated. See J.L. Schrader, 'Antique and Early Christian Sources for the Riha and Stuma Patens', *Gesta* 18 (1979), 147–56 for an overview of the different prototype theories.

112. Another exceptional example is the Sion censer with scenes from the life of the Virgin in Antalya (Boyd, 'A "Metropolitan" treasure', no. 19). This, like the Communion of the Apostles patens, is in gilded repoussé and shows the Annunciation, Visitation, Journey to Bethlehem and Nativity. For illustrations see N. Firatli, 'Un trésor du VIe siècle trouvé à Kumluca en Lycie', *Akten des VII. Internationalen Kongress für Christliche Archäologie*, 2 vols (Vatican City, 1969), 523–25.

113. The mosaic programme of S. Apollinare Nuovo is a good example, where unidentifiable figures of saints with books in the middle tier of the wall decoration serve as a mediator between the upper and lower tiers. See Elsner, *Art and the Roman Viewer*, 234–35, also F.W. Deichmann, *Ravenna, Hauptstadt des spätantiken Abendlandes*, Kommentar I (Wiesbaden, 1974), 141–54.

114. The 'Stuma paten' (Mango, *Silver from Early Byzantium*, no. 34) has a diameter of 36.5–36.8 cm and weighs 836 g. The 'Riha paten' (Mango, *Silver from Early Byzantium*, no. 35) has a diameter of 35.0 cm and weights 904 g.

115. Examples include the Kaper Koraon chalice no. 3, and flask no. 15; the three identical chalices in the Beth Misona Treasure (Mango, *Silver from Early Byzantium*, nos 57, 58,

59), the Syrian ewer in the Louvre known as the 'Homs Vase' (Mango, *Silver from Early Byzantium*, no. 84), and a censer in the Sion Treasure (Boyd, 'A "Metropolitan" treasure', no. 18). Cf. the hexagonal censer from the 1st Cyprus Treasure (British Museum) although this hoard is considered to be domestic: Kent and Painter, *Wealth of the Roman World*, no. 176, 102–03.

116. E.g. Eutychianos, most humble bishop [presents this] to the Lord for the forgiveness of [his] sins. (Ἐυτυχίανος ἐλάχιστος ἐλάχιστος ἐπίσκοπος τῷ μεγάλῳ θεῷ ˙ ὑπὲρ ἀφέσεως ἁμαρτιων, Boyd, 'A "Metropolitan" treasure', no. 2). [Treasure] of St Sergios. For the memory of Baradatos, son of Heliodoros. (+ Τοῦ ἁγίου Σεργίου. Ὑπὲρ μνήμες Βαραδάτον υἱοῦ Ἡλιοδόρου', Mango, *Silver from Early Byzantium*, no. 4).

117. C. Roueché, *Aphrodisias in Late Antiquity: the Late Roman Inscriptions including texts from the excavations of Aphrodisias conducted by Kenan T. Erim*, Journal of Roman Studies Monographs (London, 1989), xix–xxiii. For St Polyeuktos see R.M. Harrison et al., *Excavations at Saraçhane in Istanbul I, The Excavations, Structures, Architectural Decoration, Small Finds, Coins, Bones and Molluscs* (Princeton, NJ, 1986), 117–21.

118. Inscriptions on silverware before the fourth century AD are very rare; where they occur (e.g. the skeleton cups from Boscoreale; the dedicatory inscriptions in the Berthouville Treasure) they are not a prominent feature of the decoration and are executed in pointillé rather than being incised or inlaid, the favoured techniques of late antiquity. In the later period, pointillé lettering is only used for inscriptions located on the undersides of vessels.

119. Cf. Cutler's remarks on the epigraphic skills of the ivoryworkers who carved consular diptychs and were not specialist epigraphers/calligraphers: 'The Making of the Justinian Diptychs', 92–95.

120. R.R.R. Smith, 'Late antique portraits in a public context: honorific statuary at Aphrodisias in Caria AD 300-600', *JRS* 89 (1999), 174–75.

121. The text of the inscription in St Polyeuktos is preserved in the Palatine Anthology I.10; for that of SS. Sergius and Bacchus see J. Ebersolt & A. Thiers, *Les églises de Constantinople*, (Paris, 1913), 24.

122. Gregory of Tours, *Glory of the Martyrs* 84, trans. R. Van Dam, Translated Texts for Historians, Latin Series III (Liverpool, 1988), 109.

123. H. Buschhausen, *Die spätrömischen Metallscrinia und frühchristlichen Reliquiare* (Vienna, 1971) is a comprehensive catalogue of all sacred and secular metal caskets from that period. He also wrote the entries for the early Christian reliquary caskets included in K. Weitzmann, ed., *Age of Spirituality: Late Antique and Early Christian Art, 3rd to 7th Century* (New York, 1979). As few other scholars have studied these objects in depth, it is perhaps unfortunate that his theories about them are rather eccentric, especially his view that Christian reliquaries developed from a supposed pagan practice of burying metal caskets with the dead. Equally unfortunate is his failure to discuss the dating of these caskets.

124. A. Gnirs, 'Frühchristliche Denkmäler in Pola', *Jahrbuch der K. K. Zentral-Kommission für Erforschung und Erhaltung der Kunst-und Historischen Denkmale*, neue Folge 4 (1906), 230–31 with refs.

125. Reliquaries have been found in this context at a sixth-century church of Zanavartepe, near Varna, Bulgaria (Buschhausen, *Die spätrömischen Metallscrinia*, C1); a church in Chersonesus in the Crimea (idem. B21); the basilica of San Nazaro Maggiore, Milan (idem. B11); and the sixth-century basilica of St Euphemia in Grado (idem. B18, 19).

There is also plenty of textual evidence for such deposits elsewhere in the West in the late sixth century, e.g. England, where Gregory the Great sent Augustine 'relics of the holy apostles and martyrs' with instructions to place them in the altars of the churches which he finds (Bede, *History of the English People*, i. 29–30) and Merovingian Gaul, where Gregory of Tours installed various relics in the church of St Martin of Tours, the cathedral residence of Tours and other local churches. See D. Rollason, *Saints and Relics in Anglo-Saxon England* (Oxford, 1989), 23–59, and R. Van Dam, *Saints and their Miracles in Late Antique Gaul* (Princeton, NJ, 1993), 33–34, 65–66.

126. The standard work on these is the catalogue by A. Grabar, *Ampoules de Terre-Saint (Monza, Bobbio)* (Paris, 1958). Grabar erroneously identifies their material as silver (11). A. Merati, *Il Tesoro del Duomo di Monza* (Monza 1963) 11, and J. Engemann, 'Palästinensische Pilgerampullen im F.J. Dölger–Institut in Bonn', *JbAC* 16 (1973), 7 state that it is a tin-lead alloy. For a recent discussion of the ampullae in Monza and Bobbio, see J. Elsner, 'Replicating Palestine and Reversing the Reformation: Pilgrimage and Collecting at Bobbio, Monza and Walsingham', *Journal of the History of Collections* 9 (1997), 117–30.

127. On this see H. Delehaye, *Les origines du culte des martyrs*, Subsidia Hagiographia 20, 2nd edn, Brussels, 1933, and Brown, *The Cult of the Saints*.

128. E. Dassmann, 'Ambrosius und die Märtyrer', *JbAC*, 18 (1975), 49–68, esp 52–57. Also see Brown, *The Cult of the Saints*, 36–37.

129. Miracles involving the eucharist are another aspect of this relationship. One such miracle is recounted in the *Life of St Theodore of Sykeon*: consecrated bread jumps up and down on the paten to show that 'the offering of the celebrant was acceptable' (*Vie de Théodore*, 126). The miracle is explicitly connected with the fact that the saint is officiating over the offering, setting up a relationship between saint, altar/liturgy, and miracle, which could also be said to exist in the case of the relics of saints enclosed in altars.

130. See A. Angenendt, 'Der Kult der Reliquien', in A. Legner, ed., *Reliquien: Verehrung und Verklärung. Skizzen und Noten zur Thematik* (Cologne, 1989), 10–16. Body-part reliquaries offer the most literal example of the reliquary providing a context for relics: see *Gesta* 36.1 (1997), a special issue devoted to this category of object. Also see A.G. Remensnyder, 'Legendary Treasure at Conques: Reliquaries and Imaginative Memory', *Speculum* 71 (1996), 884–906 on the relationship between relics and reliquaries in the later middle ages in the West.

131. Buschhausen in Weitzmann, *Age of Spirituality*, no. 568. It should be noted however that except in the case of two caskets which have Byzantine control stamps, dating must be on stylistic grounds and can therefore be subjective.

132. P.L. Zovatto, *Grado. Antichi monumenti* (Bologna, 1971), 24.

133. Buschhausen's entry for this reliquary (*Die spätrömischen Metallscrinia*, B16) seems (erroneously) to imply that it was found in the grave of Leo III ('als das Altargrab Leo III geöffnet war'). He also gives the date of discovery as 1906; however as an unpublished paper by D. Buckton makes clear, the cupboard beneath the altar was first opened in 1903, so that a Jesuit who was writing a biography of St Agnes could examine her head, which the altar also contained. In 1905, Grisar was allowed to examine the altar's contents in the chapel and make an inventory, after which all the objects were removed to the Vatican. See Grisar, *Die römische Kapelle Sancta Sanctorum und ihr Schatz* (Freiburg, 1908). P. Lauer, a scholarly rival of Grisar's, who had also been trying to gain access to the treasure during the first years of this century, viewed it (in the Vatican) in 1906 and published his own account, 'Le trésor du Sancta Sanctorum', *Mon. Piot* 15 (1906), 7–140.

134. Lauer, 'Le trésor du Sancta Sanctorum', 7, 72. For the appearance of the cupboard see his figs 5–8.

135. See J. Duffy and G. Vikan, 'A Small Box in John Moschus', *GRBS* 24 (1983), 93–99 for literary evidence for the use of small boxes (of unspecified material) as containers for valuables, offerings to a church, and consecrated bread (in a private devotional context).

136. On this see B. Kiilerich, *Late Fourth Century Classicism in the Plastic Arts: Studies in the So-Called Theodosian Renaissance* (Odense, 1993), 181–86.

137. The Adoration as depicted on the Palestinian ampullae shows both magi and shepherds, the latter wearing short tunics, with their flocks depicted in the exergue, the former in their traditional oriental costume. See Grabar, *Ampoules*, 53–54.

138. Buschhausen, *Die spätrömischen Metallscrinia*, 223–24. The Ambrosian basilica was destroyed in the eleventh century, and rebuilt in the sixteenth, when its relics (including the casket) were translated to a new altar, where the casket was rediscovered in 1894. The authenticity of the casket has sometimes been doubted, but the most recent study rejects the idea that it could be a sixteenth-century fake: see G. Sena Chiesa & F. Slavazzi, 'La capsella argentea di San Nazaro. Prima risulati di una nuova indagine', *Antiquité Tardive* 7 (1999), 187–204.

139. Grabar, *Ampoules*, 55–58.

140. On the function of the ampullae as a metonymic representation of the Holy Land, see Elsner, 'Replicating Palestine'.

141. G.B. De Rossi, *La Capsella Argentea Africana offerta al Sommo Pontefice Leone XIII dall' emo Sig. Card. Lavigerie Arcivesco di Cartagine, Memoria* (Rome, 1889); Buschhausen, *Die spätrömischen Metallscrinia*, B15. As the title of De Rossi's work suggests, this box was presented in 1889 to Pope Leo XIII on the 50th anniversary of his ordination by Cardinal Lavigerie (1825–92), Archbishop of Algiers, who played a leading role in organizing the archaeological exploration of the early Christian monuments of North Africa, which had heavy missionary and colonial overtones. See W.C.H. Frend, *The Archaeology of Early Christianity: a History* (London, 1996), 67–81. The supposed sixth-century date of the church where it was found is a 19th century assignation, and may well not be accurate. See Frend, 127–29, on weakness of nineteenth-century archaeological dating in North Africa generally.

142. A. Grabar in *Martyrium: recherches sur le culte des reliques et l'art chrétien antique*, 2 vols (Paris, 1946), vol. 2, 56–57, says this is 'Christ as a martyr', rather than a generic male martyr, though the reasoning behind his statement is unclear.

143. See Maguire, *Earth and Ocean*, 38, figs 43, 50 (examples of this motif in early Byzantine church mosaics).

144. Dodd, *Byzantine Silver Stamps*, no. 86, 157.

145. The inscription reads: SAN(c)TUS CANTIUS SAN(ctus) (Can)TIANUS SANCTA CANTILLA SAN(c)TUS QUIRINUS SANC(c)TUS LATINUS.

146. Found in the ruins of a Syrian village church in the nineteenth century. See Mango, *Silver From Early Byzantium*, 255–56 with bibliography.

147. Grabar, *Ampoules*, Monza ampullae 1, 13, Bobbio ampulla 1; pls. X, XXII, XXV.

148. Compare the ivory pyxis in the British Museum which depicts the martyrdom of St Menas, and which is sometimes for that reason considered to have been a reliquary. A. Eastmond in Buckton, *Byzantium*, no. 65, 74, prefers to see it as a votive gift to a church from the family who are represented on one side of the pyxis, although this does not rule out the possibility that it could have been used for relics.

149. P. Lasko, *Ars Sacra 800–1200*, Pelican History of Art, 2nd edn (New Haven and London, 1994) (1st edn, 1972).

3

Representing myth in late antique silver: the role of *paideia*

In focusing first on largitio silver, then on Christian liturgical vessels, I have explored types of silverware that represent late antique innovations in this medium. In becoming a site for the representation of the imperial image, and a means of defining and articulating sanctity in the Christian Church, silverware was extending its meanings beyond the traditional sphere which it had occupied for many centuries in the Mediterranean world, namely: the domestic. In the final two chapters of this book, I want to focus on the function and meanings of late antique silver in its domestic context, and more specifically on the way that it continued to represent the traditional iconographic repertoire of Graeco-Roman mythology. This chapter will examine the use of such iconography in the fourth and early fifth centuries AD, through a close study of the large display plates which are a typical component of the major domestic hoards of this period, such as the Kaiseraugst, Sevso, and Mildenhall Treasures, and which also survive as lone pieces, such as the Corbridge Lanx and the Parabiago plate.[1] The following chapter will trace their sucessors into the sixth and early seventh centuries and examine an exceptional set of display plates – the so-called David Plates from Cyprus – which replaces the heroes of classical mythology with a biblical one.

The surviving display plates of the fourth and early fifth centuries are decorated lavishly with a range of mythological images: the deeds of heroes, the Olympian gods and their attributes, the revels of Dionysos and his followers. Such images proliferated in the domestic sphere in late antiquity. As well as on silver, they appear on mosaics, in wall-painting, on ivory boxes and plaques, and on textiles (both for furnishing and for wear).[2] What significance did this traditional iconography have for its late antique viewers in a period when the context in which it had existed for centuries was being transformed, not least by the establishment of a new religion, Christianity, which called into question the validity of the mythological tradition? One answer is that it disguised such changes by maintaining continuity with the past. This analysis of silverware will focus on one of the means by which continuity was maintained and will show that the traditional education of the elite in the Graeco-Roman world, a process commonly referred to as *paideia*, can provide a useful tool for understanding the way myth was employed in the domestic sphere. The components of *paideia* were highly standardized, and had changed little since the second century BC; yet despite the political and social changes in the Graeco-Roman world between the Hellenistic and late Roman periods *paideia* continued to be valued in the eyes of the elite as an important part of their self-definition.[3] *Paideia* was as much a training in ways of behaving, in a particular mode of social interaction, as in specific knowledge, which is reflected in the dual use of the term to denote culture as well as education.[4] It is not unreasonable to suppose that it fostered – not necessarily consciously – specific modes of viewing art. There is also an important analogy to be made between the traditions of education and of the mythological iconographic repertoire: their traditionalism was valued as a mark of stability in what was in many ways a changing society.[5]

In late antiquity, the lengthy educational training that constituted *paideia* consisted of two stages, as it had from the time of the Hellenistic period in the second century BC. Instruction by a grammarian (*grammaticus*, γραμματικός) in the rules of language and literature, followed by training in oratory under a rhetor (σοφιστής, ῥήτωρ).[6] The process began typically around the age of seven or eight and could last into the early twenties.[7] Not all of those who attended the school of the grammaticus went on to rhetorical education, which usually required travel to a major centre of study such as Athens or Antioch, since within the elite classes of the Roman Empire there were of course a variety of economic levels. However, even the grammarian's training was sufficient to distinguish those who had undergone it as men of 'culture', as opposed to those further down the social scale who had undergone only basic instruction in literacy at the second-class 'schools of letters' (*ludi litterati*, γραμματοδιδασκαλεῖα).[8] This was especially important at the beginning of late antiquity, when after the loosening of the structures of upper class society in the third century, the grammarian's training helped to re-identify the elite.[9]

In the past, classical scholarship has tended to dismiss *paideia* from serious consideration as a means of understanding the ancient world. The narrowness of its curriculum does not correspond to modern ideas of a liberal education, while the absence of 'professional' training from its curriculum has been seen as a failing by those who believe education should be practical and skill-based.[10] Such judgements are anachronistic and do not take into account the function education served in the ancient world, where extended education was the exclusive preserve of the elite and as such a mode of access to power, while the idea of supporting oneself through the practice of a profession was disdained.[11] Recently a number of studies have appeared which analyse the very different social functions of education in late antiquity.[12] One important point to arise from them is Peter Brown's observation that the uniformity of *paideia* across the Roman Empire, both East and West, allowed it to serve as a unifying bond between members of the elite, who might have rather different interests at stake (e.g. the local aristocracy of a province and their Roman governor).[13] Thus, although apparently unrelated to the concerns of the 'real' world, *paideia* served an active political function there. Brown's concept of *paideia* as a common bond, providing set formulas of reference by which members of the elite could recognize one another, can be applied productively to the visual sphere. In this study of silverware with mythological themes I want to examine the possibility that visual as well as literary culture could serve as a means of unification and communication, not in the public sphere of city politics but in its counterpart, the private politics of the dining rooms of the elite (where key political issues and alliances were as likely to be enacted).[14]

Perhaps the most explicit involvement of *paideia* in visual culture is that displayed in the *Imagines* of Philostratus the Elder. The author presents his work, a series of *ekphraseis* of pictures in a friend's house, as a lecture given to the friend's son together with an audience of local young men eager to hear a virtuoso sophist speak.[15] It is a context which is explicitly private (a house), elite (the house is rich enough to possess a large picture gallery) and exclusive (an invited audience), a display of *paideia* in its most desirable form as the master sharing his wisdom (without remuneration) in a bond of class-solidarity.[16] Philostratus' *Imagines* are a rhetorical display, corresponding to the ancient rhetorical category of *ekphrasis*, or description.[17] They are far from simple 'descriptions' of pictures in a modern sense, but rather play with the relationship between the viewer and the image in a complex way.[18] Philostratus' discourses upon the pictures are as much a contribution to the rhetorical education of his youthful listeners, as they are a training in how to look at art. Nevertheless, the fact that the Philostratus' rhetorical skills can be exercised on images in the context of an elite villa does have implications for the way owners of such villas might have understood the function of the mosaics, wall paintings, statues, textiles and silverware with which they adorned them.[19] Rather than saying that the *Imagines* show that training in art criticism was a part of *paideia* (which it arguably was not for the majority), we can say that its forms of training could predispose its recipients to employ visual culture in certain ways.

Narratives of *paideia*: the example of Achilles

I would now like to turn to one of the examples of silverware which I cited above, the Kaiseraugst Achilles plate (Fig. 3.1), and show how this approach might work in practice. The imagery on this object lends itself especially well to an analysis in terms of *paideia*, since it not only represents the education of Achilles (a slightly unusual form of *paideia*), but Achilles, as the central character of the Iliad, lies at the heart of the traditions and values of *paideia*.[20] In the Greek-speaking parts of the Roman Empire, Homer was the primary text of the grammarian's instruction and also played a key role in the teaching of Greek to Latin speakers in the Western part of the empire.[21] The Kaiseraugst Treasure, of which the plate in question forms a part, is a large hoard of domestic silver which was buried in the mid-fourth century inside the walls of the Rhine frontier fort of Augusta Rarica (about 10 km from Basle in modern Switzerland) and rediscovered in the early 1960s.[22] The Achilles plate itself

3.1 Kaiseraugst
Treasure, Augst,
Römermuseum:
Achilles Plate
(E. Schulz/Foto
Römerstadt
Augusta Rarica)

is octagonal (maximum diameter 53 cm), with a high ring foot and a slightly
convex surface. It weighs 4.643 kg. There are two main zones of decoration:
the broad rim, which has a circular inner edge, and a central medallion. These
are both decorated with figures in high relief which are formed by chasing
and carving the metallic surface. A single scene, the discovery of Achilles on
Skyros, occupies the central medallion, while the rim is divided by spiral-
fluted columns into ten sections of unequal length. Beginning from the bottom
right-hand corner of the octagon (which is nearly aligned with the ground-
line of the central medallion) the scenes are arranged anti-clockwise; their
subjects are as follows:

1. The birth of Achilles
2. Thetis dips Achilles in the river Styx
3. Thetis hands over Achilles into the care of the centaur Chiron
4. Chiron kills wild animals to feed the child Achilles on their marrow
5. Chiron teaches Achilles to hunt and ride
6. Chiron teaches Achilles to read
7. Chiron teaches Achilles to use weapons
8. Chiron returns Achilles to Thetis
9. Achilles is taken to the court of King Lykomedes, disguised as a girl
10. Achilles plays the lyre to the daughters of King Lykomedes.

These ten scenes, together with the central medallion of the Discovery on Skyros represent a remarkably full account of the life of Achilles before he realizes his destiny by going to fight at Troy. It is an upbringing which will prepare him for his future heroic deeds.[23] While certain scenes, like the discovery on Skyros, are a familiar part of the Graeco-Roman iconographic repertory in Campanian wall painting, others like the Birth of Achilles seem to be a late antique innovation.[24] The extent to which these scenes form a narrative cycle is unusual both for late antiquity and earlier periods, the more so because that cycle shows no scenes of Achilles' activities at Troy. This is in contrast to the two closest parallels to the Kaiseraugst plate, a fourth-century marble table rim in Rome, known as the 'Capitoline Puteal', and a series of rectangular terra sigillata dishes made in North Africa in the fourth and fifth centuries, both of which incorporate Achilles' deeds at Troy.[25]

The marble table rim (Fig. 3.2) has eight scenes: Birth, Immersion in Styx, Handover to Chiron, Hunt, Deidameia and Nurse on Skyros, Discovery on Skyros, Duel with Hector, and Dragging the Body of Hector. This represents a smaller total than the Kaiseraugst plate and thus the account of Achilles' training with Chiron is considerably abbreviated, although it still predominates over the Trojan scenes. The terra sigillata dishes, which would have been mass-produced using a single stamp for each scene, come in different sizes so there is some variation in the spacing and the order of the episodes. However 14 different scenes can be identified in the surviving fragments of this type, ten of which span the time between Achilles' birth and his discovery on Skyros, and another four of which show Thetis bringing arms for Achilles, Achilles and Priam (the central image), Muses and Fates (?) and Musicians. Here again the emphasis is on Achilles' earliest years, but two Iliadic episodes are also shown, as well as two scenes with only a loose connection to the narrative. While these two comparanda are clearly related to the Kaiseraugst plate both in their domestic context and iconographically, the designer of the Kaiseraugst plate seems to have made a deliberate decision not to represent Achilles at Troy.

The special character of this plate also comes across in a comparison with Roman sarcophagi of the second and third centuries AD. Achilles is very popular in this context and is represented on some examples of particularly high quality, such as the sarcophagus from the Borghese collection now in

3.2 'Capitoline Puteal', Rome, Capitoline Museum (Singer / Deutsches Archäologisches Institut, Rome, neg. 70.35)

the Louvre.[26] On these, the scene of the discovery on Skyros plays a key role, inevitably occupying the front panel of the sarcophagus. It is typically combined with the ransoming of Hector on the back panel and scenes of the arming of Achilles, the daughters of Lykomedes with Achilles, or his farewell to Lykomedes on the side panels.[27] A less common variant for a side panel is Chiron teaching Achilles to throw the javelin, an example of which is to be found on a sarcophagus in the National Museum of Naples.[28] Thus there are areas of overlap between the sarcophagi and the Kaiseraugst plate: the Discovery on Skyros is central in both cases, but does it work in the same way in each? Richard Brilliant has interpreted the Discovery on Skyros on the sarcophagi as a scene which refers simultaneously to Achilles' past and future, thereby giving a heroic allure to his uneventful early life. In the context of the memorial function of sarcophagi, this simultaneously pro- and retrospective interpretation has its attractions, but it works less well when Brilliant tries to apply it to the Kaiseraugst plate, which he believes shows 'the dependency of the narrative cycle of Achilles' early life on the Skyrian episode for its meaning and form'.[29] This interpretation ignores the detail with which the early life and upbringing of Achilles is depicted on the Kaiseraugst plate and thereby excludes the possibility that they had a value in themselves for the late antique viewer.

Rather, as I have already suggested in my comparison of the Kaiseraugst plate with Achilles cycles in other media, it is the upbringing of Achilles that forms the key narrative interest. Here there is a double appeal to the viewer's *paideia*: first in depicting the heroic *paideia*, and second in elaborating upon a short period in the hero's life, which is usually summarized in fewer scenes. This would seem to have parallels both with rhetorical composition and with the grammaticus' exegesis of texts, where accurate knowledge of minor incidents and personalities was often prized.[30] The education of Achilles is both archaic (in that it consists mainly of hunting, riding and learning to fight) and idiosyncratic (in that having completed his time with Chiron, Achilles is disguised as a girl and lives a woman's life at the court of King Lykomedes).[31] It thus appeals to a knowledge of 'how heroes were brought up'. At the same time, there is one scene which appeals more directly to the viewer's own experience: Achilles reciting his letters to Chiron from a writing tablet which he holds. The artist has even engraved the first five letters of the Greek alphabet on its leaves, while Chiron holds up two fingers in the standard gesture of a classical teacher while holding a rod in his other hand. A female figure, probably correctly identified as a muse, also attends the proceedings, suggesting that Achilles is not merely learning his alphabet but being 'educated in the muses', that is, receiving a proper literary education – like that of the viewer![32]

Although the absence of any representations of Achilles' deeds in the Trojan war on this plate is one of its distinguishing features, this is not to say that the later career of Achilles would necessarily have been absent from the viewer's mind. If we return to Philostratus' *Imagines*, his second book contains the description of a painting called 'The Upbringing of Achilles', whose subject matter is composed of scenes clearly related to those on the plate: the boy Achilles bringing back to Chiron's cave the animals he has caught whilst hunting, and Chiron teaching Achilles to ride on his own back.[33] Philostratus' response to these scenes begins with a contrast between Achilles as he is in the picture, and as he will be at Troy. The booty of the child Achilles' hunting (a fawn and a hare), and the rewards which Chiron gives him (apples and honey), are compared to the taking of 'cities and horses and the ranks of men', and his rewards of 'Briseis and the seven women from Lesbos and gold and tripods'.[34] The passage forms an excuse for a Homeric digression on Philostratus' part (a feature of several of his ekphraseis), and his language actually evokes that of the Iliad. But this is part of another picture, he tells us, one which is painted/written by Homer (Philostratus uses the Greek verb γράφω with the dual meaning of 'paint' and 'write').[35] The picture of the non-Homeric episode of the upbringing of Achilles evokes Homer's written picture of his manhood at Troy. This type of response is typical of the culture of *paideia*. One scene evokes another, not present but remembered, from a different medium, writing not painting. The Kaiseraugst plate presents us with a domestic version of a Homeric hero's *aristeia* (display of prowess), in a manner analogous to that of children's 'vita' sarcophagi, where the events of their short lives are presented as a career.[36]

Another relevant aspect of this ekphrasis is Philostratus' discription of Chiron. The centaur is shown with a gentle expression in his eye, which, Philostratus opines, is the result of 'justice, and the wisdom that he has acquired through justice', as well as his training in the lyre through which he has become cultured (literally 'ἐκμεμούσωταί').[37] Here Chiron's qualities as a good teacher are stressed, both to distinguish him from the type of centaur who is uncivilized and does not know justice, but also because those are the values which matter to Philostratus' audience. They want to know what sort of a teacher Achilles had, and that this teacher – like their own – was a civilized and cultivated man. In describing Chiron, Philostratus describes himself. This is in some ways a parallel to the scene on the Achilles plate where Chiron is shown in the guise of a *grammatikos* teaching Achilles his letters. It is worth noting in this context the popularity of the belief in the heroizing power of culture expressed in Greek funerary epigrams from the Imperial period.[38]

Even a cursory look, such as I have made above, at this particular extract from Philostratus, shows that Brilliant is wrong to see the decoration on the rim of the Kaiseraugst plate in 'subservience' to its central medallion. Of course this is still important and the visual significance of its position on the plate cannot be ignored. It would probably be fair to say that in the ancient world, in late antiquity and earlier, the Discovery on Skyros was seen as the pivotal moment of Achilles' life, its *kairos*, so to speak.[39] It was the event which bridged his childhood/adolescence and his manhood, but in late antiquity at least that childhood was seen as equally full of event and significance as his life and death at Troy.

Excerpting the narrative: the Sevso Achilles plate

A second 'Achilles plate' appeared on the art market in the late 1980s as part of the Sevso Treasure (Fig. 3.3).[40] Unlike the Kaiseraugst Achilles plate, it is circular not octagonal, but it resembles the Kaiseraugst plate in having a central medallion showing the discovery of Achilles on Skyros and an outer rim decorated with figures. The central medallions are very similar, using the same compositional formula of Achilles leaping up with shield and spear, ineffectually held back on the left by the daughter of King Lykomedes, while Diomedes, accompanied by Odysseus, blows a trumpet on the right. Iconographically, the Sevso plate medallion differs only in showing three

3.3 Sevso Treasure, private collection: Achilles Plate (courtesy of the Trustees of the Marquess of Northampton 1987 Settlement)

of King Lykomedes' daughters rather than one, and giving the scene an architectural backdrop. The border of the Sevso plate, however, includes only one of the episodes featured on the Kaiseraugst plate, the birth of Achilles. It is combined with the discovery of Ariadne by Dionysus, a Dionysiac procession with sacred snakes, and the contest between Athena and Poseidon for Athens, separated and framed by four masks placed on rectangular podiums or altars. The scene of Achilles' birth on the Sevso plate differs from this episode on the Kaiseraugst plate in several ways. As with the scene of the discovery on Skyros, the basic compositional formula is elaborated upon. Instead of the single attendant to Thetis on the Kaiseraugst version of the scene, one woman holds the baby Achilles, another pours water for his bath, and a third stands behind Thetis' couch. A more significant difference, however, is the addition of six gods – Heracles, Zeus, Apollo, Hermes, Poseidon and Helios – who flank the scene, three on either side. Their presence adds divine overtones to this domestic scene, which are entirely absent on the Kaiseraugst plate. The Achilles narrative of the Sevso plate is thus telescoped, representing only the first and last scenes of the cycle on the Kaiseraugst plate, and in the process elevating Achilles' birth from the first stage in his domestic *aristeia* to an event of cosmological significance.

Unlike the Kaiseraugst plate, the Sevso Achilles plate is not a narrative about *paideia*, instead it engages with its viewers' *paideia* in different ways. One of these is through the plate's strategy of excerpting episodes from mythical narratives and juxtaposing different myths. This strategy is not in itself unusual in Roman art, indeed it is probably more common than the continuous narrative of the Kaiseraugst plate. Pompeian wall painting offers many examples of the way images from different myths could be combined in a domestic setting, and much scholarly attention has been devoted to trying to understand what principles determined the selection and combination of myths.[41] Most recently emphasis has been placed on the importance of formal and compositional similarities in signalling thematic links between different images. These principles for combining images carry on into the second and third centuries, attested by such monuments as the Spada Reliefs, and texts such as Philostratus' *Imagines* and Lucian's *De Domo*, where the thematic connections between the different pictures described tend to be implicit and depend upon the reader's cultural knowledge for their articulation.[42] The continuation of such strategies into late antiquity can be traced not only in examples of silverware such as the Sevso Achilles plate and its companion piece in the hoard, the Meleager plate (which displays an even greater diversity of scenes on its rim), but also in mosaics of the period – such as the splendid early fourth-century mosaic from the House of Aion in Nea Paphos on Cyprus.[43] I shall discuss these examples in more detail later, but first I want to focus on the representation of a single scene from a myth, the Birth of Achilles, and the significance of its transformation between the Kaiseraugst and Sevso plates.

In iconographic terms, depictions of the birth of Achilles are a late antique phenomenon. It has been suggested that the form of the scene is derived from that of the birth of Dionysus, which although not especially common does occur periodically in the earlier Roman period.[44] The main features which these depictions have in common are Semele / Thetis reclining on a couch, and female attendants waiting to bathe Dionysus / Achilles. A late antique example of the birth of Dionysus can be seen on the fifth-century ivory pyxis in the Museo Civico in Bologna (Fig. 3.4).[45] But recognizing the links between iconographies does not explain why a schema which had been used for Dionysus should be extended to represent Achilles, or why within the depiction of Achilles' birth there should be the variations found on the Sevso Achilles plate. Nor is it only Achilles whose birth is represented for the first time in late antiquity. A mosaic from Baalbek-Soueidié shows the newborn Alexander the Great being bathed in a circular fluted basin – like those on the Bologna pyxis and the Capitoline Puteal – by a female figure labelled 'Nymphe', while his mother Olympias reclines on a bed watched by an attendant.[46] All the figures in the mosaic have name-labels, a common characteristic of mosaics of the Greek East of the third to fifth centuries. In this case the name-labels seem to serve an obvious and important purpose: how otherwise is the viewer to recognize the scene as the birth of Alexander rather than Achilles or Dionysus?[47] At the same time the borrowing of the iconographic schema hints at analogies between Alexander, Achilles and Dionysus, analogies which were also suggested in the various accounts of Alexander's life.[48] This mosaic thus appeals to the viewer's visual memory of iconographic schemata, and his or her knowledge of the biography of Alexander the Great. The latter can convincingly be placed in the context of *paideia*, since the exercises of the progymnasmata required students to be familiar with a repertoire of characters, events and aphorisms from literature, history and myth, and Alexander and his life was certainly part of the canon of these.[49]

A similar use of analogy can be seen when comparing a fifth-century mosaic representation of the birth of Achilles from the House of Theseus at Nea Paphos on Cyprus, with a fourth-century child's sarcophagus in the Vatican (Figs 3.5, 3.6).[50] Some aspects of the mosaic are very similar to the representations of this scene on silverware; in the left half, Thetis reclines on a couch, while the baby Achilles is held by a women labelled 'Anatrophe', and another labelled 'Ambrosia' approaches with a jug of water for the bath, which is a cylindrical cauldron placed below Thetis' couch. The right half of the mosaic, however, is occupied by the seated figure of Peleus and behind him the standing figures of the Three Fates, each labelled with her name. Their presence here is easily explicable in terms of Achilles' destiny of a heroic but short life; the same idea also accounts for their appearance on the Vatican sarcophagus in the scene of its occupant's birth. This scene shows the mother seated in an upright chair rather than reclining on a couch with a swaddled child, while in front of her the same child is bathed. The Fates stand in the background, their presence lending heroic overtones to the dead child's short life by suggesting that, like Achilles, he too could not escape his destiny. Moving from the Fates to consider the parade of gods who accompany Achilles' birth on the Sevso plate, it is worth noting that the names of the two women who prepare the bath for Achilles on the House of Theseus mosaic, Ambrosia and Anatrophe, occur on another mosaic at Nea Paphos, from the House of Aion (Fig. 3.7). On this mosaic they are shown on a panel which depicts the baby Dionysus presented by Hermes to the nymphs, who prepare a bath for him, a variant on the birth scene already described.[51] Although the Achilles mosaic from the House of Theseus is later than that from the House of Aion, the two houses are located close to each other, and suggests the possibility of a workshop tradition that names the attendants of divine or semi-divine children Ambrosia and Anatrophe. That this stress on the semi-divine nature of Achilles was not merely a local Cypriot phenomenon seems confirmed by the gods on the Sevso plate, who might be intended to recall the attendance of the gods at the wedding of Peleus and Thetis, but also include Heracles, a hero who became divine.[52] The parade of gods is marked as characteristically

3.4 Ivory pyxis depicting Birth of Dionysos, Bologna, Museo Civico Archeologico (Museo Civico Archeologico, Bologna)

3.5 House of Theseus, Nea Paphos, Cyprus: mosaic depicting Birth of Achilles (Department of Antiquities, Cyprus)

3.6 Child's sarcophagus with the Three Fates, Pisa, Campo Santo (Felbermeyer/Deutsches Archäologisches Institut, Rome, neg. 42.101)

3.7 House of Aion, Nea Paphos, Cyprus: detail of triclinium mosaic depicting Hermes presenting the baby Dionysus to the nymphs (Department of Antiquities, Cyprus)

late antique by the inclusion of Helios, who is shown with his right hand raised in the Sol Invictus salute. Thus while the Sevso plate's central scene of Achilles on Skyros belongs within the static traditions of *paideia*, this birth as represented on its rim hints at the way those traditions could be subtly changed in the context of late antique conceptions of divinity.

But since the scenes relating to Achilles form only one part of the Sevso Achilles plate's decoration, let us now turn to the way scenes from different mythological narratives are juxtaposed on the plate. How do the scenes with Achilles relate to the two Dionysiac scenes and the scene of Athena and Poseidon that are also part of the decorative scheme, and do these scenes in themselves make any appeal to *paideia*? First, there are thematic correspondences between the different scenes which parallel the connections between the diverse pictures which we find in Lucian and Philostratus' descriptions of art galleries. There are two scenes of 'discovery on islands', Ariadne on Naxos and Achilles on Skyros; Poseidon appears twice, as an onlooker at Achilles' birth and as a competitor against Athena; the two Dionysiac scenes share the same characters, though without any narrative continuity.[53] Discovering and articulating these correspondences offers the viewer of the plate an opportunity to display his (or her?) *paideia*. The relatively uncommon scene of the contest between Athena and Poseidon also has its own particular appeal to *paideia*. This myth is intimately connected with Athens: it is one of the founding legends of the city, explaining how Athena came to be Athens' patron, and for this reason it was represented on the west pediment of the Parthenon. Athens in the fourth century AD, while politically and economically insignificant, nevertheless held immense cultural capital in the eyes of the elite of the Roman Empire, both for its past achievements and as a centre for studying rhetoric and philosophy: a centre of *paideia*, in fact.[54] Among those who attended its schools around the middle of the fourth century were Libanius, the future emperor Julian, Basil the Great and Gregory of Nazianzus, while in the fifth century the neoplatonic school under Proclus flourished.[55] Thus the choice of this scene suggests an appeal to *paideia* through one of its centres in the late antique world, Athens.

Like the scene of the birth of Achilles on this plate, the representation of the contest between Athena and Poseidon has some specifically late antique features. The contest appears to have been decided by vote: a female figure standing by a small table with a voting urn on it holds up the winning pebble and a palm-bearing Nike presents a crown to Athena. As far as we know, these were not features of the scene on the Parthenon pediment.[56] They are found however in late antique representations of a much less well-known contest, that between Cassiopeia – a legendary queen of Ethiopia or Palestine, and in some versions the mother of Andromeda – and the Nereids, which is known from three mosaics of the later third and fourth centuries, including that from the House of Aion in Nea Paphos.[57] In each, this beauty contest is being decided by a vote, and the winner Cassiopeia is presented with her crown by Nike, while a variety of gods and personifications witness the scene. The theatricality of these depictions suggests that they might have been influenced by stage productions, since we know many myths were acted as 'spectacles' both in the theatre and as subsidiary entertainment in the amphitheatre and circus.[58] The appeal of a beauty contest in this context is obvious. It is possible that theatrical performances also influenced the depiction of the Athena-Poseidon contest on the Sevso Achilles plate. But ultimately this does not detract from its appeal to *paideia*. Rather, it presents the scene in a mode familiar to the late antique viewer, which interacts with experiences in other areas of visual culture.

Thus both the scenes of the birth of Achilles and the contest between Athena and Poseidon scene, appeal to the traditions of *paideia*, while at the same time their iconography is shaped by contemporary factors. In contrast, the central image of Achilles on Skyros and the Dionysiac scenes employ traditional and standardized iconography and appeal to *paideia* above all through such traditionalism. The variety of these appeals to *paideia* was the organizing principle which determined the combination of these five scenes on the plate. The craftsman selected scenes from his repertoire, either at the request of a patron or following his knowledge of what would be acceptable to potential customers of his workshop. The scenes are meaningful individually or in pairs; the plate as a whole is a compendium, a florilegium of the mythological repertoire.[59] The same principles can also be seen operating in the decoration of the Sevso Meleager plate (Fig. 3.8), to which I will now turn to provide further insight into this strategy of design.

The Sevso Achilles and Meleager plates are similar in many ways: in size, shape and in the way their decoration is distributed over their surface. Their diameters are 72 and 69.4 cm respectively, and they stand 5.9 and 5.8 cm high. Both plates have a relatively high, flaring foot-ring and a gently concave interior. Each has a broad horizontal rim, the outer edge of which is decorated with heavy beading. In the centre of each plate is a medallion, with a diameter of 26.1 and 21.3 cm respectively, framed by a foliate border. A single figural scene is depicted within the medallion, while the rim carries a series of scenes, separated by masks or heads standing on altars. Despite the slightly smaller size of the Meleager plate, six separate scenes are depicted on its rim, while on the Achilles plate there are only four. The Meleager plate also differs from the Achilles plate in that the remainder of the plate's surface is covered with a design of centrally radiating incised acanthus leaves, while that of the Achilles plate is left undecorated. It is named after the scene in the central medallion, which shows Meleager, Atalanta and four other hunters of the Calydonian boar after the animal's capture. The scenes on the rim, however, depict a wide range of mythological personalities and events, which have been identified by Marlia Mango as follows:[60]

1. The Judgement of Paris
2. Perseus and Andromeda
3. Phaedra and Hippolytus
4. Pyramus and Thisbe
5. Composite scene with the Dioscuri, Paris(?), Helen(?) and the Eurotas River(?)

6. Composite scene with three couples: Leda and the swan, with Eros; Atalanta and Meleager; and Aphrodite and Adonis.

What significance do these different scenes have, both individually and as a group? It is worth noting first that, unlike the Achilles plate, none of the scenes are taken from the same narrative. Some individual scenes however show more than one stage of a narrative within them: the group of Perseus rescuing Andromeda from the sea monster is preceded within the same segment of the plate's rim by a group of three figures – Perseus' mother Danaë with her baby son, pursued by her father with drawn sword – while the Hippolytus and Phaedra scene conflates two stages of the narrative, Phaedra's confession of love to her nurse and Hippolytus' angry rejection of Phaedra's love letter which he receives as he is about to go hunting. At the same time there are scenes in which no narrative unifies all the figures; like that of the three couples, for instance, one pair of which – Meleager and Atalanta – are excerpted from the central medallion.

Mango has suggested that the twin themes of love and hunting, exemplified by the story of Meleager and Atalanta, provide a common link between the diverse scenes on the plate.[61] While this is undoubtedly true, given the fact that hunting was often used as a metaphor for amorous pursuit in classical literature, the different resonances of the individual scenes, and in particular their engagement with *paideia*, deserve further exploration.[62] We might observe that while some of the myths chosen are extremely common in late antique art (Meleager and Atalanta, Hippolytus and Phaedra, Venus and Adonis, Leda and the Swan), and others relatively so (Judgement of Paris, Perseus and Andromeda), some are distinctly obscure (Pyramus and Thisbe, and the 'Helen, Paris, and Dioscuri' group, whose identification does not seem very secure). So if the plate's overall theme is love and hunting, the choice of myths used to exemplify it is quite eclectic. Some of the myths on the Meleager plate are popular on sarcophagi, not least those of Meleager, Hippolytus, and Venus and Adonis. The schema of the Hippolytus scene on the plate often appears on sarcophagi of the second and third centuries AD, while the iconography of Meleager's companions – who include the Dioscuri, identifiable by their conical hats – can be matched on the Meleager sarcophagus in the Capitoline Museum.[63] Meleager himself, however, is usually represented differently in this medium, either in the act of spearing the boar or on his premature deathbed.[64] Hippolytus and Meleager are also depicted on other examples of silverware. The Sevso hoard contains a set of two situlae and a ewer, each of which depicts the same scene of Phaedra with her attendants and Hippolytus rejecting the letter.[65] Meleager features together with Atalanta on an early seventh-century plate in the Hermitage Museum (Fig. 3.9), and alone with the boar on a sixth- or seventh-century plate in the Bayrisches Nationalmuseum in Munich.[66] Venus and Adonis are also the subject of a sixth-century plate in the Cabinet des Médailles of the Bibliothèque National in Paris, while Hippolytus and Phaedra (in a different iconographic schema) appear on one of a pair of sixth-century plates in Dumbarton Oaks.[67]

Thus for some of the scenes on the Meleager plate there is a strong iconographic tradition continuing into the early Byzantine period. In this context we should note that the stories of Hippolytus and Phaedra, and Meleager and Atalanta, exist in famous literary versions by authors widely-read in antiquity. The former features in Euripides' play *Hippolytus*, as well as Seneca's Latin work on the same theme, while the latter is described at length in Ovid's *Metamorphoses*, together with the story of Venus and Adonis (Met. X.519–739). The *Metamorphoses* is also a source for the story of Perseus and Andromeda (IV.670ff) and for the myth of Pyramus and Thisbe (IV.55–167).[68] Euripides' now lost play, the *Andromeda*, was also renowned in antiquity. This is not to say that the myths on the Meleager plate 'illustrate' the works of these authors, but simply that they provide links with the works of two

3.9 Meleager Plate, St Petersburg, Hermitage Museum

widely read authors who would have formed part of the syllabus of the grammaticus, again calling upon the viewer to interpret his visual experience through the lens of his *paideia*. Since these works of literature continued to be studied by pupils of the grammaticus well into the sixth century – at least in the eastern empire – a taste for the classicizing representations of the myths on which such literature was based continued to flourish among the recipients of *paideia* in early Byzantium. This interpretation does not require there to be any further unifying theme connecting the myths on the Sevso Meleager plate, although it seems unlikely that the associations of love and hunting would have been ignored.

Here it is worth considering an interpretation of a late antique sculptural programme which invokes *paideia* as a factor governing the choice of images in an artistic programme. Sarah Guberti Bassett's study of the sculptural programme of Constantine's renovation of the Baths of Zeuxippos in Constantinople has suggested that rather than relating to a single theme, as some earlier scholars had suggested, the vast array of statues of gods, heroes and famous Greeks and Romans placed in the baths were intended to appropriate the cultural and intellectual heritage of the Graeco-Roman world for the emperor's new capital.[69] In doing this, she argues, Constantine was motivated by contemporary assumptions about the close relationship between political power and *paideia*: the baths' statue collection of mythological and heroic figures embodied that *paideia*, and lent his city the authority of tradition.[70] It is possible to study the sculptural programme of the Baths of Zeuxippos, not because the sculptures themselves survive but because they are recorded in a poem by the late fifth/early sixth-century poet Christodorus of Coptos in the Greek Anthology, which is itself an example of *paideia* (the few inscribed bases which have been recovered from the site of the baths testify to the reliability of Christodorus' description). Basset points out that mythological figures have clearly been selected from at least two epic cycles, the Theban and the Trojan cycles, but that not all statues mentioned can be fitted into this category. And while some of these figures are well known, others are obscure, even to Christodorus.[71] This is a useful parallel to the mixture of well-known and less well-known scenes on the Meleager plate, and it is also worth noting that Christodorus' poem implies several statues were formed of pairs of figures, such as Poseidon and Amymone, Heracles and Auge, and Menelaus and Helen. Clearly in the baths of Zeuxippos the ideological strength of the sculptural programme lay not in its thematic groups, but in its massing of the widest possible range of figures from the mythological and literary traditions. This offers a clear analogy – on a larger scale – to the way in which the Sevso Meleager and Achilles plates (as well as the House of Aion mosaic) depict a range of different myths. Obviously the politics of an imperially sponsored public bath in the new capital are different from those operating in the domestic context where the Sevso plates would have been displayed. But the private sphere in late antiquity was a site where elite politics of power and status were enacted, and it seems highly likely that the political appeal of *paideia* as a confirmation of the right to power – articulated through visual means – would have operated there, as it did on a higher level in Bath of Zeuxippos.

Hellenism, paganism and *paideia*

So far I have focused on silver depicting episodes in mythological narratives, such as the life of Achilles, or the myth-history of Athens. The two Dionysiac scenes on the Sevso Achilles plate fit less comfortably in this category than the other scenes on this plate, as their narrative character is rather different. While Dionysus' birth, or his discovery of Ariadne, can be recognized as episodes in his 'career', Dionysiac processions like that on the Sevso plate are usually not identifiable as specific temporal events occurring at a definite point within the god's history. They also employ iconography which alludes to the worship of Dionysus, such as the baskets and sacred snakes on the Sevso Achilles plate. Should Dionysiac imagery be considered as a generic category on its own, with cultic as well as mythological overtones? Perhaps, but at the same time Dionysiac scenes were clearly not perceived by late antique artists and viewers to be unrelated to the type of mythological narrative already discussed, since they appear frequently juxtaposed with this type of scene, as on both the Sevso Achilles plate and the House of Aion mosaic. Is Dionysiac imagery related to the appeal to *paideia* which I have traced in such artworks?

This section will try to answer the above question, and some related ones about the role of imagery with religious overtones on silverware designed for use in a domestic context. It will focus upon the Mildenhall Great Dish with its two smaller companion plates (Figs 3.10, 3.11) as examples of Dionysiac iconography; and the Corbridge Lanx (Fig. 3.12), the Parabiago plate (Fig. 3.13), and a plate from Ballana in Nubia (Fig. 3.14) as examples of a different type of religious imagery. These plates are products of the late fourth and early fifth centuries, and since this period more than any other time in late antiquity witnessed much debate about the place of the traditional *paideia* in an increasingly Christian society, they raise issues about the role of *paideia* in understanding the significance of such imagery for their viewers and owners.[72] In particular they allow us to confront the problem of the relationship between traditional classicizing imagery of gods such as Dionysus, and the religious affiliations of those who chose to adorn their homes with such imagery. Generally these objects have been studied with an insufficient understanding of the nature of late antique paganism, and an under-valuation of the social role of *paideia*, and various conclusions have been drawn about their 'religious' character which I consider untenable. With the benefit of the insights of recent scholarship in these fields, we can revise our understanding of the social and intellectual contexts in which they might have been viewed, and thus of their function in late antique society.

The nature of the late antique debate about classical *paideia* and its relationship with Christianity has been greatly elucidated by Glen Bowersock's work on late antique forms of 'Hellenism' (Greek *hellenismos*), a term originally denoting Greek language and culture, but by the fourth century carrying an additional meaning of paganism.[73] Bowersock argues that the reason for this linguistic shift lay in the role of the Greek language in preserving local pagan cults in the Greek East and making them universally comprehensible within the Greek world. The vast range of different cults and religious practices in the Greek-speaking world, which modern scholars call paganism, was for the ancients simply an aspect of Hellenism; the uniformity of elite training in *paideia* was another.[74] Bowersock's work represents a valuable contribution to our understanding of late antique paganism, and yet in one crucial way it is flawed: the artistic evidence which Bowersock often incorporates to support his argument is of a type that is inappropriate for the points which he is trying to make. This is especially true when he uses examples of art from domestic contexts – one case being the House of Aion mosaic – to suggest the

strength of pagan cults in late antiquity.[75] For Bowersock, there is a divide in Hellenism between 'literature and intellectual reflection, and mythology *with its concomitant cults*' [my emphasis].[76] Because of the links he assumes between mythology and cult, art which depicts mythological scenes must always provide a connection to cult, regardless of the context where it is displayed. In my opinion this assumption is unwise: rather it is precisely the degree of connection between visual representations of myth and cult practices which needs to be a subject of investigation. Dionysus is a case in point, because he is represented so frequently in a domestic context, in a way that is neither exclusively narrative nor cultic. Bowersock's conception of the visual dimension of Hellenism is not well-suited to dealing with the complexities of Roman art in the domestic sphere.[77]

3.10 Mildenhall Treasure, London, British Museum: Great Dish (© The British Museum)

Mythological imagery on silver has also frequently been the subject of such over-simplistic assumptions about the relationship between artistic representation and cult practice. A common trend in the scholarship on the Mildenhall plates, the Corbridge Lanx and the Parabiago plate has been the 'strong' reading of their imagery as evidence of pagan beliefs, and the subsequent connection through such readings with supposed 'pagan revivals' in the fourth century. The silver from Mildenhall and Corbridge has been linked with the revival initiated by the emperor Julian during his reign of 361–363 AD; the Parabiago plate with that among the aristocracy of Rome in the 380s and early 390s.[78] Before exploring why these silver vessels have been so persistently associated with manifestations of late paganism, I shall give a brief description of each piece, and the context in which it was discovered.

(a)   The Mildenhall plates
The three Mildenhall plates form part of the much larger Mildenhall Treasure, comprising 28 items of tableware: plates, bowls, spoons and cups. It was discovered accidentally in 1942 in Mildenhall, Suffolk, and was subsequently acquired by the British Museum.[79] The so-called 'Great Dish' is the largest and heaviest item in the hoard, weighing 8.256 kg and measuring 60.5 cm in diameter (Fig. 3.10). It is a circular plate with a large beaded rim and a flat surface, covered with low relief decoration arranged in two concentric bands. In the centre of the plate the frontal head of Oceanus is represented in a circle, surrounded by a sea-thiasos of four Nereids riding on two tritons, a sea-stag and a hippocamp respectively. A border of scallop-shells separates this narrower band from the Dionysiac thiasos which is the most prominent decoration on the plate. Dionysus is represented together with maenads, satyrs, Pan, the drunken Hercules, and a wide variety of Bacchic implements. The two smaller companion dishes (Fig. 3.11) stand in a clear stylistic relation to the Great Dish. They each measure 18.8 cm in diameter and weigh 539 g and 613 g respectively. Each has a flat surface bordered by a beaded rim and depicts a male and a female figure: on one Pan and a maenad play pipes and flutes, in the presence of the female personification of a spring; on the other a satyr and maenad dance. In both cases paraphernalia associated with the Dionysiac thiasos – *syrinx*, castanets, tambourine, *pedum* – is included in the ground. The two smaller dishes both have a Greek graffito engraved on the reverse: 'ἐυθηρίου', the genitive of the name Eutherios. The other objects in the hoard are decorated either with geometric patterns or imagery of wild and domestic animals, interspersed with heads, possibly of mythological figures. Significantly in this context, three of the hoard's nine cochlearia-type spoons have bowls decorated with a chi-rho flanked by an alpha and omega.

(b)   The Corbridge Lanx
The Corbridge Lanx (Fig. 3.12) is the sole survivor of five silver vessels discovered in the eighteenth century in or near the bank of the river Tyne at Corbridge, in Northumberland, all presumably part of a hoard that had been concealed in the river bank.[80] The Lanx is a rectangular dish, 37.8 x 50.6

3.11 Mildenhall Treasure: small plates with maenad and satyr (left) and maenad and Pan (right) (© The British Museum)

3.12 Corbridge Lanx, London, British Museum (© The British Museum)

cm, with an oblong footrest, a convex inner surface and a horizontal rim; its weight is 4.633 kg. The rim has small beading on its inner and outer edges, and is decorated with an undulating vine scroll. The scene on the plate's inner surface shows five deities in a setting of an outdoor shrine: from left to right these are Artemis, Athena, Ortygia (Leto's sister), Leto and Apollo, although the identities of the third and fourth figures are less certain. Between Artemis and Athena is a tree filled with birds and an altar beneath it; behind Apollo is a small temple with a high staircase and a pillar surmounted by a globe. A lyre rests at Apollo's feet. In the foreground beneath the figures are from left to right: an urn spilling water (representing a spring), a dog, a palm tree, a fallen stag, an altar, a griffin and a tree with fan-shaped leaves. On the reverse is a Latin weight inscription.

(c)   The Parabiago plate
The Parabiago plate (sometimes misleadingly referred to as a patera) (Fig. 3.13) was found in 1907 in Parabiago, near Milan, on the site of a Roman cemetery.[81] It is a circular plate 39 cm in diameter, with a 2.6 cm high foot-ring, and weighing 3.555 kg. The surface of the plate, framed by an vertical grooved rim, is covered with figures in high relief. Occupying the central left part is a group of Cybele and Attis riding in a chariot pulled by four lions, accompanied by three Corybantes. To the right, also in the central register, a naked youth rises out of the ground supporting a zodiacal ring in which stands a youthful figure in a chiton, possibly Aion, holding a sceptre. At the far right is an obelisk with a snake entwined around it. The upper register contains two chariot groups: on the left, that of the sun rising; on the right that of the moon, sinking. Both are preceded by winged, torch-bearing genii, representing the morning and the evening stars, Phosphorus and Hesperus. In the centre of the lower register are figures of Neptune and Thetis. To their left are two river nymphs, to the right Tellus with two erotes who point upwards at Cybele. Above Neptune and Thetis are four erotes representing the seasons. Above Tellus' head are the small figures of a grasshopper and a lizard. The extraordinary classicism of the figures (especially the complex postures of the Corybantes) has led to much uncertainty about the plate's date. Many of the earlier scholars who discussed the piece believed that its classicism must place it in the second century; claims for later dates have been supported by iconographic or stylistic criteria.[82] But these features in themselves cannot support a late date, because of their retrospective and traditional character. However, in the last ten to fifteen years, studies of the techniques and forms of late Roman silver, as well as advances in late Roman pottery studies, allow this plate to be securely dated to the fourth to fifth centuries, despite the fact that it is stylistically distinct from all other surviving silver in that century.[83]

(d)   The Ballana plate
The silver plate from Ballana (Fig. 3.14), unlike the other pieces described so far, has received very little scholarly attention. It was found in 1932 in a tumulus tomb which formed part of a high-status necropolis on the west

bank of the Nile in Lower Nubia.[84] It was one of several pieces of late Roman tableware in silver and bronze which this richly endowed tomb contained. The occupants of the necropolis were the rulers of the Lower Nubian kingdom of Nobatia and their courtiers in the period around 420–50. Although some of the items in the tombs may have been official gifts to the rulers from the Byzantine governor of Egypt and/or high officials in the Thebaid, the tomb in which the Ballana plate was found also contained several pieces of church silver, which were most likely acquired in raids on the churches of Upper Egypt during the first half of the fifth century (papyri of the period attest to these).[85] The plate is 38.8 cm in diameter, with a slightly concave surface and a moulded rim. It has a flaring ring-foot, 5 cm in height. Its surface is decorated with the image of a syncretistic male deity (identified variously as Hermes or Apollo Alexikakos), who is shown seated on a globe with draped legs.[86] His ankles are winged, and on his nimbed head is the winged *modius* of Serapis. In his left hand he holds an ear of corn, in his right a stemless cup, which he appears to be offering to a large snake, entwined around a tree on the left side of the

3.13 Parabiago Plate, Milan, Civico Museo Archaeologico

3.14 Plate from
Necropolis at
Ballana, Cairo,
Egyptian
Museum
(Deutsches
Archäologisches
Institut, Cairo)

plate. A lion skin is draped over a lower branch of the tree. To the right of the
deity is a seated griffin with one paw raised, touching the globe on which he
sits. In the lower part of the plate are a hammer, tongs, a shield and a cuirass.
The tomb in which the plate was buried has been dated to 450–60, but the date
of its manufacture was probably between the end of the fourth century and
the beginning of the fifth. Similarities in figure style with the Corbridge Lanx
argue for a late fourth-century date, but conversely could suggest an early
fifth-century dating for the Lanx.[87]

The three Mildenhall plates, the Corbridge Lanx, and the Parabiago and
Ballana plates all represent gods and their adherents, and clearly this lies at
the core of scholars' attempts to associate them with fourth-century pagan
revivals. Let us look more closely at the sort of reasoning which lies behind
such interpretative strategies. Jocelyn Toynbee in the early 1960s saw the
iconography of the Mildenhall Great Dish in funerary terms as 'the journey
of the souls of the departed to the Blessed Isles' and 'the Dionysiac paradise

which the dead attain in the after-life', an interpretation based on similarities between the plate's iconography and that of contemporary sarcophagi.[88] Such readings of Dionysiac imagery on sarcophagi as symbolic of the afterlife have been the subject of some criticism and Toynbee's interpretation of the plate, with its connotations of ritual use, is not generally followed.[89] However this strong pagan reading influenced Kenneth Painter when he proposed a theory that saw the Great Dish and its companion plates as a gift of the emperor Julian to his *cubicularius*. Painter's interpretation rests on the two graffiti of the name Eutherios on the smaller plates. He identifies this individual with Julian's *cubicularius* Eutherios, and suggests that they were given by Eutherios to the *magister militum* Lupicinus, who brought them to Britain, since Eutherios is not known to have visited Britain. As Lupicinus was a Christian this also allows him to explain the presence of spoons with Christian symbols in the Mildenhall hoard.[90] This theory has rightly been dismissed as fantasy by Alan Cameron, but I cite it here as an example of the tendency to involve the agency of Julian in 'explaining' the presence of 'pagan' imagery on fourth-century silver, a reading which for the Mildenhall dishes derives ultimately from Toynbee.[91]

The Corbridge Lanx has also been associated with Julian on equally spurious grounds, in an attempt to explain its admittedly baffling iconography.[92] Otto Brendel in 1941 was the first to propose that the scene represented the sanctuary of Apollo on Delos. This represented an advance on earlier interpretations, since it recognized the attempt to portray a cult site rather than a narrative event on the plate. But in suggesting why Delos should be chosen he invokes Julian on the following grounds:

One effect of the religious policy of Julian seems to have been a final renewal of interest in … the cult of Apollo. At that moment Delos once again rose to honour and the last official sacrifice to Apollo of which we know was made there by Julian before his unfortunate Persian war … .[93]

The plate thus becomes some kind of commemoration of Delos' last moment of glory. Unfortunately this theory is based on evidence as flimsy as that associating Eutherios with the Mildenhall plates. For Julian's 'sacrifice on Delos', understood by subsequent readers as an actual visit by the emperor to that island, is attested in only one of the many sources for Julian's reign: the mid-fifth century *Historia Ecclesiae* by Theodoret of Cyrus.[94] Brendel cites a reference to a passage which describes Julian's actions before declaring war on Persia: 'He sent first, however, to the oracles of Delphi, of Delos, of Dodona, and of other places, to enquire whether he ought to enter upon the war' (iii, 21). There is no suggestion that Julian himself went to Delos, and no explicit mention of sacrifice, though that may be implied in the process of consulting the oracle.[95] Delos does not have special prominence, but is one of a list of places mentioned. But most telling is the absence of any mention of Julian's consultation with the oracles in any other historical accounts of his reign, especially that of his contemporary and great admirer, Ammianus Marcellinus. Theodoret, as a Christian writing a history of the Church, cannot in any sense be considered a reliable source for Julian's reign; later episodes describe 'abominable sorceries detected after the death of Julian at Carras' and 'heads of men found in the palace of Antioch'. While less sensational, the assumption that Julian consulted oracles before setting off on campaign may be nothing more than a topos of behaviour associated with pagans. It is true that Julian did try to promote the cult of Apollo, both at his shrine at Daphne near Antioch where he offered sacrifices to the god during his stay in the city, and at Delphi and Didyma where steps were taken on his behalf to restore the shrines.[96] But this does not mean that he was the only person to take an interest in Apollo in the latter half of the fourth century, and it is unrealistic to credit an emperor who reigned a bare 18 months with developing an artistic programme to support his religious reforms.

And yet it is not wrong to bring Julian and his policies into the debate about the significance of this type of iconography; it is simply a mistake to seek a concrete association between Julian's actions and particular pieces of silverware. As Marlia Mango has noted, Brendel's interpretation of the Corbridge Lanx rests in part on the unproven assumptions that an object as large as the Lanx must have imperial connections and that Julian's reign was the only time of pagan observance in the later fourth century.[97] The same points can be made for the Mildenhall plates. Yet we should not underestimate the continuing strength of paganism in the fourth century, despite its being increasingly disadvantaged by the state's support of Christianity. Julian's reign was a symptom, rather than a cause, of that strength. Continuing sympathy with his defence of paganism is revealed in his positive presentation in the works of the pagan historians of the later fourth and fifth centuries, Ammianus Marcellinus, Eunapius of Sardis and Zosimus, as well as the contemporary letters and speeches of his personal friend, the sophist Libanius.[98] Likewise we should think of a wider chronological range for works of art that seem to admit pagan affiliation by their owners; figures like Julian can help us understand the cultural milieu in which such works were created.

This is another way in which *paideia* can be used as a tool for reading the iconography of silver. Julian's religious beliefs were intimately linked with his concept of *paideia*, grounded in his rhetorical and philosophic training, an education he shared with many of his contemporaries in the upper classes of the empire, including many fourth-century Christian bishops (if not with many of his recent imperial predecessors). The connection for him between paganism (or as he would have said, Hellenism) and *paideia* is expressed in his most famous piece of anti-Christian legislation, the edict which effectively forbade Christians to teach grammar or rhetoric. A quotation from his anti-Christian polemic, 'Against the Gallileans', exemplifies the nature of his argument: 'Was it not the gods who revealed all their learning to Homer and Hesiod? ... It is absurd that men who expound the work of such writers should dishonour the gods whom those same writers honoured.'[99] To what extent were such feelings shared by Julian's contemporaries? His educated Christian contemporaries – such as Gregory of Nazianzus, who had attended the schools at Athens at the same time as Julian – were indignant: 'Julian has wickedly transformed the meaning of "Greek" so as to represent a religion but not a language, and accordingly, like a thief of someone else's goods, he has stripped us of our speech.'[100] A different sort of defence of a Christian reading of the Greek classics by another fellow student of Julian at Athens is Basil the Great's *Address to Young Men on Reading Greek Literature*, a letter addressed to his nephews on the benefits to be gained from such reading.[101] It is however a selective reading that he advises: the poets are to be treated with especial caution, and all mentions of the gods and their activities are to be avoided.[102] Nevertheless, he insisted on the importance of *paideia* as the foundation of a Christian education, rather than affirming an antithesis between non-Christian *paideia* and true Christianity, which fourth-century ecclesiastical writers in the West such as Augustine and Jerome, were inclined to posit.[103] Julian's pagan contemporaries also do not seem to have supported his edict on the schools, at least if we take the reaction of Ammianus – in so many other respects an admirer of Julian – as typical. But unlike Gregory, he does not explain what he found so deplorable about the edict, leaving it to historians to guess whether he disliked the intrusion of religion on public policy, or perhaps felt that divisions between pagans and Christians were being formed unnecessarily. It does seem to suggest that not all pagans made the same associations between religious tradition and literary – and also artistic? – tradition. It is perhaps more accurate to envisage a range of pagan attitudes on this subject, just as a range of Christian attitudes also prevailed.

If Julian's reign has been seen as one 'pagan revival' in the fourth century, a second has been posited among the senatorial aristocracy of the city of Rome in the 380s and 390s. Proponents of this theory have interpreted classicizing artistic and literary productions of the late fourth century as evidence of a pagan resistance to the Christian emperor Theodosius among the leading senatorial families in Rome, such as the Symmachi and Nicomachi. Such ideas were first suggested by Andreas Alföldi, who in his 1943 study of contorniate medallions, argued that these were distributed as propaganda for the pagan cause in Rome.[104] He also discussed the Parabiago plate in this work, and believed that it too was commissioned by a member of the pagan aristocracy in Rome, serving a similar function to the contorniates, some of which also feature the lion-drawn chariot of Attis and Cybele.[105] Luisa Musso, in her study of the Parabiago plate, accepts Alföldi's attribution of the vessel to a Roman workshop, but like many scholars is more cautious about his claims that the contorniates were a form of political propaganda. Instead she follows an interpretation of them as commemorative tokens distributed at spectacles, which represent some feature of the show, and extends this to the Parabiago plate. It was, she suggests, made by a member of the pagan aristocracy to commemorate the *Hilaria*, the major Roman festival of Cybele, and speculates further that this festival may have involved a performance in which actors dressed as Cybele and Attis rode through the city in a chariot pulled by lions, to which the plate refers.[106] Its findspot near Milan raises the possibility in this context that it was a gift from Symmachus in Rome to his friend Nicomachus Flavianus at the court of the usurper Eugenius in Milan.[107]

There are several reasons why this interpretation is not convincing. Musso's model for the plate as commemorative gift is that of silver largitio plates. But this model is inappropriate, since there is no evidence that largitio items of any type (whether silver plates or ivory diptychs) were given on occasions outside the assumption of public office which they advertised and commemorated and around which their iconography revolves. The fact that silverware was a medium for largitio does not allow us to argue that all late antique silver was given as gifts.[108] The idea that the festivities of the *Hilaria* included a re-enactment of Attis and Cybele's chariot is also ill-founded. Certainly there is literary evidence for the staging of myths involving the impersonation of the gods, but in the context of the theatre and other types of public spectacle (which were often held in conjunction with religious festivals), not as part of their worship. Thus even if such a re-enactment had been part of the entertainment on the Hilaria, it is hard to see how its representation on a plate could be the 'document of faith' which Musso claims it is.[109] Finally, and most importantly, while Musso rejects Alföldi's claims for the late fourth-century pagan revival as a political phenomenon, she retains the traditional concept of a religio-cultural revival centred around a 'circle of Symmachus', which was criticized by Alan Cameron as early as 1977. In Cameron's view, the claims for a 'circle of Symmachus' leading a pagan revival are unsupported by the historical evidence. Rather, as had been the case under Julian in the early 360s, there was no united 'pagan front'. Instead, a range of attitudes to religion and cult existed among the upper classes in Rome.[110] Regarding a literary revival in this period, Christians played as important a role as pagans in patronizing writers. In terms of artistic patronage, the case is also more complex, since the concept of the 'pagan revival' is often evoked as a reason to date classicizing works of late antique art – such as the diptych of the Symmachi and the Nicomachi, divided between the Victoria and Albert Museum and the Cluny Museum – to the late fourth century.[111] These works in turn are used to support the case for a revival, making the argument circular. Again it is more helpful to see the popularity of classicism in art and literature as a more diffuse phenomenon in late antiquity, which can in part at least be linked to the role of *paideia* in fostering continued interest in the classical.[112] And yet the appeal to the classical was also an appeal to tradition, and respect for tradition was one defence often mounted in support of paganism. What was the relationship between *paideia* and pagan religious practice in late antiquity? And can these silver plates tell us anything about it?

Let us return to the idea which lies behind so many interpretations of the plates in this section, that they in some way attest their owners' religious beliefs. Although in each case there have been flaws in the grounds for this assumption, can we rule out any connection between the decoration of these plates and religious practice in late antiquity? The Corbridge Lanx does after all represent a shrine inhabited by gods, wherever (if indeed anywhere) it is supposed to be located. Literary and epigraphic evidence attests to the continuing worship of Cybele and Attis in late antiquity, especially in Rome.[113] It would be wrong to ignore such evidence; however we can look for alternative ways of reading it. What other functions, besides that of a statement of adherence, can religious imagery serve? One such function, I would like to suggest, is as a subject for discussion and interpretation. A key text here is Macrobius' *Saturnalia*, which gives an insight into the way religion could be a topic of discussion at a gathering of educated aristocrats. It takes the form of a dialogue between a number of well-known members of the aristocracy in Rome in the house of one of them, Vettius Angorius Praetextatus on the occasion of the festival of the Saturnalia in 384 AD. For a long time it was assumed to have been written by a contemporary of theirs, but more recently has been shown to be a work of the subsequent generation in the fifth century.[114] Despite the degree of idealization which it undoubtedly incorporates, the *Saturnalia* is still valuable as a source for late antique ideals of intellectual culture in the West, in which ideals of *paideia* are combined with knowledge of religious traditions. Here I shall focus on the first book of the *Saturnalia*, which is taken up with discussion about the origin of the Saturnalia festival, the temple of Saturn, Janus, the Roman calendar, and perhaps most importantly, a lengthy theological explanation of why all gods can be identified with the sun. It may be that the imagery on the Corbridge Lanx and the Parabiago and Ballana plates could have been a focus for this type of theological discussion.

Apollo plays an important role in the discussion about the identification of different gods with the sun, as befits one of the principal deities of the Graeco-Roman pantheon to be equated with the sun. Macrobius devotes a whole chapter of his first book to the different reasons for associating Apollo with the sun.[115] Some of these are philological, interpreting Apollo's many names and epithets (1.17.7–50); others are cosmological, such as the explanation of the myth of Apollo and Artemis' birth, which is read as an allegory of the natural processes which created the sun and moon (1.17.52–56). Macrobius also devotes quite a lengthy passage to an interpretation of the statue of a bearded Apollo in the Syrian holy city of Hierapolis, which he claims embodies all the powers and activities of the sun.[116] The statue has a pointed beard and a basket on its head, on its torso a breastplate, in its right hand a spear topped with a figure of victory, and in its left hand a flower. On its shoulders it wears a gorgoneum or aegis, beside it are two flying eagles and at its feet is the image of a woman, flanked on the left and right by two female figures encircled by a snake (1.17.66–70). The explanation that Macrobius gives for these features is as follows:

The downward-pointing beard represents the rays which shoot from above to the earth. The golden basket rising high above the head denotes the height of heaven, whence the essence of the sun is believed to come. By the evidence of the spear and the breastplate a representation of Mars is added, and Mars … is to be identified with the sun. The figure of Victory bears witness to the universal sovereignty of the sun. The likeness of a flower represents the flowering of all that the god sows and engenders and fosters, nourishes and ripens. The likeness of a woman is a representation of the earth, to which the sun gives light from above; and in like manner the two female figures on each side represent matter and nature, which together serve the earth. The representation of a serpent points to the serpentine course of the sun. The eagles by the great speed and height of their flight indicate the great height of the sun. The statue also has a gorgonlike vesture, because Minerva, to whom we know this vesture belongs, is a power of the sun; for we have it on the testimony of Porphyrius that Minerva is the power of the sun which gives a right judgement to the minds of men, and that is why this goddess is said to have been born from the head of Jupiter, or, in other words, to have issued from the highest part of the heavens where the sun derives its origins.[117]

The way in which Macrobius interprets this cult image offers a visually grounded model for a late antique reading of the composite iconography of the Corbridge Lanx and the Ballana plate.[118] The Hierapolis Apollo is represented with a multitude of attributes, each of which Macrobius' speaker explains as a different powers of the sun. In a similar way the Corbridge Lanx depicts a large number of attributes of Apollo and Artemis. Apollo holds his bow and a laurel branch, his lyre is shown by his feet, and directly beneath him is a griffin. The birds in the tree may well be crows, which are also associated with Apollo. Artemis holds a bow and an arrow while in the lower part of the plate a hound and a stag, which are both associated with her, are depicted. These offer a potential exegete of the plate a chance to discourse on the range of these two deities' powers. The iconography of the plate also incorporates gods who are not traditionally associated with Apollo and Artemis in myth or cult. One of the problems associated with the interpretation of the Lanx's imagery has been how to explain the presence of Athena. But Macrobius' description of the Hierapolitan statue of Apollo includes a neoplatonic interpretation of Athena (Minerva) as an aspect of the sun, thus connecting her with Apollo. On this model I think it likely that Athena, and the other standing female figure on the Lanx who has been (not entirely convincingly) identified as Leto's sister Ortygia, were intended to be associated with Apollo, Artemis and Leto through allegory rather than myth or cult.

The Ballana plate represents a syncretistic god with composite features. It is worth noting that the findspot of the plate suggests the possibility of Egyptian manufacture, since the winged modius on the head of the god is itself an attribute of the Graeco-Egyptian syncretistic deity Serapis, which was also used in some representations of Hermes in Graeco-Roman Egypt, while the wings on the ankles of the seated figure are an attribute of the traditional Graeco-Roman Hermes.[119] In this context it is more persuasive to read the figure as some sort of syncretistic Hermes rather than Apollo Alexikakos, since this epithet of the god is not, to the best of my knowledge, associated with any visual tradition, syncretistic or otherwise.[120] However, in the end it is more important to understand the sort of interpretations to which the image on the Ballana plate appealed, than to make a firm identification of the deity represented.

The possibility of a similar syncretistic reading of the Parabiago plate is also suggested in Macrobius when Praetextatus argues for Attis' assimilation with the sun in his discussion about the identification of gods with the sun:

To the sun, under the name of Attis, are given the emblems of a shepherd's pipe and stick, the pipe indicating a series of uneven blasts (because the winds derive their properties and essential nature from the sun and do not blow with uniformity) and

the stick declaring the power of the sun which controls all things. But that these ceremonies are to be regarded as referring chiefly to the sun can be inferred from the fact that, by the usage of that people [i.e. the Phrygians], on the eighth day before the Kalends of April, the 'Descent' being ended and the symbolic mourning over, a period of rejoicing begins; and the day, as marking the time when the sun first makes the day longer than the night is called the 'Festival of Joy' (*Hilaria*).[121]

3.15 Parabiago Plate, detail of zodiac ring, Milan, Civico Museo Archaeologico

Attis is shown to be a manifestation of the sun through his iconography (his pipes and stick) and through his festival, the date of which coincides with the spring equinox. A cosmological explanation of the relationship between Attis and Cybele is not at odds with the iconography of the Parabiago plate, with its representations of sun, moon, earth, ocean, seasons and zodiac. It might be noted that the hand of the figure within the zodiac ring is placed between the signs of Aries and Taurus, which are placed at the top of the ring (Fig. 3.15). These signs denote the months of March and April. The Zodiac ring is placed so that the signs of spring and summer, Aries, Taurus, Gemini, Cancer, Leo and Virgo, are visible, and those of the winter are hidden. This seems consistent with an explanation of the Hilaria as a festival celebrating the sun's return at the beginning of spring.

Macrobius' interpretation of Attis and Cybele was not the only one current in late antiquity. Julian, for example, had proposed a neoplatonic (predominantly Iamblichean) allegory of their myth and festival in his 'Hymn to the Mother of the Gods'. In another work he writes of the need for non-literal readings of religious myths: 'Whenever myths on the sacred are incongruous (ἀπεμφαίνων) in thought, by that very fact they cry aloud, as it were, and summon us not to believe them literally but to study and track down their hidden meaning.'[122] Julian's writings are not considered philosophically innovative, but they argue for the wider currency of such ideas in late antique thought. It seems likely that there existed a range of interpretations of a topic like Attis and Cybele all of which depended on the idea of myth as allegory, and that the Parabiago plate was open to interpretation within this range. Someone viewing the plate and offering an interpretation would be displaying *paideia* as much as support for the traditional gods of Rome. Thus the Parabiago plate, the Ballana plate and the Corbridge Lanx can be understood in the context of late antique religious syncretism where the attributes and cults of diverse pagan deities are incorporated into a unifying allegory of fundamental truths about the nature of the universe. Macrobius is by no means the only source attesting the popularity of this type of religious thought in the period, but he presents it within the context of a gathering in a private house of a cultured Roman aristocrat, where we might expect such silver vessels to be displayed.

The objection might be raised that this strategy of interpretation is too sophisticated and that the average elite *paideia* did not allow for this type of philosophical allegory. While it is certainly true that Macrobius' text represents an ideal of erudition which most members of the elite were unlikely to attain, the prescription of certain modes of interpretation as an ideal to aspire to should not be overlooked. In any case, my aim is not to propose a single, fixed, interpretation for the three plates but rather to attempt to define the mode of interpretation to which their iconography seems to best lend itself. Certainly a range of interpretations in an allegorical mode were available, and the level of sophistication would vary according to different viewers. Too often the interpretation of artworks is polarized between the esoteric and the philistine, ignoring the range of options between the two.[123] The cosmic iconography of the Parabiago plate may seem obscure, but in fact can be paralleled in mosaics from Spain, Syria and Italy.[124] Such images are arguably part of the same late antique trend towards religious allegory and syncretism.[125]

I have deliberately omitted the Mildenhall plates from the above discussion, for while they have in the past provoked interpretations similar to those proposed for the Corbridge Lanx and Parabiago plate, I do not think that they can be accounted for in the same way. Why is this? For a start there are important iconographic differences between the three Mildenhall plates and the Corbridge, Parabiago and Ballana plates. The iconography of the latter three, while not unparalleled, is relatively unusual and specifically late antique. Such syncretistic imagery accounts for a tiny proportion of the iconography of surviving silverware. Dionysiac imagery on the other hand not only occurs frequently on late antique silver, but is recognizable as a distinct (although not static) genre in Graeco-Roman art, going back ultimately to the sixth century BC. This genre, while featuring images of objects associated with the Dionysiac mysteries, was always popular in a domestic context, continuing to be so well into late antiquity. Thus a strong religious reading of the Mildenhall Plates – which as we saw was influenced by readings of Dionysiac imagery in a funerary context – is problematic. The generic quality of the iconography of the Mildenhall plates also makes an allegorical reading, of the type discussed above, seem unlikely.[126] What sort of reading, therefore, is appropriate for these plates?

Many claims have been made for the importance of Dionysus in late antique paganism. Consider Bowersock's summary:

The Neoplatonists knew an Orphic tradition according to which Zeus had designated his son Dionysus as king of all the gods of the world down to the sixth generation. For other late pagans Dionysus embodied in himself all the other gods and was at the same time in his own person the intelligence of the world. Macrobius makes the interesting distinction … that the world itself was designated Jupiter or Zeus, whereas the intelligence of that world was Dionysus (Dios Nous).[127]

This may sound impressive, but it should be put in context. Dionysus was not the only pagan god in late antiquity for whom such claims were advanced. They were typical of a syncretistic approach to religion. Macrobius' comment appears in the context of his discussion on solar syncretism to which I have already referred, where Dionysus/Liber is identified with Apollo and consequently with the sun. It is also important to bear in mind that while Dionysus did play a role in late pagan thought, he also flourished outside specifically religious contexts. It is in such areas that we should look to understand the continued popularity of the genre of Dionysiac imagery in the visual arts in late antiquity, of which the Mildenhall plates are but one example, for Dionysus and the legends associated with him continued to be of interest in an increasingly Christianized society. The best evidence for this is the fifth-century neo-Homeric epic, the *Dionysiaca*, by Nonnus of Panopolis, an author who was probably a Christian and also wrote a verse paraphrase of the Gospel of St John. While it is hard to find echoes of the visual repertoire of Dionysus in the *Dionysiaca*, since the narratives of Dionysus' adventures which it recounts go far beyond the timeless processions, revels and drinking contests depicted in art, the poem engages with the powerful tradition of Homeric epic, which lay at the heart of *paideia*, as well as showing considerable erudition in a range of other Greek poetry, philosophy, and astronomy/astrology.[128] Arguably, Nonnus used a Homeric model to write about Dionysus because for him, both were representatives of a respected tradition, within which he wished to situate himself. Nonnus' self-positioning through his literary models makes the fact that, to modern readers, his Dionysus is no more like the classical Dionysus than his poetry is like Homer's, almost irrelevant. His ancient readers would not have seen any incongruity. Nor would it have seemed strange to them that living in a Christian society, Nonnus should write an epic about a pagan god. Recent scholars have tried to read the *Dionysiaca* as a 'Christianization' of Dionysus, where the god is made into a polytheist Christ for pagans.[129] This is surely to misunderstand Nonnus' display of *paideia*. For just as in the time of Julian, educated Christians and pagans alike had rejected his claim that to read Homer one should believe in Homer's gods, when Nonnus chose Dionysus as the subject of his epic, he is unlikely to have thought that writing about Dionysus also required that he worship him.[130] He chose a topic that was deemed appropriate for his genre.

There are clear parallels for this in the panegyrics and epithalamia of the poet Claudian, a fellow-countryman of Nonnus who wrote in Latin for the Christian court of Honorius in the early fifth century. His invocation of pagan deities in his poems has been shown convincingly to be a function of the highly traditional genres in which he worked.[131] Thus Venus and Cupid play active roles in an epithalamium for Honorius and his bride, just as they figure prominently on the casket given to the Christian couple Secundus and Proiecta as a wedding gift in the 390s.[132] Likewise in his panegyric on the fourth consulship of Honorius, the emperor in his jewelled consular robes is compared to Dionysus:

Were you to have passed through the cities of Maeonia in this robe, Lydia would have handed over the thyrsus of vine-tendrils to you, Nyssa performed her dances in your honour, the Bacchanals would have wondered to whom they owed their frenzy, the tigers meekly accepted your bands. Just so does Liber in fawnskin embroidered with Red Sea pearls drive in his chariot ...[133]

Dionysus' embeddedness in literary tradition offers an insight into the persistence of the generic imagery of Dionysus and his followers from the fourth century into the early seventh century, as silver, ivory and textiles all attest.[134] His popularity in late antique art is best understood through his association with Hellenism in its secular sense of Greek language and literary culture, not to mention the theatre. Thus the Mildenhall plates with their Dionysiac iconography should be seen neither as a statement of a particular pagan world-view, nor as objects whose fine craftsmanship caused their Christian owners to tolerate their pagan subject matter.[135] Rather they should be seen as objects which could be appreciated by pagan and Christian owners alike, since their decoration proclaimed that their owners valued the traditions of culture, and invited those who saw them to show in their speech and actions that they did the same.

Paideia and visual culture

In the course of this chapter, I have surveyed some of the ways in which *paideia* operated as a factor in determining the choice of imagery with which the silver of the fourth and early fifth centuries was decorated, and how that imagery might be received by its viewers. Several different aspects of *paideia*, however, are encompassed in the different pieces of silverware which I have analysed. The Kaiseraugst Achilles plate actually represents *paideia*, by showing episodes in the upbringing of the young Homeric hero which both contrasted with and evoked the upbringing of its elite viewers. A different strategy can be traced in the Sevso Achilles and Meleager plates, which call upon their viewers to use their *paideia* as a tool in reading and understanding the connections between the diverse mythological scenes which they display. These plates offered viewers an opportunity to display their knowledge of the literary tradition, which formed such an important part of the initial stages of *paideia* under the instruction of the grammaticus. Because using such silver in effect challenged the viewer to a display of *paideia*, it is not hard to imagine how such objects could function in the projection of status in the domestic sphere, since *paideia* in late antiquity, as in earlier periods, served to distinguish the elite from those lower in the social scale. Although *paideia* encompassed an essentially conservative set of cultural values, my analysis has shown how it could accommodate change and innovation: the development of a narrative cycle for the childhood of Achilles on the Kaiseraugst plate; the presence of gods at his birth on the Sevso Achilles plate; the religious allegory and syncretism of the Parabiago, Corbridge and Ballana plates are all examples of visual imagery peculiar to the late antique period. Yet it was not presented as an innovation, but interpreted through the lens of tradition that *paideia* provided. The Parabiago, Corbridge and Ballana plates are examples of *paideia* as knowledge of pagan religious lore; by contrast the Mildenhall plates show how *paideia* could contribute to the secularization of the imagery and myths of traditional pagan deities like Dionysus. This impression is reinforced by the inclusion of Dionysiac scenes on the border of the Sevso Achilles plate, and the use of 'masks' on altars to divide the scenes of the border there and on the Meleager plate. Although unlike the two Sevso plates, the Mildenhall plates do not have a 'narrative', the way in which they appeal to *paideia* is very similar.

What are the broader implications of this admittedly limited analysis of a small group of objects? Foremost I would highlight the importance for modern scholars of recognizing the role of *paideia* as a tool for interpreting the visual culture of the late antique elite. *Paideia* – both the educational training, and the concept of culture shared by individuals who had participated in this training – was an important area of continuity between late antiquity and earlier centuries, from the Hellenistic era through to more recent periods in Graeco-Roman cultural history, such as the Second Sophistic of the second and early third centuries. While the written word and the orator's speech were the means by which *paideia* was acquired, it would be wrong to think that *paideia* operated only in the realm of the text. By recognizing its role in broader perceptions of culture – including the visual – in the late antique world, we borrow from the late antique viewer an important tool for our interpretation of that culture. Silverware is not the only visual medium where it is possible to do this; however, it is a good example because as an expensive luxury product its owners are likely to have used silver as a way of advertising their membership of a late Roman elite. Whether in all cases their education matched the aspirations implied in the decoration of the silverware we cannot know; but we can at least be reasonably confident that in displaying such objects, they intended to give the impression that it did.

Notes

1. A comprehensive catalogue of examples of this type of vessel can be found in J.M.C. Toynbee and K.S. Painter, 'Silver Picture Plates of Late Antiquity: AD 300 to 700', *Archaeologia* 108 (1986), 15–65, although this also includes a number of similarly shaped vessels with non-mythological imagery.

2. Mosaics: D. Levi, *Antioch Mosaic Pavements*, 2 vols (Princeton, NJ, 1947), C. Kondoleon, *Domestic and Divine: Roman Mosaics in the House of Dionysos* (Ithaca and London, 1995). Wall-painting: V.M. Strocka, *Forschungen in Ephesos VIII.i : Die Wandmalerei der Hanghäuser in Ephesos* (Vienna, 1977). Textiles: M.-H. Rutschowscaya, *Tissus Coptes* (Paris, 1990). Ivories: W.F. Volbach, *Elfenbeinarbeiten der Spätantike*.

3. On the continuity in rhetorical education (a key part of *paideia*) from the Hellenistic period onwards see H.I. Marrou, *A History of Education in Antiquity*, trans. G. Lamb (Madison, WI, 1982), 194–205.

4. Marrou, *History of Education*, 196. For the role of ancient education in teaching modes of social interaction, see the perceptive study of T. Morgan, *Literate Education in the Hellenistic and Roman Worlds* (Cambridge, 1998).

5. On continuity and change see F.M. Clover, R.S. Humphreys, eds, *Tradition and Innovation in Late Antiquity* (Madison, 1989); A. Cameron, *The Mediterranean World in Late Antiquity AD 395–600* (London, 1993), 1–11. G. Bowersock, *Hellenism in Late Antiquity* (Cambridge, 1990) is also relevant.

6. Grammarians are recorded well into the first half of the sixth century: see the prosopography in R.A. Kaster, *Guardians of Language: the Grammarian and Society in Late Antiquity* (Berkeley, CA, 1988). A similar study has yet to be carried out for rhetors, but it seems likely that they too persisted until then: see P. Lemerle, *Byzantine Humanism: The First Phase. Notes and Remarks on Education and Culture in Byzantium from its Origins to the 10th Century*, trans. H. Lindsay and A. Moffatt. Byzantina Australiensia 3 (Canberra, 1986), 87–93. For details of syllabuses, teaching methods etc. see Marrou, *History of Education*, 160–75, 194–205, 274–91.

7. Some evidence of the normal length of time spent in formal education is provided by the atypical example of Libanius: in Or. 1.8–9 he presents himself as a late starter, studying under a grammarian from the ages of 15 to 20, and then going to Athens to study oratory. He puts down this delay to his earlier neglect of his studies, and the lack of good teachers of rhetoric in Antioch.

8. Kaster, *Guardians of Language*, 24–26.

9.   Kaster, *Guardians of Language*, 29.

10. For a summary of some of the standard criticisms see Kaster, *Guardians of Language*, 12–14 and bibliography.

11. Interestingly enough, this can be seen in upper-class attitudes to those who taught the arts of *paideia* for remuneration, especially the grammarians, who represented the bottom rung of its ladder. See Kaster, *Guardians of Language*, esp. 99–134.

12. The different social functions of ancient education were already acknowledged by Marrou, *History of Education*, 217–26. In addition to Kaster, *Guardians of Language*, important studies of these functions in a late antique context include P. Brown, *Power and Persuasion in Late Antiquity: Towards a Christian Empire* (Madison, WI, 1992). S. Swain, *Hellenism and Empire: Language, Classicism and Power in the Greek World AD 50–250* (Oxford, 1996) is also valuable, although it deals with the earlier period of the Second Sophistic, as is Morgan, *Literate Education*.

13. Brown, *Power and Persuasion*, 35–41.

14. Cf. Kaster, *Guardians of Language*, 210–15 on the importance of personal over professional qualities in making appointments and promotions.

15. Philostratus the Elder, *Imagines I*, preface 4–5. For the identity and date of this author see G. Anderson, *Philostratus: Biography and Belles Lettres in the Third Century AD* (London, 1986).

16. For a sophist delivering speeches to a private invited audience cf. Libanius *Ep.* 37 in the Loeb *Selected Letters*, ed. and trans. by A.F. Norman (Cambridge, MA, and London, 1992).

17. The category of *ekphrasis* is defined in the rhetorical handbooks (progymnasmata) of Hermogenes of Tarsus (second century AD) and Aphthonius (fourth/early fifth century AD), which have been translated respectively in C.S. Baldwin, *Medieval Rhetoric and Poetic (to 1400): Interpreted from Representative Works* (New York, 1928), 23–38 (Hermogenes) and R. Nadeau, 'The Progymnasmata of Aphthonius in Translation', *Speech Monographs* 19 (1952), 264–85. There is further discussion of progymnasmata in D.L. Clark, *Rhetoric in Graeco-Roman Education* (New York, 1957). On Philostratus and *ekphrasis* see R.H. Webb, *The Transmission of the* Eikones *of Philostratus and the Development of* Ekphrasis *from Late Antiquity to the Renaissance* (Ph.D, Warburg Institute, University of London, 1992).

18. See Elsner, *Art and the Roman Viewer*, 23–39.

19. Even if the villa and the painting collection which Philostratus describes is in fact another rhetorical device, and never existed (there has been considerably controversy over the question: see the bibliography in Elsner, *Art and the Roman Viewer*, 313–14) Philostratus' choice of a domestic rather than a public context for the setting of his work remains relevant.

20. The evocation of *paideia* in the Kaiseraugst Achilles plate was first noted by M.A. Manacorda in *La paideia di Achille* (Rome, 1971), although he interprets the term in a rather narrow philosophical sense and uses it principally to argue that Julian the Apostate was the patron of the plate.

21. Marrou, *History of Education*, 9–10, 162–63, 258–62. The phrase 'the educator of Greece' [τὴν Ἑλλάδα πεπαίδευκεν] is used in Plato, *Rep.* 10, 606e as an example of the conventional admiration of Homer, of which Plato is of course ultimately critical. Cf.

R. Lamberton and J.J. Keaney, eds, *Homer's Ancient Readers: the Hermeneutics of Greek Epic's Earliest Exegetes* (Princeton, NJ, 1992).

22. Cahn, Kaufmann-Heinimann et al., *Der spätrömische Silberschatz.*

23. For identification and discussion of the iconography of these scenes see V. von Gonzenbach, 'Achillesplatte', in Cahn, Kaufmann-Heinimann et al., *Der spätrömische Silberschatz*, 225–308, with the extensive annotated bibliography, 225–26.

24. For example, a room in the Domus Uboni at Pompeii where the Discovery on Skyros is paired with scenes of Thetis in the workshop of Hephaistos, and carrying arms to Achilles at Troy. See M.L. Thompson, 'The Monumental and Literary Evidence for Programmatic Painting in Antiquity', *Marsyas* 9 (1960/61), 36–77. More examples in R. Ling, *Roman Painting* (Cambridge ,1991), figs 137, 138. The major surveys of the iconography of Achilles are F. Brommer, A. Peschlow-Bindokat and D. Lindemann, *Denkmälerlisten zur griechischen Heldensage 2: Theseus, Bellerophon, Achill* (Marburg, 1974); D. Kemp-Lindemann, *Darstellung des Achilleus in griechischer und römischer Kunst*, Diss. Mainz, 1975, Archäologische Studien 3 (1975); A. Kossatz-Deissmann, 'Achilles', *LIMC I* (Zurich, 1981), 37–200, pls 56–145. On late antique Achilles cycles, see W. Raeck, *Modernisierte Mythen. Zum Umgang der Spätantike mit klassischen Bildthemen* (Stuttgart, 1992), 122–38.

25. Capitoline Puteal': W. Helbig, rev. W. Amelung et al., *Führer durch die öffentlichen Sammlungen klassischer Altertümer in Rom* I (3rd edn, Leipzig, 1912), 419, no. 766; H. Stuart Jones, *Catalogue of the Ancient Sculpture, Museo Capitolino* (1912), 45–47; G.A.S. Snyder, 'The So-Called Puteal in the Capitoline Museum at Rome', *JRS* 13 (1923) 56–68. Terra Sigillata plates: J.W. Salomonson, 'Late Roman Earthenware with Relief Decoration Found in Northern Africa and Egypt', *Oudheidkundige mededelingen uit het Rijksmuseum von oudheden te Leiden* 43 (1962), 53–95; idem, 'Spätrömische rote Tonware mit Reliefverzierung', 4–109; J.W. Hayes, *Late Roman Pottery* (London 1972). The cycles of both the 'Puteal' and the plates are discussed in L. Guerini, 'Infanzia di Achille e sua educazione presso Chirone', *Studi Miscellanei* (1958/9), 43–53 and J. Garbsch, 'Spätantike Keramik aus Nordafrika in der Prähistorische Staatsammlung: ein spätantike Achilles-Zyklus', *Bayerische Vorgeschichtsblätter* 45 (1980), 155–60.

26. C. Robert, *Die antiken Sarkophagreliefs II: Mythogischen Cyklen* (Rome 1968) no. 26 (=*ASR II*).

27. For example, the Louvre Borghese sarcophagus (*ASR II* no. 26); Capitoline Museum 'Alexander Severus' sarcophagus (*ASR II* no. 25).

28. *ASR II*, no. 22

29. R. Brilliant, *Visual Narratives: Storytelling in Etruscan and Roman Art* (Ithaca and London, 1984), 14–35.

30. Compare Hermogenes' prescriptions for the genre of encomium: 'Topics for encomia of a man are his race, as Greek; his city, as Athens; his family, as Alcmaeonidae. You will say what marvellous things befell his birth, as dreams or signs or the like. Next his nurture, as in the case of Achilles, that he was reared on lions' marrow and by Chiron. Then training, how he was trained and educated ....' Translation from Baldwin, *Medieval Rhetoric*, 31–32. Achilles is mentioned in a similar context in the third-century rhetor Menander's discussion of the *basilikos logos*; see the edition of D.A. Russell and N.G. Wilson (Oxford, 1981). On the methods of literary exegesis, see Marrou, *History of Education*, 166–69; F.M. Young, *Biblical Exegesis and the Formation of Christian Culture* (Cambridge, 1997), 76–96.

31. Gregory Nazianzus, in his funeral oration for Basil the Great, describes his '*enkuklios paideusis*' as superior to Achilles' rough, primitive education, describing all its components – living in a cave, taught by a centaur, learning to hunt and fight, eating the marrow of wild animals – without once mentioning Achilles' name (*Or.* 43.12, ed. and trans. J. Bernadi, Sources Chrétiennes no. 384 [Paris, 1992]). He clearly expected his listeners to be familiar enough with the tradition of Achilles' upbringing to pick up the allusion to the hero, which suggests that it was firmly embedded in the mythological repertoire of the men of *paideia* to whom Gregory addresses himself. Also see Libanius *Or.* 59.30 (Panyegyric for Constantius II and Constans), which makes a similar comparison.

32. Identification of woman as muse: von Gonzenbach in Cahn, Kaufmann-Heinimann et al., *Der spätrömische Silberschatz*, 253–54.

33. Philostratus, *Imagines* II.2. The relationship between this section of the *Imagines* and Roman visual representations of Achilles and Chiron, including those on the Kaiseraugst plate, has been explored by Letizia Abbondanza, in 'Immagini dell'infanzia di Achille in età imperiale: continuità di un paradigma educativo', *Ocnus: Quaderni della Scuola di Specializzazione in Archeologia* 4 (1996), 9–33.

34. Philostratus, *Imagines* II.2.1.

35. *ibid.*

36. See J. Huskinson, *Roman Children's Sarcophagi: Their Decoration and its Social Significance* (Oxford, 1996), 9–24, 85–91.

37. Philostratus, *Imagines* II.2.4

38. H. I. Marrou, *MOYΣIKOΣ ANHP, étude sur les scènes de la vie intellectuelle figurant sur les monuments funéraires romains* (Grenoble, 1938), 231–57.

39. On the concept of *kairos* or the crucial moment of opportunity, and its personification see A.F. Stewart, 'Lysippan Studies I. The Only Creator of Beauty', *AJA* 82 (1978), 63–71.

40. Bennet and Mango, *The Sevso Treasure*, cat. 3, 153–80.

41. Some important contributors to the debate have been, K. Schefold, *Pompejanische Malerei: Sinn und Ideengeschichte* (Basel, 1952), Brilliant (n. 29 supra), 53–89, and B. Bergmann, 'The Roman House as Memory Theatre: The House of the Tragic Poet in Pompeii', *Art Bulletin* 76 (1994), 225–56.

42. See Z. Newby, 'Reading Programs in Graeco-Roman Art: Reflections on the Spada Reliefs', in D. Fredrick, ed., *The Roman Gaze: Vision, Power and the Body* (Baltimore, 2001).

43. Meleager plate: Bennet and Mango, *The Sevso Treasure*, cat. 2, 98–152. The House of Aion mosaic is most fully published in W.A. Daszewski, *Dionysos der Erlöser: griechische Mythen im spätantiken Cypern* (Mainz, 1985).

44. L. Kötzsche-Breitenbruch, 'Geburt III (ikonographisch)' in *Reallexikon für Antike und Christentum* 9 (Stuttgart, 1976), 172–216. Also see A. Greifenhagen, 'Kindheitsmythos des Dionysos', *RM* 46 (1931), 27–43; G.M.A. Hanfmann, 'Notes on the Mosaics from Antioch', *AJA* 43 (1939), 229–39; Kossatz-Deissmann (n. 24 supra), 42–43; F. Matz, *Die antiken Sarkophagreliefs IV: Die Dionysischen Sarkophage* 4 vols (Berlin, 1969), vol. 3, nos 195–99; A. Veneri, 'Dionysos', *LIMC* III (Zurich, 1986), 478–82.

45. Volbach, *Elfenbeinarbeiten der Spätantike*, no. 95.

46. D.J.A. Ross, 'Olympias and the Serpent. The Interpretation of a Baalbek Mosaic and the Date of the Illustrated Pseudo-Callisthenes', *Journal of the Warburg and Courtauld Institutes* 26 (1963), 1–21.

47. In this context note that some scholars have read the birth scene on the Sevso Achilles plate as that of Dionysus in the context of the Dionysiac scenes on the plate. See H.A. Cahn, A. Kaufmann-Heinimann, and K. Painter, 'A Table Ronde on a Treasure of Late Roman Silver', *JRA* 4 (1991), 189.

48. Arrian, *Anabasis* I.12, VII.11, 14, 20. Plutarch, *Alexander* 15, 67. Another source for the life of Alexander in this period was the highly coloured Alexander Romance, which Ross (n. 46 supra) believes influence the scene on the Baalbek Mosaic. Cf. W. Kroll, *Historia Alexandri Magni* (Berlin, 1926); R. Stoneman, ed. and trans., *The Greek Alexander Romance* (Harmondsworth, 1991), section 1–13. On the concept of visual analogy see M. Koortbojian, *Myth, Meaning and Memory on Roman Sarcophagi* (Berkeley, CA ,1995), 1–18.

49. One example is Basil the Great, *Address to Young Men on Reading Greek Literature*, VII.9, which cites as an example of virtue Alexander's continence regarding the daughters of Darius after they were taken prisoner by his army. Cf. Plutarch, *Alexander* 21.

50. W.A. Daszewski, 'Polish Excavations at Kato (Nea) Paphos in 1970–1971', *Report of the Department of Antiquities, Cyprus* (1972), 208–17; W. Amelung, *Die Sculpturen des Vaticanischen Museums I* (Berlin, 1903), 591, no. 424, pl 61. Also see Huskinson, *Roman Children's Sarcophagi*, 10–15, 87–91, 101–02 for the representation of the young Achilles and Dionysus on children's sarcophagi.

51. The complete mosaic depicts five scenes in three registers, the central register containing a single scene and the top and bottom register two each. The scenes depicted are: Leda and the Swan, Hermes Presenting Dionysus to the Nymphs, Contest between Cassiopeia and the Nereids, Triumph of Dionysus, Apollo and Marsyas. The classicism of the mosaic echoes the classicizing tendencies of much late antique silverware. See Daszewski, *Dionysos der Erlöser*.

52. Julian the Apostate in *To the Cynic Heraclius* (*Or. VIII* 220a–221c) cites Dionysus' birth as an example of a theophany, and contrasts it with that of Heracles which he claims was merely physical, deification taking place subsequently. While visual representations of Dionysus' birth which depict Semele imply its physicality, the scene of Hermes and Dionysus on the House of Aion mosaic includes a female figure labelled 'Theogonia'.

53. Compare this with the room of pictures described in Lucian, *De Domo*, which includes only two scenes linked by narrative continuity: Perseus slaying the Gorgon, and Perseus rescuing Andromeda, which are described in reverse order. Several pictures are connected by the appearance of Athena in them, who is also represented by a marble statue in a shrine. Hephaistos appears twice, pursuing Athena, and watching Orion being cured of his blindness. The pictures of the Madness of Odysseus and Medea preparing to kill her sons contrast Medea's murderous intent towards her children with Odysseus' fatherly instinct to protect Telemachus when threatened by Palmedes, which reveals that his madness is feigned. However, for the most part, the text does not make these connections explicit, leaving that task to the reader.

54. Athens had one state-endowed chair in rhetoric and four in philosophy, which were bestowed upon the city by Marcus Aurelius, an honour shared only with Rome, which had chairs in Latin and Greek rhetoric, until the founding of similar chairs in

Constantinople in the fifth century. See Marrou, *History of Education*, 303, 307; more generally A. Frantz, *Late Antiquity AD 267–700: Excavations of the American School in Athens in the Athenian Agora* (Princeton, NJ, 1988).

55. Cf. Gregory Nazianzus, *Or.* 43.13–14.

56. For the reconstruction of the west pediment see F. Brommer, *The Sculptures of the Parthenon: Metopes, Frieze, Pediment, Cult Statue* (London, 1979), 47–52; and J. Boardman, *The Parthenon and Its Sculptures* (London, 1985), 229–30.

57. The other two are in Apamea and Palmyra. See J.C. Balty, 'Une version orientale méconnue du mythe de Cassiopée', in L. Kahil and C. Augé, eds, *Mythologie gréco-romaine, mythologies périphériques: études d'iconographie* (Paris, 1981), 95–106; and H. Stern, *Les mosaïques des maisons d'Achille et de Cassiopée à Palmyre* (Paris, 1977), 26–42. On their relationship to the Paphos mosaic, see W.A. Daszewski, 'Cassiopeia in Paphos – a Levantine Going West', in V. Karageorghis, ed., *Acts of the International Archaeological Symposium 'Cyprus Between the Orient and the Occident'* (Nicosia, 1986), 454–70.

58. Martial, *De Spectaculis* describes some instances of the 'staging' of myths at the opening games in the Colisseum. Cf. K. Coleman, 'Fatal Charades: Roman Executions Staged as Mythological Enactments', *JRS* 80 (1990), 44–73; C. Kondoleon, 'Signs of Privilege and Pleasure: Roman Domestic Mosaics', in E.K. Gazda, ed., *Roman Art in the Private Sphere* (Ann Arbor, MI, 1991) 105–15. On theatrical spectacles in a domestic context see C.P. Jones, 'Dinner Theatre', in W. Slater, ed., *Dining in a Classical Context* (Ann Arbor, MI, 1991), 185–98.

59. The genre of the florilegium or anthology can be traced back as far as the fourth century BC and seems to have been developed in an educational context as a means of presenting selected passages from admired authors, generally with a moral theme. Both poets and prose writers were anthologized, as well as the gnomic maxims of sages like Socrates and Diogenes. The wide distribution and popularity of such anthologies continued into late antiquity, and they continued to be compiled in this period, for example Stobaios' mixed anthology of prose and poetry, compiled at the end of the fourth/beginning of the fifth century AD, or the fourth century prose anthology of Sopater of Apamea. See H. Chadwick, 'Florilegium', *Realexikon für Antike und Christentum* 7 (Stuttgart, 1969), 1131–60; J. Barns, 'A New Gnomologium: with Some Remarks on Gnomic Anthologies' *CQ* 44 (1950), 126–48, esp. 132–37 and 45 (1951), 1–19.

60. Bennet and Mango, *The Sevso Treasure*, 121–47.

61. M.M. Mango, *The Sevso Treasure: A Collection from Late Antiquity*, Sotheby's Catalogue (London, 1990), 15.

62. Love and hunting: a good example is Philostratus' ekphrasis of a painting of hunters (*Imagines*, I.28); also see A. Schnapp, 'Eros the Hunter' in C. Bérard et al., ed., *A City of Images: Iconography and Society in Ancient Greece* (Princeton, NJ, 1989), 71–88; idem, *Le Chasseur et la cité: chase et érotique en Grèce ancienne* (Paris, 1997).

63. *ASR* XII.6.12.

64 For the iconography of the Meleager sarcophagi see G. Koch, *Die antiken Sarkophagreliefs XII.6: die mythologischen Sarkophage: Meleager* (Berlin, 1975); Brilliant, *Visual Narratives*, 145–61.

65. Bennet and Mango, *The Sevso Treasure*, cats 8, 9, 10, 319–401.

66. Toynbee and Painter, 'Picture Plates', cat. 28, 29, 33–34.

67. Toynbee and Painter, 'Picture Plates', cat 27, 33, 33, 35–36 (the other plate of the pair, cat. 34, shows Hippolytus with his mother Hippolyta).

68. An alternative version of the Pyramus and Thisbe legend existed in the eastern half of the empire, preserved in several late antique sources including Nonnus' *Dionysiaca*, in which the lovers were actually two rivers that sought and eventually flowed into each other. Christine Kondoleon has argued that the Pyramus and Thisbe scene on the Meleager plate, like the one represented in the House of Dionysus at Nea Paphos, is a conflation of western and eastern artists models, and is only indirectly inspired by Ovid's poem. See Kondoleon, *Domestic and Divine*, 148–56.

69. S. Guberti Bassett, '*Historiae custos*: Sculpture and Tradition in the Baths of Zeuxippos', *AJA* 100 (1996), 491–506.

70. Guberti Bassett, '*Historiae custos*', 505–06.

71. Guberti Bassett, '*Historiae custos*', 502–04.

72. The Parabiago plate is sometimes dated to the second century AD but as I argue below there are several reasons for rejecting such an early date. Proponents of the early date include A. Levi, *La patera d'argento di Parabiago*, R. Instituto d'Archeologia e Storia dell'Arte, Opera d'Arte v (Rome, 1935); M.J. Vermaseren, *Corpus Cultus Cybelae Attidisque IV* (Leiden, 1978), 109; Kiilerich, *Late Fourth-Century Classicism*, 175–77.

73. Bowersock, *Hellenism in Late Antiquity*, 9–10.

74. Bowersock, *Hellenism in Late Antiquity*, 1–13.

75. Bowersock, *Hellenism in Late Antiquity*, 4–5, where the House of Aion mosaic is compared as 'a revelation of late antique paganism' to accounts of pagan cults surviving into the sixth century in John of Ephesus' *Eccesiastical History*. Cf. Bowersock's longer discussion of the mosaic, 49–52.

76. Bowersock, *Hellenism in Late Antiquity*, 12.

77. A more persuasive use of visual evidence by Bowersock is his invocation of Hellenism to explain the co-existence of iconic and aniconic representations of the Nabatean god Dusares on the coinage of that region: see *Hellenism in Late Antiquity*, 8–9.

78. For pagan revival see generally P. Chuvin, *A Chronicle of the Last Pagans* (Cambridge, MA, 1990); on Julian's revival G.W. Bowersock, *Julian the Apostate* (London, 1978); P. Athanassiadi-Fowden, *Julian and Hellenism: an Intellectual Biography* (London, 1981); R.B.E. Smith, *Julian's Gods: Religion and Philosophy in the Thought and Action of Julian the Apostate* (London, 1995); on the Roman revival: A. Alföldi, *Die Kontorniaten: ein verkanntes Propagandamittel der stadtrömischen heidnischen Aristokratie in ihrem Kampfe gegen das christliche Kaisertum* (Budapest, 1943), esp. 48–84, revised and reprinted with E. Alföldi and C.L. Clay as *Die Kontorniat-Medallions* 3 vols (Berlin, 1976–90) ,esp. vol. 2, 7–74; H. Bloch, 'The Pagan Revival in the West at the End of the Fourth Century', in A.D. Momigliano, ed., *The Conflict Between Paganism and Christianity in the Fourth Century* (Oxford, 1963), 193–218.

79. J.W. Brailsford, *The Mildenhall Treasure: A Handbook*, 2nd edn (London, 1955); Painter, *The Mildenhall Treasure*.

80. The four items now lost were a basin, a two-handled cup, a bowl with a projecting rim decorated with chi-rhos, and a silver vase bearing the inscription 'DESIDERI VIVAS'. See F.J. Haverfield, 'Roman Silver in Northumberland', *JRS* 4 (1914), 1–12; also O. Brendel, 'The Corbridge Lanx', *JRS* 31 (1941), 100–27.

81. Levi, *La patera d'argento*; Kiilerich, *Late Fourth Century Classicism*, 174–77; Vermaseren, *Corpus Cultus Cybelae*, no. 268, 107–09. On the findspot see also L. Musso, *Manifattura suntuaria e committenza pagana nella Roma del IV Secolo: indagine sulla Lanx di Parabiago* (Rome, 1983), 3, n. 1.

82. Levi, *La patera d'argento*, dated it as to the Antonine period. H.P. L'Orange in *Der spätantike Bildschmuck des Konstantinsbogens* (Berlin, 1939), 164, n. 1 claimed that its style is typical of later fourth-century 'renaissance' tendencies. J.M.C. Toynbee, in a review of L'Orange, suggested in turn a late third-century date (*JRS* 35 [1941], 192). Another early supporter of the fourth century date was Alföldi, *Die Kontorniaten*, 47–48. Vermaseren, *Corpus Cultus Cybelae*, follows Levi. Most recently Kiilerich, *Late Fourth Century Classicism*, has doubted the fourth-century date on stylistic grounds.

83. The shape of the vessel – a circular, flat, or nearly flat, plate with a high foot-ring slightly less than half the diameter of the plate – can be matched by many other silver plates datable to the fourth and early fifth centuries, such as the Missorium of Theodosius, the Missorium of Ardabur Aspar, the Mildenhall Great Dish, and the Kaiseraugst Achilles plate, as well as two silver plates from the necropolis at Ballana in Nubia. This shape is also known in late Roman terra sigillata: Hayes forms 89 A and B. For a full discussion of ceramic and metal parallels see Musso, *Manifattura suntuaria*, 15–22. Moreover although the plasticity with which the figures are modelled is unusual, they are considerably embellished with surface detail – for example, borders on clothing – created with punches in a manner entirely typical of fourth and fifth century silver. These techniques are well illustrated in Cahn, Kaufmann-Heinimann et al., *Der spätrömische Silberschatz*, and Bennet and Mango, *The Sevso Treasure*, 30–33, and *passim*. It is worth noting that while the plasticity of the figures is not matched in other late antique silver, the depth of relief is, for example in the Kaiseraugst Achilles and the Sevso Meleager plates' central medallions.

84. W.B. Emery and L.P. Kirwan, *The Royal Tombs of Ballana and Qustal. Mission archéologique de Nubie 1929–1934*, 2 vols (Cairo, 1938), vol. I, 273–74, vol. II, pl. 65, figs B, C. The plate was found in tomb B-3.

85. See L. Török, 'Egyptian Late Antique Art from Nubian Royal Tombs', in C. Moss and K. Kiefer, eds, *Byzantine East, Latin West. Art-Historical Studies in Honour of Kurt Weitzmann* (Princeton, 1995), 91–92; idem. *Late Antique Nubia. History and Archaeology of the Southern Neighbour of Egypt in the Fourth-Sixth Century AD*, with a preface by Sir Laurence Kirwan, Antaeus 16 (Budapest, 1988), 51ff.

86. The figure is identified as Hermes in Emery and Kirwan, *Royal Tombs*, 175, and in Weitzmann, *Age of Spirituality*, 189–90. F.W. Von Bissing, 'Die Funde in den Nekropolen von Kostol, Ballana und Firka am II Nilkatarakt und ihre zeitliche und kunstgeschichtliche Stellung', *AA* (1939), 576–77, and Toynbee and Painter, 'Picture Plates', no. 58, 45–46 identify him as Apollo Alexikakos.

87. See Török, 'Egyptian Late Antique Art', 93. In addition to the bibliography cited there, W.F. Volbach, 'Silber- und Elfenbeinarbeiten vom Ende des 4. bis zum Anfang des 7. Jahrhunderts', *Beiträge zur Kunstgeschichte und Archäologie des Frühmittelalters. Akten zum VII internationalen Kongreß für Frühmittelalterforschung 21.–28. September 1958* (Cologne, 1962), 27, also noted technical similarities between the Ballana and Corbridge plates. On the dating of this plate see also Musso, *Manifattura suntuaria*, 141 n. 282.

88. J.M.C. Toynbee, *Art in Britain Under the Romans* (Oxford, 1964), 309–10. For such interpretations of Dionysiac sarcophagi see K. Lehmann-Hartleben and E.C. Olsen, *Dionysiac Sarcophagi in Baltimore* (Baltimore, 1942), R. Turcan, *Les sarcophages romains à représentations dionysiaques: essai de chronologie et d'histoire religieuse* (Paris, 1966).

89. For a useful comment on Toynbee's position in relation to the trends in interpreting Roman funerary art, see S. Walker, 'Aspects of Roman Funerary Art', in J. Huskinson, M. Beard and J. Reynolds, eds, *Image and Mystery in the Roman World* (Gloucester, 1988), 23–25.

90. Painter, *The Mildenhall Treasure*, 18–23.

91. Cameron, 'Distribution and Ownership', 182–83.

92. For a summary of eighteenth- and nineteenth-century attempts at interpretation see Haverfield, 'Roman Silver in Northumberland'.

93. Brendel, 'The Corbridge Lanx', 127.

94. A *locus classicus* for this reading of Brendel is Toynbee, *Art in Britain Under the Romans*, 307, which refers to 'the sacrifice offered to Apollo on Delos by Julian the Apostate in 363, when he was en route for the Persian War'. The claim is repeated most recently in a publication by the British Museum, which owns the Lanx: see T. Potter, *Roman Britain* 2nd edn (London, 1997), 81, caption to fig. 76.

95. For a fuller discussion of the untenability of Brendel's reading of this passage, see O. Nicholson, 'The Corbridge Lanx and the Emperor Julian', *Britannia* 26 (1995), 312–15. The problem was also noted by Musso, *Manifattura suntuaria*, 130.

96. Smith, *Julian's Gods*, 169.

97. M.M. Mango in Buckton, *Byzantium*, 38–39. Her entry there on the Mildenhall plates is also relevant, 40.

98. This view has been convincingly stated in Smith, *Julian's Gods*. See esp. xi–xvi, 9–22, 210–11, 219–24. Ammianus' positive view of Julian is less influenced by religious considerations than the others: J. Matthews in *The Roman Empire of Ammianus* (London, 1989), 113, concludes that 'intensity of religious feeling forms no part of Ammianus' view of what makes a good emperor. Both Julian and Constantine are criticized in their obituary notices for their 'superstition' (21.16.8; 25.4.17)'. See further 115–29.

99. *Against the Gallileans*, 423ad.

100. Gregory Nazianzus *Or.* 4 (*Inv. against Jul.* 1), 5.79–81.

101. See N.G. Wilson, *Address to Young Men: Saint Basil on the Value of Greek Literature* (London, 1975) for text and commentary.

102. Basil, *Address To Young Men*, iv 30–36, v 1–4. Cf the importance of classical philosophy in the theology of Gregory Nazianzus, Basil and the other Cappadocians, detailed in J. Pelikan, *Christianity and Classical Culture: the Metamorphosis of Natural Theology in the Christian Encounter with Hellenism* (New Haven and London, 1993), esp. 1–21, 169–83; also more generally W. Jaeger, *Early Christianity and Greek Paideia* (Cambridge, MA, 1961).

103. Cf. Brown, *Power and Persuasion*, 122–23, S. MacCormack, *The Shadows of Poetry: Vergil in the Mind of Augustine* (Berkeley, CA, 1998). Also see R.A. Markus, 'Paganism,

Christianity and the Latin Classics in the Fourth Century', in J.W. Binns, ed., *Latin Literature of the Fourth Century* (London, 1974), 1–21.

104. Alföldi, *Die Kontorniaten*, 48–84; also see Alföldi, Alföldi and Clay, *Die Kontorniat-Medallions*, vol. 2, 25–62.

105. Alföldi, Alföldi and Clay, *Die Kontorniat-Medallions*, vol. 1, nos 23–26, 194.

106. Musso, *Manifattura suntuaria*, 106–35.

107. Musso, *Manifattura suntuaria*, 146–48.

108. Cameron, 'Distribution and Ownership', 178–85, has argued this case convincingly against similar suggestions made by Kenneth Painter.

109. Musso, *Manifattura suntuaria*, 131.

110. A. Cameron, 'Paganism and Literature in Late Fourth Century Rome', in M. Fuhrmann, ed., *Christianisme et formes littéraires de l'antiquité tardive en Occident*, Entretiens Fondation Hardt 23 (Geneva, 1977) ,1–30; idem, 'The Latin Revival of the Fourth Century', in W. Treadgold, ed., *Renaissances Before the Renaissance: Cultural Revivals of Late Antiquity and the Middle Ages* (Stanford, 1984), 42–58; idem, 'The Last Pagans of Rome' in W.V. Harris, ed., *The Transformations of Urbs Roma in Late Antiquity*, *JRA* Supplement 33 (Portsmouth, RI, 1999), 109–21.

111. Volbach, *Elfenbeinarbeiten der Spätantike*, no. 50, 39.

112. Cf. Comments by L. Stirling in her review of Kiilerich, *Late Fourth Century Classicism*, in *JRA* 8 (1995), 538.

113. On the cult of Cybele generally see H. Graillot, *Le Culte de Cybéle mère des dieux à Rome et dans l'Empire romain* (Paris, 1912); M.J. Vermaseren, *Cybele and Attis: the Myth and the Cult* (London, 1977). The late antique evidence (esp. inscriptions by members of the senatorial aristocracy commemorating the performance of the Taurobolium) is discussed by Smith, *Julian's Gods*, 172–76.

114. A. Cameron, 'The Date and Identity of Macrobius', *JRS* 56 (1966), 25–38. For an overview of Macrobius studies see P. De Paolis, 'Macrobio 1934–1984', *Lustrum* 28/29 (1986/87), 107–249.

115. Macrobius, *Saturnalia* 1.17.

116. The bearded Apollo is mentioned in Lucian's account of the cults at Hierapolis, *De Dea Syria* 35. His statue is said to stand behind the throne of Helios in the temple of the Syrian goddess, who herself is interpreted as a syncretism of different Greek goddesses (Hera, Athena, Aphrodite, Selene, Rhea, Artemis, Nemesis and the Fates), and whose statue combines a selection of their different attributes (*De Dea Syria* 33).

117. Macrobius, *Saturnalia* 1.17.68–70. Trans. P.V. Davies (New York, 1969).

118. It is worth noting that this composite character was recognized by the Corbridge Lanx's earliest modern interpreter, Roger Gale in 1735, who rejected any mythological explanation, and considered it 'onely an assemblage of the Deitys it represents' (*sic*). Quoted in Haverfield, 'Roman Silver in Northumberland', 10.

119. Hermes is shown with a similar winged modius and a cadduceus on a fragment of a silver bowl from the Traprain Law hoard: see A.O. Curle, *The Treasure of Traprain*

(Glasgow, 1923), 40. Hermes himself was a focus for syncretism in late antique Egypt in the context of the literature attributed to Hermes Trismegistus: see G. Fowden, *The Egyptian Hermes: a Historical Approach to the Late Pagan Mind* (Cambridge, 1986), 177–86.

120. The epithet of Apollo, 'alexikakos' (warding-off evil) is known chiefly from Pausanias, who says that the Athenians worshipped Apollo under this name in thanks for turning away the plague during the Peloponnesian war. He records a statue of the god under this name in front of the temple of Apollo Patroos in the Athenian Agora, but does not describe it. Paus. I.3.4, VI.24.6, VIII.41.8.

121. Macrobius, *Saturnalia* 1.21.9–10. Trans. adapted from Davies (as above).

122. Julian, *To the Cynic Heraclius (Or. VII)*, 222c (Loeb translation). On the *Hymn to the Mother of the Gods* and its neoplatonic elements see Smith, *Julian's Gods*, 159–62.

123. The response by J.G. Deckers to Daszewski's esoteric interpretation of the mosaic in the House of Aion is a case in point. See 'Dionysos der Erlöser? Bemerkungen zur Deutung der Bodenmosaiken im "Haus des Aion" in Nea-Paphos auf Cypern durch W.A. Daszewski', *Römische Quartelschrift* 81 (1986), 145–72.

124. For full discussion of parallels see Musso, *Manifattura suntuaria*, 25–64.

125. Another manifestation of this in late antique art is the personification of abstract qualities such as Megalopsychia, Euteknia, Dikaiosyne, and Philosophia on mosaics. The first appears on a fifth-century mosaic at Antioch (the Megalopsychia Hunt), the other three as a tableau on an early fourth-century mosaic from the House of the Banquet at Shabba-Philopolis. These are only two of the many Syrian examples. See Levi, *Antioch Mosaic Pavements*, and J. Balty, *Mosaiques Antiques de Syrie* (Brussels, 1977), 42–43. The qualities represented on these mosaics belong to the ethical, moral aspect of *paideia*, rather than the aspect of religious tradition that we have been looking at on silver, but they allow us to suppose that abstract and allegorical modes of viewing would have come easily to more than a minority of the elite.

126. The images of the Nereids and Oceanus which also form part of the decoration of the Great Dish are equally generic, and can be found on sarcophagi, mosaics, textiles and silver of this period (e.g. the Projecta casket, the Conçesti Amphora).

127. Bowersock, *Hellenism in Late Antiquity*, 41.

128. See the essays in N. Hopkinson, ed., *Studies in the Dionysiaca of Nonnus*, Camb. Phil. Soc. Suppl. Vol. 17 (Cambridge, 1994); W. Liebeschuetz, 'The Use of Pagan Mythology in the Christian Empire with Particular Reference to the *Dionysiaca* of Nonnus', in P. Allen and E.M. Jeffreys, eds, *The Sixth Century – End or Beginning?*, Byzantina Australiensia 10 (Brisbane, 1996), 75–91, esp. 76–81.

129. Bowersock, *Hellenism in Late Antiquity*, 41–42; idem, 'Dionysos as Epic Hero' and P. Chuvin, 'Local Traditions and Classical Mythology in the *Dionysiaca*', both in Hopkinson, ed., *Studies in the Dionysiaca*, 156–66, 167–76.

130. A strong argument for the secular character of the *Dionysiaca* is given by Liebeschuetz, 'The Use of Pagan Mythology', 77, 81–84.

131. A. Cameron, *Claudian: Poetry and Propaganda at the Court of Honorius* (Oxford, 1970), 189–227.

132. Cameron, *Claudian*, 194. On the Projecta casket see Shelton, *The Esquiline Treasure*, no. 1, 72–75; and the discussion in Elsner, *Art and the Roman Viewer*, 251–55.

133. Claudian, *Panegyricus de Quarto Consulatu Honorii Augusti*, ll 602–607, ed. and trans. W. Barr, Translated Texts for Historians, Latin Series 2 (Liverpool, 1981).

134. Silver: Toynbee and Painter, 'Picture Plates', nos 39–42 are four plates with Dionysiac imagery dating to the sixth to seventh centuries. Textiles: a square wool emblema with Dionysus and a Satyr surrounded with cultic paraphernalia in the Museum of Fine Arts, Boston could date anywhere between the fifth and seventh centuries (Rutschowscaya, *Tissus Coptes*, 19); also see V.F. Lenzen, *The Triumph of Dionysos on Textiles of Late Antique Egypt* (Los Angeles and Berkeley, CA, 1960). Ivory: the sixth-century carvings incorporated in the pulpit of Henry II in Aachen Cathedral (Volbach, *Elfenbeinarbeiten der Spätantike*, nos 72–77).

135. As suggested by Painter in Kent and Painter, *Wealth of the Roman World*, 33.

4

4

The persistence of *paideia*: the David Plates and the transformation of the secular in early Byzantium

In the Kunsthistorisches Museum in Vienna there is a silver bucket or *situla*, discovered in 1814 in Kuczurmare (to the east of the Carpathian Mountains, now in the Ukraine). It is decorated in relief with a frieze of six pairs of mythological figures: Hercules and Minerva, Apollo and Diana, and a third less easily identifiable pair, who are possibly Venus and Adonis (Fig. 4.1).[1] The figures are executed in a style that is recognisable as an example of late antique classicism, while some evoke classical models more directly: the pose of Hercules, for example, clearly imitates the much-copied Lysippean form used (for instance) in Farnese Hercules of the early third-century AD. The bucket's non-narrative display of pairs of related mythological figures is reminiscent of the scene on Corbridge Lanx, which it also resembles stylistically. One could be forgiven for suggesting, on the basis of a stylistic and iconographic comparison, that the Kuczurmare situla must be close to the Corbridge Lanx in date. In fact, the underside of the situla carries a set of control stamps which date it to between 613 and 629–30 AD, in the reign of the Byzantine emperor Heraclius.[2] What are the implications of this extraordinarily late date for our understanding of late antique silver? Initially it suggests that, in the eastern part of the empire at least, the culture of *paideia* continued to influence the decoration of silver plate into a period which many historians have considered after the 'end' of late antiquity and the 'beginning' of the middle ages proper.[3] This is a period when, we are told, mythological poetry (like Nonnus' *Dionysiaca* of the fifth century AD) was no longer being written, and mythological allusions disappeared from other types of writing.[4] In the previous chapter, I argued that in the fourth and fifth centuries the generic imagery associated with a god such as Dionysus had occupied a neutral ground, where it was acceptable in a domestic context to both pagans and Christians. Yet the decoration of the Kuczurmare situla consists of a mini-pantheon. Its assemblage of gods in statuesque poses can perhaps be compared most productively with early Byzantine collections of classical statuary, such as that of Theodosius II's chamberlain Lausus in fifth-century Constantinople.[5] Nor is this an isolated example: a total of 11 pieces of silverware carry control stamps of the sixth and seventh centuries and display the same continuity with the fourth- and fifth-century repertoire of

4.1 Kuczurmare
Situla, Vienna,
Kunst-
historisches
Museum

classicizing mythological imagery.[6] Among these is the plate in the Hermitage showing Meleager and Atalanta departing for the hunt, a subject also featured on the fourth-century Sevso Meleager plate (Figs 3.8, 3.9).[7] Another plate in the Hermitage depicts a mythological scene traditionally known as 'Venus in the Tent of Anchises', where Venus appears in the same long-sleeved robe and Phrygian cap that she wears in the Kuczurmare situla (Fig. 4.2).[8] A Justinianic plate recalls the traditions of classical pastoral with its elegant image of a shepherd with his dog and two goats in a landscape (Fig. 4.3).[9] Generic Dionysiac and marine imagery are also well-represented, and adorn some of the latest surviving examples of Byzantine silver plate – a jug with nereids

4.2 Plate with mythological scene, so-called 'Venus in the tent of Anchises', St Petersburg, Hermitage Museum

riding sea monsters (Fig. 4.4), and a trulla with similar marine scenes, both of which were stamped in the reign of Constans II (641–651 AD).[10]

The apparent continuity of the classical tradition of Hellenism between the fourth and the seventh centuries presented by this aspect of early Byzantine domestic silverware is at variance with the conventional image of Byzantine art and society in this period. The latter represents Christian discourse and the religious image increasingly coming to dominate all areas of life, including domestic life.[11] The silver suggests that a secular culture survived in the eastern empire into the first half of the seventh century. This has wide-reaching implications for our understanding of the nature of Christianization in early Byzantium, since historians have identified the disappearance of the cultural category of the secular as one of the key developments which mark

4.3 Plate
with Goatherd
from Klimova,
St Petersburg,
Hermitage
Museum

the transformation from the 'classical' to the 'mediaeval' world.[12] Without
necessarily questioning the general validity of this premise, it should also
be noted that much work in this area has been predominately text-based.
Domestic art offers an alternative perspective from which to assess effect
of Christianization on the private sphere in early Byzantium. It has been
suggested, for example, that the reign of Justinian in the sixth century marked
a watershed in the Christianization of the Byzantine empire, when the realm
of the secular was increasingly permeated by Christianity and its rhetoric.[13]
However, as we have seen, classical mythological imagery did not disappear
from domestic silver plate in the sixth century, but continued to be used
through into the seventh century. In fact, it is the silver of the seventh century,
especially that produced in the reign of Heraclius (610–641 AD), which offers
the richest material for understanding the transformation of the secular art of

the domestic sphere in the early Byzantine period and gives new perspectives on the Christianization of Byzantium.

The quantity of stamped silver surviving from the reign of Heraclius exceeds that remaining from the reign of any other emperor except Justinian.[14] While this may be a result of accidents of survival, it nevertheless offers us a broad base from which to draw conclusions.[15] It is also notable that only two out of a total of 38 objects can clearly be identified as serving a liturgical or sacred function; again, this cannot be seen as representative of the period as a whole, but it means that we are dealing with a large sample of domestic silver plate. This silver encompasses a variety of different types of decoration, for while vessels with mythological imagery are an important aspect of early Byzantine silver, they do not represent the only type of domestic silver to be produced in this period. Instead, they should be considered alongside a group of less elaborate silver vessels which survive in far greater quantities than those with mythological scenes: the 'cross-monogram plates', plain circular plates with a slightly concave surface, a rounded rim and a foot-ring, their only decoration consisting of a central medallion with a cross or cross-monogram surrounded by a wreath or scroll executed in niello (Figs 4.5, 4.6). The earliest datable example of this type is from the reign of Anastasius (491–518 AD), and they are produced throughout the sixth century but survive in much greater numbers after 578.[16] There are in total fourteen stamped examples from the reign of Heraclius, the largest single category of vessel among the stamped silverware of his reign. Marlia Mango has argued convincingly for the domestic function of these plates, pointing out that early Byzantine patens (with which they have sometimes been identified) are shaped quite differently, with a flat inner surface and high raised sides, while the decoration of patens occupies a much larger proportion of the interior surface and is usually accompanied by a dedicatory inscription. Furthermore the monograms which characterize many of the plates can be seen as a typical feature of private dining vessels; sets of monogrammed plates appear, for example, in the fourth-century Esquiline Treasure.[17]

The cross-monogram plates present a very different perspective on the Christianization of the domestic sphere from that offered by the mythological silverware with which they are contemporary. They are highly standardized in their sizes and decoration and were probably produced in quite large quantities.[18] Their production required a less skilled craftsmanship than that of silver decorated in relief. What does it mean, therefore, that the cross – either in itself or as a bearer of the owner's name – was chosen for their sole decoration? Here silverware does seem to reflect Christianity's encroachment upon the realm of the secular in the private sphere, which has been observed in other aspects of early Byzantine society. This can be seen by comparing the cross-monogram plates with earlier domestic silver decorated with Christian symbols. There are numerous examples of domestic silver of the fourth century decorated with the chi-rho symbol, either as the primary decoration of the object – as on the spoons in the Mildenhall and Hoxne hoards (Figs 2.6, 2.7) – or as part of a larger decorative scheme, as on the Sevso Hunting Dish,

4.4   Jug with Nereid riding Sea Monster, St Petersburg, Hermitage Museum

4.5   Plate with cross-monogram in ivy-wreath, New York, Metropolitan Museum, stamped between 610 and 613 (The Metropolitan Museum of Art, Fletcher Fund, 1952 [52.25.2])

4.6   Plate with cross in ivy-wreath, London, British Museum, stamped between 578 and 582 (© The British Museum)

where it punctuates the inscription encircling the central figural medallion (Fig. I.1). These suggest that the erosion of the secular in the private sphere began much earlier than the sixth century. However, the different stages in this complex process should be distinguished. In the fourth century, the use of the chi-rho symbol on silver can be seen as an advertisement of the owner's Christianity at a time when, although on the ascendant and imperially supported, Christianity was by no means universal in Roman society. Although the display of such symbols of religious affiliation in a non-religious context marks an important shift in the visual culture of the Roman world, this is because – as Jaś Elsner has argued – the objects bearing these symbols were not restricted to an initiate audience, but could be seen and used 'by anti-pagan Christians ... by anti-Christian pagans ... and by anyone in between'.[19] By the seventh century this spectrum of viewers could be said to have contracted considerably, and the situation consequently reverses itself: all viewers and users of the cross-monogram plates are (or can be assumed to be) initiates, since they are members of a society that only recognizes one religion, Christianity. The cross symbolizes Christianity as the norm rather than the exception.

How can we reconcile the evidence offered by the Kuczurmare situla and related items, of the survival from the fourth to the seventh century of the secular use of traditional mythological imagery in the private sphere, with the transformations over the same period that we see in the decoration of the cross-monogram plates? One approach would be to see the 'cultural contradictions' of a society in transition between classical and Christian traditions, which Averil Cameron has traced for the reign of Justinian, as continuing into the seventh century.[20] It is perhaps possible to argue that such contradictions were always to some extent present in a society that saw itself at once as the preserver of the Roman Empire and as the centre of the Christian world. For although there was clearly some contraction of the secular sphere in this period, the evidence that we have suggests that a different sort of transformation occurred in comparison to that in the West. To understand fully the character of this transformation in Byzantium, a study in its own right is needed – ideally one that puts equal weight on artistic and textual evidence. Here I can only focus briefly on one difference between the East and the West that is particularly significant in this context: education.

The previous chapter outlined the connection between the secular culture of Hellenism and the education of the elite classes in the Roman Empire in grammar and rhetoric. This education system appears to have come to an end in the West after the 530s, a result of the damage inflicted on the senatorial class in the Gothic wars and later by Justinian's war of reconquest, both of which encouraged an exodus of aristocrats to the East. Education in the West became (and for much of the middle ages there remained) the preserve of the monasteries, which developed a new curriculum based on Christian texts.[21] In the East however, education was never Christianized in the same way. Schools continued to remain outside the control of the Church (at least until the eleventh or twelfth century), and were never associated

with monasteries.[22] There was also little change in the curriculum: grammar and rhetoric continued to be taught, and we probably owe the survival of the progymnasmata and related rhetorical treatises to their continued use in Byzantine schools.[23] The continuity of the structures and substance of traditional Graeco-Roman education in Byzantium makes the use of classical subjects to decorate silverware in the sixth and seventh centuries less surprising than it at first appears. It also suggests that the role of traditional education as an instrument of elite self-definition and cohesion, which could be projected through the luxury art of the domestic sphere, lasted longer in the Byzantine world than some scholars have allowed.[24]

The acceptability of the traditional Graeco-Roman education for the Christian society of Byzantium, where some of its main beneficiaries were clerics, suggests that the secular underwent a transformation but was not

4.7 The David Plates: *Fight between David and Goliath,* New York, Metropolitan Museum (The Metropolitan Museum of Art, Gift of J. Pierpont Morgan, 1917 [17.190.396])

completely effaced or rejected. It should be possible, therefore, to identify points of intersection between the persistence of *paideia* in the silver of the first half of the seventh century and the Christianized domestic sphere implicit in the cross-monogram plates. The David Plates, also produced in the early seventh century, like the Kuczurmare situla and many of the cross-monogram plates, provide a unique insight into the way in which the classical culture of *paideia* and the new all-embracing Christian culture could interact on a highly sophisticated level. These plates, which are the most outstanding examples of silverware surviving from the early middle ages, play an important role in helping us to understand the nature of the transformation of the secular in early Byzantium. They comprise a set of nine plates in three different sizes: one large plate (diameter 49.4 cm), four medium size plates (diameter 26 cm) and four small plates (diameter 14 cm) (Figs 4.7–4.15). The shape of each is similar, with a slightly concave surface, a rolled rim, and a high foot-ring. Each plate is marked on the reverse inside the foot-ring with control stamps from the years 613–629/30 in the reign of Heraclius.[25] Between them, the plates depict a series of events in the early life of David, as related in chapters 16.12–18.27 of the Old Testament book 1 Samuel (in the Septuagint, 1 Kings), from David's anointing by Samuel to his fight with Goliath and his marriage to Saul's daughter. The most important event of the narrative is clearly the battle with Goliath, which is depicted in three registers on the largest plate (Fig. 4.7). The top register shows David's challenge to Goliath, the central register (where the figures are largest) the combat between the two, with Israelite and Philistine soldiers as spectators, and the lower register shows David decapitating Goliath. The four medium-sized plates depict ceremonial events: the anointing of David by Samuel (Fig. 4.8), the introduction of David to Saul (Fig. 4.9), Saul arming David (Fig. 4.10), and the marriage of David and Michal (Fig. 4.11), over which Saul presides. The four smallest plates depict David fighting a lion and a bear (Figs 4.12, 4.13), a harp-playing David summoned by a messenger to be anointed (Fig. 4.14), and David in conversation with a soldier, whose identity is much disputed (Fig. 4.15).

The Second Cyprus Treasure, of which the David Plates form part, was discovered in 1902 in the ruins of the Byzantine town of Lambousa, where a few years earlier another hoard of sixth- and seventh-century Byzantine silver, known as the First Cyprus Treasure, had been found.[26] In both cases the hoards were discovered casually by labourers from the nearby village of Karavas who were quarrying the ruins for building stone. As well as the David Plates, the Second Cyprus Treasure contained at least two cross-monogram plates and a quantity of elaborate gold jewellery.[27] According to the son of one of the finders, the jewellery was discovered in a pot hidden beneath a floor, while the plates were found walled up in a niche.[28] No investigation of the findspot was ever carried out by archaeologists, and some uncertainty must remain as to whether the two caches were the property of the same individual and even whether they were concealed at the same time. The finders did not report their discovery to the Cypriot authorities. On learning of it subsequently, the authorities managed to confiscate three of the David Plates, as well as the two

cross-monogram plates and a few small items of jewellery which are now in the Museum of Antiquities in Nicosia. The rest was smuggled out of Cyprus and sold to a dealer in Paris, where most of it was bought by J. Pierpoint Morgan for a large sum and given by his heirs to the Metropolitan Museum of Art, New York, which today owns six of the David Plates, one plate with a niello cross monogram, and much of the jewellery. Dumbarton Oaks acquired a gold encolpium medallion and a girdle of gold medallions and solidi.[29]

The David Plates differ from other late antique silver in two key ways. First, the nine plates combine to form a narrative sequence, instead of that sequence being contained on a single vessel, as we saw with the representation of the upbringing of Achilles on the Kaiseraugst Achilles plate. Vessels produced as a set with related imagery are known, but in these cases the relationship between them is thematic rather than narrative.[30] Second, the narrative which the nine David Plates depict is taken from the Old Testament. The only other

4.8   The David Plates: *Samuel anoints David in the presence of his father and brothers*, New York, Metropolitan Museum (The Metropolitan Museum of Art, Gift of J. Pierpont Morgan, 1917 [17.190.398])

4.9 The David Plates: *David is introduced to Saul*, New York, Metropolitan Museum (The Metropolitan Museum of Art, Gift of J. Pierpont Morgan, 1917 [17.190.397])

type of silver object where scenes from the Old Testament are depicted is the reliquary casket, which typically features single scenes like the Hebrews in the Furnace or Daniel in the Lions' Den, but not complex narratives.[31] Reliquary caskets had a sacred function, but it seems likely that the David Plates – which in shape resemble contemporary plates decorated with mythological imagery and the cross-monogram plates, and not the forms of liturgical vessels in this period – were not intended for use in an ecclesiastical context, especially if both plates and jewellery in the Second Cyprus Treasure were the property of the same person.[32] Not surprisingly, the David Plates have been the subject of considerable scholarly attention. Most of this has been concerned with the sources of the plates' iconography, its interpretation and issues of patronage and ownership. This chapter's approach to the plates is very different as it considers them in the context of other contemporary silver, and focuses on the contribution that they can make to our understanding of the Christianization of the domestic sphere. In effect, it is a critique of the prevailing academic opinion of the plates' meaning and function – until now unchallenged – which sees them in the context of imperial self-representation, rather than in the tradition of silverware in the domestic sphere. But first, some discussion of the conventional interpretation of David Plates is necessary, if only to show why an alternative approach is desirable.

Imperial readings of the David Plates and their problems

After their 1906 publication by O.M. Dalton, the David Plates were often cited in discussions of Byzantine art, but were not studied as an independent entity until the 1970s, when a series of five articles by different authors appeared.[33] Apart from Kurt Weitzmann's 'Prolegomena', which was concerned only with the iconographic sources for the plates' imagery, all attempted to make connections between the subject matter of the David Plates and the emperor Heraclius during whose reign they were produced, as the control stamps indicate. Although they differ in details, the authors of these articles all agree that Heraclius was the most likely patron of this set of plates, which are thought to evoke certain key victories in his reign (his overthrow of his imperial predecessor Phocas; his fight in single combat with the Persian champion Razatis; and his ultimate victory in the Persian wars have all been proposed). Although it is sometimes suggested that the plates were for Heraclius' own use, more often they are envisaged as a commemorative gift to a high-ranking court official (or, according to one interpretation, a cleric).[34] In effect the plates are seen as a form of largitio, in the tradition of the Missorium of Theodosius and related fourth-century plates. Is the analogy with fourth-century largitio silver really valid, however? Marlia Mango stated the problem astutely when she wrote: 'If the theory that the plates refer to Byzantine imperial victory and were made for imperial distribution is correct, then the subtlety of their message is a marked departure from the overt imperial images and legends adorning fourth-century largitio silver.'[35] To see these plates as largitio would imply that the form in which the emperor represented himself on official art had changed radically since the fourth century. That the forms of imperial self-representation had changed somewhat over this period certainly cannot be denied, but when we compare the David Plates with the coinage of Heraclius, we can find little evidence of the close iconographic relationship that existed between fourth-century largitio plates and contemporary coinage. Nor does the coinage of Heraclius match the 'subtlety' of the David Plates: obverses feature frontal portraits of the emperor and his sons, reverses a cross on a stepped base.[36] To see the David Plates as largitio in the fourth-century sense, when largitio vessels were produced in workshops connected to the imperial mint, is clearly problematic. In any case, the available evidence suggests that the institution of largitio was in decline by the end of the sixth century.[37] Imperial gold medallions of multiple solidus weights (a form of largitio

4.10 The David
Plates: *Saul arms
David*, New York,
Metropolitan
Museum (The
Metropolitan
Museum of Art,
Gift of J. Pierpont
Morgan, 1917
[17.190.399])

of which there are examples surviving beyond the fourth century) become
increasingly rare after the mid-fifth century, with only four sixth-century
types known, the latest of which is the 8-solidus medallion of Maurice,
probably issued for his first consulship in 583. This medallion is known from
four examples, which form part of the girdle found with the jewellery of the
Second Cyprus Treasure. Its iconography of the emperor in the consular toga
with a mappa and sceptre on the obverse, and riding in a quadriga with a
victory on a globe on the reverse, follows the standard late-Roman tradition
of consular iconography.[38] The largitio model must therefore be approached
with caution as the David Plates are so different both from fourth-century
largitio silver and the gold largitio medallions which are closer to them in
date, and since there is so little evidence for the operation of that institution in
the seventh century.

However, the interpretation of the plates as largitio is only one aspect of the problematic reading of them as imperial art. There are several ways in which scholars define works of art as 'imperial'. The term can encompass art made for an emperor's private use, for public display in his palace, as a gift to him or from him, or a number of variations within these parameters.[39] Usually such definitions depend on some clear evidence to associate the artwork with an emperor, like the presence of his image or an inscription, or information about its production or commission. Factors such as the quality of workmanship and the cost of materials can also argue for a work of art's availability being restricted to the emperor and senior members of his family and court.[40] What sort of evidence is available to associate the David Plates with Heraclius? The idea that the plates might have been largitio has already been questioned as

4.11 The David Plates: *Marriage of David and Michal*, Nicosia, Archaeological Museum (Department of Antiquities, Cyprus)

4.12 The
David Plates:
*David fights
lion*, New York,
Metropolitan
Museum (The
Metropolitan
Museum of Art,
Gift of J. Pierpont
Morgan, 1917
[17.190.394])

unproven. Nor do the plates bear Heraclius' name or his image, except on the control stamps on their reverses which are found on many other silver objects of this period that no-one would think of associating with the emperor. While a case for an imperial connection could be made through the superlative quality of the David Plates, this has rarely been more than implicit in the literature on them. An argument for imperial ownership from value has been made, using an extension of Philip Grierson's assertion that the girdle of gold medallions and solidi in the Second Cyprus Treasure could only have been afforded by a very small number of dignitaries in the empire.[41] But the majority of scholars has chosen to substantiate the case for the imperial associations of the David Plates iconographically, seeing the figure of David as standing for Heraclius. These interpretations combine modern perceptions of the historical analogies between David and Heraclius with textual evidence of contemporary modes

4.13 The David Plates: *David fights bear*, Nicosia, Archaeological Museum
(Department of Antiquities, Cyprus)

4.14 The David Plates: *David is approached by messenger while playing the harp*, Nicosia,
Archaeological Museum (Department of Antiquities, Cyprus)

of praising the emperor. Can the individual arguments which have been made in this context support the association of Heraclius with the plates?

Van Grunsven-Eygenraam, in her study of the David Plates, develops what she sees as 'the analogy between the persons of the biblical champion, David, and the emperor Heraclius, [and] the analogous course of events in both lives.'[42] In particular she refers to the circumstances under which Heraclius overthrew his predecessor Phocas in 610. He was invited to do so by the Senate of Constantinople, the Deme of the Greens and the patriarch Sergius. After Phocas was defeated, he was captured and beheaded. Shortly after ascending the throne, his first wife having died, Heraclius married again. Van Grunsven-Eygenraam proceeds to identify these episodes with different plates: the appeal to Heraclius is represented by the Anointing and the Harp-Playing scene; the actual overthrow by the fight with Goliath; Heraclius' marriage by David's marriage; his friendship with the patriarch Sergius by the covenant of Jonathan with David (her reading of the arming plate).[43] An obvious problem with this interpretation is that some plates make better analogies to events in Heraclius' life than others: the marriage and the fight with Goliath are at least plausible, but the anointing, the harp-playing or the covenant with Jonathan are less persuasive. Moreover in the case of these last two plates, van Grunsven-Eygenraam's identification of the subject matter is eccentric and has not found any adherents.

Wander, whose article on the David Plates was published in the same year as that of van Grunsven-Eygenraam, suggests another historical event in Heraclius' reign which the plates might evoke. During the long war which Heraclius fought against the Sassanian rulers of Persia from 621–628 AD

4.15 The David Plates: *David in conversation with soldier*, New York, Metropolitan Museum (The Metropolitan Museum of Art, Gift of J. Pierpont Morgan, 1917 [17.190.395])

he was challenged to single combat by the Persian general Razatis, whom he fought successfully and beheaded.[44] The analogy with the combat of David and Goliath is clear. Unlike van Grunsven-Eygenraam, Wander does not ascribe individual meanings to the other eight plates; these provide the narrative context for the combat with Goliath. The historical analogy lies with the central event – single combat with the enemy champion – depicted on the largest plate. Although none of the Byzantine sources which describe the duel makes the comparison between Heraclius and David, Wander later found a reference to Heraclius as 'a second David' in a seventh-century Merovingian chronicle which recorded this event.[45]

Alexander also sees the war against the Persians as central to an understanding of the David Plates. But rather than trying to connect the narrative of the plates with specific events in the Persian war, as Wander does, she focuses on how the identification between David and Heraclius was 'nurtured' during that period. As an example, she cites a sermon delivered by Theodore Synkellos in 627 to commemorate the anniversary of the lifting of the Avar siege of Constantinople the previous year, where Heraclius is compared to David:

For our *basileus* is also [like] David in his piety toward the divine and in his gentleness. But may the Lord crown him with victories, just as with David; may he make his son who reigns with him [Heraclius Constantine, regent in Constantinople in his father's absence] both wise and peaceful like Solomon, granting him piety and orthodoxy, just as with his father.

Alexander also believes that analogies are to be found between Heraclius' restitution of the True Cross (which had been captured by the Persians) to Jerusalem at the end of the war, and David's installation of the Ark of the Covenant there after it had been recovered from captivity (2:Sam.6), despite a lack of contemporary comparisons of Heraclius with David in this context (although the Cross and the Ark are compared).[46] It is somewhat hard to see how this latter episode can be relevant to the David Plates, since it is not portrayed on the plates and occurs much later in the biblical narrative than the events which the plates do depict. Thus the choice of the early episodes in David's life for the narrative on the plates is not really accounted for. The comparison between David and Heraclius made by Theodore Synkellos, on the other hand, does not refer to any specific event in the life of David, but suggests that because Heraclius' shares David's virtues, he will also share his rewards, namely God-given victory over his enemies. Part of the reason that Alexander focuses on the period of the Persian wars is because she favours a date for the plates at the very end of the span provided by the control stamps. She argues that if the plates had been made before 621, they would have been confiscated to fund the war effort, that they are unlikely to have been made during the war, and must therefore be a production of the years 628–629/30. In fact we know only that the patriarch Sergius appropriated the silver reserves of the churches in Constantinople on Heraclius' behalf for the war effort; there is no evidence of confiscation from private individuals, though it is possible that silver would have been in short supply during the Persian wars.[47]

Trilling, like Alexander, focuses predominately on the role of texts from the reign of Heraclius to understand the function of the plates. But instead of looking for specific references to David or analogies with particular events, he compares the visual metaphors used on the plates to associate David with heroes of Classical antiquity and the Byzantine emperor (the classicizing style, the imperial iconography of the ceremonial scenes), with the metaphorical techniques of seventh-century Byzantine court poetry, especially that of George of Pisidia. Underlining the way that George combines the Christian and Classical traditions to celebrate Heraclius' victories over the Persians and the Avars, he argues that 'both poet and silversmith base their work on three elements, biblical, classical and imperial, each of which serves as a commentary on the others'.[48] The battle with Goliath is chosen as the focal point of the narrative on the plates because it represents victory, not as a historical event, but as an emblem of the ruler's need for unceasing watchfulness and vigour to preserve his kingdom and protect his people. In Trilling's view, both the plates and the poetry articulate this concept of victory in a similar fashion, employing the range of cultural resources at their disposal. This is by far the most subtle of the four arguments – yet Trilling still depends on the largitio theory for his initial association of the plates with the emperor.

The problems implicit in these readings are highlighted in a recent critique of the way later representations of David in Byzantine art have been understood. John Hanson, in his unpublished PhD dissertation, has noted that modern scholars have most often understood the function of Old Testament imagery in the middle Byzantine period as a type of *speculum principis* (that is, a model of qualities desirable in a ruler), and has identified what he describes as 'a sort of virulent strain of the notion of the *speculum principis*', whereby characters from the Old Testament are proposed to refer to specific rulers and specific events, rather than general types.[49] This idea lies behind van Grunsven-Eygenraam's and Wander's readings of the plates, and to a lesser extent Alexander's and Trilling's, although they associate the plates more with Heraclius in general than with any specific event(s) in his reign. Focusing on the interpretation of the Palazzo Venezia Casket, a ninth-century ivory box with scenes from the life of David around its sides, an image of an emperor and empress crowned by Christ on the lid, together with an honorific inscription addressed to the imperial couple (Fig. 4.16), Hanson's study shows that the interpretation of the David Plates is an issue of wider relevance for Byzantine art and raises questions about the plates' relationship to a later example of Byzantine luxury art. Hanson cites two theories concerning the Palazzo Venezia Casket: the first sees the David narrative as a standard flattering allusion to the mystic coronation of the emperor and empress represented on the lid, with no reference to a specific emperor, and the second interprets it as an allegory of the succession of Basil I (869–886) to Michael III, justifying his compliance in the latter's murder and identifying the unnamed emperor on the lid accordingly.[50] In each case, Hanson demonstrates that modern scholars have perceived the David narrative in Byzantine society as having a fixed meaning, which could be employed as a commentary on the current emperor

4.16 Palazzo Venezia Casket, Rome, Palazzo Venezia (A. Cutler)

to enhance his status.[51] However, he suggests that the comparison should be seen to operate in the other direction, with the emperor as the 'constant and immutable reality' modifying the meaning of David.[52]

There are several relevant points here for the David Plates. All four interpretations of the plates outlined above consider the plates' narrative as a comment on Heraclius' achievements (whether these be overthrowing Phocas, fighting Razatis, or winning the war against the Persians). These differing views are all problematic, as suggested, because there is no clear evidence that the primary purpose of these plates was to make a statement about Heraclius. However, following Hanson, we may ask: to what extent is the image of the emperor used to modify the biblical narrative of David on the plates? The figures on the plates certainly wear contemporary costume rather than some imagined version of biblical costume. David appears consistently in a short tunic with segmenta, boots and a cloak, except in the arming scene where he wears a cuirass and cloak in the Roman military tradition (Fig. 4.10), and in the marriage scene where he wears a long-sleeved tunic and full-length cloak with a diagonally placed segmentum at waist-height, fastened at the shoulder with a cross-bow fibula (Fig. 4.11). But while this is Byzantine costume, it is not specifically imperial. Only in the marriage scene does David acquire the costume of a court dignitary (the long cloak with segmentum and the fibula). This plate is clearly meant to represent the immediate outcome of his victory over Goliath: marriage with Saul's daughter and a place of honour at court. David's role as future king of Israel is conveyed less by his clothing than by the nimbus that he bears in every scene except that of the anointing. Saul also is nimbed and might seem like another promising candidate to be depicted as a Byzantine emperor. When David is presented to him, he appears sitting on a cushioned seat on a dais in the centre of an arcaded pediment and is shown on a larger scale than the other figures (Fig. 4.9). He wears a long cloak with a segmentum and a long-sleeved tunic. However his cloak is fastened by a cross-bow fibula, and on his head he wears a plain band as a diadem. If we compare this with the representation of Theodosius and his two co-emperors on the Missorium of Theodosius (Fig. 1.1), as scholars have frequently done, or Justinian in the San Vitale mosaics (Fig. 1.13), we can observe several significant differences: in both cases the emperors wear circular fibulae decorated with jewels and pearls, not cross-bow fibulae. On their heads, the emperors on the Missorium have pearl diadems while Justinian wears an elaborate jewelled crown. Justinian's attendants, and the official receiving a codicil on the Missorium, wear cross-bow fibulae which here clearly mark their lesser rank. Thus, while the plate of the presentation to Saul clearly borrows from the iconography of late Roman ceremonial – as exemplified in the Missorium of Theodosius – using features like ceremonial architecture, frontality, a large central enthroned figure, and flanking body guards, it does not employ specific details of imperial costume, in contrast to the Palazzo Venezia casket.[53] The modification of the biblical narrative through imperial ceremonial is of a more general character, which seems to preclude a close identification of either David or Saul with the Byzantine emperor. Instead the court of Saul is seen through the lens of contemporary perceptions of the ceremonial appropriate to any court, which naturally derived from that of the Byzantine emperor. This may well have reminded the Byzantine viewer that Saul and David were precursors of the emperor in his role of monarch sanctioned by God, but does not lend itself to any closer reading.

Another aspect of the iconography of the David Plates which has been over-interpreted as imperial is the group of a basket flanked by two bags, which appears in the exergue of the presentation and marriage plates. The bags are tied at the neck and the basket is shown full of small round objects resembling coins. Weitzmann was the first to suggest that these items, which do not appear in the manuscript tradition of these scenes, are taken from the representation of the *sparsio* (the scattering of money among the people) on consular diptychs.[54] Wander follows his argument when he suggests that they are meant to represent the reward offered by Saul to the slayer of Goliath, but in the process misunderstands the imagery of the consular diptychs. He describes *sparsio* as 'the money distributed to the Roman populace at the *imperial* games' (my italics), and goes on to say that on diptychs, '*sparsio* carries associations of victory and regal munificence'.[55] However the games depicted on the consular diptychs are not necessarily imperial; they are those hosted by the consul – who might or might not be the emperor – on taking office. It was the major financial obligation of the office to fund these games, their prizes and the accompanying largesse to the populace who attended.[56] Diptychs frequently represent the money given at the games to commemorate this munificence on the part of the consul. It is more common to find non-imperial consuls commemorating their own munificence in this way: although the Codex Calendar of 354 shows Constantius II as consul with a stream of coins flowing from his hand, there are no surviving diptychs that represent the emperor thus.[57] The consuls on the diptychs in their official robes, presiding over the games from a dais, framed with an architectural pediment, are a reminder that the iconography of late antique ceremonial – as used in the presentation and marriage plates – was not restricted to an imperial context.[58] Ceremonial was a feature of official life in late antiquity and early Byzantium which achieved its most elaborate forms in the imperial court but was not restricted to them.[59] The ceremonial iconography of the David Plates therefore does not seem to provide sufficient basis for a strong imperial reading of them, since such imagery could, as we have seen, have non-imperial secular sources.

Re-examining the David Plates in the light of Hanson's analysis of the function of the David narrative on the Palazzo Venezia casket serves to highlight a key difference between the casket and the plates: the casket represents both the emperor and David, while the David Plates do not. It is valid, therefore, to ask in what way the image of the emperor on the casket relates to the scenes from the David narrative which are also part of its decoration. In the case of the David Plates, however, where the emperor is not represented, his covert presence can only be justified by the assumption that the plates were largitio, or a private imperial commission. Such assumptions are based on the quality of the plates, and on their supposed use of imperial iconography, which, as we have just seen, has been over-estimated. Quality too is a difficult factor to judge without securely identified examples of court art from this period.[60] Van Grunsven-Eygenraam's and Wander's readings of the David Plates as referring to specific events in Heraclius' reign suffer from the circularity of this argument – not to mention the common assumption that Roman and Byzantine art is full of 'hidden' messages of imperial propaganda[61] – as to a lesser degree do the readings of Alexander and Trilling. In the face of the absence of evidence to support a strong imperial reading, I would question whether the David Plates do in fact derive their primary meaning from the role of David as the type of an ideal king.

David as emperor

Skeptics may see this criticism of the prevailing scholarship on the David Plates as extending Thomas Mathews' controversial attack on what he

4.17 Monastery of St Catherine, Mt Sinai, medallion bust of David in apse mosaic (courtesy Michigan-Princeton-Alexandria Expedition to Mount Sinai)

terms 'the emperor mystique' in early Christian art – that is, the theory that Christian iconography derived many of its forms and their meanings from imperial imagery.[62] Certainly my analysis of the David Plates seems to support Mathews' claim that imperial readings are often built on insufficient evidence, and has obscured other possible interpretations. Mathews' mistake is in going to the opposite extreme and denying any interpenetration of imperial and Christian imagery. In fact, there is good evidence that the figure of David could serve as a type of the emperor in the early Byzantine period. The mid sixth-century mosaic decoration of the monastery church of St Catherine on Mount Sinai and *codex purpureus* known as the Sinope Gospels represent David in a manner that is clearly imperial. By showing how their representation of David differs from that on the plates, I shall make the case that by the seventh century there was more than one meaning that could be read in the figure of David and the narrative of 1 Samuel. This highlights some of the complexities in the development of Christian imagery that Mathews' rejection of the 'emperor mystique' ignores.

The mosaics of St Catherine of Sinai are located in the church's apse. Within the apse-conch the Transfiguration is depicted, framed by medallion-busts of apostles (along the upper edge) and prophets (along the lower edge). A total of 17 prophets are represented; in the central position, directly below the figure of Christ in the Transfiguration, is a bust of David (Fig. 4.17), labelled with his name (as are all the busts).[63] David is shown as a young, beardless figure with short dark hair. He wears a purple chlamys, fastened at the shoulder (though no fibula is represented), beneath which a white and golden-yellow garment can be seen. On his head he wears a jewelled crown with pearl pendants,

surmounted by a cross. This is clearly imperial costume, rather than the court costumes worn by David and Saul on the plates. The similarities with the contemporary image of Justinian in San Vitale are striking: the purple chlamys, the white and gold tunic, the jewelled crown with pendant pearls. Here David is unequivocally represented in the guise of a Byzantine emperor. What purpose does this serve? One should first note that the David roundel is vertically aligned not only with the figure of Christ in a mandorla in the Transfiguration scene, but also with the central roundel on the upper edge of the conch, which depicts a cross (Fig. 4.18). Kurt Weitzmann was inclined to read the vertical axis as an allusion to the two natures of Christ, a doctrine formulated at the Council of Chalcedon in the mid-fifth century, and still of considerable relevance during Justinian's reign in the sixth. Thus David stands for the human nature of Christ ('Born of the tree of David according to the flesh', Rom. 1:3), while the cross-roundel represents his divine nature, and the Transfiguration represents the occasion on which Christ revealed his dual nature to his disciples.[64] He saw the costume of David as an allusion to the imperial founder of the monastery, Justinian. There is surely more mileage in this suggestion than Weitzmann allowed, for in representing David as a *Christian* emperor (note the cross surmounting his crown), he is evoked not merely as a human ancestor of Christ, but as a type both of Christ as universal ruler *and* of the emperor as his representative on earth. The image of David on the Sinai mosaics fits well with Hanson's preferred model of an Old Testament figure modified by the imagery of the Byzantine emperor in an abstract sense.

The Sinope Gospels, now preserved in the Bibliotheque Nationale in Paris, is a fragment of a sixth-century Gospel book written on purple parchment in

4.18 Monastery of St Catherine, Mt Sinai, apse mosaic (courtesy Michigan-Princeton-Alexandria Expedition to Mount Sinai)

gold letters.[65] Five of its surviving 44 pages are illustrated. In each case the illustration has the same format: a scene illustrating an event described in the text of that page, flanked on either side by figures of Old Testament prophets holding scrolls, whose texts act as a commentary on the New Testament scene depicted. On four out of the five illustrated pages David is one of these prophets, holding a scroll with verses from the Book of Psalms (Fig. 4.19). He is depicted almost identically each time: young, beardless and nimbed, wearing a gold and pearl diadem, a purple chlamys fastened with a large circular fibula with pendant pearls, underneath which a gold or gold and white tunic is visible. This portrayal is strikingly similar to that of the Sinai mosaics, and here again David functions in relation to Christ, as author of the Psalms, which were seen to prophesy Christ's deeds. By dressing David in contemporary imperial costume, the artist has added another layer of meaning to an already complex visual message, reminding the viewer that David was a king as well as a prophet and that as a divinely ordained king he is also a type of the Byzantine emperor, who in his turn represents the divine ruler Christ on earth.[66]

The context of the Sinai mosaic and the Sinope Gospels is important for understanding the circumstances in which the figure of David was used as a type of the emperor in early Byzantine art. The mosaic shows David in an unambiguously imperial guise in a monument whose imperial patronage is attested in Procopius' *Buildings* (5.8.1–9). He is no less imperial in the Sinope Gospels; although we do not know their patron, it is worth remembering that the purple parchment and gold used in their production have imperial connotations.[67] More important still, the images of David on Mount Sinai and in the Sinope Gospels were used in a sacred context, clearly subordinated to the image of Christ. It is perhaps no coincidence that the most imperial representations of David are closely associated with those of Christ. This is the case with the Palazzo Venezia casket whose lid shows Christ crowning an emperor and empress, as well as in the two sixth-century art-works discussed above. As the narrative of the David Plates makes no reference to David's relationship with Christ, it is unlikely that the plates were intended for use in a sacred context.

The evidence of the Sinai mosaics and the Sinope Gospels demonstrates how the David Plates differ from early Byzantine representations of David as a type of the emperor and by implication justifies a non-imperial reading of them. The idea that the David narrative does not always have to have an imperial meaning is supported by the medium of textiles. Scenes from the life of David are depicted on the so-called 'Coptic textiles' of the sixth to eighth centuries (Fig. 4.20).[68] The designs are quite schematic, even crude in their style of representation, and it is not always easy to decipher them. It would not be accurate to place them in the same luxury category as silver, although it has been suggested that the wool and linen textiles which survive in relatively large numbers represent mass-produced adaptations of designs in silk, which *was* a known luxury textile of early Byzantium.[69] Clearly imperial connotations would be inappropriate for these widely available images which

4.19 Sinope Gospels, Paris, Bibliothèque Nationale Suppl. gr. 1286, folio 29r (Bibliothèque Nationale de France)

4.20 *David Before Saul and David Summoned to Be Anointed*, Coptic textile, London, British Museum (© The British Museum)

could be worn by people with no connections with the emperor or the court. These textiles are also of considerable interest as a comparison with the David Plates because their design consists of a series of individual scenes in roundels (about 20 cm in diameter, at least on the two examples in the Walters Art Gallery), the circular shape of which echoes that of the plates. Thomas Dale has examined a group of 25 David textiles, and identified a total of five scenes represented on them, all of which also occur on the David Plates: David summoned to be anointed, David volunteering to fight Goliath, David slaying the lion, Samuel anointing David, and a two-figure scene possibly showing David confronting Goliath.[70]

Although the Coptic textiles are not luxury items, they belong, as the David Plates probably do, to the domestic sphere. This brings me back to the suggestion at the beginning of this chapter that the David Plates could help us understand the Christianization of the domestic sphere in early Byzantium. Attempts at imperial readings of the plates have obscured this issue, and are in any case – as I have tried to show – not supported by the available evidence. In proposing my alternative reading of the David Plates, I want to focus on their role as luxury items in a secular context, and how this might have shaped their meaning for a Byzantine viewer, while bearing in mind that the biblical narrative of the plates challenges the concept of the domestic as a secular sphere. The relationship between the David Plates and the luxury illustrated manuscripts of late antiquity offers some important insights on this topic.

Old Testament narratives and luxury art

Ever since the discovery of the David Plates, scholars have suggested that they owe some of their iconography to illustrated manuscripts.[71] There are a number of problems with this theory: not only are there no surviving manuscripts with a David cycle earlier than the ninth century, but the idea (developed to its fullest extent by Kurt Weitzmann) that manuscripts should be seen as an iconographic 'source' for images in other media has been the subject of increasing criticism.[72] However a different sort of comparison can be made productively between the David Plates and illustrated manuscripts, namely, the comparison of two forms of luxury art which are experimenting with different ways of representing the narratives of the Old Testament. As both silverware and illustrated manuscripts require considerable expense and skill in materials and labour, they can reasonably be considered luxury objects, and just as silver was used in both sacred and secular contexts, luxury manuscripts – even of sacred texts – could find a place in a private library as well as a church.[73] Rather than looking at the manuscripts from the middle Byzantine period which display iconographic similarities with the plates, I want to compare the plates with Old Testament manuscripts of the fifth and sixth centuries, which are more relevant to the artistic context in which the plates were produced.

Among the illustrated manuscripts surviving from this early period are some of single books or groups of books from the Old Testament. The Cotton and the Vienna Genesis are well-known, less so the Quedlinburg Itala, which from its surviving fragments seems to have consisted of the books 1 and 2 Samuel and 1 and 2 Kings, in a pre-Vulgate Latin translation. The status of such manuscripts remains a much-debated question. Most recently it has been suggested that the two Genesis manuscripts are by no means 'typical' of the period when they were produced; that is, they are not surviving representatives of much-reproduced 'types', but are probably unique experiments in producing illustrated books of Genesis.[74] The implication is that this was a period when there was considerable artistic experimentation with the illustration of biblical narratives (themselves rather new to the public visual repertoire) in the manuscript codex, which was a relatively recent development in book production. The Quedlinburg Itala, though about a century earlier than the Genesis manuscripts and produced in the West not the East, is nevertheless best understood within the same context of experimentation in representing Old Testament narratives.[75] A full understanding of this unique manuscript is hampered by the extremely fragmentary form in which it survives: five folios, four of which carry a full page illustration on one side. Two of these depict events in the reign of Saul from 1 Samuel, one an episode in 2 Samuel from the civil wars between David and Saul's sons that followed Saul's death, and one the building of the Temple by Solomon in 1 Kings.[76] These, and other features of the manuscript, have led scholars to conclude that the Quedlinburg Itala contained only the four books of Samuel and Kings. It is impossible to tell, however, what the original density of the illustrations was and how many illustrations the manuscript originally contained, as those surviving relate to widely varying amounts of text. For example, the story of Saul, Samuel and Agag is told in 24 verses of a single chapter of 1 Samuel, while the building of the Temple extends over four chapters of 1 Kings.[77] Although the Quedlinburg Itala does not preserve any of the episodes depicted on the David Plates, it is likely that the complete manuscript would have contained them. But while 'illustrated books of Kings' have in the past been suggested as sources for the images on the David Plates, here I want to compare the Quedlinburg Itala's approach to illustrating the narratives of Old Testament history in Kings with that displayed on the David Plates.[78]

The illustrations of the Quedlinburg Itala are notable for their classicizing style and their use of iconography and compositional features borrowed from the Roman tradition of imperial imagery.[79] Most noticeable is the way that all the kings in the surviving illustrations (including David on folio 3) wear the full dress uniform of a late-Roman emperor: a short white tunic decorated with coloured bands around the hem, a cuirass, a belt tied at the waist, a purple-red paludamentum fastened on the shoulder with a round, gem-encircled fibula, a plain gold diadem with ribbon ends fluttering behind the head, laced boots, and a gold spear (Fig. 4.21). The closest fifth-century parallel for this costume worn by a living emperor is the portrait of Honorius on the Probus diptych (Fig. 1.15), probably made in 406 AD in a Roman workshop, like the

4.21 Quedlinburg Itala, folio 1r, Berlin, Staatliche Bibliothek (Staatsbibliothek zu Berlin, Preussicher Kulturbesitz)

Quedlinburg Itala which is thought to have been made in Rome around 420–30 AD.[80] While incorporating elements special to the late-Roman period, such as the circular fibula, it is essentially a version of the traditional Roman military commander's uniform, which had represented one of the available modes for portraying Roman emperors ever since the time of Augustus, as exemplified in the Prima Porta statue of Augustus in the Vatican. The classicizing chiastic stance of this figure, with the weight placed on the right leg and the left, non-weight-bearing leg bent at the knee and held at a slight angle to the line of the body, derives from the fifth-century BC Doryphoros of Polykleitos, and is used both for the figure of Honorius, and the royal figures in the manuscript.

The Quedlinburg Itala would appear to be another case where the kings of the Old Testament are presented as contemporary emperors. Yet unlike the figure of David in the Sinai mosaics or the Sinope Gospels, the emperor-kings in the Quedlinburg Itala are integrated into narrative scenes, not removed from a narrative context to form a component of a Christian exegesis. This suggests that although Saul, David and the other kings represented in the Quedlinburg Itala fragments are more explicitly imperial than the figures of the David Plates – for whom I would prefer to use the term 'courtly' – in function they may be more closely related to the images of the plates than to overtly imperial images of David. What is their function, though? Why did the artist of the Quedlinburg Itala choose to depict not only Saul, David and Solomon, but also their enemies such as Agag, in imperial costume? Clearly the identification of the emperor with a single biblical individual is not intended. Instead we should consider the comparison in more general terms. One possible explanation, proposed by Inabelle Levin, is that the illustrators of the manuscript borrowed from the aura and prestige of official court and military imagery to enhance their luxury product.[81] This makes a connection between the manuscript's status as a luxury object and its artist's choice of classicizing imperial imagery. Levin herself suggests that the classicism of the manuscript's illustrations should be seen in the larger context of late fourth and fifth-century silver and ivories, where a taste for this retrospective style is apparent among imperial, pagan and Christian patrons alike.[82] The Probus diptych, although it represents a late antique emperor, combines the symbols of a Christian empire – the labarum bearing a chi-rho and the inscription 'may you always be victorious in the name of Christ' held by Honorius – with a style of representation from the high and early empire. The 'imperialism' of the Quedlinburg Itala illustrations, which have been compared to the campaign narratives on the columns of Trajan and Marcus Aurelius, is similarly backward-looking.[83] Levin is right, therefore, to see the imperial imagery employed in Quedlinburg Itala as evoking an aura of the Roman imperial past in the historical past of the Old Testament. In a wider sense, the use of such imagery gives a biblical sanction to Byzantine imperialism, which – insofar as it was a Roman system of rule – was non-Christian. Like the Probus diptych, the Quedlinburg Itala presents a visual fusion of Christian ways of thinking about government with Roman ones, and thus operates as an instrument of Christianization.

How does this aspect of the Quedlinburg Itala help us understand the David Plates? The key area of comparison is the perspective provided by these two different representations of Old Testament narratives on an important aspect of Christianization in late antiquity and early Byzantium. Both show how the increasingly Christianized culture of the Roman Empire between the fifth and the seventh centuries absorbed and interpreted Christianity's legacy of the Jewish scriptures.[84] The first stage of this process had begun much earlier, when episodes of the Old Testament (such as Jonah, Abraham's sacrifice of Isaac) had been interpreted typologically as prefigurations of Christ. Such interpretative strategies continued into the early Byzantine period (a good example being the Sinope Gospel illustrations). But the Quedlinburg Itala and the David Plates represent a second stage in the assimilation of the Old Testament, where it was deployed outside the context of explicit Christian exegesis, as the need to contest a Christian rather than a Jewish meaning for it diminished.[85] It can be argued that one of its functions in this context was to provide the basis for a new Christian culture, an alternative to the traditional pagan secular culture. For the artist of the Quedlinburg Itala, this was achieved by using traditional Roman imperial costume and settings to construct a visual analogy between the kingdom of Israel and the Roman Empire. For the designer of the David Plates, it was achieved by presenting David's youthful adventures as an alternative to the exploits of the heroes of classical myth traditionally depicted on domestic silverware. This, I am convinced, is the reading to which the plates best lend themselves.

Christian *paideia*

A striking feature of the David narrative as it is depicted on the plates is the lack of interest shown in David's eventual status as king. This contrasts with the David cycles of the middle Byzantine period: both the Palazzo Venezia casket and Paris Psalter feature images of the coronation of David, and almost half of the scenes on the casket are of events occurring during David's conflict with Saul.[86] David's combat with Goliath is presented on the plates as a circumscribed episode, with no reference to his subsequent conflict with Saul as a result of his victory. The interest is not in how David finally became king, but in the combat, the events which prepared him for it – physically and spiritually – and its reward. A similar situation can be observed in the scenes from the life of David depicted on Coptic textiles, although this is more complicated because no one surviving garment displays all five scenes identified by Dale (which do not in any case seem to represent the outcome of the contest between David and Goliath) and there is a preference for the repetition of single scenes over narrative continuity.[87] Nevertheless, here too the focus is on the earliest events in David's life. The previous chapter discussed how the Kaiseraugst Achilles plate chose to represent the events in Achilles' life *before* he went to Troy. Like the David Plates, it represented those events as a continuous narrative cycle, albeit contained on one plate instead of spread over nine. I suggested that the scenes on the Kaiseraugst plate were chosen because the education of the Homeric hero Achilles had a double appeal to its viewers' *paideia*: it represented a heroic *paideia* that was very different from their own, and at the same time their interpretation of the different episodes shown on the plate (themselves a virtuosic expansion of the basic myth) relied on the literary knowledge which was part of *paideia*. The Sevso Achilles plate, although it represents only the first and last scenes in the Kaiseraugst cycle, further confirms the interest in the early lives and education of heroes which seems to have flourished in late antiquity.

It is possible, therefore, to interpret the events depicted on the David Plates as David's *paideia*. The plates represent his youthful preparation for his subsequent role as king of Israel, which like the education of Achilles, is not a conventional *paideia*. Three of the plates show David's simple beginnings as a shepherd boy, playing the harp to his flocks and defending them against the lion and bear that attack them. In the biblical narrative these last two events are offered by David to Saul as evidence of his ability to kill Goliath, despite his lack of conventional military training (1 Sam. 17:36). Another key event in David's *paideia* depicted on one of the plates is his anointing by Samuel, which marks his election by God as the future king of Israel. The later plates in the series represent David's transition from shepherd boy to killer of Goliath, shown through his encounter with the soldier (who is most likely Eliab, as Wander suggests, or one of the soldiers in the camp from whom David learns of Goliath's challenge), his presentation to Saul and his arming by Saul.[88] The fight with Goliath is the culminating stage in this *paideia* where David proves his worthiness to be king through his personal heroism.[89] The combat with Goliath is followed by marriage to Saul's daughter. In all the plates except this one, David is shown wearing a boy's tunic, which has short sleeves and reaches to the knee; he is also shown about a head shorter than the older male figures in authority, Samuel and Saul. On the marriage plate, this height difference is reduced and seems to serve more to emphasize Saul's position as the central figure in the scene. David wears the adult dress of a Byzantine courtier consisting of an ankle-length chlamys and a long-sleeved tunic. Through these visual details, as well as through the narrative, the plate indicates that David's *paideia* is now completed; he has become the Saul's son-in-law, and has a place in his court.

David's marriage marks a transition to a later and more difficult stage of his life when he begins to realise his ordained role as king through his struggle with Saul, which the David Plates do not represent.[90] In the case of the Kaiseraugst Achilles plate, I cited the ekphrasis of a picture of 'The Upbringing of Achilles' in Philostratus' *Imagines*, as an example of how *paideia* might allow a viewer to respond to an image by evoking a text which describes not what is represented in that image but related events. Thus Achilles' upbringing under Chiron evokes a Homeric description of his behaviour at Troy. Christian *paideia* would allow the viewers of the David Plates to respond to them either in terms of what is actually shown, or by referring to the later chapters in the narrative of Samuel and Kings. This model was also informed by Christian typological thinking, which would have seen not only David's end in his beginning but also Christ's kingdom which David presages. Such a response seems to be indicated in the way the plates allude to David's future destiny as king of Israel, as when they consistently represent David with a nimbus. Saul and his daughter are also shown nimbed, but not Samuel, which indicates that here the nimbus is used as a sign of royal, not holy, status. Because these and other signs of royal status borrow from those of the Byzantine emperor, in this sense my interpretation of the David Plates accommodates – on a secondary level – a reading of David as a Byzantine emperor. David's *paideia* could be read as a model (metaphorical as well literal) for the emperor's *paideia*. But this should be seen in general terms, not as an allegory of one specific emperor.

The evidence offered by the David Plates, that multiple ways of deploying the figure of David had developed by the first half of the seventh century, provides an important insight into the process of Christianization in early Byzantium. As more areas of Byzantine culture became explicitly Christian rather than neutral, biblical figures and narratives were adapted to new contexts. In the case of David, the Sinai mosaic and the Sinope Gospels are examples of a strong tradition which existed in an ecclesiastical context of typological readings of David as prophet of Christ and author of the Psalms, not as a character within the narrative of Kings. In the domestic context of silverware, however, the figure of David takes on a different meaning. The events in 1 Samuel are presented as an independent narrative, a 'Christian Homer', executed in a classical style which evoked the mythological heroes who traditionally decorated silver for domestic use.

Challenging the conventional interpretation of the David Plates, not only places them in a wider context of artistic production in early Byzantium, but also questions assumptions about the absence of a secular culture in Byzantium. Like the David Plates, the bone and ivory caskets of the middle Byzantine period – of which the Palazzo Venezia Casket is an outstanding, if exceptional example – were luxury art objects for display in a domestic (albeit aristocratic or courtly) context, and they had an iconographic repertoire that included both mythological and Old Testament subjects .[91] The David Plates represent an attempt to adapt the traditions of late antique domestic silver plate, which was still flourishing in the seventh century, to a changing concept of 'secular' culture. In art-historical terms they are essentially a transitional, experimental work. Like the early illustrated manuscripts, they may well have been unique.[92]

The secular tranformed

In this chapter I have used domestic silver from the first half of the seventh century in Byzantium to focus on the survival of ideals of classical *paideia* in the private sphere over a much longer period than is generally supposed and to examine the way that Christianization affected the visual expression of these ideals.[93] At its core has been a lengthy discussion of one particular example of seventh-century silver – the David Plates – whose exceptional quality and unique iconography can give important insights into the transformation of the secular in Byzantium through the Christianization of the private sphere in this period. Examining the David Plates in these terms offers, to my mind, a more productive reading of them than has been achieved by comparing them to later, iconographically related, images in other media, or by constructing a political symbolism in their iconography. The David Plates are a remarkable work of art because they can be seen as simultaneously 'classical' and 'medieval'. The metamorphosis of the classical traditions of *paideia*, which the plates' theme represents is simultaneously the beginning of a medieval Byzantine tradition of the secular use of Old Testament subjects in the context of luxury art. Overall, the challenge is not only to conventional interpretations of the David Plates, but also to assumptions about the existence of a secular culture in Byzantium.

This is not to say that Byzantium retained the Graeco-Roman construction of the secular intact. The Kuczurmare situla, with which I began this chapter, represents an aspect of *paideia* which cannot be traced beyond the seventh century. Arguably it was excluded from the new formation of the secular in Byzantium, most probably because its representations of deities – even in the context of a collection of statues – were too closely linked to what Byzantium defined as pagan 'idolatry'.[94] Seventh-century silver reveals more than one aspect of the process of Christianization in the domestic sphere in early Byzantium, as the comparison between the David Plates and the plates with niello crosses or monograms in wreaths shows. The cross-monogram plates are explicitly Christianizing, whereas the choice of subject matter for the David Plates is an implicit result of Christianization. In this sense, the cross-monogram plates are typical of Byzantine art before iconoclasm, when the use of Christian images and symbols was more flexible and less strictly controlled. This is demonstrated even more clearly in the bowl from the First Cyprus Treasure, now in the British Museum (Fig. 4.22), which has a half-length image of a military saint (probably St Sergius) in a medallion in the base of the interior and stamps from the reign of Constans II (641–651).[95] There is no evidence within the bowl itself, or in the rest of the First Cyprus Treasure, that it was intended for church use. Yet even if such evidence existed, this use of a saint's image on a functional vessel would have been inconceivable after iconoclasm. So while this bowl and the cross-monogram plates do represent an important aspect of the Christianization of the domestic sphere in early Byzantium, they are in a sense an abortive beginning, since this form of visual expression did not have a lasting influence on visual art in the private sphere in Byzantium. Their most important contribution was to the dismantling of the Graeco-Roman construction of the secular, not to its rebuilding.

The David Plates, on the other hand, did contribute to this rebuilding. This can be seen in their relationship with Middle Byzantine bone and ivory boxes, which with their iconographic repertoire of both mythological and Old Testament subjects, constituted an important form of secular art in later Byzantium.[96] These boxes were luxury products, aimed at an aristocratic or court milieu, the area where a secular art can be argued to have existed

4.22 First
Cyprus Treasure,
London, British
Museum: bowl
with bust of a
military saint
(© The British
Museum)

in Byzantium. It is indicative of the difference between Byzantium and the medieval West as regards the secular that in the West these boxes frequently ended up in an ecclesiastical context in church treasuries (for example as reliquaries).[97] This study of seventh-century silver and its descendants has shown that it is inappropriate to apply Robert Markus' model of the drainage of the secular to Byzantium. My case study of the David Plates suggests that the secular in Byzantium is far better perceived in terms of transformation or metamorphosis of that late antique concept. A full history of this transformation remains to be written, but this chapter has shown that such a study cannot afford to ignore the visual arts, least of all silverware.

Notes

1   See Matzulewitsch, *Byzantinische Antike*, 15, 38, 41. Matzulewitsch identifies the male figure with Venus as Mars, but I think an identification as Adonis is more likely, as the figure is a young, beardless man wearing hunting boots and a cloak, and carrying a spear and shield.

2.   Dodd, *Byzantine Silver Stamps*, no. 56, 174–75.

3.   Examples include, A.H.M. Jones, *The Later Roman Empire 284–602. A Social, Economic and Administrative Survey* (Oxford 1964), and more recently A. Cameron, *The Mediterranean World in Late Antiquity AD 395–600* (London, 1993), who explicitly accepts Jones' chronological limit of the death of Maurice in 602 for the end of the period (5, cf. 7–8).

4.   Liebeschuetz, 'The Use of Pagan Mythology', 91.

5.   See C. Mango, M. Vickers, and E.D. Francis, 'The Palace of Lausus at Constantinople and its Collection of Ancient Statues', *Journal of the History of Collections* 4 (1992), 89–98; S. Guberti Bassett, ' "Excellent Offerings": The Lausos Collection in Constantinople', *Art Bulletin* 82 (2000), 6–25.

6.   This body of material was first discussed in detail by Matzulewitsch, together with similar unstamped material which may be of the same date. A more recent overview is provided by M.M. Mango, 'Continuity of Fourth/Fifth Century Silver Plate in the Sixth/Seventh Centuries in the Eastern Empire', *Antiquité Tardive* 5 (1997), 83–92. The authoritative study of the identification and dating of the stamps is Dodd, *Byzantine Silver Stamps* and its supplements, 'Byzantine Silver Stamps: Supplement I. New Stamps from the Reigns of Justin II and Constans II', *DOP* 18 (1964), 239–48; 'Byzantine Silver Stamps: Supplement II. More Treasure from Syria', *DOP* 22 (1968), 141–50. The 11 pieces are her nos 1, 9, 10, 14, 16, 26, 56, 57, 70, 75, 77.

7.   Dodd, *Byzantine Silver Stamps*, no. 57, 176.

8.   Dodd, *Byzantine Silver Stamps*, no. 16, 84. There is not space in this chapter to discuss the problems of the identification of this scene, or the unusual iconography of Venus on this plate and the Kuczurmare situla. See also Matzulewitsch, *Byzantinische Antike*, 26–29.

9.   Dodd, *Byzantine Silver Stamps*, no. 9, 70.

10.   Dodd, *Byzantine Silver Stamps*, nos 1, 10, 14, 70, 75, 77. She argues that the stamping system ended under Constans II (32–33), and there are certainly no stamped examples of Byzantine silver after this date.

11.   For a sophisticated account of this (from a textual point of view) see A. Cameron, *Christianity and the Rhetoric of Empire: the Development of Christian Discourse* (Berkeley CA 1991).

12.   This has been explored most fully for the empire in the West in R.A. Markus, *The End of Ancient Christianity* (Cambridge, 1990). No comparable study exists for the eastern empire, although some of the same issues are raised in Cameron, *Rhetoric of Empire*.

13.   Cameron, *Rhetoric of Empire*, 193–94.

14.   Dodd, *Byzantine Silver Stamps* lists a total of 38 pieces (136–210). An equal number of stamped pieces survives from the reign of Justinian, of which about two-thirds are

liturgical vessels from the Sion Treasure. The stamps of the latter have not been fully published, but can be inferred from the table in Appendix IV of Boyd, 'A "Metropolitan" Treasure', 37, and Dodd's article 'The Question of Workshop: Evidence of the Stamps on the Sion Treasure', in Boyd and Mango, eds, *Ecclesiastical Silver Plate*, 57–63.

15. The Kama region of Russia, the findspot of much early Byzantine silver of the sixth and seventh centuries, has produced a particularly high concentration of finds from the reign of Heraclius. This possibly indicates increased imports into the region at that period, especially as the objects with Heraclian stamps tend to be grouped together in finds, and accompanied by coins of Heraclius, which are the only early Byzantine coins to have been found in the region. See L. Matsulevich, 'L'antique byzantin et la region de Kama', in *Monuments Archéologiques de l'Oural et du Pays de la Kama. Materiaux et Recherches d'Archéologie de l'URSS* No. 1 (Moscow and Leningrad, 1940) 139–58 [Russian with French summary].

16. Dodd, *Byzantine Silver Stamps*, no. 5 (Anastasius), no. 12 (Justinian), no. 28 (Tiberius II), nos 32, 33, 36 (Phocas), nos 37–42, 45, 46, 51, 54, 55, 67, 68, 73 (Heraclius), 76 (Constans II).

17. M.M. Mango in Buckton, *Byzantium*, no. 96, 93. For the Esquiline plates see Shelton, *The Esquiline Treasure*, nos 5–12, 80–81.

18. Mango suggests that those with plain crosses were bought 'off the shelf', those with monograms finished to order (Buckton, *Byzantium*, 93).

19. Elsner, *Art and the Roman Viewer*, 259–60 (quotation from 260).

20. Cameron, *Rhetoric of Empire*, 191.

21. Markus, *The End of Ancient Christianity*, 217–19. Also see J. Lowden, 'Concerning the Cotton Genesis and Other Illustrated Manuscripts of Genesis', *Gesta* 31 (1992), 47–48 on some of the late antique Latin reworkings of the biblical narrative which were subsequently used for didactic purposes in the monasteries in the West, and the lack of comparable texts for the East.

22. P. Lemerle, *Byzantine Humanism*, 47, 111–16.

23. This is clear from the description of Byzantine education in H. Maguire, *Art and Eloquence in Byzantium* (Princeton, 1981), 13–15, although he does not specifically make this point. The progymnasmata also found later imitators in Byzantium: Maguire cites a twelfth-century teacher, Nikephoros Basilakes, who wrote his own collection of progymnasmata after the categories of Aphthonius, on a mixture of mythological and Christian subjects. See also Webb, *The Eikones of Philostratus*, 88–89, 105–41.

24. Averil Cameron, for example, claims that learning became 'increasingly the preserve of the church and was expressed in theological works and learned sermons, when it was not being deployed in the doctrinal battles of the seventh and eighth centuries'. Cameron, *Rhetoric of Empire*, 221. This fundamentally text-based view underestimates the significance of the continuity in forms of education. Liebeschuetz, 'The Use of Pagan Mythology', 91 draws similar conclusions, suggesting that 'the perceived object of education' must have changed. However N.H. Wilson, *Scholars of Byzantium* (London, 1983) goes too far in the opposite direction, overemphasizing classical attitudes to education at the expense of Christian ones.

25. Dodd, *Byzantine Silver Stamps*, nos 58–66.

26. See O.M. Dalton, 'A Byzantine Silver Treasure from the District of Kyrenia, Cyprus, now preserved in the British Museum', *Archaeologia* 57 (1900), 159–74; *Catalogue of Early Christian Antiquities and Objects from the Christian East in the Department of British and Mediaeval Antiquities and Ethnography of the British Museum* (London, 1909), nos 397–424, 86–90.

27. The complete find is listed in A. Stylianou and J. Stylianou, *The Treasures of Lambousa* (Lapethos, 1969) [Greek with English preface and summary]. For the cross-monogram plates see Dodd, *Byzantine Silver Stamps* nos 33 and 54. No. 33 has stamps from the reign of Phocas (602–610 AD), no. 54 has stamps from the earlier part of the reign of Heraclius, like the David Plates (613–629/30 AD). The Stylianous also identify Dodd nos 37–39 (also with stamps from 613–629/30) as part of the hoard, though Dodd is less certain of their provenance.

28. Stylianou and Stylianou, *The Treasures of Lambousa*, preface ix–x. The Stylianous are responsible for tracing this descendant of one of the finders and establishing what is probably the most reliable account of the hoard's discovery. The pot with the jewellery and the plates were apparently discovered on subsequent workdays in February 1902.

29. Two of the items of jewellery, a girdle and a medallion (now in Dumbarton Oaks), contain coins issued in 583 and 584, almost 30 years before the earliest possible date for the David Plates. See P. Grierson, 'The Kyrenia Girdle of Byzantine Medallions and Solidi', *Numismatic Chronicle* (6th ser.) 15 (1955), 55–70; and 'The Date of the Dumbarton Oaks Epiphany Medallion', *DOP* 15 (1961), 223, n. 18. It is unclear whether when he suggested 609/10 as a possible concealment date for the girdle ('The Kyrenia Girdle', 70) he was aware of the dating of the stamps on the plates.

30. Examples include the Great Dish and the two smaller Dionysiac plates from the Mildenhall Treasure, and a set of six plates from Egypt with medallions depicting a range of marine imagery (see S. Pelekanides, ''Αργυρά πινάκια τού Μουσείου Μπενάκη', 'Αρχαιολογική 'Εφημερίς 1942–44 (1948), 37–62). The Sevso Treasure contains two situlae and a jug, each bearing a near-identical scene of Phaedra and Hippolytus, probably worked by three different craftsmen from the same design (Bennet and Mango, *The Sevso Treasure*, 319–401, figs 8.33–8.35).

31. Examples include the fourth-century San Nazaro and Thessalonike reliquaries: see Buschhausen, *Die spätrömischen Metallscrinia*, 223–39. A fourth-century flask from the Traprain Law hoard which combines the Fall and Moses striking water from the rock with two New Testament scenes belongs in the same category as the reliquary caskets, though its function is unclear. See Curle, *The Treasure of Traprain*, 13–19, no. 1.

32. A secular use was recognized in the first article published on the plates, O.M. Dalton, 'A Second Silver Treasure from Cyprus', *Archaeologia* 60 (1906), 1–24, and has been accepted by all subsequent scholars working on the plates.

33. Dalton (n. 32 supra); K. Weitzmann, 'Prolegomena to a Study of the Cyprus Plates', *Metropolitan Museum Journal* 3 (1970), 97–111; M. van Grunsven-Eygenraam, 'Heraclius and the David Plates', *BABesch* 48 (1973), 158–74; S.H. Wander, 'The Cyprus Plates: The Story of David and Goliath', *Metropolitan Museum Journal* 8 (1973), 89–104; S.S. Alexander, 'Heraclius, Byzantine Imperial Ideology and the David Plates', *Speculum* 52 (1977), 217–37; J. Trilling, 'Myth and Metaphor at the Byzantine Court: a Literary Approach to the David Plates', *Byzantion* 48 (1978), 249–63.

34. Van Grunsven-Eygenraam, 'Heraclius and the David Plates', 174, suggests that the plates were given to the patriarch of Constantinople, Sergius (with whom Heraclius had a close relationship), or John the Almoner, whom he appointed patriarch of Alexandria in 612. The latter was a Cypriot by birth, and although he died in 619, she proposes that the plates might have passed to another member of his family resident

in Cyprus, resulting in their burial there. Wander also entertains the possibility that the plates could have been made for the emperor's own use ('The Cyprus Plates', 103), while Alexander ('Imperial Ideology and the David Plates', 239) suggests that they are 'a superlative, multi-partite, highly personalized variety of the imperial medallion, which Heraclius commissioned as his predecessors had commissioned in order to bestow them as gifts.'

35. M.M. Mango, 'Imperial Art in the Seventh Century', in P. Magalino, ed., *New Constantines: The Rhythm of Imperial Renewal in Byzantium, 4th–13th Centuries* (Aldershot, 1994), 131.

36. See P. Grierson, *Catalogue of Byzantine Coins in the Dumbarton Oaks Collection. Volume Two: Phocas to Theodosius III 602–717. Part I: Phocas and Heraclius (602–641)* (Washington, DC, 1968), 65–103.

37. See Delmaire, 'Largesses impériales', 113–22, and 'Le déclin des largesses sacrées', 265–77.

38. Grierson, 'The Kyrenia Girdle' and 'Epiphany Medallion'.

39. This has been argued for medieval book-making by J. Lowden, 'The Royal/Imperial Book and the Image or Self-Image of the Medieval Ruler', in A.J. Duggan, ed., *Kings and Kingship in Medieval Europe* (London, 1993), 213–40. Also see the definition in Mango, 'Imperial Art in the Seventh Century', 110.

40. For some examples see H. Belting, 'Kunst oder Objekt-Stil? Fragen zur Funktion der "Kunst" in der "makedonischen Renaissance"', in I. Hutter, ed., *Byzanz und der Westen: Studien zur Kunst des europäischen Mittelalters* (Vienna, 1984), 65–83.

41. Wander, 'The Cyprus Plates', 102–03, Trilling, 'Myth and Metaphor', 249. Cf. Grierson, 'The Kyrenia Girdle', 69. The inclusion of imperial largitio medallions of a high value in the girdle certainly argues for an owner with close connections to the court. Neither Wander nor Trilling note the difference of 30 years between the minting of the medallions (583) and the earliest possible date for the plates (613). This means that if the gold jewellery and the plates were the property of a single individual or family (which we do not know for certain), we must envisage a collection accumulated over at least two generations, each of which had links to the court.

42. Van Grunsven-Eygenraam, 'Heraclius and the David Plates', 173.

43. Van Grunsven-Eygenraam, 'Heraclius and the David Plates', 173–74.

44. Wander, 'The Cyprus Plates', 103–04.

45. S. Wander, 'The Cyprus Plates and the *Chronicle* of Fredegar', *DOP* 29 (1975), 345–46.

46. Alexander, 'Imperial Ideology and the David Plates', 226–27.

47. Theophanes, *Chronographia* records that in 622 'the emperor Heraclius after celebrating the Easter feast, straight away set out against the Persians on Monday evening. Being short of money he took on loan the moneys of religious establishments, and he also took the candelabra and other vessels of the holy ministry from the Great Church [i.e. Hagia Sophia], which he minted into a great quantity of gold and silver coin' (AM 6113). Translation from: C. Mango and R. Scott, with the assistance of G. Greatrex, *The Chronicle of Theophanes Confessor: Byzantine and Near Eastern History AD 284–813* (Oxford, 1997). Also see Dodd, *Byzantine Silver Stamps*, 32–33.

48. Trilling, 'Myth and Metaphor', 161.

49. J. Hanson, *The Ivory Casket in Sens known as La Sainte Chasse* (unpublished PhD dissertation, Courtauld Institute, University of London, 1996), 160–211.

50. A. Cutler and N. Oikonomides, 'An Imperial Byzantine Casket and its Fate at a Humanist's Hands', *Art Bulletin* 70 (1988), 77–87; and in the same issue H. Maguire, 'The Art of Comparing in Byzantium', 88–103. Hanson, *The Ivory Casket*, 167–69. Cutler does identify the imperial couple, but on the evidence of the inscription alone.

51. Hanson, *The Ivory Casket*, 171.

52. Hanson, *The Ivory Casket*, 174–76.

53. As regards the relationship between the David Plates and the Missorium of Theodosius, I would not accept the claim put forward by Ernst Kitzinger that these are a deliberate attempt to imitate the classicism of the Theodosian period. See E. Kitzinger, 'Byzantine Art in the Period Between Justinian and Iconoclasm', *Berichte zum XI Byzantinistenkongress* (Munich, 1958), 5–6.

54. Weitzmann, 'Prolegomena', 110–11.

55. Wander, 'The Cyprus Plates', 90.

56. For the representation of money-bags as prizes cf. the mid-third century mosaic of Magerius from Smirat (N. Africa), which commemorates a *venatio* given by Magerius, and features a figure holding a tray of money-bags, the prizes awarded by the patron to the performers. See K. Dunbabin, *The Mosaics of Roman North Africa: Studies in Iconography and Patronage* (Oxford, 1978), 67–69.

57. Possibly this is because emperors could represent themselves as consuls on the coins which they distributed at consular sparsiones, an option that was not open to non-imperial consuls. On the difference between the largitio of imperial and non-imperial consuls, see Chapter 1.

58. For a discussion of representations of sparsio on diptychs see Delbrueck, *Die Consulardiptychen*, 68–70. The diptych-leaf of Flavius Anastasius (consul in 517) in the Victoria and Albert Museum (Delbrueck, no. 20, 127) shows the consul framed by an especially elaborate pediment.

59. Cf. M. McCormick, 'Clovis at Tours: Byzantine Public Ritual and the Origins of Medieval Ruler Symbolism', in E.K. Chrysos, ed., *Das Reich und die Barbaren* (Vienna, 1989), 164.

60. On this problem see Mango, 'Imperial Art in the Seventh Century'.

61. Hanson makes a similar criticism of Maguire's reading of the Palazzo Venezia casket: *The Ivory Casket*, 171.

62. Mathews, *The Clash of Gods*, with the reviews by Brown in *Art Bulletin* and Kinney in *Studies in Iconography*.

63. Full illustrations of the mosaics can be found in G.K. Forsyth and K. Weitzmann, *The Monastery of St Catherine at Mount Sinai: The Church and the Fortress of Justinian* (Ann Arbor, MI, 1973).

64. Forsyth and Weitzmann, *The Monastery of St Catherine*, 15; also in K.A. Manafis, ed., *Sinai: Treasures of the Monastery of St Catherine* (Athens, 1990), 62. Also see Elsner, *Art and the Roman Viewer*, 99–123.

65. A. Grabar, *Les peintures de l'évangéliaire de Sinope* (Bibliothèque nationale, Suppl. gr. 1286) (Paris, 1948).

66. The illustrations of the Rossano Gospels, another *codex purpureus*, are structured similarly to those of the Sinope Gospels (though they are on full pages forming a preface, rather than accompanying text). David features frequently on them, but his costume – while courtly – is not as explicitly imperial as in the Sinope Gospels. See A. Muñoz, *Il Codice purpureo di Rossano e il frammento sinopense* (Rome, 1907), pls I–VIII and XI–XII.

67. It has also been suggested that the primary connotation of these materials was heavenly, not earthly, kingship: see Lowden, 'The Royal/Imperial Book', 236–39.

68. See T.E.A. Dale, 'The Power of the Anointed: The Life of David on Two Coptic Textiles in the Walters Art Gallery', *Journal of the Walters Art Gallery* 51 (1993), 23–41. Another Old Testament character who is represented on Coptic textiles is Joseph: see G. Vikan, 'Joseph Iconography on Coptic Textiles', *Gesta* 18 (1979), 99–108. Unfortunately the dating of these textiles is extremely imprecise, to the extent that it is hard to assign them even to a single century.

69. Dale, 'The Power of the Anointed', 24.

70. Dale, 'The Power of the Anointed', 25–35.

71. This was first suggested by Dalton, 'A Second Silver Treasure', and was taken up by K. Weitzmann in 'The Psalter Vatopedi 761. Its Place in the Aristocratic Psalter Recension', *Journal of the Walters Art Gallery* 10 (1947), 21–51, and 'Prolegomena'.

72. See for example J. Gutmann, 'The Dura Europos Synagogue Paintings: The State of Research', in L.I. Levine, ed., *The Synagogue in Late Antiquity* (Philadelphia, PA, 1987), 61–72; D.M. Wright, 'The School of Princeton and the Seventh Day of Creation', *University Publishing* 9 (1980), 7–8; J. Lowden, *The Octateuchs: a Study in Byzantine Manuscript Illustration* (University Park, PA, 1992), 79–104.

73. The majority of manuscripts were not luxury objects, of course. I am referring to those distinguished by features such as dyed parchment, gold and silver lettering, and painted illustrations, which set them apart from books produced for purely functional purposes. For a good general survey of the surviving luxury manuscripts of the sixth century, see J. Lowden, *Early Christian and Byzantine Art* (London, 1997), 83–95. On illuminated manuscripts as luxury objects in later Byzantine culture see A. Cutler, 'Uses of Luxury: on the Functions of Consumption and Symbolic Capital in Byzantine Culture', in A. Guillou and J. Durand, eds, *Byzance et les images* (Paris, 1994), 310–11.

74. Lowden (n. 21 supra), 40–53. This article is a response to Weitzmann's theory that the illustrations of these manuscripts represent a standard 'cycle' which was reproduced in other manuscripts, now lost.

75. See H. Degering and A. Boeckler, *Die Quedlinburger Italafragmente*, 2 vols (Berlin, 1932); I. Levin, *The Quedlinburg Itala: the Oldest Illustrated Biblical Manuscript* (Leiden, 1985).

76. The episodes depicted are: folio 1r, the fulfilment of the three prophetic signs which Samuel had indicated to Saul would prove that God had chosen him, and Saul's introduction to the Israelites by Samuel (1 Sam. 10); folio 2r, Saul sacrificing after his victory over the Amalichites, Samuel announcing that God has rejected Saul's kingship, renouncing Saul, and slaying the Amalechite king Agag with his own hands (1 Sam 15:9–33); folio 3v, the story of Abner, a military commander who switches his allegiance to David during the civil war with Saul's heirs, is assassinated by Joab and mourned by David (2 Sam. 3:6–39); folio 4r, the building of the temple by King

Solomon, from the first requests to King Hiram for materials and skilled workers to its final dedication (1 Kings 5:1–8.66).

77. Degering's suggestion that the original manuscript contained sixty illustrations, based on an average of one illustration to 5–6 pages of text must remain a hypothesis, although his calculation that the full text of Kings would have occupied about 190 folios in this manuscript can be considered reliable, as it is based on the size of the letters and their spacing in the surviving pages of text. See Degering and Boeckler, *Die Quedlinburger Italafragmente*, 110–19.

78. The existence of 'illustrated books of Kings' as a category is perhaps dubious. Apart from the fragments of the Quedlinburg Itala, only one other such manuscript exists, Vatican gr. 333 (the Vatican Kings), dating to the mid-eleventh century. The density of illustrations in this ambitious manuscript declines rapidly after 1 Samuel, and it is worth speculating whether the same thing happened in the Quedlinburg Itala. The two are not iconographically related, and it seems possible that they may both represent 'one-off' experiments. For other early David cycles in non-luxury media (and including some in ecclesiastical contexts) see A. Cutler, 'A Psalter from Mar Saba and the Evolution of the Byzantine David Cycle', *Journal of Jewish Art* 6 (1979), 39–63, who argues that a David cycle, isolated from the Book of Kings but following the narrative order of that text, existed as an independent entity from an early point in late antiquity.

79. Levin, *The Quedlinburg Itala*, 48–52.

80. On the Probus diptych see Delbrueck, *Die Consulardiptychen*, no. 1, 84–87; W.F. Volbach, *Elfenbeinarbeiten der Spätantike*, no. 1, 22; Kiilerich, *Late Fourth Century Classicism*, 65–67. On the date of the Quedlinburg Itala see Levin, *The Quedlinburg Itala*, 67–71.

81. Levin, *The Quedlinburg Itala*, 62.

82. Levin, *The Quedlinburg Itala*, 32. Cf. Kiilerich, *Late Fourth Century Classicism*, esp. 199; Belting, 'Kunst oder Objekt-Stil?'.

83. Levin, *The Quedlinburg Itala*, 48. Note how in folio 2r, Saul is shown pouring a libation from a patera onto an altar according to the long-established formula for a sacrificing emperor. In the Christian empire of the fifth century, however, this imperial gesture was obsolete.

84. This process began as early as Christianity itself. For a perceptive analysis of its development up to the fourth century, see F.M. Young, *Biblical Exegesis and the Formation of Christian Culture* (Cambridge, 1997), esp. 9–28, 49–75.

85. Again, on this see Young, *Biblical Exegesis*, 9–28. The mosaic in the fourth-century basilica of Misis/Mopsuestia representing the life of Samson is also relevant in this context: see L. Budde, *Antike Mosaiken in Kilikien I: frühchristliche Mosaiken in Misis-Mopsuhestia* (Recklinghausen, 1969), 67–72; and Ernst Kitzinger, 'Observations on the Samson Floor at Mopsuestia', *DOP* 27 (1973), 135–44.

86. The cycle here ends not with David's coronation but his encounter with Saul in the cave at Engedi. See Hanson, *The Ivory Casket*, 208.

87. Dale, 'The Power of the Anointed', 35–39. Dale accounts for the preference of repetition over narrative by suggesting that David images on clothing served an apotropaic function, following a theory of apotropaic textile designs first proposed by H. Maguire, 'Garments Pleasing to God: The Significance of Domestic Textile Designs in the Early Byzantine Period', *DOP* 44 (1990), 215–24. Although we have no way of knowing whether the David Plates as they survive today represent the complete set

made in the seventh century, there are no obvious lacunae among the episodes which
they represent, and nothing to suggest – beyond a comparison with Middle Byzantine
material – that the series should have continued beyond the marriage with Michal.
Moreover, none of the early cycles cited by Cutler, 'A Psalter from Mar Saba', go
beyond the immediate aftermath of David's victory over Goliath.

88. Wander, 'The Cyprus Plates', 91–93.

89. Cf. Trilling, 'Myth and Metaphor', 262–63, who notes that David is a biblical type of
kingship bestowed by divine grace but earned by personal heroism.

90. It is worth noting how the narrative sequence on the plates moves directly from the
victory over Goliath to marriage with Saul's daughter, considerably simplifying the
biblical narrative, and masking the tensions between Saul and David which begin at
this point.

91. See I. Kalavrezou, 'Luxury Objects', in H.C. Evans and W.D. Wixom, eds, *The Glory of
Byzantium: Art and Culture of the Middle Byzantine Era, A.D. 843–1261* (New York, 1997),
219–23. With the exception of the Veroli Casket, all surviving Middle Byzantine boxes
with mythological subjects are made of bone, rather than ivory, which was reserved
for those with sacred subjects: see A. Cutler, *The Hand of the Master: Craftsmanship,
Ivory and Society in Byzantium (9th–11th Centuries)* (Princeton, NJ, 1994), 59–60.

92. The existence of further sets of David Plates has sometimes been hypothesized from
a single plate found in the Kama region of Russia which seems to show David killing
a lion in a composition which is the mirror image of the plate with that subject from
Cyprus. There are some differences however: David is armed with a sword and
shield, the lion leaps against him instead of his leaping on top of it, and the animal
has a smaller mane and is covered with spots; no lamb is shown; instead a snake
is depicted near David's foot. The study of this plate is obstructed by the fact that
its whereabouts, dimensions and the presence or absence of stamps on it are all
unknown. The article by Matzulewitsch, 'L'antique byzantin et la region du Kama',
in which it was published, is in Russian with a French summary. The summary does
not state whether Matzulewitsch was able to examine the piece himself, but I think it
is unlikely, since given his interests in Byzantine silver stamps and the precision of his
scholarship, he would undoubtedly have recorded whether any were present, as well
as the dimensions of the piece. In these circumstances it is hard to decide what the
relationship between the Kama plate and the Cyprus plates might be, and it is not safe
to assume that another *set* of David Plates did exist.

93. Compare my discussion in Chapter 3 of related claims made for Hellenism by
Bowersock in *Hellenism in Late Antiquity*.

94. On the Byzantine relationship with classical statues see C. Mango, 'Antique Statuary
and the Byzantine Beholder', *DOP* 17 (1963), 53–67; L. James, ' "Pray Not to Fall into
Temptation and Be on Your Guard": Pagan Statues in Christian Constantinople', *Gesta*
35 (1996), 12–20.

95. Dodd, *Byzantine Silver Stamps*, no. 78, 220; Dalton, *Catalogue of Early Christian
Antiquities,* no 398, 87. These stamps mean that is it one of the latest pieces of datable
silver: see Dodd, 22–23 on the demise of the stamping system under Constans II.

96. Hanson, *The Ivory Casket*, 192, notes that the most common subject-matter for
decoration on Byzantine bone and ivory caskets is mythological, with Old Testament
themes coming second: cf. Cutler, *The Hand of the Master*.

97. The Sens Casket is an excellent example of this: see Hanson, *The Ivory Casket*.

Conclusion

Huc vetus argentum formas speciesque novatum
in varias, pressum titulis sculptumque figuris
excelcis portant umeris …

Here they brought on their tall shoulders old silver
renewed in different shapes and forms, embossed with legends
and engraved with figures …

The above description by the sixth-century panegyric poet Corippus, of the
silver vessels presented as largitio by the emperor Justin II on assuming the
consulate, makes an especially apt conclusion for this book.[1] Throughout, I
have sought to 'renew' the silver of late antiquity – not in the poet's literal
sense of melting down and reshaping, but by through the creation of a new
intellectual framework for understanding this medium. A synthetic approach
has been adopted, where case studies of a range of different types of late antique
silverware have drawn on multiple methodological approaches to elucidate
different aspects of this material. Together the individual (and to some extent
independent) case studies provide a complex picture of the extent and nature
of the deployment of silverware in late antiquity. From the internalization of
the image of the late antique emperor through the development of a Christian
art in a context which implied worldly (and sometimes pagan) luxury, and the
close and interactive relationship between the visual and literary culture of
late antiquity to the survival of secular culture in Byzantium, the issues raised
in this book have significance beyond the narrow confines of silver studies.
Here I wish to dwell briefly on some of their wider implications.

My approach to late antique silver has been iconographic rather than
stylistic, and, as this book's title suggests, has been conceived primarily
in socio-cultural terms. Nevertheless, it has at least some bearing on the
subject which has been the traditional concern of historians of late antique art
since Alois Riegl wrote his seminal 'Late Roman Art Industry', namely, the
understanding of the stylistic changes of this period. The relationship between
the decoration of domestic silverware and *paideia*, traced in the second half of
the book, includes many examples of silver plate which scholars have singled
out as examples of the use of a classicistic style in the early Byzantine period,
and have contrasted with the move towards abstraction and formalization in
other types of art of the period.[2] The role of the educational culture of *paideia*
in elite self-definition in late antiquity suggests that the use of such styles can
be understood not simply in terms of a workshop tradition associated with a

particular medium and iconography, but as part of a cultural phenomenon. The demand for such objects among the elite may well have ensured the continuity of such artistic traditions – including classicizing style – until the middle of the seventh century. Interpreting the meaning of late antique classicism outside the conventional 'renaissance' framework allows us to understand the use of this style within its cultural context in late antiquity, rather than in relation to the Graeco-Roman past which it deliberately evokes or the Italian Renaissance which it has been deemed to anticipate.[3]

An understanding of late antique silver has implications for the study of the medieval art of Western Europe as well as Byzantium. At the end of Chapter 2, I suggested that the use of silver in Christian contexts in late antiquity could be seen as an important transitional stage in the development of the *ars sacra* of the early middle ages. In fact, one might extend this observation to all of the silverware and other forms of applied art which I have explored. Lasko's *ars sacra* is characterized by its reproduction and transformation of classical models. While they were employed in producing art for sacred functions and contexts, these models were not taken exclusively from the Christian art of late antiquity. If both the sacred and secular art of late antiquity helped to shape the art of the Carolingian and subsequent periods, which Lasko has described as predominately 'the art of the goldsmith, the metalworker, and the ivory carver',[4] then potentially the whole tradition of late antique luxury arts – of which silver plate was a prominent part – can help in understanding the formation of *ars sacra*.

Although the study of late Roman and early Byzantine silver plate might seem a rather restricted specialization, this book has shown that the range of its meanings and associations is very wide. This, I would argue, is the result of an approach which is neither strictly archaeological nor purely concerned with stylistic development. Such an approach could be productively extended to the silverware of earlier periods, but we have seen that silver plate served an especially wide range of functions in late antiquity, and for that reason should occupy a particularly prominent role in our understanding of art in that period.[5] That such breadth can be encompassed in a medium which some would still label a 'minor' art is significant, and reminds us how inappropriate it is to apply the hierarchies of post-enlightenment aesthetic canons to the luxury arts of late antiquity. The aim of this book has been not just to provide a more extensive knowledge of late Roman and early Byzantine silver, but to shed through that knowledge a light on that fascinating and complex period when the Roman empire was making its long, and often painful, transition between the classical and medieval worlds.

Notes

1.   Corippus, *In Laudem Iustini Augusti Minoris* 4.109–110. The translation is adapted from that of Averil Cameron.

2.   Kitzinger, *Byzantine Art in the Making*; Volbach, 'Silber- und Elfenbeinarbeiten'.

3.   Compare some recent approaches to the question of 'renaissances' in later Byzantine
      art: Belting, 'Kunst oder Object-Stil?'; Cutler, 'Uses of Luxury'.

4.   Lasko, *Ars Sacra*, xi.

5.   On silver plate in classical Greece, see M. Vickers & D. Gill, *Artful Crafts: Ancient Greek
      Silverware and Pottery* (Oxford, 1994). There is surprisingly little recent work on Roman
      silver of the first century AD, perhaps because – unlike late antique silver – there has
      not been the stimulus of new discoveries in this century. Although its surviving range
      may not be as great as late antique silver, it offers a rich and complex iconography,
      which deserves fuller study. For some possible directions this might take, see Elsner,
      Art and the Roman Viewer, 261–66; V. Huet, 'Stories One Might Tell of Roman Art:
      Reading Trajan's Column and the Tiberius Cup', in J. Elsner, ed., *Art and Text in Roman
      Culture* (Cambridge, 1996), 9–31.

Bibliography

Alexander, S.S., 'Heraclius, Byzantine Imperial Ideology and the David Plates', *Speculum* 52 (1977), 217–37.

Alföldi, A., *Die Kontorniaten: ein verkanntes Propagandamittel der stadtrömischen heidnischen Aristokratie in ihrem Kampfe gegen das christliche Kaisertum* (Budapest, 1943).

—, *Die monarchische Repräsentation im römischen Kaiserreiche* (Darmstadt, 1970).

—, Alföldi, E., and Clay, C.L., *Die Kontorniat-Medallions*, 3 vols (Berlin, 1976–1990).

Almagro-Gorbea, M., Alvarez Martinez, J.M., Blazquez Martinez, J.M. and Rovira, S., eds, *El Disco de Teodosio* (Madrid, 2000)

Amelung, W., *Die Sculpturen des Vaticanischen Museums I* (Berlin, 1903)

Anderson, G., *Philostratus: Biography and Belles Lettres in the Third Century AD* (London, 1986).

Angenendt, A.,'Der Kult der Reliquien', in A. Legner, ed., *Reliquien: Verehrung und Verklärung. Skizzen und Noten zur Thematik* (Cologne, 1989), 10–16.

Athanassiadi-Fowden, P., *Julian and Hellenism: an Intellectual Biography* (London, 1981).

Babelon, E., *Le Trésor d'argenterie de Berthouville près Bernay (Eure), conservé au Department des médailles et antiques de la Bibliothèque nationale* (Paris, 1916).

Baldwin, C.S., *Medieval Rhetoric and Poetic (to 1400): Interpreted from Representative Works* (New York, 1928).

Balty, J., *Mosaiques Antiques de Syrie* (Brussels, 1977).

Balty, J.C., 'Une version orientale méconnue du mythe de Cassiopée', in L. Kahil and C. Augé, eds, *Mythologie gréco-romaine, mythologies périphériques: études d'iconographie* (Paris, 1981), 95–106.

Baratte, F., 'La vaisselle d'argent dans le monde romain: bilan et perspectives', *Antiquité Tardive* 5 (1997), 25–28.

—, *La vaiselle d'argent en Gaule dans l'antiquité tardive (IIIe–Ve siècles)* (Paris, 1993).

—, 'Les trésors de temples dans le monde romain: une expression particulière de la piété', in S.A. Boyd, and M.M. Mango, eds, *Ecclesiastical Silver Plate in Sixth Century Byzantium* (Washington, DC, 1992), 111–21.

—, 'Vaisselle d'argent, souvenirs littéraires et manières de table: l'example des cuillers de Lampsaque', *CA* 40 (1992), 5–20.

— et al., *Le trésor de la Place Camille-Jouffray à Vienne [Isère]*, Gallia Supplement 50 (Paris, 1990).

— and Painter, K., eds, *Trésors d'orfèvrerie gallo-romains* (Paris, 1989).

—, ed., *Argenterie romaine et byzantine: actes de la table ronde, Paris 11–13 octobre 1983* (Paris, 1988).

—, Beck, F., et al.,*Orfèvrerie gallo-romaine: le trésor de Rethel* (Paris, 1988).

—, *Le trésor d'argenterie gallo-romaine de Notre-Dame-d'Allençon*, Gallia supplement 40 (Paris, 1981).

Barns, J., 'A New Gnomologium: with Some Remarks on Gnomic Anthologies', *CQ* 44–45 (1950–51), 126–37, 1–19.

Barr W., ed. and trans., *Claudian: Panegyricus de Quarto Consulatu Honorii Augusti*, Translated Texts for Historians, Latin Series 2 (Liverpool, 1981).

Bastien, P., and Metzger, C., *Le trésor de Beaurains (dit d'Arras)* (Wettern, 1977).

Beard, M. and North, J., eds, *Pagan Priests: Religion and Power in the Ancient World* (London, 1990).

Belting, H., 'Kunst oder Objekt-Stil? Fragen zur Funktion der "Kunst" in der "makedonischen Renaissance" ', in I. Hutter, ed., *Byzanz und der Westen: Studien zur Kunst des europäischen Mittelalters* (Vienna, 1984), 65–83.

Bergmann, B., 'The Roman House as Memory Theatre: The House of the Tragic Poet in Pompeii', *Art Bulletin* 76 (1994), 225–56.

Bernardi, J., ed. and trans., *Grégoire de Nazienze, Discours 42–43*, Sources Chrétiennes 384 (Paris, 1992).

Bianchi Bandinelli, R., *Rome: The Late Empire AD 200–400* (New York, 1971)

Binns, J.W., ed., *Latin Literature of the Fourth Century* (London, 1974)

Binsfeld, W., 'Der 1628 in Trier gefundene römische Silberschatz', *Trierer Zeitschrift* 42 (1979), 113–27.

Bland, R. and Johns, C., *The Hoxne Treasure: An Illustrated Introduction* (London, 1993).

—, 'The Hoxne Late Roman Treasure', *Britannia* 25 (1994), 165–73.

Bloch, H., 'The Pagan Revival in the West at the End of the Fourth Century', in A.D. Momigliano, ed., *The Conflict Between Paganism and Christianity in the Fourth Century* (Oxford, 1963), 193–218.

Boardman, J., *The Parthenon and Its Sculptures* (London, 1985).

Bowersock, G.W., 'Dionysos as Epic Hero', in N. Hopkinson, ed., *Studies in the Dionysiaca of Nonnus*, Cambridge Philological Society Supplementary vol. 17 (Cambridge, 1994), 156–66.

—, *Hellenism in Late Antiquity* (Cambridge, 1990).

—, *Julian the Apostate* (London, 1978).

Boyd, S.A., 'A "Metropolitan" Treasure from a Church in the Provinces: an Introduction to the Study of the Sion Treasure', in S. Boyd & M.M. Mango, eds, *Ecclesiastical Silver Plate in Sixth Century Byzantium* (Washington, DC, 1992), 5–38.

— and Mango, M.M., eds, *Ecclesiastical Silver Plate in Sixth Century Byzantium* (Washington, DC, 1992).

Bracci, D.A., *Dissertazione sopra un clipeo votivo, spettante alla famiglia Ardaburia trovato l'anno 1769, nelle vicinanze d'Orbetello ora essistente nel museo di S.A.R. Pietro Leopoldo* (Lucca, 1771).

Brailsford, J.W., *The Mildenhall Treasure: a Handbook*, 2nd edn (London, 1955).

Bréhier, L., 'Les trésors d'argenterie syrienne et l'école artistique d'Antioche', *Gazette des beaux arts* 62 (1920), 173–96.

Brendel, O.J., 'The Corbridge Lanx', *JRS* 31 (1941), 100–27.

Brilliant, R., *Visual Narratives: Storytelling in Etruscan and Roman Art* (Ithaca and London, 1984).

—, *The Arch of Septimius Severus in the Roman Forum*. Memoirs of the American Academy in Rome 29 (Rome, 1967).

—, *Gesture and Rank in Roman Art: Use of Gestures to Denote Status in Roman Sculpture and Coinage* (New Haven, 1963).

Brommer, F., *The Sculptures of the Parthenon: Metopes, Frieze, Pediments, Cult-statue* (London, 1979).

—, Peschlow-Bindokat, A. and Lindemann, D., *Denkmälerlisten zur griechischen Heldensage 2: Theseus, Bellerophon, Achill* (Marburg, 1974).

Brooks, E.W., ed. and trans., *John of Ephesus: Lives of the Eastern Saints*, Patrologia Orientalis 19 (Paris, 1925).

Brown, P., review of Thomas F. Mathews, *The Clash of Gods: A Reinterpretation of Early Christian Art* (Princeton, NJ, 1993), *Art Bulletin* 77 (1995), 499–502.

—, *Power and Persuasion in Late Antiquity: Towards a Christian Empire* (Madison WI, 1992).

—, *The Body and Society: Men, Women & Sexual Renunciation in Early Christianity* (London, 1988)

—, *The Cult of the Saints: Its Rise and Function in Latin Christianity* (Chicago, 1981).

Bruhn, J.A., *Coins and Costume in Late Antiquity*. Dumbarton Oaks Byzantine Collection Publications no. 9 (Washington, DC, 1993).

Buckton, D., ed, *Byzantium: Treasures of Byzantine Art and Culture from British Collections* (London, 1994).

Buschhausen, H., *Die spätrömischen Metallscrinia und frühchristlichen Reliquiare* (Vienna, 1971).

Cahn, H.A., Kaufmann-Heinimann, A., and Painter, K, 'A Table Ronde on a Treasure of Late Roman Silver', *JRA* 4 (1991), 184–91.

—, Kaufmann-Heinimann, A., et al., *Der spätrömische Silberschatz von Kaiseraugst*, Baseler Beiträge zur Ur- und Frühgeschichte 9 (Derendingen, 1984).

Cameron, Alan, 'The Last Pagans of Rome, in Harris, W.V., ed., *The Transformations of Urs Roma in Late Antiquity*, *JRA* Supplement 33 (Portsmouth, RI, 1999), 109–21 (p. 168, n.110).

—, 'Observations on the Distribution and Ownership of Late Roman Silver Plate', *JRA* 5 (1992), 178–185.

—, 'The Latin Revival of the Fourth Century', in W. Treadgold ed., *Renaissances Before the Renaissance: Cultural Revivals of Late Antiquity and the Middle Ages* (Stanford CA, 1984), 42–58.

—, 'Paganism and Literature in Late Fourth Century Rome', in M. Fuhrmann ed., *Christianisme et formes littéraires de l'antiquité tardive en Occident*, Entretiens Fondation Hardt 23 (Geneva, 1977), 1–30.

—, *Claudian: Poetry and Propaganda at the Court of Honorius* (Oxford, 1970).

—, 'The Date and Identity of Macrobius', *JRS* 56 (1966), 25–38.

Cameron, Averil, *The Mediterranean World in Late Antiquity AD 395-600* (London, 1993).

—, *The Later Roman Empire AD 284-430*. Fontana History of the Ancient World (London, 1993).

—, *Christianity and the Rhetoric of Empire: the Development of Christian Discourse* (Berkeley, CA, 1991).

—, ed. and trans., *Corippus: In Laudem Iustini Augusti Minoris* (London, 1976).

Cameron, Averil and Hall, S.G., introduction, trans. and commentary, Eusebius, *Life of Constantine* (Oxford, 1999).

Caprino, C., *La Colonna di Marco Aurelio* (Rome, 1955).

Castriota, D., *The Ara Pacis Augustae and the Imagery of Abundance in Later Greek and Roman Imperial Art* (Princeton, NJ, 1995).

Chadwick, H., 'Florilegium', in *Reallexikon für Antike und Christentum 7* (Stuttgart, 1969), 1131–60.

Chiesa, G.L., and Pedrazzini, M.P.L., eds, *Milano, capitale dell' impero romano 286–204 d.c.* (Milan, 1990).

Chuvin, P., *A Chronicle of the Last Pagans* (Cambridge MA, 1990).

—, 'Local Traditions and Classical Mythology in the *Dionysiaca*', in N. Hopkinson, ed., *Studies in the Dionysiaca of Nonnus*. Cambridge Philological Society Supplementary Vol. 17 (Cambridge, 1994), 167–76.

Cichorius, C., *Die Reliefs der Traianssäule*, 2 vols (Berlin, 1896–1900).

Clark, D.L., *Rhetoric in Graeco-Roman Education* (New York, 1957).

Clover, F.M. and Humphreys, R.S., eds, *Tradition and Innovation in Late Antiquity* (Madison, WI, 1989).

Coleman, K., 'Fatal Charades: Roman Executions Staged as Mythological Enactments', *JRS* 80 (1990), 44–73.

Cormack, R., *Writing in Gold: Byzantine Society and its Icons* (London 1985).

Curle, A.O., *The Treasure of Traprain* (Glasgow, 1923).

Cutler, A., *The Hand of the Master: Craftsmanship, Ivory and Society in Byzantium (9th–11th Centuries)* (Princeton, NJ, 1994)

—, 'Uses of Luxury: on the Functions of Consumption and Symbolic Capital in Byzantine Culture', in A. Guillou & J. Durand, eds, *Byzance et les images* (Paris, 1994), 287–328.

—, 'Barberiana: Notes on the Making, Content and Provenance of Louvre OA 9063', in *Tesserae. Festschrift für J. Engemann*. JbAC Ergänzungsband 18 (Münster, 1991), 329–39.

— and Oikonomides, N., 'An Imperial Byzantine Casket and its Fate at a Humanist's Hands', *Art Bulletin* 70 (1988), 77–87.

—, 'The Making of the Justinian Diptychs', *Byzantion* 54 (1984), 104–12

—, 'A Psalter from Mar Saba and the Evolution of the Byzantine David Cycle', *Journal of Jewish Art* 6 (1979), 39–63

Dale, T.E.A., 'The Power of the Anointed: The Life of David on Two Coptic Textiles in the Walters Art Gallery', *Journal of the Walters Art Gallery* 51 (1993), 23–42.

Dalton, O.M., *Catalogue of Early Christian Antiquities and Objects from the Christian East in the Department of British and Mediaeval Antiquities and Ethnography of the British Museum* (London, 1909).

—, 'A Second Silver Treasure from Cyprus', *Archaeologia* 60 (1906), 1–24.

—, 'A Byzantine Silver Treasure from the District of Kyrenia, Cyprus, now preserved in the British Museum', *Archaeologia* 57 (1900), 159–74.

Dassmann, E., 'Ambrosius und die Märtyrer', *JbAC*18 (1975), 49–68.

Daszewski, W.A., 'Cassiopeia in Paphos — a Levantine Going West', in V. Karageorghis, ed., *Acts of the International Archaeological Symposium 'Cyprus Between the Orient and the Occident'* (Nicosia, 1986), 454–70.

—, *Dionysos der Erlöser: griechische Mythen im spätantiken Cypern* (Mainz, 1985).

—, 'Polish Excavations at Kato (Nea) Paphos in 1970–1971', *Report of the Department of Antiquities, Cyprus* (1972), 204–36.

Davies, P.V., ed. and trans., Macrobius, *Saturnalia* (New York, 1969).

Davis, R., ed. and trans., *The Book of Pontiffs (Liber Pontificalis)*. Translated Texts for Historians, Latin Series 5 (Liverpool, 1989).

Dawes, E. and Baynes N.H., eds and trans., *Three Byzantine Saints: Contemporary Biographies* (Oxford, 1948).

De Paolis, P., 'Macrobio 1934–1984', *Lustrum* 28/29 (1986/87), 107–249.

De Rossi, G.B., *La Capsella Argentea Africana offerta al Sommo Pontefice Leone XIII dall' emo Sig. Card. Lavigerie Arcivesco di Cartagine. Memoria* (Rome 1889).

—, *Inscriptiones Christianae Urbis Romae*. Vol. II.1 (Rome 1881).

Deckers, J.G., 'Dionysos der Erlöser? Bemerkungen zur Deutung der Bodenmosaiken im 'Haus des Aion' in Nea-Paphos auf Cypern durch W.A. Daszewski', *Römische Quartelschrift* 81 (1986), 145–72.

—, 'Die Wandmalerei im Kaiserkultraum von Luxor', *JdI* 94 (1979), 600–52.

Degering, H., and Boeckler, A., *Die Quedlinburger Italafragmente*, 2 vols (Berlin, 1932).

Deichmann, F.W., *Ravenna, Hauptstadt des spätantiken Abendlandes*, Komentar I (Wiesbaden, 1974).

Delbrueck, R., *Antike Porphyrwerke* (Berlin, 1932).

—, *Die Consulardiptychen und verwandte Denkmäler*, 2 vols (Berlin and Leipzig, 1929).

Delehaye, H., *Les origines du culte des martyrs*, Subsidia Hagiographica 20, 2nd edn (Brussels, 1933).

Delgado y Hernandez, A., *Memoria historico-critica sobre el gran disco de Theodosio, encontrado en Almendralejo* (Madrid, 1849).

Delmaire, R., *Largesses sacrées et res privata: l'aerarium impérial et son administration du IVe au VIe siècle* (Paris, 1989).

—, 'Le déclin des largesses sacrées', in C. Morrisson & J. Lefort, eds, *Hommes et richesses dans l'empire byzantin I: IVe–VIIe siècle* (Paris, 1989), 265–77.

—, 'Les largesses impériales et l'émission d'argenterie du IVe au VIe siècle', in F. Baratte, ed., *Argenterie romaine et byzantine* (Paris, 1988), 113–22.

Diehl, C., 'L'école artistique d'Antioche et les trésors d'argenterie syrienne', *Syria* 2 (1921), 81–95.

Dodd, E.C., 'The Question of Workshop: Evidence of the Stamps on the Sion Treasure', in S.A. Boyd & M.M. Mango, eds, *Ecclesiastical Silver Plate in Sixth Century Byzantium* (Washington, DC, 1992), 57–63.

—, *Byzantine Silver Treasures*, Monographien der Abegg Stiftung 9 (Bern, 1973).

—, 'Byzantine Silver Stamps: Supplement I. New Stamps from the Reigns of Justin II and Constans II', *DOP* 18 (1964), 239–48.

—, 'Byzantine Silver Stamps: Supplement II. More Treasure from Syria', *DOP* 22 (1968), 141–50.

—, *Byzantine Silver Stamps. With an excursus on the Comes Sacrarum Largitionum by J.P.C. Kent*, Dumbarton Oaks Studies 7 (Washington, DC, 1961).

Duffy, J., and Vikan, G., 'A Small Box in John Moschus', *GRBS* 24 (1983), 93–99.

Dunbabin, K., *The Mosaics of Roman North Africa: Studies in Iconography and Patronage* (Oxford, 1978).

Duval, N., 'La place de Split dans l'architecture antique du bas-empire', *Urbs* 4 (1961–62), 67–95.

Ebersolt, J., and Thiers, A., *Les églises de Constantinople* (Paris, 1913).

Effenberger, A., 'Bemerkungen zur "Kaper-Koraon-Schatz"', in *Tesserae. Festschrift für J. Engemann*, JbAC Ergänzungsband 18 (Münster, 1991), 241–77.

Effenberger, A., et al., *Spätantike und früh-byzantinische Silbergefässe aus der Staatlichen Ermitage, Leningrad* (Berlin, 1978).

Ellis, S.P., 'Late-Antique Dining: Architecture, Furnishings and Behaviour', in R. Laurence & A. Wallace-Hadrill eds, *Domestic Space in the Roman World: Pompeii and Beyond*, JRA Supplement 22 (Portsmouth RI, 1997), 41–51.

—, 'Power, Architecture and Decor: How the Late Roman Aristocrat Appeared to his Guests', in E.K. Gazda, ed., *Roman Art in the Private Sphere* (Ann Arbor, MI, 1991), 117–34.

Elsner, J., 'Frontality in the Column of Marcus Aurelius', in V. Huet & J. Scheidt, eds, *La Colonne Aurélienne: autour de la Colonne Aurélienne. Geste et image sur la colonne de Marc Aurèle à Rome* (Brussels, 2000), 251–64.

—, 'Replicating Palestine and Reversing the Reformation: Pilgrimage and Collecting at Bobbio, Monza and Walsingham', *Journal of the History of Collections* 9 (1997), 117–30.

—, *Art and the Roman Viewer: The Transformation of Art from the Pagan World to Christianity* (Cambridge, 1995).

Emery, W.B. and Kirwan, L.P., *The Royal Tombs of Ballana and Qustul. Mission archéologique de Nubie 1929–1934*, 2 vols (Cairo, 1938).

Engemann, J., 'Palästinensische Pilgerampullen im F.J. Dölger Institut in Bonn', *JbAC* 16 (1973), 1–27.

—, 'Anmerkungen zu spätantiken Geräten des Alltagslebens mit Christlichen Bildern, Symbolen und Inschriften', *JbAC* 15 (1972), 154–73.

Evans, H.C. andWixom, W.D., eds, *The Glory of Byzantium: Art and Culture of the Middle Byzantine Era, A.D. 843–1261* (New York, 1997).

Fairbanks, A., ed. and trans., *Philostratus the Elder and Philostratus the Younger, Imagines. Callistratus, Descriptiones*. Loeb Classical Library (Cambridge, MA, 1931).

Festugière, A.-J., ed. and trans., *La Vie de Théodore de Sykéon*, Subsidia Hagiographica 48, 2 vols (Brussels, 1970).

Finley, M.I., *The Ancient Economy*, 2nd edn (London, 1985).

Firatli, N., 'Un trésor du VIe siècle trouvé à Kumluca en Lycie', in *Akten des VII Internationalen Kongress für Christliche Archäologie*, 2 vols (Vatican City, 1969), 523–25.

Forsyth, G.K. and Weitzmann, K., *The Monastery of St. Catherine at Mount Sinai: The Church and Fortress of Justinian* (Ann Arbor, MI, 1973).

Fowden, G., *The Egyptian Hermes: a Historical Approach to the Late Pagan Mind* (Cambridge, 1986).

Frantz, A., *Late Antiquity AD 267–700: Excavations of the American School in Athens in the Athenian Agora* (Princeton, NJ, 1988).

Frend, W.C.H., *The Archaeology of Early Christianity: a History* (London, 1996).

Fuhrmann, H., 'Studien zu den Consulardiptychen verwandten Denkmälern II: Tönerne Missoria aus der Zeit der Tetrarchie', *RM* 55 (1940), 92–99.

—, 'Studien zu den Consulardiptychen verwandten Denkmälern I. Eine Glasschale von der Vicennalienfeier Constantins des Grossen zu Rom im Jahre 326 nach Chr.', *RM* 54 (1939), 161–75.

Gajdukerič, V.F., *Das Bosporanische Reich* (Berlin and Amsterdam, 1971).

Galinsky, K., *Augustan Culture: an Interpretative Introduction* (Princeton, NJ, 1996)

Garbsch, J. and Overbeck, B., *Spätantike zwischen Heidentum und Christentum* (Munich, 1989).

Gazda, E.K., ed., *Roman Art in the Private Sphere: New Perspectives on the Architecture and Decor of the Domus, Villa and Insula* (Ann Arbor, MI, 1991).

M. Gibson, *The Liverpool Ivories: Late Antique and Medieval Ivory and Bone Carving in Liverpool Museum and the Walker Art Gallery* (London, 1994).

Giovagnoli, D.E., 'Una collezione di vasi eucaristici scoperti a Canosca', *Rivista di Archeologia Cristiana* 12 (1935), 313–28.

Gordon, R., 'The Veil of Power: Emperors, Sacrificers and Benefactors', in M. Beard and J. North, eds, *Pagan Priests: Religion and Power in the Ancient World* (London, 1990).

Gnirs, A., 'Frühchristliche Denkmäler in Pola', *Jahrbuch der K. K. Zentral-Kommission für Erforschung und Erhaltung der Kunst-und Historischen Denkmale* (neue Folge) 4 (1906), 230–55.

Grabar, A., *Ampoules de Terre-Saint (Monza, Bobbio)* (Paris, 1958).

—, 'Quelques reliquaires de Saint Démétrios et le martyrium du saint à Salonique', *DOP* 5 (1950), 1–28.

—, *Les peintures de l'Evangéliare de Sinope (Bibliothèque nationale, Suppl. gr. 1286)* (Paris, 1948).

—, *Martyrium: recherches sur le culte des reliques et l'art chrétien antique*, 2 vols (Paris, 1946).

—, *L'empereur dans l'art byzantin* (Paris, 1936).

Graillot, H., *Le Culte de Cybéle mère des dieux à Rome et dans l'Empire romain* (Paris, 1912).

Greifenhagen, A., 'Kindheitsmythos des Dionysos', *RM* 46 (1931), 27–43.

Grierson, P., 'The Role of Silver in the Early Byzantine Economy', in S.A. Boyd & M.M. Mango, eds, *Ecclesiastical Silver Plate in Sixth Century Byzantium* (Washington, DC, 1992), 137–46.

—, *Catalogue of Byzantine Coins in the Dumbarton Oaks Collection. Volume Two: Phocas to Theodosius III 602–717. Part I: Phocas and Heraclius (602–641)* (Washington, DC, 1968).

—, 'The Date of the Dumbarton Oaks Epiphany Medallion', *DOP* 15 (1961), 221–24.

—, 'The Kyrenia Girdle of Byzantine Medallions and Solidi', *Numismatic Chronicle (6th ser.)* 15 (1955), 55–70.

Grisar, H., *Die römische Kapelle Sancta sanctorum und ihr Schatz* (Freiburg, 1908).

Grünhagen, W., *Der Schatzfund von Groß Bodungen*. Römisch-Germanische Forschungen 21 (Berlin, 1954).

Guberti Bassett, S., '"Excellent Offerings": The Lausos Collection in Constantinople', *Art Bulletin* 82 (2000), 6–25.

—, '*Historiae custos*: Sculpture and Tradition in the Baths of Zeuxippos', *AJA* 100 (1996), 491–506.

Guerrini, L., 'Infanzia di Achille e sua educazione presso Chirone', *Studi Miscellanei* (1958/9), 43–53.

Guidi, I., ed. and trans., Severus of Antioch, *Homiliae Cathedrales*. Patrologia Orientalis 22 (Paris, 1930).

Gutmann, J., 'The Dura Europos Synagogue Paintings: The State of Research', in I. Levine, ed., *The Synagogue in Late Antiquity* (Philadelphia, 1987), 61–72.

Hamberg, P.G., *Studies in Roman Imperial Art, with special reference to the State Reliefs of the Second Century* (Uppsala, 1945).

Hanfmann, G.M.A., 'Notes on the Mosaics from Antioch', *AJA* 43 (1939), 229–46.

Hanson, J., *The Ivory Casket in Sens known as La Sainte Chasse* (unpublished PhD dissertation, Courtauld Institute, University of London, 1996).

Harden, D.B., ed., *Glass of the Caesars* (Milan, 1987).

Harrison R.M., et al., *Excavations at Saraçhane in Istanbul I. The Excavations, Structures, Architectural Decoration, Small Finds, Coins, Bones and Molluscs* (Princeton, NJ, 1986).

Harvey, S.A., *Asceticism and Society in Crisis: John of Ephesus and the 'Lives of Eastern Saints'* (Berkeley and Los Angeles, CA, 1990).

Hauser, S.P., *Spätantike und frühbyzantinische Silberlöffel: Bemerkungen zur Produktion von Luxusgütern im 5. bis 7. Jahrhundert*, *JbAC* Ergänzungsband, 19 (Münster, 1992).

Haverfield, F.J., 'Roman Silver in Northumberland', *JRS* 4 (1914), 1–12.

Haynes, D.E.L. and Hirst, P.E.D., *Porta Argentariorum* (London, 1939).

Helbig, W., rev. Amelung, W., et al., *Führer durch die öffentlichen Sammlungen klassischer Altertümer in Rom* I, 3rd edn (Leipzig, 1912).

Hellenkemper, H., 'Ecclesiastical Silver Hoards and their Findspots: Implications for the Treasure found at Korydalla, Lycia', in S.A. Boyd & M.M. Mango, eds, *Ecclesiastical Silver Plate in Sixth Century Byzantium* (Washington, DC, 1992), 65–70.

Hendy, M.F., 'The Administration of Mints and Treasuries, Fourth to Seventh Centuries, with an Appendix on the Production of Silver Plate', in M.F. Hendy, *The Economy, Fiscal Administration and Coinage of Byzantium* (Northampton, 1989), VI, 1–18.

—, *Studies in the Byzantine Monetary Economy c. 300–1450* (Cambridge, 1985).

Hilgers, W., *Lateinische Gefässnamen. Bezeichnungen, Funktion und Form römische Gefässe nach den antiken Schriftquellen.* Beihefter Bonner Jahrbuch 31 (Dusseldörf, 1969).

Hopkins, K., *Conquerors and Slaves: Sociological Studies in Roman History*, vol. 1 (Cambridge, 1978).

Hopkinson, N., ed., *Studies in the Dionysiaca of Nonnus.* Cambridge Philological Society Supplementary vol. 17 (Cambridge, 1994).

Huet, V., 'Stories One Might Tell of Roman Art: Reading Trajan's Column and the Tiberius Cup', in J. Elsner, ed., *Art and Text in Roman Culture* (Cambridge, 1996), 9–31.

Huskinson, J., *Roman Children's Sarcophagi: Their Decoration and its Social Significance* (Oxford, 1996).

Jaeger, W., *Early Christianity and Greek Paideia* (Cambridge, MA, 1961).

James, L., '"Pray Not to Fall into Temptation and Be on Your Guard": Pagan Statues in Christian Constantinople', *Gesta* 35 (1996), 12–20.

Janes, D., *God and Gold in Late Antiquity* (Cambridge, 1998).

Johansen, I.M., 'Rings, Fibulae and Buckles with Imperial Portraits and Incriptions', *JRA* 7 (1994), 223–42.

Johns, C., *The Jewellery of Roman Britain: Celtic and Classical Traditions* (London, 1996).

— and Painter, K., 'The Risley Park Lanx: Bauge, Bayeux, Buch or Britain?', in *Orbis Romanus Christianusque ab Diocletiani aetate usque ad Heraclium. Travaux sur l'Antiqué Tardive rassemblés autour des recherches de Noël Duval* (Paris, 1995), 175–87.

—, 'Research on Roman Silver Plate', *JRA* 3 (1990), 28–43.

— and Potter, T., *The Thetford Treasure: Roman Jewellery and Silver* (London, 1983).

—, 'The Risley Park Lanx: a Lost Antiquity from Roman Britain, *Antiquaries Journal* 61 (1981), 53–72.

Jones, A.H.M., *The Later Roman Empire 284–602. A Social, Economic and Administrative Survey*, 2 vols (Oxford, 1964).

Jones, C.P., 'Dinner Theatre', in W. Slater, ed., *Dining in a Classical Context* (Ann Arbor, MI, 1991), 185–98.

Kane, J.P., 'The Mithraic Meal in its Greek and Roman Environment', in J.R. Hinnells, ed., *Mithraic Studies: Proceedings of the First International Conference of Mithraic Studies*, 2 vols (Manchester, 1975), vol. II, 311–51.

Kaster, R., *Guardians of Language: The Grammarian and Society in Late Antiquity* (Berkeley, CA, 1988).

Kaufmann-Heinimann, A., 'Eighteen New Pieces from the Late Roman Silver Treasure of Kaiseraugst: First Notice', *JRA* 12 (1999), 333–41.

Kent, J.P.C., *The Roman Imperial Coinage VIII: the Family of Constantine I AD 337–364* (London, 1981)

— and Painter, K., eds, *The Wealth of the Roman World: Gold and Silver AD 300–700* (London, 1977).

Kiilerich, B., *Late Fourth Century Classicism in the Plastic Arts: Studies in the So-Called Theodosian Renaissance* (Odense, 1993).

Kinney, D., review of Thomas F. Mathews, *The Clash of Gods: A Reinterpretation of Early Christian Art* (Princeton, NJ, 1993), *Studies in Iconography* 16 (1994), 237–42.

Kitzinger, E., *Byzantine Art in the Making: Main Lines of Stylistic Development in Mediterranean Art, 3rd–7th century* (London, 1977).

—, 'Byzantine Art in the Period Between Justinian and Iconoclasm', in *Berichte zum XI. internationalen Byzantinistenkongress* (Munich, 1958), 1–50.

Kleiner, D.E.E., *Roman Sculpture* (New Haven & London, 1992).

Koch, G., *Die Antiken Sarkophagreliefs XII.6. Die mythologischen Sarkophage: Meleager* (Berlin, 1975).

Kondoleon, C.,*Domestic and Divine: Roman Mosaics in the House of Dionysos* (Ithaca & London, 1995).

—, 'Signs of Privilege and Pleasure: Roman Domestic Mosaics', in E.K. Gazda, ed., *Roman Art in the Private Sphere* (Ann Arbor, MI, 1991), 105–15.

Koortbojian, M., *Myth, Meaning and Memory on Roman Sarcophagi* (Berkeley, CA, 1995).

Kötzsche-Breitenbruch, L., 'Geburt III (ikonographisch)', in *Reallexikon für Antike und Christentum 9* (1973), 172–216.

Kossatz-Deissmann, A., 'Achilles', in *LIMC 1* (1981), 37–200.

Kraft, K., 'Eine spätantike Glaspaste', *Jahrbuch für Numismatik und Geldgeschichte* 2 (1950–51), 36–42.

Krautheimer, R., 'The Architecture of Sixtus III: a fifth century renaissance?', in R. Krautheimer, *Studies in Early Christian, Medieval and Renaissance Art* (New York, 1969).

—, Corbett, S. and Frankl, W., *Corpus Basilicarum Christianarum Romae. The Early Christian Basilicas of Rome (IV–IX Centuries)*, 5 vols (Vatican City, 1937–77).

Kroll, W., *Historia Alexandri Magni* (Berlin, 1926).

Künzl, E., 'Römische Tempelschätze und Sakralinventare: Votive, Horte, Beute', *Antiquité Tardive* 5 (1997), 57–81.

Kuttner, A., *Dynasty and Empire in the Age of Augustus: The Case of The Boscoreale Cups* (Berkeley, CA, 1995).

Lamberton, R. and Keaney, J.J., eds, *Homer's Ancient Readers: the Hermeneutics of Greek Epic's Earliest Exegetes* (Princeton, NJ, 1992).

Lasko, P., *Ars Sacra 800-1200*, Pelican History of Art, 2nd edn (New Haven & London, 1994 [1st edn 1972]).

Lauer, P., 'Le trésor du Sancta Sanctorum', *Mon. Piot* 15 (1906), 7–140.

Lawrence, M., 'Columnar Sarcophagi in the Latin West: Ateliers, Chronology, Style', *Art Bulletin* 14 (1932), 103–85.

Lehmann-Hartleben, K., 'The Dome of Heaven', *Art Bulletin* 27 (1945), 1–27.

— and Olsen, E.C., *Dionysiac Sarcophagi in Baltimore* (Baltimore, MD, 1942).

—, *Die Trajanssäule: ein römisches Kunstwerk zu Beginn der Spätantike*, 2 vols (Berlin and Leipzig, 1926).

Lemerle, P., *Byzantine Humanism: The First Phase. Notes and remarks on education and culture in Byzantium from its origins to the 10th century*, trans. H. Lindsay & A. Moffatt, Byzantina Australiensia 3 (Canberra, 1986).

—, ed. and trans., *Les plus anciens recueils des miracles de S. Démétrios*, 2 vols (Paris, 1979).

Lenzen, V.F., *The Triumph of Dionysos on Textiles of Late Antique Egypt* (Los Angeles and Berkeley, CA, 1960).

Leontsini, S., *Die Prostitution im frühen Byzanz* (Vienna, 1989).

Levi, A., *La patera d'argento di Parabiago*, R. Instituto d'Archeologia e Storia dell'Arte, Opera d'Arte V (Rome, 1935).

Levi, D., *Antioch Mosaic Pavements*, 2 vols (Princeton, NJ, 1947).

Levin, I., *The Quedlinburg Itala: the Oldest Illustrated Biblical Manuscript* (Leiden, 1985).

Lexicon Iconographicum Mythologiae Classicae (LIMC), 8 vols (Zurich, 1981–1999).

Liebeschuetz, W., 'The Use of Pagan Mythology in the Christian Empire with Particular Reference to the *Dionysiaca* of Nonnos', in P. Allen & E.M. Jeffreys eds, *The Sixth Century — End or Beginning?* Byzantina Australiensa 10 (Brisbane, 1996), 75–91.

Ling, R., *Roman Painting* (Cambridge, 1991).

L'Orange, H.P., *Art Forms and Civic Life in the Late Roman Empire* (Princeton, NJ, 1965).

L'Orange, H.P. and von Gerkan, A., *Der spätantike Bildschmuck des Konstantinsbogens* (Berlin, 1939).

Lowden, J., *Early Christian and Byzantine Art* (London, 1997).

—, 'The Royal/Imperial Book and the Image or Self-Image of the Medieval Ruler', in A.J. Duggan, ed., *Kings and Kingship in Medieval Europe* (London, 1993), 213–40.

—, *The Octateuchs: a Study in Byzantine Manuscript Illustration* (University Park, PA, 1992).

—, 'Concerning the Cotton Genesis and Other Illustrated Manuscripts of Genesis', *Gesta* 31 (1992), 40–53.

MacCormack, S., *The Shadows of Poetry: Vergil in the Mind of Augustine* (Berkeley, CA, 1998)

—, *Art and Ceremony in Late Antiquity* (Berkeley, CA, 1981).

MacMullen, R., 'The Emperor's Largesses', *Latomus* 21 (1962), 159–66.

Maguire, H., 'Magic and Money in the Early Middle Ages', *Speculum* 72 (1997), 1037–54.

—, 'Garments Pleasing to God: The Significance of Domestic Textile Designs in the Early Byzantine Period', *DOP* 44 (1990), 215–24.

—, 'The Art of Comparing in Byzantium', *Art Bulletin* 70 (1988), 88–103.

—, *Earth and Ocean: The Terrestrial World in Early Byzantine Art* (University Park, PA, 1987).

—, *Art and Eloquence in Byzantium* (Princeton, NJ, 1981).

Manacorda, M.A., *La paideia di Achille* (Rome, 1971).

Manafis K.A., ed., *Sinai: Treasures of the Monastery of St Catherine* (Athens, 1990).

Mango, C., Vickers, M., and Francis, E.D., 'The Palace of Lausus at Constantinople and its Collection of Ancient Statues', *Journal of the History of Collections* 4 (1992), 89–98.

— and Scott, R., with the assistance of Greatrex, G., *The Chronicle of Theophanes Confessor: Byzantine and Near Eastern History AD 284–813* (Oxford, 1997).

—, ed., *The Art of the Byzantine Empire 312–1453. Sources and Documents* (Englewood Cliffs, NJ, 1971).

—, 'Antique Statuary and the Byzantine Beholder', *DOP* 17 (1963), 55–75.

Mango, M.M. and Bennet, A., *The Sevso Treasure: Part I, Art Historical Description and Inscriptions, Methods of Manufacture and Scientific Analyses, JRA* Supplementary Series no. 12.1 (Ann Arbor, MI, 1994).

—, 'Imperial Art in the Seventh Century', in P. Magdalino ed., *New Constantines: The Rhythm of Imperial Renewal in Byzantium, 4th–13th Centuries* (Aldershot, 1994), 109–38.

—, 'The Monetary Value of Silver Revetments and Objects Belonging to Churches, AD 300–700', in S.A. Boyd & M.M. Mango, eds, *Ecclesiastical Silver Plate in Sixth Century Byzantium* (Washington, DC, 1992), 123–36.

—, 'The Purpose and Places of Byzantine Silver Stamping', in S.A. Boyd & M.M. Mango, eds, *Ecclesiastical Silver Plate in Sixth Century Byzantium* (Washington, DC, 1992), 203–16.

—, 'The Uses of Liturgical Silver, 4th–7th Centuries', in R. Morris ed., *Church and People in Byzantium* (Birmingham, 1990), 245–61.

—, *The Sevso Treasure: a Collection from Late Antiquity.* Sotheby's Catalogue (London, 1990).

—, 'The Origins of the Syrian Ecclesiastical Silver Treasures of the Sixth-Seventh

Centuries', in F. Baratte ed., *Argenterie romaine et byzantine* (Paris, 1988), 163–78.

—, *Silver from Early Byzantium: the Kaper Koraon and Related Treasures* (Baltimore, MD, 1986).

Markus, R.A., *The End of Ancient Christianity* (Cambridge, 1990).

—, 'Paganism, Christianity and the Latin Classics in the Fourth Century', in J.W. Binns, ed., *Latin Literature of the Fourth Century* (London, 1974), 1–21.

Marrou, H.I., *A History of Education in Antiquity*, trans., G. Lamb (Madison WI, 1982).

—, *Histoire de l'education dans l'antiquité* (Paris, 1948).

—, *ΜΟΥΣΙΚΟΣ ΑΝΗΡ, étude sur les scènes de la vie intellectuelle figurant sur les monuments funéraires romains* (Grenoble, 1938).

Mathews, T.F., *The Clash of Gods: A Reinterpretation of Early Christian Art* (Princeton, NJ, 1993).

Matthews, J.F., *The Roman Empire of Ammianus* (London, 1989).

—, *Western Aristocracies and the Imperial Court, AD 364–425* (Oxford, 1975).

—, 'The Letters of Symmachus', in J.W. Binns, ed., *Latin Literature of the Fourth Century* (London, 1974), 58–99.

Matz, F., *Die antiken Sarkophagreliefs IV: die Dionysischen Sarkophage*, 4 vols (Berlin, 1969).

Matzulewitsch, L.A., 'L'antique byzantine et la region de Kama', in *Monuments Archéologiques de l'Oural et du Pays de la Kama*, Materiaux et Recherches d'Archéologie de l'URSS No. 1 (Moscow and Leningrad, 1940), 139–51.

—, *Byzantinische Antike: Studien auf Grund der Silbergefässe der Ermitage* (Berlin and Leipzig, 1929).

McCormick, M., 'Clovis at Tours: Byzantine Public Ritual and the Origins of Medieval Ruler Symbolism', in E.K. Chrysos & A. Schwartz, eds, *Das Reich und die Barbaren* (Vienna, 1989).

Meischner, J., 'Das Missorium des Theodosius in Madrid', *JdI* 111 (1996), 389–432.

Merati, A., *Il Tesoro del Duomo di Monza* (Monza, 1963).

Meyer, R.T. trans. Palladius, *The Lausiac History*, Christian Writers 34 (New York, 1964).

Milliken, W.H., 'The Cleveland Byzantine Silver Treasure', *Bulletin of the Cleveland Museum of Art* 38 (1951), 142–45.

Milojčić, V., 'Zu den spätkaiserzeitlichen und merowingischen Silberlöffeln', *Bericht der Römisch-Germanischen Kommission* 49 (1968), 111–33.

Montserrat, D., 'Early Byzantine Church Lighting: A New Text', *Orientalia* 64 (1995), 430–44.

Morgan, T., *Literate Education in the Hellenistic and Roman Worlds* (Cambridge, 1998)

Morrisson, C. and Lefort, J., eds, *Hommes et richesses dans l'empire byzantin I, IVe–VIIe siècle* (Paris, 1989).

Muñoz, A., *Il Codice purpureo di Rossano e il Frammento sinopense* (Rome, 1907).

Musso, L., *Manifattura suntuaria e committenza pagana nella Roma del IV Secolo: indagine sulla lanx di Parabiago* (Rome, 1983).

Nadeau, R., 'The Progymnasmata of Aphthonius in Translation', *Speech Monographs* 19 (1952), 264–85.

Newby, Z., 'Reading Programs in Graeco-Roman Art: Reflections on the Spada Reliefs', in D. Fredrick, ed., *The Roman Gaze: Vision, Power and the Body* (Baltimore, MD, 2001).

Nicholson, O., 'The Corbridge Lanx and the Emperor Julian', *Britannia* 26 (1995), 312–15.

Nixon, C.E.V., and Rogers, B.S., eds and trans., *In Praise of Later Roman Emperors: The Panegyrici Latinii* (Berkeley, CA, 1994).

Ognenova, L., 'Plats en argent du décennaire de l'empereur Licinius', *Bulletin d'Institut Archéologique Bulgare* 19 (1955), 233–43.

Overbeck, B., *Argentum Romanum: ein Schatzfund von spätrömischen Prunkgeschirr* (Munich, 1973).

The Oxford Dictionary of Byzantium 3 vols. (New York, 1991).

Painter, K.S., 'The Silver Dish of Ardabur Aspar', in E. Herring, R. Whitehouse & J. Wikins, eds, *Paper of the Fourth Conference of Italian Archaeology 2: The Archaeology of Power, part 2* (London, 1991), 74–79.

—, 'The Seuso Treasure', *Minerva* 1 no. 4 (April, 1990), 4–11.

—, 'Roman Silver Hoards: Ownership and Status' in F. Baratte, ed., *Argenterie romaine et byzantine* (Paris, 1988), 97–111.

—, *The Mildenhall Treasure. Roman Silver from East Anglia* (London, 1977).

—, *The Water Newton Early Christian Silver* (London, 1977).

Panofsky, E., *Renaissance and Renascences in Western Art*, 2nd edn (Stockholm, 1960).

Patlagean, E., *Pauvreté économique et pauvreté sociale à Byzance, 4e–7e siècles* (Paris, 1977).

Pelekanides, S., ''Αργυρὰ πινάκια τοῦ Μουσείου Μπενάκη', *Ἀρχαιολογικὴ Ἐφημερίς* 1942–44 (1948), 37–62.

Pelikan, J., *Christianity and Classical Culture: the Metamorphosis of Natural Theology in the Christian Encounter with Hellenism* (New Haven, CT, 1993).

Pharr, C., with Davidson, T.S. and Pharr, M.B., eds, *The Theodosian Code and Novels: and the Sirmondian constitutions. A translation with commentary, glossary and bibliography* (Princeton, NJ, 1952).

Pirzio Biroli Stefanelli, L., *L'argento dei romani: vasellame da tavola e d'apparato* (Rome, 1991).

Potter, T.W., *Roman Britain*, 2nd edn (London, 1997).

Remensnyder, A.G., 'Legendary Treasure at Conques: Reliquaries and Imaginative Memory', *Speculum* 71 (1996), 884–906.

Riegl, A., *Die spätromische Kunstindustrie nach den Funden in Osterreich-Ungarn* (Vienna, 1901).

Robert, C., *Die antiken Sarkophagreliefs II: Mythologischen Cyklen* (Rome, 1968).

Roberts, M., *Poetry and the Cult of the Martyrs: the Liber Peristephanon of Prudentius* (Ann Arbor, MI, 1993).

Rodenwaldt, G., 'Säulensarcophage', *RM* 38/39 (1923–24), 1–40

Rogers, G.M., *The Sacred Identity of Ephesos: Foundation Myths of a Roman City* (London, 1991).

Rollason, D., *Saints and Relics in Anglo-Saxon England* (Oxford, 1989).

Rosenthal, E., *The Illuminations of the Vergilius Romanus (Cod. Vat. Lat. 3867). A Stylistic and Iconographical Analysis* (Zurich, 1972).

Ross, M.C., *Catalogue of Byzantine and Early Medieval Antiquities in the Dumbarton Oaks Collection I* (Washington, DC, 1962).

—, 'A Silver Treasure Found at Daphne Harbiye', *Archaeology* 6 (1953), 39-41

—, 'A Second Byzantine Treasure from Hama', *Archaeology* 3 (1950), 162–63.

Roueché, C., *Aphrodisias in Late Antiquity: the Late Roman Inscriptions including texts from the excavations of Aphrodisias conducted by Kenan T. Erim, JRS* Monographs (London, 1989).

Russell, D.A. and Wilson, N.G., eds and trans., *Menander Rhetor* (Oxford, 1981).

Rutschowscaya, M.-H., *Tissus Coptes* (Paris, 1990).

Salomonson, J.W., 'Kunstgeschichtliche und ikonographische Untersuchungen zu einem Tonfragment der Sammlung Benaki in Athen', *BABesch* 47 (1973), 3–82.

—, 'Spätrömische Tonware mit Reliefverzierung aus nordafrikanischen Werkstätten: entwicklungeschichtliche Untersuchungen zur reliefgeschmückten Terra Sigillata "C" ', *BABesch* 44 (1969), 4–109.

—, 'Late Roman Earthenware with Relief Decoration Found in Northern Africa and Egypt', *Oudheidkundige mededelingen uit het Rijksmuseum von oudheden te Leiden* 43 (1962), 53–95.

Salzman, M.R., *On Roman Time: The Codex Calendar of 354 and the Rhythms of Urban Life in Late Antiquity* (Berkeley, CA, 1990).

Schefold, K., *Pompejanische Malerei: Sinn und Ideengeschichte* (Basel, 1952).

Schnapp, A., *Le chasseur et la cité: chase et érotique en Grèce ancienne* (Paris, 1997).

—, 'Eros the Hunter', in C. Bérard et al., eds, *A City of Images: Iconography and Society in Ancient Greece* (Princeton, NJ, 1989), 71–88.

Schrader, J.L., 'Antique and Early Christian Sources for the Riha and Stuma Patens', *Gesta* 18 (1979), 147–56.

Ševčenko, I., 'The Sion Treasure: the Evidence of the Inscriptions', in S.A. Boyd & M.M. Mango, eds, *Ecclesiastical Silver Plate in Sixth Century Byzantium* (Washington, DC, 1992), 49–56.

— and Ševčenko, N.P., eds and trans., *The Life of St. Nicholas of Sion* (Brookline, MA, 1984).

Shapiro, M., 'The Place of the Joshua Roll in Byzantine History', *Gazette des beaux arts (6th ser.)* 35 (1949), 161–76.

Shelton, K., *The Esquiline Treasure* (London, 1981).

Smith, R.B.E., *Julian's Gods: Religion and Philosophy in the Thought and Action of Julian the Apostate* (London, 1995).

Snyder, G.A.S., 'The So-Called Puteal in the Capitoline Museum at Rome', *JRS* 13 (1923), 58–68.

Spon, J., 'Sur un Bouclier antique d'argent appellé par les Latins CLYPEUS VOTIVUS qui se voit à Lyon dans le Cabinet de M. Octavio Mey', in *Recherches curieuses d'antiquité: contennues en plusieurs dissertations, sur des médailles, bas reliefs, statues, mosaiques et inscriptions antiques* (Lyon, 1683), 3–32.

—, *Recherches des antiquités et curiosités de la ville de Lyon: ancienne colonie des Romains et capitale de la Gaule celtique* (Lyon, 1673).

Stemmer, K., *Untersuchungen zur Typologie, Chronologie und Ikonographie der Panzerstatuen* (Berlin, 1978).

Stern, H., *Les mosaiques des maisons d'Achille et de Cassiopée à Palmyre* (Paris, 1977).

—, *Le Calendrier de 354: étude sur son texte et ses illustrations* (Paris, 1953).

Stewart, A.F., 'Lysippan Studies I. The Only Creator of Beauty', *AJA* 82 (1978), 63–71.

Stirling, L., 'Theodosian "Classicism" (review of: B. Kiilerich, *Late Fourth Century Classicism in the Plastic Arts* [Odense, 1993])', *JRA* 8 (1995), 535–38.

Stoneman, R., ed. and trans., *The Greek Alexander Romance* (Harmondsworth, 1991).

Strocka, V.M., *Forschungen in Ephesos VIII.i. Die Wandmalerei der Hanghäuser in Ephesos* (Vienna, 1977).

Strong, D.E., *Greek and Roman Gold and Silver Plate* (London, 1966).

Stuart Jones, H., *Catalogue of the Ancient Sculpture, Museo Capitolino* (1912).

Stukeley, W., *An Account of a Large Silver Plate of antique basso relievo, Roman Workmanship, found in Derbyshire, 1729* (London 1736).

Stylianou, A., and Stylianou, J., *The Treasures of Lambousa* (Lapethos, 1969).

Swain, S., *Hellenism and Empire: Language, Classicism and Power in the Greek World AD 50–250* (Oxford, 1996).

Taft, R.F., 'Byzantine Communion Spoons: a Review of the Evidence', *DOP* 50 (1996), 209–38.

Thompson, M.L., 'The Monumental and Literary Evidence for Programmatic Painting in Antiquity', *Marsyas* 9 (1960–61), 36–77.

Torelli, M., *Structure and Typology of Roman Historical Reliefs* (Ann Arbor, MI, 1982).

Török, L., 'Egyptian Late Antique Art from Nubian Royal Tombs', in C. Moss and K. Kiefer, eds, *Byzantine East, Latin West. Art-Historical Studies in Honour of Kurt Weitzmann* (Princeton, NJ, 1995), 91–97.

—, *Late Antique Nubia. History and Archaeology of the Southern Neighbour of Egypt in the Fourth-Sixth Century AD*, with a preface by Sir Laurence Kirwan, Antaeus 16 (Budapest, 1988).

Toynbee, J.C.M., and Painter, K.S., 'Silver Picture Plates of Late Antiquity: AD 300–700', *Archaeologia* 108 (1986), 15–65.

—, *Art in Britain under the Romans* (Oxford, 1964).

—, 'review of H.P. L'Orange, *Der spätantiken Bildschmuck des Konstantinsbogens* (Berlin 1939)', *JRS* 35 (1941), 189–93.

—, *The Hadrianic School: a Chapter in the History of Greek Art* (Cambridge, 1934).

Treadgold, W., ed., *Renaissances Before the Renaissance: Cultural Revivals of Late Antiquity and the Middle Ages* (Stanford, CA, 1984).

Trilling, J., 'Myth and Metaphor at the Byzantine Court: a Literary Approach to the David Plates', *Byzantion* 48 (1978), 249–63.

Turcan, R., *Les sarcophages romains à représentations dionysiaques: essai de chronologie et d'histoire religieuse* (Paris, 1966).

Van Dam, R., *Saints and their Miracles in Late Antique Gaul* (Princeton, NJ, 1993).

—, ed. and trans., Gregory of Tours, *Glory of the Martyrs*, Translated Texts for Historians, Latin Series III (Liverpool, 1988).

van Grunsven-Eygenraam, M., 'Heraclius and the David Plates', *BABesch* 48 (1973), 158–74.

Veneri, A., 'Dionysos', *LIMC* III (Zurich, 1986), 478–82.

Vermaseren, M.J., *Corpus Cultus Cybelae Attidisque IV* (Leiden, 1978).

—, *Cybele and Attis: the Myth and the Cult* (London, 1977)

Vickers, M. and Gill, D., *Artful Crafts: Ancient Greek Silverware and Pottery* (Oxford, 1994).

Vikan, G., 'Joseph Iconography on Coptic Textiles', *Gesta* 18 (1979), 99–108.

Visconti, E.Q., *Lettera di Ennio Quirino Visconti intorno ad una antica supelletile d'argento scoperta in Roma nell' anno 1793*, ed. P.P. Montagnani-Mirabili (Rome, 1827).

Volbach, W.F., 'Silber- und Elfenbeinarbeiten vom Ende des 4. bis zum Anfang des 7. Jahrhunderts', in *Beiträge zur Kunstgeschichte und Archäologie des Frühmittelalters. Akten zum VII internationalen Kongreß für Frühmittelalterforschung 21.–28. September 1958* (Cologne, 1962), 21–36.

—, *Elfenbeinarbeiten der Spätantike und des frühen Mittelalters*, 2nd edn (Mainz, 1952).

von Bissing, F.W., 'Die Funde in den Nekropolen von Kostol, Ballana und Firka am II Nilkatarakt und ihre zeitliche und kunstgeschichtliche Stellung', *AA* (1939), 569–81.

von Hessen, O., Kurze, W. and Mastrelli, C.A., *Il tesoro di Galognano* (Florence, 1977).

Walker, S., 'Aspects of Roman Funerary Art', in J. Huskinson, M. Beard & J. Reynolds, eds, *Image and Mystery in the Roman World* (Gloucester, 1988), 23–36.

Wallace-Hadrill, A., 'Rome's Cultural Revolution', *JRS* 79 (1989), 157–64.

Wander, S.H., 'The Cyprus Plates and the *Chronicle* of Fredegar', *DOP* 29 (1975), 345–46.

—, 'The Cyprus Plates: the Story of David and Goliath', *Metropolitan Museum Journal* 8 (1973), 89–104.

Ward, B., *Harlots of the Desert: a Study of Repentance in Early Monastic Sources* (London, 1987).

Ward Perkins, B., *From Classical Antiquity to the Middle Ages: Urban Public Buildings in Northern and Central Italy, AD 300–700* (Oxford, 1984).

Watts, D., *Christians and Pagans in Roman Britain* (London & New York, 1991).

Webb, R.H., *The Transmission of the Eikones of Philostratus and the Development of Ekphrasis from Late Antiquity to the Renaissance* (PhD, Warburg Institute, University of London, 1992).

Weitzmann K., ed., *Age of Spirituality: Late Antique and Early Christian Art, 3rd to 7th Century* (New York, 1979).

—, 'The Heracles Plaques of St. Peter's Cathedra', *Art Bulletin* 55 (1973)

—, 'Prolegomena to a Study of the Cyprus Plates', *Metropolitan Museum Journal* 3 (1970), 97–111.

—, 'The Psalter Vatopedi 761. Its Place in the Aristocratic Psalter Rescension', *Journal of the Walters Art Gallery* 10 (1947), 21–51.

Werner, J., *Der Grabfund von Malaia Perescepina und Kuvrat, Kagan der Bulgaren*. Bayrische Akademie der Wissenschaften, phil.-hist. Klasse Abhandelungen, neue Folge, Heft 91 (Munich, 1984).

Wessel, K., 'Das Diptychon Barberini', in *Akten des XI internationalen Byzantinistenkongress* (Munich, 1960), 665–70.

Wilkes, J.J., *Diocletian's Palace, Split: Residence of a Retired Roman Emperor* (Sheffield, 1986).

Willers, D., et al., *Der Dionysos-Behang der Abegg-Stiftung* (Riggisberg, 1987).

Wilson, N.G., *Scholars of Byzantium* (London, 1983).

—, ed., *Address to Young Men: Saint Basil on the Value Greek Literature* (London, 1975).

Wölfel, C., 'Der Teller von Aquileia', in H.-H. von Prittwitz und Gaffron and H. Mielsch eds, *Das Haus lacht vor Silber: die Prunkplatte von Bizerta und das römische Tafelgeschirr* (Cologne, 1997), 149–52.

Wright, D., 'The School of Princeton and the Seventh Day of Creation', *University Publishing* 9 (1980), 7–8.

Young, F.M., *Biblical Exegesis and the Formation of Christian Culture* (Cambridge, 1997).

Zanker, P., *The Power of Images in the Age of Augustus* (Ann Arbor, MI, 1988).

Zovatto, P.L., *Grado. Antichi monumenti* (Bologna, 1971).

Index